Fifth Edition

CUSTOMER SERVICE

CAREER SUCCESS THROUGH CUSTOMER LOYALTY

Paul R. Timm
Emeritus Professor of Organizational Leadership and Strategy
Marriott School of Management
Brigham Young University

Prentice Hall

Boston   Columbus   Indianapolis   New York   San Francisco   Upper Saddle River
Amsterdam   Cape Town   Dubai   London   Madrid   Milan   Munich   Paris   Montreal   Toronto
Delhi   Mexico City   Sao Paulo   Sydney   Hong Kong   Seoul   Singapore   Taipei   Tokyo

Editor in Chief: Vernon Anthony
Senior Acquisitions Editor: Gary Bauer
Editorial Assistant: Megan Heintz
Director of Marketing: David Gesell
Marketing Manager: Leigh Ann Sims
Marketing Assistant: Les Roberts
Project Manager: Holly Shufeldt
Cover Designer: Diane Lorenzo

Inhouse Artist: Suzanne Duda
Cover Art: SuperStock, Corbis
Full-Service Project
 Management: Integra
Composition: Integra
Printer/Binder: Edwards Brothers
Cover Printer: Lehigh-Phoenix Color
Text Font: Minion

Photo Credits: Chapter 1: Banana Stock BPL012; Chapte 2: itstock free itf112006; Chapter 3: itstock free itf112074; Chapter 4: Business Corporate 068039; Chapter 5: Comstock KS13818; Chapter 6: Comstock KS13805; Chapter 7: Comstock KS13843; Chapter 8: Business Corporate 068027; Chapter 9: Comstock KS13824; Chapter 10: Comstock KS13854; Chapter 11: itstock free itf112066; Chapter 12: Comstock KS13794; Chapter 13: Goodshoot 021047; Chapter 14: Banana Stock BPL076.

Library of Congress Cataloging-in-Publication Data

Timm, Paul R.
    Customer service: career success through customer loyalty/Paul R. Timm.—5th ed.
        p. cm.
    Includes bibliographical references and index.
    ISBN-13: 978-0-13-506397-2 (alk. paper)
    ISBN-10: 0-13-506397-3 (alk. paper)
    1. Customer services.   2. Consumer satisfaction.   3. Customer relations.
4. Success in business.   I. Title.
HF5415.5.T513 2010
658.8'12—dc22

                                                                            2009047554

10 9 8 7 6 5 4 3 2 1

Prentice Hall
is an imprint of

www.pearsonhighered.com

ISBN 10:   0-13-506397-3
ISBN 13: 978-0-13-506397-2

CONTENTS

FROM THE AUTHOR

YOU MAY BE ASKING: WHAT'S IN THIS BOOK FOR ME?

Thank you for considering this book. By doing so you are making a potential investment. You may be spending some money for the book or, at least, you will be making an investment of your time to read it. You have the right to ask, "What's in it for me?" That's a fair question.

Here is a straight answer: learning to build your customer service skills will have a powerful impact on your career success as well as success in other areas of your life. An overstatement? I don't really think so. Based on my 30-plus years of organizational experience in many capacities, I feel confident in saying that there is a direct relationship between service skills and career achievement.

My reasoning lies in the fact that a loyal customer is a company's most valuable asset. Without customers, no organization can long exist. Customer loyalty is building one relationship at a time with people just like you.

Every organization talks about giving great service. Likewise, people in all kinds of professions acknowledge the importance of serving their customers, clients, patients, shareholders, passengers, employees, and other stakeholders. Despite these good intentions, everyday experience quickly shows that great service is not commonplace. Far too often, customers receive poor value, are forced to wrestle with ineffective processes, or encounter people who make them want to do business elsewhere.

You can change that. You can help your organization and your career by translating your good service intentions into a workable plan. This book provides much of what you need to devise such a plan. Build your career success by applying proven principles than create customer satisfaction and loyalty. Your customers can and will become your promoters, fueling positive word-of-mouth and repeat business.

The true winners in today's economy do more than just talk about great service—they find ways to consistently deliver it. The payoff is enormous.

Other books on customer service often take one of two forms: either they give an assortment of tips and techniques for boosting service quality or they describe the story of one company's successes. Such books can have value, of course, so long as the reader can effectively apply these ideas to his or her own organization. But such books seldom show a systematic way to build the specific skills needed to succeed with customers.

This book is a response to the need for a different approach to learning the skills needed to be an exceptional service provider. It is skill based and offers practical, immediately applicable information. In *Customer Service*, I tie together the best information from bookstore trade books and school textbooks—and present it in an easy-to-remember format. Reading this, you will find a clear and usable process for developing the skills, attitudes, and thinking patterns needed to win customer satisfaction and loyalty.

Some of what you'll learn includes ways of developing

- A heightened awareness of the challenges and opportunities in customer service
- The willingness and ability to gather performance-enhancing feedback
- Specific personal and communication behaviors that engage customers
- Telephone techniques for excellent service
- The ability to create friendly Web sites, personable email, and clear written messages that delight customers
- The tools for dealing with and recovering unhappy customers
- An understanding of the powerful impact of exceeding expectations—giving customers more than they anticipate.

- Specific techniques for exceeding expectations in value, information, convenience, and timing, thus creating greater customer loyalty
- Tactics for dealing with the challenge of "emotional labor"
- The ability to lead, expand, and empower the service process
- Skills for managing others in the pursuit of service excellence
- An understanding of the future directions in customer service

Key Features of this Book

I have worked hard to make this book enjoyable and engaging with features like these:

The Way It Is . . . What Happened to the "Service Economy"?

Picture this: Two characters show up on your doorstep from the appliance repair service. They have the appearance and demeanor of a pair of street thugs, but they smile and say hello. One of them looks at the worksheet and mispronounces your name. You ask if they could identify themselves and, although one of them looks insulted, he fishes around under his shirt and produces a plastic card on a silver necklace. The other points a thumb over his shoulder to his truck, implying that that should be identification enough. Are you getting nervous yet?

But you need the refrigerator fixed, so you let them in. They wipe their feet on the mat, carefully

---

- **The Way It Is** stories and illustrations start each chapter by showing the current state of customer service in a variety of organizations, large and small.

SERVICE SNAPSHOT

Burgers Supreme

Steve and Debby K. owned an independent fast-food restaurant called Burgers Supreme. For more than six years they built up a loyal clientele, many of whom ate there almost every day. Not only did these customers buy lunch at Burgers Supreme, but they also brought friends and fellow workers. Some of the regulars were teased about owning stock in the restaurant, although none did.

The menu was broad, covering dozens of sandwiches, salads, soups, desserts, and specialty foods like gyros, onion rings, and frozen yogurt. Everything was prepared fresh. But

in, but it did reflect the owners' belief in recognizing customer loyalty. It also reflected their willingness to empower their employees to give something away now and then.

The counter help at Burgers Supreme learned service behaviors from Debby's example. She was always right there beside them on the firing line. She taught by example and freely dispensed compliments and corrective suggestions. She taught (and modeled the behaviors) as her people greeted customers by name, smiled, cheerfully fixed any mistakes, and kept hustling to make sure the restaurant was clean,

---

- **Service Snapshots** briefly cite innovative ideas and practices of real people giving real service.

ACTION TIPS FOR IDENTIFYING TELEPHONE USE ATTITUDES

Action Tip 1—Check Your Phone Use Attitudes

Many people are phone-shy—they see calls as interruptions.

Many people have a love–hate relationship with the telephone. Of course, we all know that the telephone can be a powerful tool for sales, information gathering, and relationship building. By receiving and initiating calls, we can accomplish a lot. Yet some people are phone-shy. They are hesitant to call others and sometimes hesitant about answering incoming calls. They perceive the phone call as an intrusion on their other activities. Perhaps this attitude is reinforced by the annoyance of dinnertime telemarketers.

Check your telephone-use attitudes using the self-evaluation that follows. It can help you understand some of your attitudes toward using the telephone. It can also help you improve your telephone techniques by showing what you may be doing wrong.

- **Action tips** show you, the reader, how to apply specific ideas discussed.

LOOK INSIDE

Applying the Mrs. Williams Example to Your Company

Let's take a few moments and go back to the Mrs. Williams example, but instead use your own organization. Suppose that you lose one customer and the other statistics hold true. Take a few moments to calculate the numbers as they apply to your organization. If you work for a nonprofit or government

agency where the dollar sales are not a relevant measure, calculate the number of people who may be aggravated or upset with you and your organization. Think in terms of the psychological price that must be paid as you deal with frustrated, angry, upset patrons on a day-to-day basis.

- **Look Inside** activities are a series of self-evaluations that can help you better understand your own behaviors and attitudes about service.

ANOTHER LOOK

Why Customer Satisfaction Is Not Enough

Several studies by the Gallup polling organization look at the connection between customer satisfaction and customer loyalty. Data from a leading supermarket chain supports the importance of an emotional connection on the frequency of customers' visits and the amount of money they spent during those visits. Shoppers who reported being *less than* "extremely satisfied" visited this chain about 4.3 times per month, spending an average of $166 during that month. Those who reported being "extremely satisfied" but did not also have a strong emotional connection to the chain actually went to the store less often (4.1 times per month) and spent less ($144). In this case, extreme satisfaction represented no added value to the store.

visited the grocery chain 32 percent more often and spent 46 percent more money than those without emotional bonds. Their conclusion is that satisfaction without engagement is basically worthless. Satisfaction with engagement (stemming from some **emotional attachment**), however, is priceless.

Probes

1. What does this research suggest about companies that simply measure customer satisfaction?
2. What are the key challenges facing organizations that want to build customer loyalty?

- **Another Look** segments feature the thinking of people with fresh ideas and, sometimes, contrasting opinion. These can stimulate your thinking about fresh and creative applications of ideas.

Reviewing the Facts

1. What defines a customer (using this term in the broad sense)?
2. What are some attitudes or orientations that define a customer relationship? What factors account for a strengthening of this relationship?
3. How can customer skills be valuable even in nonprofit organizations (or organizations that have no competitors)?
4. Why does word-of-mouth "advertising" work so effectively?
5. How can a person build his or her "social capital"?

6. How do diversity, age, globalization, and work–life balance issues impact a company's ability to give great service to both internal and external customers?
7. How do ripple effects escalate the problem of the lost customer?
8. What three key characteristics define real customer loyalty?
9. What do we mean by an "engaged" customer, and how does this relate to customer loyalty?
10. What characteristics are often confused with customer loyalty but do not represent real loyalty?

Applying the Ideas: Interview Service Providers

1. Interview five people about their customer service attitudes. Specifically, ask them to describe their internal and external customers and what they feel about the importance of serving them.
2. Ask two businesspeople to estimate the typical amount customers spend with them. Then calculate the "cost of a lost customer" based on the scenario in this chapter. Ask each businessperson to react to this estimate. Does it seem plausible? Too high? Too low?

3. Describe three businesses that have won your customer loyalty—places you enjoy doing business and are likely to remain a customer. What, specifically, causes you to give them your loyalty? (Note: Often it's subtle little things that win you over.)
4. What major corporations that you've heard of seem to be doing the best job of building customer loyalty? In what ways do they attempt to build long-term relationships with customers?

- **Reviewing the Facts** and **Applying the Ideas** sections at the end of each chapter recap and let you test yourself for comprehension of key points.

- **Consider This Case** presents brief application cases at the end of each chapter, followed by a few probing questions designed to stimulate your thinking.

Overall, I believe these features make for a more enjoyable learning experience. I think you'll agree.

New to the Fifth Edition

This fifth edition of *Customer Service* reflects a major revision with extensive new material.

Overall, the structure of the material has been reorganized to build around an easy-to-remember acronym. The acronym is the simple word **LIFE** (so I guess we'll be talking about the meaning of life!). I have found this acronym to be useful as I teach, train, and consult with businesses across the United States and in Europe. Participants have expressed appreciation for this memory aid.

LIFE stands for *little things, insight, feedback,* and *expectations.* These will become more meaningful to you as you read the book. The last two chapters talk about tips for *living* **LIFE**— applying the principles and helping others (such as employees who may report to you) do so as well.

Chapter 1 presents a compelling case for the importance of providing excellent customer service in today's economy. In the chapter, I refer to Ockham's razor—the notion that often the simplest explanation for an outcome is the best one. Simply put, good service distinguishes successful companies (and people) from the less successful.

I have added material about the importance of good service to internal customers—employees. The best companies to work for succeed in large measure by the relationships they build with employees. Good "service" to employees leads to lower turnover, better recruits, and higher productivity—all of which contribute to the bottom line.

The central challenge of many organizations is to get beyond good intentions and slogans to clear strategies for winning customer and employee loyalty. I include some updated information about changes in the diverse nature of today's customers.

The goal remains the same: attracting and keeping long-term, loyal customers.

Chapters 2 through 5 focus on some of the "little things" that can make or break an organization's service efforts. Chapter 2 describes specific behaviors and communication techniques that create customer engagement through the power of personality. Chapter 3 presents material on the critical importance of listening as we seek to create customer loyalty. The reader will gain specific tactics (action tips) for improving this key communication skill.

Chapter 4 delves into telephone techniques and offers additional specific action tips. Phone responsiveness can be an important first step toward customer loyalty. New material on using better phrasing and on the importance of call centers is added to this edition.

Chapter 5 has been extensively reworked to show how today's organizations can make the most of those increasingly important service delivery options: Web sites and electronic communication. Today's customer demands almost instant responses to requests. I also talk about the role of social networking sites (SNS) such as Facebook, MySpace, and others in customer loyalty. Today's "Net-generation" holds expectations about service that have not been common in the past.

Finally, Chapter 5 has specific action tips for making the most of e-commerce as we attempt to better serve customers.

Chapters 6 and 7 address the third letter of our LIFE acronym: Insight. Two kinds of insight are of particular value: insight into the kinds of things that are likely to turn our customers off and insight into emerging trends in our ever-changing economy. Chapter 7 considers possible future changes that can have a dramatic impact on a company's success. The possible changes are widespread, although some service factors will remain the same.

Consider this Case

Costco and the Power of High-Quality Relationships

Retailing giant Costco has enjoyed substantial success at building customer loyalty. The warehouse outlets spend almost nothing on traditional advertising but have grown dramatically largely by word of mouth. In short, enthusiastic Costco customers tell other people.

Costco, the wholesale club company, is a real-life example of how great customer relationships generate economic benefits. More than 80 percent of customers report a willingness to recommend Costco to their friends and associates. The company has grown to almost 50 million members despite spending next to nothing on advertising or marketing. While a typical discounter carries 40,000 SKUs (stock keeping units—essentially the number of products sold), Costco stores have only 4,500—only those items where it can provide outstanding value. Sales per store are almost twice those at Sam's Club, its closest competitor. Costco's success funds a generous compensation package for its employees. New hires start at $10 an hour—high for the retail industry—and progress to $40,000 a year after three years. They receive a benefits package virtually unequalled in the industry. Low turnover and long tenure reduce hiring and training costs and boost productivity; they also contribute to Costco's remarkably low inventory-shrinkage rate, which is only 13 percent of the industry average. The company eliminates bad profits through a generous return policy—there is no time limit on returns except for a limit of one year on computer technology items. Costco's earnings have grown at about 12 to 17 percent a year, over the past decade, even in a difficult economic environment.

Probes

1. Describe any experiences you have had with Costco. Generally, are you satisfied when shopping there?
2. Would you describe yourself as a promoter for Costco—someone who would willingly recommend it to friends?
3. How does Costco appear to be aware of the importance of its internal customers?
4. What challenges do you think Costco will face in the future regarding its customer loyalty?

The third letter of our **LIFE** acronym refers to feedback and that is the theme addressed in Chapters 8 and 9. Chapter 8 stresses the importance of being open to customer complaints and to accept such feedback as a form of coaching. Companies improve to the degree that they get and use customer feedback. They also build stronger loyalty through this two-way communication. Chapter 9 further explains how to use feedback as we attempt to recover potentially lost customers. Studies show that customers who complain and experience some of these simple recovery tactics discussed in this chapter are actually more likely to be loyal to a company than customers who never have a complaint! Service recovery is a critical key to success.

The fourth letter of our **LIFE** acronym stands for expectations. Chapters 10, 11, and 12 deal with the most powerful ways to create customer loyalty, "exceeding customer expectations." Chapter 10 shows ways we can surprise the customer with an enhanced sense of value. Chapter 11 explains how to use enhanced information to exceed expectations, and Chapter 12 talks about giving better convenience and attention to timing. These chapters explain why this works and specifically how you can do it. These updated chapters provide powerful ideas based on the author's years of experience as a consultant and not found anywhere else.

Chapters 13 and 14 are organized under a part heading called living LIFE. The first of these chapters introduces the concept of "emotion labor" and explains how the stresses of giving good service can be difficult if not carefully managed. But, alas, the chapter gives some in-target action tips for better time and stress management—tips that you can apply immediately.

And, of course, one way to reduce stress and get more done is to effectively manage the efforts of other people, the topic of Chapter 14. Managers can do much to hire service-oriented people (those with high "emotional intelligence," for example, direct their efforts to create a culture that reinforces individual efforts to give great service).

Overall, this book reflects substantial enhancements over the already successful earlier editions. It provides a comprehensive and up-to-date look at customer service and the skills needed in today's economy.

Student and Instructor Resources

COMPANION WEB SITE   A companion Web site located at *www.prenhall.com/timm* contains student materials, such as templates, forms, checklists, self-quiz questions, and links to helpful sites.

POWERPOINT LECTURE PRESENTATION PACKAGE   High quality lecture presentation screens for each chapter are available online and on the Instructor Resource CD.

INSTRUCTOR'S MANUAL   The instructor's manual for this text is available as a downloadable Word document at *www.prenhall.com* under instructor resources and is also on the Instructor's Resources CD. It contains multiple-choice and true/false test questions, chapter outlines and lecture notes, answers to discussion questions and case problems, and comments about the exercises.

ELECTRONIC TEST GENERATOR   This computerized text generation system is available as a downloadable file at *www.prenhall.com* under instructor resources. The program gives the instructor maximum flexibility in preparing tests. It can create custom tests and print scrambled versions of a test at one time, as well as build tests randomly by chapter, level of difficulty, or question type. The software also allows online testing and record-keeping and the ability to add problems to the database.

VIDEOS FROM JWA CATALOG   JWA is a producer of professional commercial training films on customer service, workplace communication, and management topics in VHS or DVD format. Up to three video selections are available free-of-charge upon adoption of this text. Please contact your local representative for details. To see complete listing of JWA videos, visit *www.jwavideo.com*.

DISTANCE LEARNING SOLUTIONS: CONVENIENCE, SIMPLICITY, SUCCESS Ready-made **WebCT** and **Blackboard** online courses! If you adopt a course, student access cards will be packaged with the text. Courses include Research Navigator, a premium online research tool, and access to the Paralegal Professional Classroom Video Series via streaming video.

Special Thanks

This book was developed with the help of many people. I want to especially thank my editors, Gary Bauer and Christina Taylor, for their valuable input. Thanks also to the good people who took the time to review the manuscript as it developed and provide excellent guidance. These reviewers include:

Jenell Bramlage—University for Northwestern Ohio, OH

Yvonne Drake—Pensacola Junior College, FL

Steven H. Eichmeier—Weber State University, UT

James R. Ellis—Lamar State College, CA

Stephanie Emrich—Metropolitan Community College, NE

Beverly A. Forsberg—Metropolitan Community College, NE

Ross R. Higa—Leeward Community College, HI

Grace J. Johnson—University of Wisconsin, Milwaukee, WI

Patricia Morrow —Middlesex Community College, MA

Lizzie Scoburgh—University for Northwestern Ohio, OH

Bernard Skown—Steven Institute of Technology, NJ

Art Weinstein—Nova Southeastern University, FL

Beverly J. Yeagle—Hagerstown Community College, MD

Finally, I'd like to dedicate this book to my brilliant and talented wife, Dr. Sherron Bienvenu, and to my good friend (and the guy who got me into the study of customer service) Jack Wilson. I'd also like to thank my many students and seminar participants, especially those at Brigham Young University, the Helsinki School of Economics and Executive Education in Finland, and numerous client organizations.

I sincerely hope that you, my readers, enjoy using this book. I'd love to hear about your experiences. Feel free to contact me by visiting my Web site: *www.DrTimm.com* or by emailing me at DrTimm@aol.com.

Paul R. Timm, Ph.D.
July 2009

ABOUT THE AUTHOR

I've had the privilege of writing more than 40 books on a variety of topics dealing with challenges managers and career-oriented people deal with every day. My books on customer loyalty, human relations, management communication, and self-management have been translated into dozens of languages and sell worldwide. I have also written and appear in a series of videotape training programs produced by Jack Wilson & Associates (*www.JWAvideo.com*).

My writing is based on more than 30 years experience as a professor, trainer, consultant, and entrepreneur. I have held positions with large companies (Xerox and Bell South) and have led small organizations (such as Prime Learning, Inc.). I have consulted and trained with many companies and taught at universities in the United States, Finland, Scotland, Singapore, and Poland. In an earlier life, I served in a helicopter company in the U.S. Army in Vietnam.

For fun, I run (marathons and triathlons), play golf, read, and enjoy observing the kinds of customer service people give—or, more often, fail to give.

I strongly believe that no arena offers as much opportunity for your professional advancement as does the field of customer service and loyalty. And with the skills taught in this book, you will greatly enhance your ability to build and sustain your greatest asset—your relationships with loyal, committed customers, and employees—through exceptional service.

CHAPTER 1

Know Why Service Matters

Recognizing the Role of Customer Service in Your Career Success

Great service is about attitude. And a service attitude leads to a richer quality of life, not only in the commercial sector.

—Leonard Berry

. . . in all the [economic] gloom and doom there is one ray of light that consumers can enjoy—customer service and support should improve in a recession. And frankly the companies that don't take steps to improve customer service can—and should— find themselves out of business. As Warren Buffet, the Sage of Omaha, says, "You only find out who is swimming naked when the tide goes out."

—Stephen Lynn

After reading this chapter, you should be able to

1. Explain how no one succeeds without attracting and keeping loyal customers— people with whom we exchange value.

2. Know that customers are identified by various names and include both external and internal relationships.

3. Know how customers can become partners through service intimacy and an ongoing relationship.

4. Recognize the importance of positive word of mouth in getting and keeping customers.

5. Calculate the possible impact of lost customers on a business or organization.

6. Describe some key changes in the diverse nature of customers in today's economy.

7. Grasp the challenge of translating slogans and good intentions into a strategy for better customer loyalty.

8. Articulate how to get customers beyond mere satisfaction and develop customer loyalty.

The Way It Is . . . What Happened to the "Service Economy"?

Picture this: Two characters show up on your doorstep from the appliance repair service. They have the appearance and demeanor of a pair of street thugs, but they smile and say hello. One of them looks at the worksheet and mispronounces your name. You ask if they could identify themselves and, although one of them looks insulted, he fishes around under his shirt and produces a plastic card on a silver necklace. The other points a thumb over his shoulder to his truck, implying that that should be identification enough. Are you getting nervous yet?

But you need the refrigerator fixed, so you let them in. They wipe their feet on the mat, carefully place their toolbox on your kitchen counter, pull out the refrigerator, and set to work. While disassembling the innards of your fridge, they chat between themselves about an apparently lively weekend party but they seem to work competently. After half hour and some cussing, the older man explains to you that they had to put in a temporary part because the factory-recommended part has to be shipped from a distant city. But it's been ordered, he reassures you. They will return and install that when it comes in. They clean up their mess, push the fridge back, and leave, promising that the part would arrive shortly. Those first impressions can be so misleading, can't they? Maybe these guys are okay after all.

Maybe not. Weeks pass and you hear nothing from them. The ordered part apparently never arrived and your refrigerator is running okay, but you wonder about possible harm due to the substandard fix. You make several calls to the company and are reassured that the part will be in soon, but after months, you have never heard from them again and keep your fingers crossed that the temporary part will continue to work. How do you feel about this customer service?

Another example: Anthony recently called a major U.S. airline reservations line to book two business trips. Since he travels a lot, Anthony is one with what they call "medallion" status—a frequent flyer. He has a "special" phone number to call for "preferential" service. Unfortunately, the service he received was anything but preferential or special.

The phone connection was poor, with cross talk in the background and the faint sound of chattering on the line. He was left on hold for a long time, while being subjected to repeated (and garbled) promotional messages from the airline. Finally, a representative came online but her vocal articulation made her hard to understand. When Anthony told her the flights he would like to book, she asked him (!), quote, "Do we fly direct to Amsterdam from Salt Lake City?" At that point, he lost confidence in her ability to book his flights accurately and politely told her that he'd call back later (hoping he'd get a more knowledgeable agent). Anthony hung up and redialed. After going through all the "press one for reservations," "please enter your Sky Miles number," and so on, he got to agent number two. This man spoke with a strong Indian accent and the connection was marked by background chatter on the line. Although Anthony had looked at flight options online and gave the reservation agent several options, he was repeatedly told that he could not have that flight and that he could not use any of his hundreds of thousands of frequent flyer miles to upgrade on most of his choices. The agent "explained" this to Anthony by citing some jargon about "point-to-point" versus "destination" flight distinctions, which made no sense to his customer. After 26 minutes on the phone (he had a timer on his phone), the agent essentially tossed his hands up in defeat and announced that he was transferring Anthony to "the Medallion desk," and he was put back on hold. After a few minutes, another rep came on line, and Anthony had to begin all over again.

The call took 47 minutes. And for this he bought $4,400 worth of plane tickets. Anthony practically had to beg them to take his money! Of course, the call center contact was necessary because the airline had eliminated almost all of its regional ticket offices. Remember them? Places where you could actually talk face-to-face with human beings?

Ah, the service economy.

Some people are wondering. Where is the service in the "service economy"?

INTRODUCTION

Every person reading this book could describe customer service fiascoes. We all encounter substandard service every day, and much of that poor service can be attributed to poor attitudes among individuals and organizations. Companies make business decisions (change policies, close offices, reduce employee training, install excessively complex pricing systems, fail to follow up on commitments, etc.) with insufficient thought about the impact on customers. We've all come to expect less than optimal service despite the claims that we live in a service economy.

For several decades, enlightened companies have paid a great deal of attention to customer service and methods for improving it. The vast majority of companies have initiated customer service improvement programs or strategies. Yet despite these initiatives, customer satisfaction levels remain stubbornly low. And, in today's world of high interconnectivity, poor service experiences are readily shared in cyberspace. The impact on businesses and individuals is dramatic. Companies and people that consistently give good service succeed, while poor service providers fumble and eventually fail. It's as simple as that.

"Ockham's razor" may well apply to customer service and company success. Usually attributed to fourteenth-century English logician and Franciscan friar William of Ockham, this logical approach asserts that when trying to understand a situation, the simplest explanation is usually the right one. Put into the context of customer service, Ockham's razor can slice through the many debates about what accounts for a business's success. It's really quite simple: Satisfied, loyal customers make for successful organizations. Think about competing businesses like K-Mart and Wal-Mart, for example. They are very similar in many ways—sell the same kind of stuff for about the same prices in stores with similar locations and layouts, and so on. They are, in essence, the same, save for some small details. Given this, if you ask people which of these two they would choose to shop at (and these are the only two choices), the vast majority of people will say Wal-Mart. (Your author has asked this question to thousands of people in audiences over the past two decades, and the percentage favoring Wal-Mart is at least 80–20.) Is it any wonder, then, that K-Mart (and merger partner Sears) sales are about $50 billion a year, while Wal-Mart sells $400 billion. Sometimes the simplest explanation is the best one: People prefer to shop at Wal-Mart. The service experience is usually perceived as being better.

In fairness, there are many excellent K-Mart stores and also more than a few substandard Wal-Marts. But overall, given a choice, customers opt for the service difference provided at Wal-Mart.

> The bottom line: satisfied, loyal customers make for successful organizations.

While it is tempting to join the chorus of customer service complainers, and no one will criticize you if you do, we can also look at widespread discontent with service from another viewpoint: as an opportunity. The upside potential for those who give good service is unlimited. By making the process of satisfying customers a part of our daily lives, we can virtually guarantee our professional success.

Likewise, it's more fun to work for companies that give great service. A quick look at *Fortune* magazine's annual "Best Companies in America to Work For" shows service leaders like Nordstrom, Container Store, Marriott, eBay, FexEx, Zappos, and others—all companies that clearly illustrate the linkage between great service and great employee morale. Says consultant Chip Bell, "[these kinds of companies] boast the lowest turnover (a cost saver), the best recruits (an investment), the highest productivity (another positive hit to the balance sheet) and the greatest profits. Companies in the top 20% of the highly revered American Customer Satisfaction Index outperformed the Dow Jones industrial average by 90+%, the S&P 500 by 200+% and the NASDAQ by 350+%."[1]

> The upside opportunity for people who give great service is almost unlimited.

Clearly, customer service success pays.

NO ONE SUCCEEDS WITHOUT LOYAL CUSTOMERS

No business or organization can succeed without building **customer satisfaction and loyalty**. Likewise, no person can make a good living without meeting the needs of his or her customers. That is what people *do* in organizations: they serve others. And they succeed through service.

Those statements may seem to be rather broad generalizations, but let's consider this position a bit further. Most people would agree that a business needs customers—but not everyone works in business. What about other kinds of organizations? Does a government agency need customer satisfaction to succeed? Does a civic organization, church congregation, political party, family, service club, school, or fraternity need satisfied customers to succeed? To answer these questions, we first need to define what we mean by a customer. The common perception is that a customer is someone who buys something from you. Most people assume that to buy involves the

The broad definition of "customer" is anyone with whom we exchange value.

exchange of money. In many cases, that is true enough. But an expanded definition of "customer" can be useful. In its broadest sense, a customer is *someone with whom we exchange value.*

"Customer" Implies an Exchange of Value

As human beings, we are constantly exchanging value with each other. We are, by nature, social beings. When we exchange money for a product or service, we are customers. When we provide work in exchange for a wage, our boss and our company are our customers. When we participate in a civic organization or church group, the people to whom we give support, advice, ideas, and information are our customers. When we give of ourselves to contribute to a strong family, our spouse, parents, kids, and others become our customers. When we build and maintain networks of friends and associates, we become each others' customers.

Principles of good customer service can be applied to all kinds of relationships.

Exchanging such value involves give and take. We give and accept social support to and from friends and family. We give and take ideas and information to and from teachers or work teams. We give and accept buying recommendations to and from trusted associates; we give and take gifts and tokens of appreciation to and from others. In short, much of life involves **exchange of value**. As such, many of our interactions are with customers as we have broadly defined that term. The ideas on improving customer service found in this book can be equally applied to all kinds of relationships, not just commercial transactions.

By accepting this broader view of what it means to be and have customers, we will see that applying the principles of customer service results in much more than just business or financial success. Yes, customer service is a key to career success but, more importantly, it is a master key to success in all the relationships in one's life. By applying the customer service principles in this book to every aspect of your life, you can gain exceptional levels of success and life satisfaction.

CUSTOMERS HAVE MANY NAMES

Different names for customers can imply different kinds of transactions.

In our commercial dealings, we have a lot of names for customers, often varying by the nature of our business or organization. Some examples of these names include clients, patients, passengers, patrons, members, associates, insureds, users, buyers, subscribers, readers, viewers, purchasers, end users, guests, or cases. But, again, the commonality in all these customers is that they engage in some sort of transaction—some **exchange of value**—with us or with our organization. They give us something (often, but not always, money) in exchange for something else (usually services or goods). These are **external customers**—people outside of our company with whom we do business.

Internal customers— employees—are an equally important target for customer service efforts.

Internal customers are typically a company's employees. Employee relationships are crucial to organizational success. If a company has a high employee turnover rate, that is, the number of employees quitting and having to be replaced, it will face serious challenges. Replacement of employees involves a huge cost as the company needs to spend money and effort to attract, recruit, and train replacements.

Virtually everything we will discuss in this book about customer service also applies to employees, our internal customers.

CUSTOMER RELATIONSHIPS CAN BECOME PARTNERSHIPS

Relationships with customers can evolve into rich and fulfilling partnerships. Consultant and author Chip Bell contends that such customer partnerships arise from certain attitudes or orientations. Among these, he says that such partnerships are anchored in an attitude of generosity and trust so that the people involved find pleasure in extending the relationship beyond just meeting a need or requirement. Generally partnerships require some joint purpose and are marked by truth, candor, and straight talk mixed with compassion and care.

Is it possible to have a business that doesn't need to build relationships? Possibly. If you work for a traveling carnival and you sell cotton candy to people you will never see again, perhaps

EXHIBIT 1.1 Levels of "customer" relationships.

relationship-building is not important. If you engage in any such one-time transactions, you might argue that you'll never deal with these people again, so customer service isn't important. But such a viewpoint can be short-sighted for two reasons. First, very few businesses are one-time, isolated transactions. The potential for repeat business is always there. Second, even if your business is a transaction business, word of mouth to other customers can help or hurt you. If you are an unusually grouchy cotton candy vendor, people will tell others and those others may avoid even that one transaction with you. Or, if you are exceptional in your friendliness, positive word may get around. So, even transaction businesses have the potential for becoming relationship businesses.

> The ideal goal in most businesses is to create partnerships with customers.

Not every customer relationship becomes a partnership, but such partnerships represent the highest level of customer–provider affiliation. Exhibit 1.1 represents two dimensions that define levels of customer relationships: the degree of **service intimacy** and extent of **ongoing relationship**. When relationships evolve into something personally "intimate"—that is, people get to know each other and strive to meet the needs each has—and continue over a period of time, they can become rich and satisfying.

The earlier description of partnership attributes is echoed by research into **social capital**. In his book *Achieving Success through Social Capital*, Professor Wayne Baker defines *social capital* as the resources available in and through personal and business networks. Good networks of relationships (including customer relationships, as we have broadly defined "customer") "are vital for good health, emotional well-being, and a meaningful life—even a longer life."[2]

Notwithstanding the semantic distinctions among customers, it remains useful to agree that everyone has customers, or people we interact with who depend on us for information, guidance, services, products, or social support—in short, value. In exchange for value we provide, they will give something back. This exchange system defines, on the most basic level, what it means to be a customer. When this exchange evolves into something more than an isolated transaction, when we move up the stair steps of relationship building, we will enjoy immense levels of career and personal satisfaction.

POSITIVE WORD OF MOUTH GETS AND KEEPS CUSTOMERS

New customers can be tough to get. An oft-quoted statistic says that it costs five or six times as much to get a new customer as it does to keep an existing one. So logically, it makes sense to focus on satisfying customers you already have, thus encouraging repeat business. Without customer retention, you'll spend a lot of time and effort refilling a leaky bucket as you chase an ever-replenishing supply of new customers. (This is the dilemma faced by companies that offer shoddy products or poor service. People may buy from them one time but will not come back.)

Getting new customers and replacing those lost is an expensive part of any business.

Some people think that advertising is a good way to induce people to buy. In fact, U.S. business spends about $11.5 billion a year on advertising. Surveys, however, show that only 25 percent of those polled said that a television ad would induce them to buy a new product. Likewise, only 15 and 13 percent respectively said that newspaper or magazine ads would cause them to buy. In short, consumers have little confidence in traditional advertising. Advice or the recommendation from a friend or relative, however, scored 63 percent as a determinant of people's buying a new product.[3] This confirms what people have long known: word of mouth is still the best way to attract customers.

Advertising increases awareness of products and services, but personal referrals and recommendations by people who have had a good customer experience lead to actual decisions to purchase those products and services. Over 4,000 empirical studies document the predominant role of social networks—that is, word of mouth—in the diffusion, or spread, of products and services.[4]

To sustain repeat business, generate positive **word-of-mouth advertising** by providing exemplary service. People talk to others about a service experience when it is exceptional, out of the ordinary. You can offer the best products available, but if you fail to supplement them with a positive service experience, few customers will notice the difference between you and your competition. Service success is a matter of setting yourself apart from others through unexpected excellence.

The Impact of E-Commerce on Word of Mouth

Use of electronic media in the form of Web pages, email, **social networking** sites, and blogs are commonplace in today's business world. Such e-commerce capabilities have turbocharged the process of spreading the word about businesses—good and bad. With electronic technology, the scope of the problems and opportunities caused by word of mouth is even greater. Word of mouth becomes "word of mouse."

Spreading the word about a business is simpler than ever with forwarded emails or by copying in dozens of people in our email address book. Easier yet, posting your experiences on Face Book, MySpace, or Linked In (which together with similar sites are approaching millions of users) gets the word out with unimaginable efficiency.

Web sites and Web logs (blogs) are popping up all over for the sole purpose of praising or trashing businesses. In the mid-1990s film *Rainman*, Dustin Hoffman's character, an autistic man, repeatedly states that "K-mart sucks" and the phrase caught on, much to the chagrin of K-mart executives. Today, Web users have the opportunity to regularly rate the relative "suckiness" of any company, and they do. Numerous sites (e.g., *www.RateItAll.com*) provide the opportunity for anyone to evaluate a business, politician, product, entertainment, and much more. The Web provides an additional megaphone for personal opinion, thus turbocharging the power (for better or for worse) of word of mouse.

Companies cannot long get away with mediocre service. In this age of technology and ubiquitous communication, there are few secrets. Customers will get the word out about your company's service. The challenge is to make that the good word.

THE GOOD AND BAD NEWS ABOUT CUSTOMER SERVICE: THE COST OF A LOST CUSTOMER

As the old joke setup goes, I have good news and bad news. The bad news is that the typical company will lose 10 to 30 percent of its customers per year—mostly because of poor service. When customers have a choice, they'll go to the competition without hesitation. Customer satisfaction is like an election held every day, and the people vote with their feet. If dissatisfied, they walk (sometimes run) to another provider—a competitor. When customers don't have a choice—such as in dealing with public utilities or government agencies—they'll use their feet for something else: they'll kick back. Employees will feel the brunt of customer dissatisfaction, dealing with unhappy customers day after day. The cost to the company comes when frustrated employees get fed up with hearing customer grief and leave. The company then faces the cost and disruption of having to replace employees—their internal customers.

The good news about the relatively poor state of customer service is that organizations that initiate effective customer retention programs may see profits jump 25 to 100 percent. Nonprofit groups or organizations with no serious competition see reduced turnover, better financial results, and happier staffs. Like it or not, customer service will always be the decisive battleground where winners and losers are quickly sorted out.

Calculate the Terrible Cost of the Lost Customer

What happens when poor service causes a customer to quit being a customer? Many people don't understand the real **cost of a lost customer**. The costs can be calculated in many ways, but are invariably much greater than we might realize.

To get a clearer view of the cost impact of a lost customer, let's look at a somewhat simplified example from a business we are all familiar with: a grocery supermarket. Let me tell you the story of Mrs. Williams:

Harriet Williams, a 60-something single woman, has been shopping at Happy Jack's Super Market for many years. The store is close to home and its products competitively priced. Last week, Mrs. Williams approached the produce manager and asked, "Sonny, can I get a half head of lettuce?" He looked at her like she was crazy and curtly said, "Sorry, lady. We just sell the whole head." She was a bit embarrassed but accepted his refusal.

Later she had several other small disappointments (she wanted a quart of skim milk and they only had half-gallons), and when she checked out her groceries she was largely ignored by the clerk, who was carrying on a conversation with a fellow employee. The clerk made matters worse by abruptly demanding "two forms of ID" with Harriet's check ("What do they think I am," she thought, "a common criminal?") and failing to say "thank you."

When Mrs. Williams left the store that day, she decided that she was no longer going to do business there. Although she had shopped at Happy Jack's for many years, she realized that she had never felt that her business was appreciated. She got the overall feeling that Happy Jack's employees couldn't care less if she shopped there. She spent about 50 hard-earned dollars there every week, but to the store employees she was just another cash cow to be milked without so much as a sincere "thank you." Nobody seemed to care if she was a satisfied customer. But today is different—no more "nice" Mrs. Williams! Today she decided to buy her groceries elsewhere. Maybe—just maybe—there is a store where they'll appreciate her business.

What do the employees think about Mrs. Williams' actions? They're not worried. Life is like that. You win some; you lose some. Happy Jack's is a pretty big chain and doesn't really need Mrs. Williams. Besides, she can be a bit cranky at times and her special requests are stupid. (Who ever heard of buying a half head of lettuce!) Happy Jack's will survive just fine without her $50 a week. Too bad she's unhappy, but a big company like this can't twist itself into contortions just to save one little old lady from going down the street to the competition. Sure, we believe in treating customers well, but we're businesspeople. Let's look at the bottom line. After all, it can hardly be considered a major financial disaster to lose a customer like Mrs. Williams. Or can it?

Appreciate the Cost of the Lost

The employees at Happy Jack's need to understand some economic realities. Successful businesses look long term. They also look at the "**ripple effects**" of their service, not just at the immediate profit from an individual purchase. Just as the ripples swell when a rock is dropped into a pond, the impact of one unhappy customer can move far beyond that one person.

The shortsighted employee sees Mrs. Williams as a small customer dealing with a big company. Let's change that view: Look at the situation from another, broader perspective.

Ho hum, just the loss of one small customer . . . or is it?

products popped up that appealed to them simply because of the enormous buying power of this demographic group.

Today is no different. The boomer generation still wields a powerful economic stick. But this is not only as customers but also as employees (internal customers). Many 60-something people behave far differently from their parents' generation. Many plan to work well past the traditional retirement ages, although most of them want to cut back from full-time to part-time employment. They are not interested in the proverbial rocking chair.

Some businesses are successfully tapping this important market for employees. The American Association for Retired Persons (AARP) regularly publishes lists of companies that are friendly to older workers. They also work the problem from the other direction and show companies how to become more friendly to older potential employees (their internal customers).

Globalization

In our shrinking world, customers can easily do business with people across the globe. Your competitors are likely to be in different hemispheres. We have all heard the stories of customer service call centers serving U.S. businesses from India or China. In Thomas L. Friedman's best-selling book *The World Is Flat*, he describes how many business services are being outsourced to overseas countries. For example, he talks about an Indian firm in Mumbai (formerly Bombay) called MphasiS that "has a team of Indian accountants able to do outsourced accounting work from any state in America and the federal government." He goes on to explain how "The accountants in India call up all the raw data directly from the [computer] server in America, and they complete your tax returns . . ."[5] The book further explains how many products and services can, and increasingly will, be outsourced worldwide.

The competition for the hearts and minds of your internal customers has increased as well. More and more employees face opportunities to work in foreign lands. The job market has become broader than ever with worldwide opportunities for skilled workers.

Work–Life Balance

People's desire to balance work and other aspects of life is also having an impact on customer and employee loyalty. Employees, in particular, feel that their work must not consume their lives. Companies that recognize the need for balance are increasingly attractive to workers. Similarly, companies that provide services and goods that enable customers to enjoy an appropriate balance between the mundane and the more rewarding pursuits can thrive. By giving customers efficient services and added convenience, companies can take the burdens off people and establish a basis for strong customer loyalty.

Historically, daily chores consumed a large part of the typical person's life. Homemakers spent many hours cooking, cleaning, and doing laundry. Breadwinners toiled in unpleasant jobs long hours to bring home the bacon. But today, much of this drudgery has been alleviated—and people want even more relief. The best commercial opportunities are often ones that promise to further enable people to have balanced, fulfilling lives. Great customer service can help people achieve these objectives.

TRANSLATING SLOGANS AND GOOD INTENTIONS INTO A STRATEGY

Most companies accept, or at least pay lip service to, the idea that "the customer is the boss," that he or she is a "king" or "queen" (or at least a prince or princess!). They talk about the customer always being right. They say, ad nauseam, that the customer is "our reason for existing" as an organization. Yet despite these claims, how is the service given? Often, not great.

A significant challenge lies in translating such slogans into actions that convey these feelings and beliefs *to the customer*. Even when leaders truly believe in the importance of customer service, they still face the difficulty of getting the customer contact people to do what customers want—especially when a customer's request is a bit unusual. The problem gets trickier when you realize that the lowest-paid and least-trained employees are often those who face the customer every day. For example,

- A multibillion-dollar fast-food restaurant places its success squarely in the hands of the minimum-wage teenager taking the orders and delivering the food. The employee turnover in such businesses is huge, requiring constant training of new people.
- A huge financial institution's image is created in the mind of the customer by the entry-level teller who handles the customer's day-to-day transactions.
- A multibillion-dollar government agency is judged largely by the receptionist who answers the phone or greets the customer, thus setting a tone for any transaction. (Many a criticism of the "government bureaucracy" can be traced to a receptionist "getting off on the wrong foot" with a patron.)

> The face of a company is often that of the lowest-paid employees who meet the customers.

When you sincerely buy into the value of a happy, loyal customer and effectively communicate that value to each customer, you virtually guarantee your success. When you supervise others, you need to "infect" them with your same positive attitudes and skills.

What If You Are "Just an Employee?"

Businesses benefit from good service, but suppose you don't own a business. As "just an employee," what can you gain from developing service skills? The short answer is that customer service skills are the same skills that bring success and satisfaction to all aspects of life. The best reason for learning the processes that create customer loyalty is that *it will make you feel better about your life and yourself*. Sure, there are solid business reasons, as we've already discussed. But ultimately, the personal benefits can be even greater.

It doesn't matter whether we are the company CEO or are working in the mail room, we choose how much we want to give to the organization. Inevitably, the more effort, energy, and commitment we give, the more value we get from our association with that organization. That's a principle of life that has been proven true throughout time. The flip side—giving the least we can get away with—results in unsatisfying relationships, mind-numbing work, and low levels of satisfaction. Giving average or substandard service will be hazardous to your career health. Undistinguished service leads to unhappy and eventually extinguished careers.

> The more we commit to giving great service, the more we will get from our association with our company.

The person who makes a commitment to mastering customer skills will be light years ahead of one who fails to do so.

THE ULTIMATE GOAL: DEVELOPING CUSTOMER LOYALTY FOR LIFE

The ultimate goal of customer service is to create customer loyalty. Understanding loyalty—what makes your customer loyal and how to measure this—enables a company or person to improve customer-driven service quality. I'll talk more about this later in the book, but for now, it is important to understand what loyalty means.

To best understand what customer loyalty is, it is useful to first recognize what it is *not*. Customer loyalty is sometimes mistaken for:

- Customer satisfaction alone. Satisfaction is a necessary component, but a customer may be satisfied today but not necessarily loyal to you in the future.
- A response to some trial offer or special incentive. You can't buy loyalty; you must earn it.

SERVICE SNAPSHOT

Burgers Supreme

Steve and Debby K. owned an independent fast-food restaurant called Burgers Supreme. For more than six years they built up a loyal clientele, many of whom ate there almost every day. Not only did these customers buy lunch at Burgers Supreme, but they also brought friends and fellow workers. Some of the regulars were teased about owning stock in the restaurant, although none did.

The menu was broad, covering dozens of sandwiches, salads, soups, desserts, and specialty foods like gyros, onion rings, and frozen yogurt. Everything was prepared fresh. But the loyalty went far beyond good food and fair prices.

Almost every regular customer had the unexpected surprise of having Steve, Debby, or one of their employees say, "This meal's on me." Owners, managers, and even employees were authorized to give free lunches to loyal customers. Obviously that didn't happen every time the customer came in, but it did reflect the owners' belief in recognizing customer loyalty. It also reflected their willingness to empower their employees to give something away now and then.

The counter help at Burgers Supreme learned service behaviors from Debby's example. She was always right there beside them on the firing line. She taught by example and freely dispensed compliments and corrective suggestions. She taught (and modeled the behaviors) as her people greeted customers by name, smiled, cheerfully fixed any mistakes, and kept hustling to make sure the restaurant was clean, even during the busiest lunch hour.

Faced with tremendous competition from national chains like Wendy's, McDonald's, and others who serve similar fare, Burgers Supreme ate their lunch, so to speak, with friendly, individual, personalized service. They didn't just talk the talk of customer service. They walked the walk.

- Large share of the market. You may have a large percentage of the customers for a particular product or service for reasons other than customer loyalty to you. Perhaps your competitors are poor or your current prices more attractive.
- Repeat buying alone. Some people buy as a result of habit, convenience, or price but would be quick to defect to an alternative.

Recognizing counterfeit loyalty is important. It can lull you into a false sense of security while your competition may be building real customer loyalty.

Customer Loyalty

So, what exactly is customer loyalty? A more reliable definition has evolved in recent years. Considerable empirical research concludes that customer loyalty is best defined as a composite of three important characteristics:

- It is driven by *overall satisfaction*. Low or erratic levels of satisfaction disqualify a company from earning customer loyalty.
- It involves a commitment on the part of the customer to make a sustained *investment in an ongoing relationship* with a company.
- It is reflected by a combination of attitudes and behaviors, including:
    - *repeat buying* (or the intention to do so as needed)
    - *willingness to recommend* the company to others
    - a commitment to the company demonstrated by a *resistance to switch* to a competitor

Some customers aren't really loyal; they just haven't left—yet.

More recent research by the Gallup polling organization validates these elements and takes the concept a bit further by describing customer "engagement" as a critical variable. In a 2003 article, the *Gallup Management Journal* questions the intuitively obvious link between loyalty and profitability. The researchers conclude that some kinds of customer loyalty may not be profitable. Specifically, they say that "repeated purchase behavior [that] has been motivated—or bribed—by a company's gifts, discounts, or other purchase rewards" may not be profitable. These customers aren't really loyal; they're just customers who haven't left—yet. Behavioral measures of loyalty are often misleading because they can't differentiate between customers with allegiance to a business or brand and those with no real commitment. The uncommitted may *appear* to be loyal, but they remain customers only out of habit, convenience, or because it's a hassle to switch to another provider. Or maybe it's because the company continues to bribe them with some reward program or cost incentive. These uncommitted customers, however, are susceptible to the incentives and discounts competitors will offer them to switch.

If you fail to make an emotional connection with customers, satisfaction is worthless. Gallup concludes that customer **engagement** with the organizations they buy from becomes a priceless resource for those organizations. Several case studies reveal that fully engaged customers—that is, customers who are both satisfied and emotionally connected to a store—visit the store more often and spend more money.

> An emotional connection with customers is crucial to building loyal relationships.

Concepts of engagement, allegiance, and so on offer different ways to express levels of loyalty and commitment a customer may hold toward a company or brand. While the terminology may differ, our earlier definition of the conditions necessary for creating loyalty remains essentially intact. For now, let's agree that customer loyalty is the highest goal of our service efforts.

A FINAL THOUGHT

Customer service skill development provides the most significant arena for career success. Whether you work for a huge corporation or you run a lemonade stand, the principles of customer service remain the same. You live and die by what your customers think of you.

Service to internal customers—employees—can be equally important as service to external customers. All the principles of customer service we discuss in this book can be applied to employee relationships.

Your number-one task, regardless of your job title, organizational position, experience, or seniority, will *always* be to attract, satisfy, and preserve loyal customers.

ANOTHER LOOK
Why Customer Satisfaction Is Not Enough

Several studies by the Gallup polling organization look at the connection between customer satisfaction and customer loyalty. Data from a leading supermarket chain supports the importance of an emotional connection on the frequency of customers' visits and the amount of money they spent during those visits. Shoppers who reported being *less than* "extremely satisfied" visited this chain about 4.3 times per month, spending an average of $166 during that month. Those who reported being "extremely satisfied" but did not also have a strong emotional connection to the chain actually went to the store less often (4.1 times per month) and spent less ($144). In this case, extreme satisfaction represented no added value to the store.

However, when Gallup looked at customers who were extremely satisfied and emotionally connected to the store (what they call "fully engaged"), a very different customer relationship emerged. These customers visited the store 5.4 times and spent $210 a month.

Apparently, not all "extremely satisfied" customers are the same. Those with strong emotional connections visited the grocery chain 32 percent more often and spent 46 percent more money than those without emotional bonds. Their conclusion is that satisfaction without engagement is basically worthless. Satisfaction with engagement (stemming from some **emotional attachment**), however, is priceless.

Probes

1. What does this research suggest about companies that simply measure customer satisfaction?
2. What are the key challenges facing organizations that want to build customer loyalty?
3. How could your business apply this information to build customer loyalty?

Source: Excerpted from W. J. McEwen and J. H. Flemming, "Customer Satisfaction Doesn't Count." *Gallup Management Journal*, March 13, 2003 [Online]. Available *http://gmj.gallup.com/ management_articles/customer_engagement/article*.

Summary of Key Ideas

- Business and personal success is almost always dependent upon one's ability to build healthy relationships. In a broad sense, we succeed when we attract and keep loyal customers—people with whom we exchange value.
- Customers may be called by many names, but all are engaged in an exchange of value. External customers are those outside the company (usually purchasers); internal customers are generally employees or organization members.
- Customers can become partners through service intimacy and creation of an ongoing relationship. This happens when we are generous, trustworthy, share a joint purpose, speak with truth and candor, mixed with compassion and care, and pursue equality with grace.
- Positive word of mouth helps any business get and keep customers. E-commerce also introduces "word of mouse," which spreads the news to people's networks with unparalleled speed.

- The impact of lost customers can be calculated many ways, but a simple process is to compute lost sales, the cost of other lost customers who hear the bad news, and replacement costs of getting new customers.
- The changing nature of today's customers has been especially impacted by greater diversity, age issues, globalization, and work–life balance.
- While all companies *say* the customer's satisfaction is paramount, few successfully translate good intentions into a workable strategy or specific behavior. This presents a significant opportunity for leaders.
- Customer satisfaction, although necessary, is not sufficient to create loyalty.
- Some key elements of loyalty are a customer's general satisfaction, intention to keep doing business with us, and willingness to recommend us to others.

Key Concepts

cost of a lost customer
customer satisfaction
    and loyalty
emotional attachment

exchange of value
external customers
loyalty and engagement
internal customers

ongoing relationship
ripple effects
service intimacy
social capital

social networking
word-of-mouth
    advertising

Reviewing the Facts

1. What defines a customer (using this term in the broad sense)?
2. What are some attitudes or orientations that define a customer relationship? What factors account for a strengthening of this relationship?
3. How can customer skills be valuable even in nonprofit organizations (or organizations that have no competitors)?
4. Why does word-of-mouth "advertising" work so effectively?
5. How can a person build his or her "social capital"?

6. How do diversity, age, globalization, and work–life balance issues impact a company's ability to give great service to both internal and external customers?
7. How do ripple effects escalate the problem of the lost customer?
8. What three key characteristics define real customer loyalty?
9. What do we mean by an "engaged" customer, and how does this relate to customer loyalty?
10. What characteristics are often confused with customer loyalty but do not represent real loyalty?

Applying the Ideas: Interview Service Providers

1. Interview five people about their customer service attitudes. Specifically, ask them to describe their internal and external customers and what they feel about the importance of serving them.
2. Ask two businesspeople to estimate the typical amount customers spend with them. Then calculate the "cost of a lost customer" based on the scenario in this chapter. Ask each businessperson to react to this estimate. Does it seem plausible? Too high? Too low?

3. Describe three businesses that have won your customer loyalty—places you enjoy doing business and are likely to remain a customer. What, specifically, causes you to give them your loyalty? (Note: Often it's subtle little things that win you over.)
4. What major corporations that you've heard of seem to be doing the best job of building customer loyalty? In what ways do they attempt to build long-term relationships with customers?

Consider this Case

Costco and the Power of High-Quality Relationships

Retailing giant Costco has enjoyed substantial success at building customer loyalty. The warehouse outlets spend almost nothing on traditional advertising but have grown dramatically largely by word of mouth. In short, enthusiastic Costco customers tell other people.

Costco, the wholesale club company, is a real-life example of how great customer relationships generate economic benefits. More than 80 percent of customers report a willingness to recommend Costco to their friends and associates. The company has grown to almost 50 million members despite spending next to nothing on advertising or marketing. While a typical discounter carries 40,000 SKUs (stock keeping units—essentially the number of products sold), Costco stores have only 4,500—only those items where it can provide outstanding value. Sales per store are almost twice those at Sam's Club, its closest competitor. Costco's success funds a generous compensation package for its employees. New hires start at $10 an hour—high for the retail industry—and progress to $40,000 a year after three years. They receive a benefits package virtually unequalled in the industry. Low turnover and long tenure reduce hiring and training costs and boost productivity; they also contribute to Costco's remarkably low inventory-shrinkage rate, which is only 13 percent of the industry average. The company eliminates bad profits through a generous return policy—there is no time limit on returns except for a limit of one year on computer technology items. Costco's earnings have grown at about 12 to 17 percent a year, over the past decade, even in a difficult economic environment.

Probes

1. Describe any experiences you have had with Costco. Generally, are you satisfied when shopping there?
2. Would you describe yourself as a promoter for Costco—someone who would willingly recommend it to friends?
3. How does Costco appear to be aware of the importance of its internal customers?
4. What challenges do you think Costco will face in the future regarding its customer loyalty?

Consider this Case

The Diminished Image of Airline Travel

Once upon a time, commercial flying was thought to be prestigious, adventurous, and fun. Few people would describe it that way today. In the "old days" passengers dressed in their best clothing and enjoyed the pampering of courteous, uniformed "stewardesses" (virtually all were women and most were hired for their attractiveness). All passengers enjoyed complimentary beverages and meals and other amenities such as decks of playing cards, pillows, and blankets for adults, and activity books, crayons, and toy pilot's wings for children.

Bit by bit, the industry's landscape changed and the passenger perks disappeared. With rising costs, increased competition, and extensive security requirements, air travel has become a far less pleasant experience. Flying coach is now likened to steerage in the sailing vessels of old. Discrepancies between first class and coach amenities have reinforced for many the strict notion of social class. One airline recently floated the idea of a flight class *with no* seats! Passengers would stand like subway strap hangers. One recent columnist complains that "the airlines have raised group humiliation into an art form."

Chat with anyone at an airport about service changes and you'll get an earful. Many of these changes are not the fault of the airlines, but they get the blame. Whatever happened to "the friendly skies"?

Probes

1. What changes have you seen as an airline passenger? Which of these are most annoying? Which seem to improve service?
2. What could airline leaders do to offset the negative impression so many people have of the industry? What initiatives being taken now seem the most fruitful?
3. What do you see as the long-term impact of diminished service quality on the industry?

Notes

1. Chip R. Bell and John R. Patterson, "When More Is Less: Why Value-Added Service Won't Give You an Edge in Tough Times," *www.chipbell.com/articles* ©2009.

2. W. Baker, *Achieving Success Through Social Capital* (San Francisco: Josey-Bass, Inc., 2000). Quoted on dust jacket.

3. K. Goldman, "Study Finds Ads Induce Few People to Buy," *Wall Street Journal*, October 17, 1995, p. B6.

4. E. Rogers, *Diffusion of Innovations*, 4th ed. (New York: Free Press, 1995).

5. Friedman, Thomas L., *The World Is Flat: A Brief History of the Twenty-First Century* (New York: Farrer, Straus and Giroux, 2005, p. 12).

PART 1

LIFE: Little Things

The first letter in our acronym LIFE is **L** for "little things." In any transaction with customers, the little details can make or break you. The attention to detail in the ways we communicate with customers—even the most subtle detail—often determines whether a customer will have a positive experience. The next four chapters focus on some of the little things people value. We begin with behaviors in face-to-face interactions. Some of these behaviors are second nature to people and project pleasing personalities. Chapter 3 considers one of the most often overlooked communication skills: listening. Chapter 4 will be of particular value to readers who use the telephone in their business. Finally, in Chapter 5 we will look at the little things that make for more successful electronic communication using email, Web pages, and a variety of new media options.

So, let's consider the "little things" worth considering as we strive to provide better customer service.

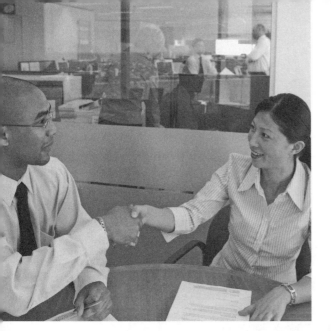

CHAPTER 2

Use Behaviors that Engage Your Customers
It's All about the Little Things You Do

Sometimes the smallest, unintended behavior can create relationship turnoffs—or trigger pleasant, positive impressions. Subtle facial expressions, gestures, vocal intonation, or appearance can make the difference between winning customer loyalty or losing it.

—Paul R. Timm

If people are good only because they fear punishment, and hope for reward, then we are a sorry lot indeed.

—Albert Einstein

After reading this chapter, you should be able to

1. Recognize the kinds of behaviors and personality factors that please customers.

2. Use 15 specific action tips that convey a positive personality.

3. Respond to difficult people with appropriate communication styles.

4. Apply six organizational behaviors that convey a customer-centered culture.

The Way It Is . . . the Power of Personality

"G'morning, Hon," "Hi, there!" and a chorus of other greetings ring out whenever customers enter a Waffle House. The ubiquitous Southern restaurants are famous for a cheery hello, especially at breakfast time. You never feel like a stranger at Waffle House.

More than 20 years ago, Ferris Beyer opened a bank account near his office. Being new to town, he needed the checking account and the branch office was close by. A week after opening the account, he walked in to make a deposit. He stated, "I'd barely cleared the door when a teller cheerfully called across the lobby, 'Good morning, Mr. Beyer.' I was stunned. She had remembered my name after only one transaction. I remained a loyal customer of that bank for decades, based largely on the personality of the employees."

The Disney organization builds incredible loyalty by providing a "happiest-place-on-earth" atmosphere in their theme parks. People enjoy themselves in large part because the employees (whom Disney calls "cast members") seem to be enjoying themselves. Smiles and greetings are exchanged freely and convey the organization's personality.

Every organization, like every individual, has a personality. This personality is conveyed by countless "little things," mostly verbal and nonverbal communication cues. Some people are unaware of how these cues work—how subtle behaviors send "messages" to others. In this chapter, we will talk about the importance of personality-projecting communication behaviors in customer service.

BEHAVIOR AND PERSONALITY FACTORS THAT PLEASE CUSTOMERS

Behavior is, of course, what people do. It is conveyed to others via both verbal (using words or language) and nonverbal (without words) communication. Even when no words are exchanged, personality can still communicate loud and clear. A salesperson who ignores a customer, an employee who routinely shows up late, a clerk wearing a "frowny" face, and a repair person who leaves a mess all communicate something. Likewise, the friendly greeter at a store or restaurant, the cheerful voice from a call center, or the associate who always has a smile and a cheerful comment communicates something as well.

While having a good attitude is important, that attitude becomes apparent to others only through behaviors. A behavior is visible—as a colleague once reminded me—"if it can't be video-taped, it isn't a behavior." Behaviors are the ways we communicate to others.

Good attitudes come across to customers via visible behaviors.

Keep in mind two important rules of communication: (1) *Anything can and will communicate*, and (2) *the receiver of the message determines what it "means."* Therefore, the projected personality is in the eyes of the beholder and what may be an attractive personality to one may be less so to another. Nevertheless, some behaviors almost always get a good response.

The remainder of this chapter looks at some kinds of **behaviors**—of **individuals and organizations**—that convey messages to customers. This is by no means an exhaustive list of all possible behaviors, but it does reflect the more common ones that associate closely with customer service.

ANOTHER LOOK
Nonverbal Communication Differences Across Cultures

Nonverbal communication is one way we convey behaviors to others. People see us doing something and extract meaning from our actions. But, the meaning of these cues is in the eyes of the beholder—what we project can come across differently in different cultures. People consider nonverbal cues even more carefully when the words we use are unclear, ambiguous, or of a different language. Nonverbal behavior arises from our cultural common sense—our ideas about what is appropriate, normal, and effective in communicating. Different cultures assign different meanings to gestures, posture, silence, spatial relations, emotional expression, touch, physical appearance, and other nonverbal cues.[1]

Some elements of nonverbal communication are consistent across cultures. For example, research has shown that the emotions of enjoyment, anger, fear, sadness, disgust, and surprise come across in similar ways by people around the world. There are, however, exceptions. In China and Japan, for example, a facial expression that would be recognized around the world as conveying happiness may actually express anger or mask sadness, both of which are unacceptable to show overtly.[2] The implication of this: Don't assume too much about the meaning of nonverbal messages.

We also tend to differ in areas such as what emotions are appropriate for expression. For example, in the United States it may be more socially acceptable for women to show fear, but not anger, and for men to display anger, but not fear.[3]

Here are several other variables across cultures that can have implications for customer service:

- *Proxemics* (ways of relating to space). In conversations, North Americans tend to position themselves about arm's-length apart. The French, Italian, Arabic, and most

(continued)

Latin American people tend to stand closer to each other when talking. Americans become uncomfortable with such "invasion of personal space," except in situations of intimacy.

- *Personal space*. If someone is accustomed to standing or sitting very close when they are talking with another, they may see attempts to create more space as evidence of coldness, condescension, or a lack of interest. Those who are accustomed to more personal space may view attempts to get closer as pushy, disrespectful, or aggressive. Neither is correct—they are simply different.
- *Furniture or other objects*. People from various cultures accept the position of furniture and artifacts in different ways. In some cultures, it would be very rude for a guest to move a chair when visiting an office. In cultures where people hold a high regard for "power difference," large furniture barriers are commonplace.

These people may be quite uncomfortable if invited to sit on a couch or around a small table.

- *Waiting in line (or "cues" as they are called in Europe)*. The British and Americans are serious about standing in lines, perhaps in accordance with their beliefs in the principle of "first come, first served." The French, on the other hand, have a practice of line jumping that irritates many British and Americans. In another example, immigrants from Armenia report that it is difficult to adjust to a system of waiting in line, when their home context permitted one member of a family to save spots for several others.

These are, of course, just a few examples of nonverbal differences across cultures. To reduce the risk of offending customers, it makes sense to become aware of such differences and work to avoid giving or taking offense at what are simply differences.

Each customer is likely to encounter two interrelated personalities: the personality of the individual who provides service and the overall personality of the organization. This organizational personality reflects the company's "culture." Culture is a composite of many factors that project the shared values of the people who work there. The culture can strengthen and reinforce individual behaviors and, of course, individual behaviors reinforce the culture. For example, if a company is an enjoyable, fun-loving place to work, its people will convey a sense of enjoyment to customers. If the culture is more formal (say, at a law firm or medical facility), this personality—these shared values—may be reinforced by employee behaviors that convey competence and professionalism. (Of course, lawyers and medical-office employees can also be fun-loving and personable.)

A company's "personality" comes across through its organizational culture.

One company recently cited for its exceptional culture is Zappos, the Las Vegas–based e-commerce company selling shoes. In its annual feature on the 100 best companies to work for in America, the *Fortune* magazine featured Zappos, "the quirky retailer," which appeared for the first time on the list at number 23. Why Zappos? The key factor was the company's personality described as having a reputation for flat-out fun, while still being rooted in core values. Zappos's CEO Tony Hsieh articulates his "ten commandments," which include "create fun and a little weirdness" and "deliver 'wow.'"[4]

Zappos's fun and weirdness includes parades, pajama parties, happy hours, and shaved heads. Its notion of "wowing" customers includes free returns, quick shipping, sending flowers and thank-you notes, and finding out of stock items elsewhere. Wowing the customer is their top priority. The personality of a company comes through to customers and is reinforced by the employees they hire. Zappos does its best to hire positive people and put them where positive thinking is reinforced by the culture.

Wal-Mart founder Sam Walton understood **organizational culture** when he taught his managers that "People will treat your customers the way you treat your people." Enthusiasm, comradeship, a sense of enjoyment, and humor quickly become evident to Wal-Mart's customers. Southwest Airlines, which has a culture of informality and fun at work, projects an organizational personality very different from that of many of its competitors. This personality has been useful both in attracting customers and in enlisting employees who enjoy working in such an atmosphere. Southwest has fared far better than its competitors in difficult times for the airline industry. Indeed, research studies of the best companies to work for consistently identify "having fun" as a critically important criterion.

INDIVIDUAL BEHAVIOR ACTION TIPS THAT CONVEY PERSONALITY

The rest of this chapter looks at specific behaviors—often little things—that can project powerful messages to customers. It's these kinds of little things that can make or break relationships. Awareness of these alone can improve service, yet many employees are essentially clueless about the impact of their behaviors. Below are 15 behaviors (I call them "Action Tips") that, taken together, project personality.

Action Tip 1—Greet Customers Like Guests

Woody Allen once said that 80 percent of success is just showing up. In customer service, 80 percent of success is treating the customer like a guest who just showed up. When guests come to your home, you greet them, right? You wouldn't ignore someone who comes into your living room. Yet we've all had the experience of being totally ignored by service people in some businesses. A friendly greeting, like that offered routinely at Waffle House, is one of those little things that mean a lot. Even in more subdued businesses, a welcome is appreciated.

INITIATE CONVERSATION PROMPTLY   Studies have clocked the number of seconds people had to wait to be greeted in several types of businesses. Researchers then asked customers how long they'd been waiting. In every case, the customer's estimate of the time elapsed was much longer than the actual time. A customer waiting 30 or 40 seconds often felt like it had been three or four minutes. Time drags when you're being ignored.

Customers who are ignored for even short periods feel like it is longer.

A prompt, friendly greeting can help people feel comfortable and reduce stress customers may experience. Why would customers feel stress? Because they are on unfamiliar turf. While employees work there every day, customers are just visiting. A prompt, friendly greeting can help everyone relax and grease the wheels of comfortable interaction.

SPEAK UP   Employees should **verbally greet customers** within a few seconds of entering the business or approaching a work location. Even if busy with another customer or on the phone, workers should pause to say something that acknowledges customers and lets them know that they will be ready to help them soon. The absence of any spoken greeting creates an awkward silence for customers. "Hi. I'll be right with you" is all that may be needed to comfort the customer.

GET THE CUSTOMER COMMITTED   Some fast-food restaurants send a clerk out to write your order on a sheet of paper while you are waiting in line. You tell the person what you want, she marks it on a slip of paper, and then she gives it back to you to present at the cash register where the order is called out. Why do they do this? It is a way of **getting the customer committed**. If no one greeted you or wrote your order, you might be more likely to leave, especially if the line seems long, before reaching the register. But psychologically, this strategy makes you feel as if you've "ordered," so you stay in line and follow through with your lunch purchase.

Try to get a customer to do something—physically.

Some years ago as PCs were first gaining widespread popularity, the behavior differences between the successful and unsuccessful salespeople were striking. The less successful ones rattled off a lot of techno-jargon, apparently intended to impress customers, while their successful counterparts quickly invited the novice computer user to sit down and *do something* on the computer. Research observations of auto salespeople showed similar patterns. The best car sales reps didn't spend much time talking about the car a customer was looking at. He literally tossed them the keys and invited the prospect to test-drive the car.

Employees should greet each customer promptly, verbally if possible, and try to get them doing something as soon as feasible when they come into the business or work area.

Action Tip 2—Break the Ice

The best way to start a conversation depends on what the customer needs. In many cases, especially in retail stores, customers need first to be reassured that this is a nice, friendly place to do business. They need to overcome worries about being high-pressured into buying, a major turnoff for many people. Often customers want to browse and get the feel of the place before they commit to doing business. To dispel those worries, use a nonthreatening **icebreaker**. The best icebreaker for the browser can be an off-topic, friendly comment. Some good ones might be:

- A compliment ("That's a great looking tie you're wearing" or "Your children are sure cute. How old are they?" or "I appreciate your coming in today.")
- Weather-related or local-interest comments ("Isn't this sunshine just beautiful?" or "Some snowfall, isn't it?" or "How about that game last night?")
- Small talk (Look for cues about the customer's interest in sports, jobs, mutual acquaintances, past experiences, and so on. Then initiate a relevant comment.)

If a browsing customer seems to be focusing attention on a product (say he or she is holding several shirts or is looking at a particular item), the person can be reclassified as a "focused shopper." The best icebreaker for the focused shopper is one that is more specific to the buying decision. It may:

- Anticipate the customer's questions ("What size are you looking for, sir?" or "Can I help you select a . . . ?")
- Provide additional information ("Those widgets are all 25 percent off today" or "We have those in other colors in the stockroom" or "We just got those in. They're the latest model.")
- Offer a suggestion or recommendation ("Those striped suits are really popular this season" or "If you need help with measurements, our estimators can figure out what you'll need.")

Be attentive to customers' needs. Give them time to browse if that's what they need, but be responsive in helping them make a buying decision when they are ready. Retail-industry research shows that 60 to 80 percent of all shopping decisions are made in the store at the point of sale.[5] This is precisely the point where customers come face-to-face with the employee's and the organization's personality. Reassure customers that you can help them. Ask questions to identify their needs, concerns, or problems. Oh, and *listen* to their responses (more on this in Chapter 3).

Engage your customers at the point of sale.

Action Tip 3—Compliment Freely and Sincerely

It only takes a second to say something nice to a person. Such comments can add enormous goodwill and move people toward a positive experience. Employees should look for opportunities to say something complimentary to their customers and coworkers. Safe ground for sincere compliments includes:

a. Some article of clothing or accessories they are wearing ("I like that sport coat!" or "Those shoes look really comfortable. I've been shopping for some like that" or "What a beautiful necklace.")

b. Their family ("That's a great family picture" or "How old is your daughter? She's beautiful" or "Your son looks like quite the athlete.")

c. Their behavior ("Thanks for waiting. You've been very patient" or "I noticed you checking those items. You're a careful shopper" or "Thanks for being so cheerful. Customers like you make this job much more fun.")

d. Something they own ("I like your car. What year is it?" or "I noticed your championship ring. Did you play on that team?")

One caveat: avoid compliments that might be construed as sexually suggestive or condescending.

Action Tip 4—Call People by Name

A person's name is his or her favorite sound. We appreciate it when people make the effort to use our name in addressing us. Just as in the earlier example about the bank teller calling a customer by name, this action can project a company's personality to its customers and build loyalty.

When appropriate, employees should introduce themselves to customers and ask their names. If this isn't appropriate (such as when there is a line of waiting customers), they can often get customers' names from checks, credit cards, order forms, or other paperwork.

People appreciate being called by their names.

Be careful not to become overly familiar too quickly, as some customers may feel it's disrespectful. We are generally safe calling people "Mr. Smith" or "Ms. Jones," but we may be seen as rude calling them "Homer" and "Marge." (This is especially true when younger employees are dealing with older customers.) It's better to err on the side of being too formal. If people prefer being addressed by their first name, they'll tell you so.

Action Tip 5—Talk to Customers with Your Eyes

Even in situations where you may not be able to say "hello" out loud or give undivided attention to a customer right away, you can make eye contact. Simply looking at your customer tells him or her much about your willingness to serve. Eye contact creates a bond between you and the customer. It conveys your interest in communicating further.

As with your greeting, the timing of eye contact is important. Make eye contact with your customer as soon as possible—within a few seconds—even if you are busy with another person. It's not necessary that you interrupt what you are doing with the customer at hand. Just a pause and a quick look capture new customers and reduce the chance they'll feel ignored and leave.

When working with customers, be sensitive to how you look at them. Communication expert Bert Decker says that the **three I's of eye contact** are intimacy, intimidation, and involvement. Intimacy (as when we're expressing love) and intimidation (when we want to exert power) are both communicated by looking at another person for a long period—from 10 seconds to a minute or more.[6] But most communication in business settings calls for Decker's third "I": involvement.

In Western cultures, people create involvement by looking at the other person for 5- to 10-second periods before glancing away briefly. This is generally comfortable for people. If you look away more often than that, you may be seen as shifty or suspicious; if you lock in eye contact for longer, it feels like intimidation or intimacy. These traditions vary in other countries.

Action Tip 6—Ask Often "How Am I Doing?"

Legendary politician and former New York City mayor Ed Koch would constantly ask his constituents, "How'm I doing?" The phrase became his tagline. There is some evidence that he even listened to their answers. After all, he survived as mayor of the Big Apple for many years. We can learn something from the Koch question.

LOOK INSIDE

How Often Do You Compliment?

How frequently do you compliment people? To get a better answer, try this: Carry a note card or small notebook and simply tally each time you compliment someone. After each conversation, jot down the number of compliments you included. Do this for a reasonable amount of time—an hour, half day, or full workday.

Then, to build the habit of complimenting, try this: Set a goal to give 10 sincere compliments each day. Keep track.

See what happens. You'll probably see a sharp increase in your personal popularity! People love to be complimented. And, of course, complimenting internal customers (e.g., coworkers, employees) can also help create a supportive and pleasant work climate.

People always appreciate sincere compliments and rarely get enough of them.

SERVICE SNAPSHOT

The Watch Repair Guy

Mr. Stearn ran a very small watch repair shop. The shop was no more than 10 feet square. He was a real expert at repairing timepieces, and his prices were good. Two customers squeezed into his tiny shop. They were both bent over the work counter while Mr. Stearn adjusted the one customer's watch. The second customer stood not more than 5 feet away from Mr. Stearn for several minutes without ever being acknowledged. It was so uncomfortable that the second customer was just about to step out of the shop and go elsewhere when Mr. Stearn finished with the first customer and finally acknowledged the person waiting.

Mr. Stearn ran a real risk of losing a valuable customer before he got a chance to show what he could do—simply because he made no eye contact and did not take the time to welcome a customer.

Probes

1. What should Mr. Stearn have done when the second customer came into his shop? If you were the first customer, would you be upset if he shifted his attention briefly to the second customer?
2. How does this illustrate the principle that little things can mean everything?

Businesses need to ask that question in as many ways as possible. In addition to using more formalized measurement and feedback systems, employees should demonstrate an ongoing attitude of receptiveness. Being receptive to people's comments and criticisms can be challenging and at times frustrating. It takes a lot of courage not only to accept criticism but to actually request it. Nevertheless, getting a constant flow of "how am I doing" information is a critical key to projecting an open personality. We'll talk much more about getting feedback in Chapter 8.

For now, simply be aware that being open to it is a little thing that can enhance your personality.

Action Tip 7—Listen with More than Your Ears

Since so few people are really good listeners, this skill provides an excellent opportunity to project a positive personality. There is no such thing as an unpopular listener. Everyone becomes more interesting when they stop talking and start listening—to us!

We will talk extensively about listening in Chapter 3. The minimum requirements for good listening are these:

- *Focus on the content of what people are saying, not the way they are saying it.* Customers may not have the "right" words, but they know what they need better than anyone.
- *Hold your fire.* Don't jump to make judgments or finish a customer's thought before he or she has finished talking.
- *Work at listening.* Maintain eye contact and discipline yourself to listen to what is being said. Tune out those thoughts that get you sidetracked, thinking about something else.
- *Seek clarification from customers to fully understand their needs.* Do this in a nonthreatening way using sincere, open-ended questions.

Action Tip 8—Say "Please," "Thank You," and "You're Welcome"

At the risk of sounding like a self-help book about things learned in kindergarten, "please," "thank you," and "you're welcome" are powerful words for building customer rapport and creating customer loyalty. Stick with these terms and avoid saying something like "there you go" when concluding a transaction. There is really no good substitute for these traditional terms.

When a customer thanks you, respond with "You're welcome," Or, as the Ritz Carlton hotel employees say, "It was my pleasure." Again, stick with these or similar phrases. Do not use the currently popular favorite, "no problem." "No problem" seems to imply that you expected the customers to be potential problems, but dealing with them wasn't as bad as expected. That's not the message you want to convey. Stick with the basics: Say, "You're welcome" or something equally polite.

Basic courtesy is never out of style.

Action Tip 9—Reassure Customers in Their Decision to Do Business with You

Marketers talk about the problem of **buyer's remorse**—the feeling that a purchase was a mistake. This feeling can set in pretty quickly, especially when people make a large purchase. At the time of sale, service providers can inoculate against buyer's remorse by reassuring customers that they've made a good purchasing decision.

Phrases like "I'm sure you'll get many hours of enjoyment out of this" or "Your family will love it" can help reassure and strengthen the buyer's resolve to follow through with the purchase and, as importantly, feel good about it. A government agency employee might say, "I'll bet you're glad that's over with for another year" or "I'll handle the renewal—you've done all that is necessary." Such reassurance can project your personality in positive ways.

Action Tip 10—Smile

As the old adage goes, "You are not dressed for work until you put on a smile." Or, as a more cynical person might say, "Smile—it'll make people wonder what you've been up to." But more importantly, it'll tell customers that they came to the right place and are on friendly ground. Personality is rarely projected without a smile.

Keep in mind that a smile originates in two places, the mouth and the eyes. A lips-only version looks pasted on and insincere. It's like saying "cheese" when being photographed. It doesn't fool anyone. In fact, it might scare them away!

The eyes, however, are the windows to the soul and tell the truth about your feelings toward people. So smile with your eyes and your mouth. Let your face show that you're glad your guest arrived.

Now, in fairness, some people smile more readily than others, and in some business contexts smiling may be inappropriate (at a funeral home, for example). For some people, a more serious facial expression is comfortable and natural. But in most cultures, a smile is generally both expected and appreciated when meeting people. If people don't smile spontaneously, they can practice it. This need not be a Cheshire cat, ear-to-ear grin (in fact, that may *really* get people wondering), but just a pleasant, natural smile.

Employees can work on their facial expression as an actor would. If you are a person who does not smile readily, work on it by looking into the mirror and practicing. This may sound a bit weird, but the advantages of smiling may call for such drastic measures.

Action Tip 11—Use Good Telephone Techniques

In Chapter 4, we look more extensively at telephone techniques, but, for now consider these points: Many customers make their initial contact with a company via the phone. Handling such calls requires some special behaviors, especially if it is the only contact with customers. A key to successful phone use is to make up for all that lost nonverbal communication by using the voice effectively. Here are a few key behaviors that can help project personality when on the phone:

- *Give the caller your name.* Let the caller know who you are just as you would if in a face-to-face situation (via a name tag or desk plaque). Answer the phone with your name.
- *Smile into the phone.* Somehow people can hear a smile over the phone. Some telephone pros place a mirror in front of them while they're on the phone to remind them that facial expressions can transmit through the wires.
- *Keep the caller informed.* If you need to look up information, tell the customer what you are doing. Don't leave a caller holding a dead phone with no clue as to whether you are still there.

- *Invite the caller to get to the point.* Use questions such as, "How can I assist you today?" Or "What can I do for you?"
- *Commit to requests of the caller.* Tell the caller specifically what you will do and when you will get back to them. ("I'll check on this billing problem and get back to you by five this afternoon, okay?")
- *Thank the caller.* This lets him or her know when the conversation is over.
- *Let your voice fluctuate in tone, rate, and loudness.* You hold people's attention by putting a little life into your voice. Convey honest reactions in expressive ways. Let your voice tones be natural and friendly.
- *Use hold carefully.* People hate being put on hold. When it's necessary, explain why and break in periodically to let the person know he or she hasn't been forgotten. If what you're doing will take longer than a few minutes, ask if you can call the caller back. Write down your commitment to call back, and don't miss it.
- *Use friendly, tactful words.* Never accuse the customer of anything; never convey that the person's request is an imposition.

Action Tip 12—Reach Out and Touch Them

Physical touch is a powerful form of communication that can impact customer perceptions of personality. Successful employees often take an opportunity to shake hands with a customer or even pat him or her on the back, if appropriate.

A study of bank tellers shows the power of touch. Tellers were taught to place money or receipts in the hand of the customer rather than on the counter. Researchers found that customer perceptions of the bank rose sharply among customers who had been touched in this way. In a similar study, restaurant servers who touched their customers when serving the food or while handing the customers something found that their tips increased dramatically.

Similarly, studies found that restaurant servers who touch customers received higher tips. Handing a person something or even lightly touching a shoulder while placing a dish before the customer seems to be a little behavior that strengthens the customer experience.

Among internal customers and coworkers, a literal pat on the back can build instant rapport. But don't overdo it; some people resent people who seem too touchy-feely. Recognize different preferences; try touching behavior but be willing to adjust if the person seems uncomfortable or ill at ease. And, of course, the key word here is appropriateness. Never touch a person in a manner that could be interpreted as being overly intimate or having sexual overtones.

Appropriate touching behavior can help build positive relationships.

Action Tip 13—Enjoy People and Their Diversity

J. D. Salinger said, "I am a kind of paranoid in reverse. I suspect people of plotting to make me happy." If everyone had an attitude like that, as employees we'd look forward to every meeting with every customer. Of course, we quickly learn that some customers do not seem to be plotting to make us happy. Most are very pleasant. Some are unusual. A few are downright difficult.

Every person is different; each has a unique personality. But the kinds of people who offer the richest opportunity for personal growth are the ones who are *not like us*. If we were all alike, it would be a rather uninteresting world. Accept the wide range of diversity among customers and coworkers and learn to enjoy it. Know that people's needs are basically the same at some level and that treating all people as guests will create the most goodwill.

Although enjoying people is more of an attitude than a specific behavior, some actions can reflect this enjoyment. For example, we can work on **verbal discipline**.

To be more accepting of others, focus your comments to others as well as your "self-talk"— those internal conversations in your mind—on the positive, and avoid being judgmental. Instead of saying, "Can you believe that ugly dress on that lady?" avoid comment or say in a nonjudgmental way, "She dresses interestingly." Instead of saying, "This guy will nickel-and-dime me to death," say, "This customer is very cost-conscious." Phrase potentially negative comments in neutral tones.

Pay attention to verbal discipline; resist negative comments whenever possible.

At times, you'll have to force yourself to avoid the negative and judgmental. Accept the challenge and make a game out of it. Sincerely try for one full day to avoid saying anything negative or judgmental about another person. If you make it through the day, shoot for another day. Verbal discipline can become a habit that pays off. You'll find yourself enjoying people more.

We have all read, seen, or experienced heartbreaking examples of people who look and act differently being mistreated. A recent story about a returning Iraq war veteran who was disfigured from a war injury made me stop and think about cutting people some slack. This particular story spoke of people who became impatient with the veteran, whose ability to complete his transaction was slowed by his injuries. Give diverse people the benefit of the doubt.

People come in all sizes, shapes, ages, and with a wide variety of beliefs, attitudes, and behaviors. This variety can make work fun—so long as we back off on judging and treat them like our guests.

People who are different from us are just that: different. Not better or worse. Avoid the tendency to judge; accept the diversity for the richness it brings to our lives.

Action Tip 14—Be Positive about Selling

Ultimately, great customer service is a form of selling. We want people to have a good experience with us, perhaps become repeat buyers—or at least recommend us to others. We are selling positive experiences. Despite this reality, some of us hold imagined negative stereotypes about selling. Customer contact people sometimes refuse to call themselves salespeople, preferring terms like "associate" or even "consultant." Yet everyone is in sales to some degree. We constantly sell (convince, persuade, or whatever term you prefer) other people on ourselves, our products or services, and our company.

Like any profession, selling requires certain skills and attitudes. But often these skills and attitudes are different than one might think. For example, it surprises some people to find that you do not need to be an extrovert to be successful at selling. Quiet, thoughtful people often are very successful. A quiet self-confidence is more important than "techniques." Elwood Chapman, who trained thousands of salespeople, says that you will likely be good at sales if you agree with statements like these:[7]

- I can convert strangers into friends quickly and easily.
- I can attract and hold the attention of others even when I have not met them.
- I love new situations.
- I'm intrigued by the psychology of meeting and building a good relationship with someone I do not know.

If you can't honestly agree with these statements, look inside and consider what it is about selling you dislike. Is it the "image" of manipulative people? Is it the feeling that you are trying to get something from another person unfairly? Try reframing those impressions to see selling or that it is in it most objective definition. Selling is providing people with information and encouragement so that they can make good decisions about products and services that can benefit them. While the stereotype of some salespeople may be negative in your mind (perhaps because of bad experiences), selling as a career skill is necessary, important, and a legitimate form of service.

Most customer service functions involve selling of some sort.

Action Tip 15—Watch Your Dress, Grooming, and Workplace Attractiveness

Experts on decision making talk about the "diagnosis bias"—our propensity to label people, ideas, or things based on our initial opinions of them. In other words, customers make rather quick judgments (diagnoses) about service providers they encounter. From the moment we meet people, we immediately begin to size them up and draw conclusions about them. What we decide about their character, trustworthiness, and ability is largely a factor of first impressions. And, as the old saying goes, you only get one chance to make that first impression. The way they dress is a first clue.

Looking Good at the Auto Repair Shop

"Man, some of these guys look scruffy," said Roger, the owner of Furrin Auto Repair Services. He was drinking his morning coffee and looking at his crew of mechanics, each getting to work on repair projects for customers. "I wonder what my customers think of these characters?"

Then Roger struck on an idea. He decided to try an experiment. Since each of his repair people was paid on commission for the amount of repair work done (and often, customers requested a particular mechanic to work on their car), he wondered if customers ask for guys who dressed a little better.

That evening he called the crew together and invited the mechanics to volunteer to change their dress and grooming. He would not require changes, but if they wanted to participate in the experiment, they could do so. Several agreed to cut their hair shorter, shave daily, remove some piercings, and wear clean uniforms, which Roger provided.

The outcome: Those who cleaned up their act to look more like their customers created far more repeat business than the others. Customers would ask for the better dressed mechanics, while those who chose to dress and groom themselves in the "old way" found themselves getting less work.

Appropriate dress and grooming conveys important messages to customers.

The key word in dress and grooming is "appropriate." Salespeople in a surf shop would look foolish in three-piece suits; an undertaker would look ludicrous in a tank top and shorts. Some organizations issue uniforms to standardize the look of their people. These may be coveralls, full uniforms, or partial uniforms such as blazers, vests, name badges, or logo work shirts. Some employees like these (as they save on the costs of a wardrobe), while some resist the sameness of the uniformed look.

Determine what level of professionalism you want to convey to your customers; then create a look that projects your competence and your company's personality. Pay attention to the little things that reinforce (or detract from) the look you are trying for. Your customers notice these things.

ANOTHER LOOK

Life Would Be Easy . . . If It Weren't for Difficult People

By Connie Podesta[8]

Every time we communicate with another person, we choose (often unconsciously) to use one of four communication styles: aggressive, passive, passive-aggressive, and assertive. **Assertive communication**, however, is the only one of the four that enables us to build healthy, happy, and functional relationships. The other three all involve some degree of manipulation, avoidance, or form of game playing that makes it difficult to maintain a relationship built on trust. As business owners, it is imperative we learn to communicate assertively at all times. The foundation of our business is our reputation. No matter how much we market and advertise, the strongest marketing tool we have is word of mouth. It is vital we have the respect of our customers, vendors, and associates.

Their opinion of us will determine our success and profitability. Therefore, we must learn how to avoid communicating in any way that would undermine our reputation as a fair, honest, and experienced businessperson.

To do that, we must understand how *not* to communicate. At the same time, we will be learning to recognize negative communication patterns and how to react so we will be prepared when difficult people use them to get their way.

Aggressive Communication

The only concern of those who engage in **aggressive communication** is getting their own needs met regardless of the methods used or the consequences of their actions.

The two most manipulative emotions used when communicating aggressively are *hurt* and *anger*. People who use *hurt* attempt to make people do what they want by inducing guilt (whining, crying, playing the "victim," being moody, etc.) so they can avoid responsibility for their own choices and behaviors. People who use *anger* employ intimidation and control tactics (yelling, put-downs, abuse, sarcasm, etc.) to make others feel frightened and powerless so they can get their own way.

The problem with aggressive behavior is when we use guilt or anger to get our needs met, other people begin to resent us, avoid us, or become aggressive themselves. We cannot have a healthy relationship when either party is being aggressive and using manipulative behaviors.

Passive Communication

Unlike aggressive communicators, people who communicate in the passive style seldom say what's really on their minds. **Passive communication** is based on compliance and the hope they can avoid confrontation at all costs. Passive means to take the path of least resistance by tuning out, ignoring, avoiding, or backing away and withdrawing from a person or situation rather than dealing with it head on. They often put their needs last in an attempt to be liked by everyone and to please those around them. Unfortunately, in their attempts to please everyone, they usually end up pleasing no one.

Passive-Aggressive Communication

The **passive-aggressive communication** style is probably the most difficult one to deal with in a relationship. A combination of styles, passive-aggressive avoids direct confrontation (passive), but attempts to get even through manipulation (aggressive).

Passive-aggressive communicators avoid confronting others and steer clear of face-to-face discussions, but they nevertheless want to get their own way or make others suffer. And they usually do it behind another person's back. This style of communication is usually hurtful and can even be dangerous to an organization.

As business owners, we can never afford to have people out to get us and sabotage us behind our backs. Unfortunately, I often see competitors resort to this, thinking their best way to get ahead is to belittle or demean their competitor. Please remember the best way to get ahead is to always take the high road. Have the best product and the best service available and let your actions speak for themselves. If our customers cannot trust us to be honest, then they will not trust anything else about us either.

Assertive Communication

Assertive communication is the most effective and definitely the only healthy form of communication. It's how we express ourselves when our self-esteem is intact, giving us the confidence to communicate without games, manipulation, gimmicks, threats, or hidden agendas. When we are being assertive, we work hard to create mutually satisfying solutions. We communicate our needs clearly and forthrightly. We care about the relationship and strive for a win/win situation. However, and this is the part that confuses many people, we *never* allow ourselves to be treated inappropriately or disrespectfully. Being assertive requires a sincere belief that all individuals, including oneself, are valuable people who are worthy of being treated respectfully. Being assertive uses negotiation rather than manipulation, openness rather than secrecy, and honesty rather than game playing.

Note: Assertive communication is the *only* communication effective when dealing with difficult people. When we are being assertive we understand we always have a choice of how to behave in a healthy and responsible way.

So now what?

Surely you can identify many people in your own life that favor each of the four styles. In fact, if you are honest, you yourself have communicated in all of the ways at some point or another. Most of us use a combination of these four styles, depending on the person or situation. The styles we choose generally depend on what our past experiences have taught us will work best to get our needs met in each specific situation.

The biggest problem is most of us don't even think about communication at all. We just say what comes to mind, using techniques we have thought worked the best since childhood. As a business owner, however, communication must be thought through. You cannot take a chance on alienating a customer by saying something thoughtless, cruel, or hurtful. On the other hand, you must understand how to react to people who use the techniques on you. Hopefully, you have come to the conclusion life is not about changing other people, but about changing yourself and your reactions to others. Success comes when you learn to take control of your life, your business, and your future by being assertive and making healthy choices, then taking responsibility for those choices.

ORGANIZATIONAL ACTION TIPS THAT CONVEY A CUSTOMER-CENTERED CULTURE

In addition to the individual behaviors previously described, a customer also assesses the personality of the entire organization by looking at group behaviors. The communication rule that anything can and will communicate still applies to these behaviors, of course. The composite result of group and individual behaviors conveys much about the organization's culture. If the customer likes a company's culture, that company is well on the way to building satisfaction and a loyal relationship. The following are some action tips organizations should consider.

Action Tip 16—Consider Your Company's Appearance and Grooming

What does your customer see when he or she comes to your business? Are the facilities attractive and well maintained? Is merchandise displayed in an appealing manner? Are employee desks tidy? Is the customer or employee lounge area clean and tidy? Does the work space look like an organized, efficient place? Are the restrooms clean and well maintained?

A cluttered work area conveys a sense of disorganization and low professionalism. Look around you, and see what your customer sees. If the view is unappealing, take time and spend some money to make the place look good. Be aware that you don't have to be located in five-star offices or the most exclusive retail mall to have an attractive appearance. A friend of mine in Finland named Pauli runs a small custom medical products shop located in a basement. Customers who visit don't expect the Taj Mahal but they are pleasantly surprised by the attention to detail Pauli has put forth to make them comfortable. He provides a well-lit seating area, displays interesting posters, and provides humorous reading materials for adults and toys for children. Rocket science? Of course not, but all this simply indicates attention to some little things that make customers comfortable and projects the caring personality of this small organization.

The appearance of the store, shop, or office conveys nonverbal messages to customers.

LOOK INSIDE

How Do You Measure Up?

Below is a list of many of the individual behaviors discussed thus far in this chapter. Using the following scale, evaluate how well you do with each behavior:

N = never; O = occasionally; S = sometimes; M = most of the time; A = always.

Be completely honest. There is nothing wrong with admitting shortcomings. Indeed, it is far more damaging to deny them. After rating yourself on the scale, go back through the list and circle the plus (+) or minus (−) to indicate how you *feel* about your response. If you are comfortable with your answer, circle the plus. If you wish you could honestly answer otherwise, circle the minus.

For each item where you circled a minus sign, write a goal for improvement on a separate sheet of paper. Make this specific and measurable, if possible.

Behaviors	Scale	Goal
1. I promptly greet all customers.	N O S M A + −	
2. I use appropriate icebreakers.	N O S M A + −	
3. I compliment people freely and often.	N O S M A + −	
4. I call customers by their name.	N O S M A + −	
5. I make and maintain eye contact with customers.	N O S M A + −	
6. I often ask for feedback to find out how I'm doing.	N O S M A + −	
7. I listen well.	N O S M A + −	
8. I always say "please," "thank you," and "you're welcome."	N O S M A + −	
9. I reassure customers in their decisions to do business with me.	N O S M A + −	
10. I smile freely and often.	N O S M A + −	
11. I know and use good telephone techniques.	N O S M A + −	
12. I appropriately touch customers when possible.	N O S M A + −	
13. I enjoy people and their diversity.	N O S M A + −	
14. I have good attitudes about "selling" to customers.	N O S M A + −	

SERVICE SNAPSHOT

The Lexus Dealer

When customers bring their automobiles into Lexus of Lindon (and most other Lexus dealerships) for repair, they are invited to wait in a comfortable, well-lit area near the showroom. In addition to soft couches or chairs, soft music, and interesting reading material, morning guests are also invited to help themselves to donuts, pastries, coffee, and other beverages—all complementary. The environment and the food make the normally unpleasant task of waiting for auto service not only bearable but actually enjoyable.

As you consider your organizational appearance, check, too, for barriers. Often people arrange their work space with a desk, counter, or table between them and the customer. While sometimes this is necessary, it can create a barrier—both physical and psychological—between the customer and the one serving. Companies may establish a better personality by doing the following:

- Invite customers to sit beside a desk with the employee instead of across from him or her.
- Offer a comfortable living room–type atmosphere as a place to meet customers or as a waiting area. (An auto body shop had a waiting room that looked like a living room in a nice home, complete with easy chairs, a TV, a coffee table with recent magazines, and even fresh flowers. That surprised a lot of first-time customers!)
- Do as some auto dealerships have done: remove all sales office desks and replace them with small round tables. Now the customer and salesperson sit around the table and work together to make a deal. When the table is round, they don't feel as if they are on opposite sides, engaged in "combat" with each other.

Finally, look for customer comfort. Are your customers invited to sit in a comfortable chair? Does your office or store encourage them to relax? Are waiting areas furnished with reading materials, music, or and perhaps a TV? Are vending machines or complementary snacks available? Is the area kept clean?

Recently, auto dealers have begun to emphasize ways to make their car lots and showrooms, many of which are decades old, more attractive and customer friendly. Some now feature landscaped settings with benches and pathways, different display areas for each auto brand, and interactive systems with screens that show how elements like paint colors and upholstery coordinate together. Take a look at your work areas from the customer's viewpoint.

Action Tip 17—Get Customers to Interact with Your Organization

Make it easy for customers to sample the company culture—the organizational personality. We talked earlier about getting customers to promptly order their food, try a new computer, or test-drive a car. Some high-end stores such as Brookstone (which advertises "unique gifts & smart solutions") encourage customers to "test drive" the latest games, massage chairs, or electronic gadget. Other, perhaps less obvious ways to involve customers with little things may include:

- Personally handing them a shopping cart or basket
- Asking them to begin filling out paperwork
- Inviting them to touch, taste, or sample the product
- Offering coffee, a piece of candy, or fruit while they wait
- Offering a product flyer, information packet, video presentation, or sample to review

If the organizational culture encourages such activities, the customer is increasingly likely to have a positive impression of the company's personality. It doesn't matter so much *what* they do, so long as they begin to do *something*.

Action Tip 18—Correspond Regularly—The Old-fashioned Way

An athletic shoe store and a rental car agency represent two good examples of the simple idea of correspondence. A week after purchasing some running shoes, customers receive a hand-written note from the store owner simply thanking them for buying. In no fancy prose, it expresses appreciation for the business and invites them to return via a one- or two-sentence message. Similarly, a small city airport car-rental desk has employees write thank-you notes to customers when the desk is not busy. The notes are handwritten on the company letterhead and personalized to mention the type of car rented. They thank the customer and invite them to rent again the next time they are in town. The cost of doing this is practically nil since the desk is busy when flights come in but then has slow periods in between. Why have employees sit around and waste time when it's slow? Instead, they write these notes and build customer loyalty.

"Old fashioned" written messages still convey a sense of caring.

Written messages are becoming increasingly rare in our e-world. Most of us prefer generating an email or instant message. It's efficient, easy. That said, an "old fashioned" written note may have even more impact because it takes additional effort and is so rare.

An even simpler example of the power of a brief written message is when the employee serving the customer writes "Thank you, Sharon" or "Please come again" followed by their signature. A little thing like this begins to create a bond.

A print shop sends all customers a monthly package of coupons, flyers, and samples, including a motivational quote printed on parchment paper suitable for framing. Additional copies of the quote are available free for the asking. The mailing acts as a reminder of the quality of the work the shop can do as well as a promotion.

Don't let your customer forget you. Another way to make customers remember your company is to send them information about upcoming sales, changes in policies, new promotions, and the like. Keep the customer tied in. Help him or her feel like part of the company, like an insider.

Obviously, correspondence can be done electronically so long as you gather customer email addresses. I don't mean to minimize this—it's a great tool. Send customers discount coupons or announcements of special hours for preferred customers via such media. But for special, personal, and important messages, consider the potential advantages of "snail mail."

SERVICE SNAPSHOT

Touching the Stuff at the Gap

Some retailers arrange merchandise so that customers can easily pick it up. In fact, they are encouraged to do so even though this may call for more work from employees as they continuously refold and redisplay product. Marketing expert Paco Underhill[9] describes this:

> A trademark of the Gap clothing stores, for example, is that customers can easily touch, stroke, unfold, and otherwise examine at close range anything on the selling floor. A lot of sweaters and shirts are sold thanks to the decision to foster intimate contact between shoppers and goods.

That merchandising policy dictates the display scheme (wide, flat tabletops, which are easier to shop than racks or shelves). That display scheme in turn determines how and where employees will spend their time; all that customer touching means that sweaters and shirts constantly need to be refolded and straightened. That translates into the need for lots of clerks roaming the floor rather than standing behind the counter ringing up sales, which is a big expense, but for Gap and others, it's a sound investment—a cost of doing business.

Action Tip 19—Use Hoopla and Fun

People enjoy working in an organization that has fun. We mentioned Zappos earlier as an example of a company that has grown very rapidly and is seen as a great place to work. Successful companies have regular rituals, whether they are Friday afternoon popcorn, birthday parties, or employee-of-the-month celebrations or other, more creative celebrations. Excellent organizations are fun places to work; they create rituals of their own.

As a manager at a telephone company, Jim initiated frequent sales contests, complete with skits and prizes. Each time a particular product was sold, the service representative could pop a balloon and find inside a prize ranging from a $10 bill to a coupon good for a piece of pie in the company cafeteria. Employees loved it and got involved. The rewards at such events need not be large or costly. The fact that employees are being recognized, even with little things, can be very motivating for them.

Other ideas to promote fun in the workplace include:

- Employee (or performer) of the week/month recognition
- Awards luncheons (include some tongue-in-cheek "awards")
- Win a day off with pay
- Casual dress days
- Halloween costume day
- Family picnics, after-work sports, dinner together

Don't fall into the trap of thinking these things are hokey. Employees at all levels enjoy celebrations and hoopla—and the good cheer can spread to its customers. Of course, be sure the hoopla is not distracting to customers or seen as unprofessional. One company I recently worked with found a need to dial back the Nerf gun combat in the office because clients thought it was a bit too childish. Consider the nature of your customers. How might they view your professionalism?

Have fun and celebrate at work, but maintain an appropriate level of professionalism.

Action Tip 20—Reward the Right Actions

Sometimes organizational reward systems incentivize one behavior while hoping for something else. In other words, the organization *hopes* people will do something—take right actions—but actually rewards an opposite behavior. For example, a company rewards individuals and departments for "never receiving complaints." The hope is that receiving no complaints means the company is doing a good job. In reality, however, you may well be that no complaints are heard because the complaints are simply being suppressed or ignored. Actually complaints are valuable indicators of ways we can do better. The complaining customer can be like a coach, can show us how to improve. Rewarding "no complaints" may be counterproductive.

Here are some other examples of possible reward conflicts where the wrong behaviors may be rewarded and the right behaviors ignored:

- Rewarding employees for fast transaction-handling when the customer may be left uninformed or may resent being rushed along. For instance, the restaurant that encourages employees to get the customers fed and out may make people who prefer more leisurely dining unhappy. Or, the buyer of electronic equipment who is rushed may leave the store not understanding how to work the features of his or her purchase.
- Encouraging salespeople to cooperate with each other to best meet the customer needs while paying a straight commission to just one sales person. For instance, salespeople practically trip over each other to approach the new customer before the other guy gets him. So much for cooperation.
- Encouraging employees to send thank-you notes to customers but never allowing on-the-job time to do so. This creates the impression that it really isn't that important.

- Constantly stressing the need to reduce the amount of return merchandise by punishing clerks who accept too many returns. The result: Customers encounter employees' reluctance to take back unsatisfactory products.
- Paying people by the hour instead of by the task accomplished. Hourly wages are simpler to administer, but they basically pay people for using up time!

The organization's reward system needs to be tilted to the advantage of the employee who provides excellent service. Any rewards should be given in direct relationship to the employee's contribution to customer service that is consistent with the company's mission and service theme.

Action Tip 21—Stay Close after the Sale

Customers hate a love-'em-and-leave-'em relationship, yet many companies offer just that. Once the sale is made, the customer goes back to feeling like a stranger. The relationship with the customer doesn't go beyond the current transaction. There is little or no incentive for the customer to come back or remain loyal.

Look for opportunities to contact the customer after the sale. Establish an ongoing friendship, and they'll keep coming back. Some ideas for contacting the customer after the sale might be:

- Mail thank-you notes
- Call to be sure the product/service met their needs
- Send out new-product information or advance notice of upcoming sales
- Send clippings of interest or newsworthy information that may be interesting to the customer. These clippings need not be directly related to your company.
- Send birthday and holiday cards
- Invite people to participate in focus groups or marketing research about topics of interest to them
- Call, write, or email to thank customers for referrals

A FINAL THOUGHT

The behaviors of individual employees convey impressions to customers via little things. Often employees are unaware of how they are coming across and, as such, are at a distinct disadvantage. They run a significant risk of annoying or at least failing to impress customers. Broadening our awareness of how other people read our verbal and nonverbal messages is a useful step in improving customer service.

Likewise, just as individuals project their behaviors to customers, so do organizations. The company's collective behavior patterns constitute its culture and may be perceived as favorable or unfavorable by customers and employees. The ways managers and leaders interact with subordinates and associates will have considerable impact on the way all employees behave toward customers. Like it or not, organizational leaders model the kinds of behaviors the company accepts or desires.

Behaviors such as those discussed in this chapter are often unconscious and subtle. As such, they constitute examples of the "little things" principle. Raising our awareness of these little things can go a long way toward building or damaging customer relationships.

Summary of Key Ideas

- Behavior is what people do. It is conveyed via verbal or nonverbal communication.
- Individual actions as well as organizational behaviors convey messages to customers that may be positive or

counterproductive to the customers' perception of service received.

- Any behaviors (or sometimes the lack of behaviors) can communicate; the receiver of the message (e.g., the customer) determines what the message means. Perception is reality.

- Projecting positive personality depends on both individual actions and the patterns of behavior exhibited in the organization. This reflects the organizational culture.
- Individual behaviors that impact customer service include greeting customers, appropriately initiating conversation, complimenting, calling people by name, establishing and maintaining eye contact, asking for feedback, listening skillfully, reassuring customers in their buying decisions, smiling, using good telephone techniques, using appropriate touching behaviors, enjoying people, and being positive about selling.
- Organizational behavior patterns that tell the customer about your culture include the appearance and grooming of employees, the appearance of work areas, the frequency and quality of correspondence with customers, the propensity to get customers doing something relevant to the buying decision, the use of hoopla and fun to celebrate company successes, reward systems that motivate appropriate employee behaviors, and staying close to the customer after the sale.

Key Concepts

aggressive communication
appropriate touching
assertive communication
behaviors, individual and
    organizational

buyer's remorse
getting the customer
    committed
icebreaker
organizational culture

passive communication
passive-aggressive
    communication
reward the right
    actions

three I's of eye contact
verbal discipline
verbally greet
    customers

Reviewing the Facts

1. What constitutes behavior, and how is it conveyed? How can you distinguish a behavior from an attitude?
2. What are some ways an organization's culture can impact customer loyalty?
3. What are some specific behaviors that project individual personality? How do these reflect the importance of "little things?"
4. What are icebreakers? How can they best be used with different types of customers?
5. What are the three I's of eye contact?
6. Why are listening skills important? What are some specific actions you can take to be a better listener?
7. How can physical touch be used to project positive personality?
8. What are some factors (patterns of behavior) that project a company's culture? List several examples from organizations you work in.
9. What are some examples of reward systems that encourage the wrong kinds of behaviors? How can leaders adjust these to reward more positive behaviors?

Applying the Ideas: Does Behavior Influence Customer Loyalty?

1. This chapter implies a strong relationship between behaviors (of individuals and organizations) and the likelihood of customer loyalty. Let's test that idea. The following are two simple data-gathering forms. The first lists the behaviors discussed in the chapter and invites customers to rate these. The second form asks three simple questions about customer loyalty. We call this the Customer Loyalty Index (CLI).

    Select five to ten customers of a given business at random. These may be people who frequent a nearby restaurant, customers of a popular store, or even students in the same school.

    Write the name of the company or organization in the blanks on the questionnaire. Make a copy of the following questionnaire for each respondent and administer it to your selected customers. Then score the results as described at the end of the questionnaire.

    Write a one-page summary of what you found. To what degree did your samples agree with each other? How do their answers on the first questionnaire relate to the answers on the CLI?

INTERVIEW GUIDE

Part I Behavior Questionnaire

When you last did business with [_____], did the employees there

Part II Customer Loyalty Index (CLI)

1. Overall how satisfied were you with [_____]?
Extremely unsatisfied/Unsatisfied/Neutral/Satisfied/Extremely satisfied

	Yes	No	Unsure or Does Not Apply
1. greet you promptly?			
2. use opening comments to help you feel at ease?			
3. compliment you in any way?			
4. call you by name?			
5. make and maintain eye contact with you?			
6. ask for feedback from you in any way?			
7. listen carefully to your needs or wants?			
8. say "please" and "thank you"?			
9. reassure your decisions to do business with them?			
10. smile freely and often?			
11. use good telephone techniques?			
12. appropriately touch you (with a handshake, pat on the back, etc.)?			
13. seem to enjoy people and their diversity?			
14. seem to have good attitudes about selling?			
15. keep the workplace clean and attractive?			
16. dress and groom themselves appropriately?			
17. seem to enjoy working for this company?			

2. How likely would you be to recommend [_____] to a friend or associate?
Very unlikely/Not likely/Maybe/Very likely/Certain

3. How likely are you to do business with [_____] again?
Very unlikely/Not likely/Maybe/Very likely/Certain

Scoring

• For Part I of the interview, score 1 point for each "yes" response. The total possible is 17.

• For the CLI, score each item on a 5-point scale from left to right (e.g., the most negative response is a 1, the most positive is a 5, and those in between are 2, 3, or 4).

• After you have tallied scores for your entire sample of customers (five to ten), write a brief analysis of the results. Comment especially on the behaviors that most seem to relate to customer service, as your customers see them.

Applying the Ideas: Hooray for Waffle House[10]

The Waffle House restaurants apparently have a very happy internal customer—an employee who used a blog to rave about her job. Amber, in a casual, breezy posting, explains,

> i work at waffle house i have for 2 yrs now I'm a grill op. and i love my job. I don't know many people who can be as proud of their job or love there job as much as i do. my whole family works at waffle house. I have 6 brothers and sisters I am the oldest the youngest is 7. my mom is the unit mgr.

She goes on to talk about other members of her family who work there too and the jobs they do. While the work may seem mundane, the enthusiasm for her job is real. She goes on to say

> the owners of our waffle house are so nice and friendly. we talk on! the phone every day. the customers all know us and love the fact that our whole family is there. well at least one on every shift (it's an invasion! lol).

Her enthusiasm goes on to sound like an unsolicited advertisement

> it's the only place a family can eat, talk, listen to music and enjoy the ambiance at the same time, and the show [of the personality of employees] isn't that bad either. so thanks for hearing me out.
>
> Have a great day and come back and see us soon!! (a waffle goodbye) amber grill op since 2001

1. Employees have a dramatic impact on the organization's personality. What does Amber's blog posting say about her loyalty to Waffle House? How does her personality shine through?
2. What elements of personality discussed in this chapter are evident in this blog entry?
3. As a manager of a similar organization, what could you do to encourage the display of such enthusiasm from your staff?

Consider this Case

How Difficult Is It to Treat Someone Well?

Marcia and Lamar had just moved into a larger home and wanted to furnish the family room tastefully but without spending a lot of money. Saturday was the day for their furniture shopping, so off they went.

Their first stop was a deep-discount Furniture Barn.* The place was appropriately named—it looked like a barn—and its merchandise was piled high in irregular heaps. Some were wrapped in plastic from the manufacturer, while others were uncovered. Some collected dust. The Barn had a pretty good variety of goods, but the "display" left a lot to be desired. The goods had no posted prices, although the company had a reputation for good deals.

Upon entering the Barn, a middle-aged fellow with a beard, sandals, cut-off shorts, and a sleeveless tee shirt called a greeting to Marcia and Lamar from across the cavernous room where he was stacking merchandise. "Lemme know if ya need help," he yelled from across the room. But that was the last they saw of him. They wandered around the Barn for about 10 minutes before making a hasty retreat, apparently unmissed.

Their next stop was Whooley Furniture* a few miles away. Here the merchandise was displayed attractively and prices were clearly posted on each piece. Anne, a 40-something woman, greeted them and introduced herself when they came into the store. They shook hands and Lamar introduced himself and his wife as they chatted briefly about what they were looking for. Anne invited them to look around, directed them to the family room furniture section, and said that she would be happy to answer any questions. She mentioned that they had a sale on LazyChair brand recliners and showed them where they were. The saleswoman was dressed in slacks, a yellow blouse, and wore a tactful necklace. She was quite attractive, although not a raving beauty. She smiled pleasantly and gave them some space as they strolled through the store.

Marcia and Lamar were on a pretty tight budget and the merchandise at the Barn would have probably been cheaper, but about an hour later they had spent about $2,000 with Anne at Whooley Furniture. Asked by friends why they shopped there, Lamar summed it up: We felt like they wanted our business, and Anne became a friend.

Probes

1. If you owned the Furniture Barn, what lesson would you learn from this case? What actions would you take? Identify several "little things" they could do to better serve the customer without changing their basic "stack-it-deep-and-sell-it-cheap" business approach.
2. In your opinion, how important is the personality of salespeople in a furniture business? Would Anne's approach be advantageous in all kinds of businesses? Why or why not?

*These are fictional organizations.

Consider this Case

Hospitality in the Big City

When people think of "down home" hospitality, big city hotels don't generally come to mind. But this past weekend in New York City, Midwesterners Dennis and Sylvia were downright shocked at just how friendly those big city folks can be.

They arrived in New York on a rainy Friday afternoon. The taxi from the airport took almost two hours, but the driver knew the shortcuts through Queens and gave them a running commentary on the various neighborhoods and explained why he chose to avoid the traffic-choked freeways. He also reassured them that the flat-rate fare applied and that he was as anxious as they were to get them to the hotel.

Despite the friendly cabby, their patience was wearing thin as they checked into the Manhattan hotel. But travel exhaustion soon turned to laughter as the desk clerks greeted them warmly and joked about the "liquid sunshine." The check-in process was quick and painless and they were given a choice of several room options. The bellman, a smiling giant of a fellow, welcomed them to the Big Apple and took their bags and got them settled into their room, all the while chatting pleasantly and telling them about the features of the hotel and nearby restaurants.

An hour later, when Dennis and Sylvia decided to go out to dinner, they realized they had forgotten umbrellas and the rain showed no signs of letting up. Overhearing this, the desk clerk offered his own personal umbrella with a smile. All he asked was that they bring it back before he got off duty at midnight "or else I'll have to charge you interest," he joked.

Probes

1. How does this case illustrate the importance of little things and personality?
2. How important is it to defuse unpleasantness even when the problems are not caused by you?
3. Describe any similar experiences you may have had where people surprised you with unexpected pleasantness. How did it feel?

Notes

1. Some of the ideas in this reading are adopted from LeBaron, M., "Cross-Cultural Communication," *Beyond Intractability*, Eds. Guy Burgess and Heidi Burgess. Conflict Research Consortium, University of Colorado, Boulder. Posted: July 2003, *http://www.beyondintractability.org/essay/cross-cultural_communication/*.
2. Novinger, T., *Intercultural Communication* (Austin, TX: University of Texas Press, 2001, p. 65).
3. Okun, Barbara F., J. Fried, and M. L. Okun, *Understanding Diversity. A Learning as Practice Primer* (Pacific Grove, CA: Brooks/Cole Publishing, 1999, p. 78).
4. O'Brien, Jeffrey M., "Zappos Knows How to Kick It," *Fortune*, February 2, 2009, pp. 55–56.
5. Cited in "Yamaha Merchandising Training," Yamaha Corp. Also found in S. Geist. *Why Should Someone DO Business with You Rather than Someone Else?* (Bonita Springs, FL: Addington & Wentworth, 1997, p. 98).
6. B. Decker, *The Art of Communication* (Menlo Park, CA: Crisp Publications, Inc., 1988, p. 17).
7. These ideas are found in E. N. Chapman's classic book, *The Fifty Minute Sales Training Program* (Menlo Park, CA: Crisp Publications, Inc., 1992).
8. C. Podesta "Success from Home," May 2005. Connie Podesta is an International Professional Speaker and licensed professional counselor. Connie is the author of three books, including *Life Would Be Easy If It Weren't for Other People, How to Be the Person Successful Companies Fight to Keep, and Make a Fortune Selling to Women*. For more information visit *www.conniepodesta.com*.
9. Excerpted from Paco Underhill, "What Shoppers Want." *Inc.*, July 1999, p. 76.
10. Excerpted from as posting on a pro-Waffle House blog by a truly enthusiastic "internal customer"—an employee! See: *www.geocities.com/waffleshrine/*. Downloaded April 30, 2006.

CHAPTER 3

Listen to Your Customer (a Big "Little Thing")

Better Service Means Getting Your Ears On

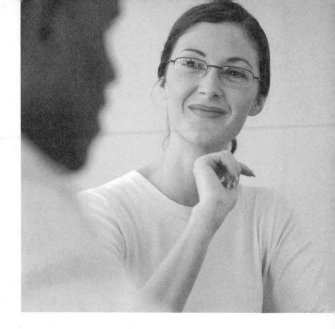

Listening, not imitation, may be the sincerest form of flattery.

—JOYCE BROTHERS

No man ever listened himself out of a job.

—CALVIN COOLIDGE

After reading this chapter, you should be able to

1. Describe the important distinction between hearing and listening.

2. Distinguish between internal, environmental, and interactional factors that complicate the listening process.

3. Assess your own listening skills and set goals for improvement.

4. Avoid five particularly ineffective behaviors that inhibit effective listening.

5. Employ four simple, positive approaches to enhance your active listening.

The Way It Is . . . How Can You Help Me? Try Listening!

SALES PERSON: Hi, I'm Jerry. Welcome to Cell Phone Kingdom. How can I help you today Mr. . . . ? [Jerry smiles and shakes hands with the customer but pulls his cell phone off his belt to glance at it at the same time.]

CUSTOMER: Nice to meet you, Jerry. I'm George Patterson. I just want a very basic cell phone with no fancy bells and whistles, okay? It's for my 75-year-old mother and she isn't interested in a built-in taking pictures or text messaging or fancy ring tones or music. All she wants is a phone that's easy to use and reliable. Oh, and it would be good if the keys were larger and the screen easy to read. Do you have anything like that?

SALES PERSON: Sure, we can get her into a nice phone like this model, Jeff. It has some pretty cool features like a built-in MP3 player and a lot of cool custom options. In fact, we have a nice deal on music downloads—unlimited songs for just a flat monthly fee. It's incredible. I can set it all up for her and make it just what she needs. We'll have her texting and sending IMs in no time—people love that once they get the hang of it. I see kids texting all the time. Everybody likes to do that.

CUSTOMER:	You're not listening to me. I want to get her something simple. The woman is 75 years old and not technologically savvy. She wants something simple.
SALES PERSON:	Not a problem, Mr. Peterson. This is real simple. Look you just turn on the feature you want from this drop-down menu on the touch screen and . . .
CUSTOMER:	It's Patterson and I don't want any of those "features." I just want a plain vanilla phone that . . .
SALES PERSON:	I'll check to see what colors it comes in but I don't think we have vanilla. We can get her a nice tan colored one—that should be close. And it'll have access to our video download option. Another nice thing we have going this week is a special deal where we'll load your choice of three games for free—it's included in our free setup. Does she play MindSweeper or FreeCell? I love those games—I can play for hours. One weekend I spent about 20 hours straight. It was awesome. Oh wait, I'm getting a text, will you excuse me for a minute. I need to answer this and then I'll check our stock for a vanilla-colored phone. You'll want a Bluetooth with that won't you, Mr. Pearson?
CUSTOMER (WALKING OUT THE DOOR):	No "Larry." I do NOT want a Blue Tooth or any other tooth from you. All I want is a plain, ordinary, simple, easy-to-use cell phone with big numbers!

DOESN'T ANYBODY EVER LISTEN?

It looks like Jerry (or was it Larry?) had a problem listening to his customer. George Patterson had some fairly clear requirements for his mother's cell phone but Jerry never quite got it. Was Patterson unclear? Did he seem to use words from a foreign language Jerry didn't speak? It doesn't appear so. Jerry just wasn't listening very well. You might think listening is easy. After all, doesn't everybody do it? Well, yes and no. The fact is that many people are confused about listening effectiveness and how best to do it. For example, listening is sometimes confused with hearing.

Think about a commercial for a product you have no interest in—it's easy to tune that information out, isn't it? You may hear the ad but you're not really listening. Listening involves mentally absorbing the message. Without listening, the commercial is just noise. As service providers, it's easy to *hear* what the customer says, but great customer service begins with great *listening* skills—an ability to absorb and digest what the customer says.

This chapter focuses on the nature of listening and the skills individual service providers need to do a better job. In Chapter 8, we will study *organizational listening*—the processes companies use to get feedback from customers.

POOR LISTENING = THE #1 COMMUNICATION PROBLEM

The lack of effective listening may be the most common human communication problem—and a significant factor in customer dissatisfaction. One of the greatest gifts we can give others is our attention. People who commit to be active listeners experience communication like never before. Everyone wants to be heard, understood, respected, and loved. A lot of us like to talk and very few choose to listen. Therein lies a huge opportunity for distinguishing yourself from the vast majority of ineffective listeners. When you become a skilled, active listener, you will become a better communicator. You will also improve your customer service skills.

Better listeners are better communicators. Better communicators give better service.

As customer service professionals, we need to have our "ears on" regularly. We need to apply effective listening in dealing with others. This chapter takes an in-depth look at listening, gives you a better understanding of the problems, and provides specific action tips you can apply to be a better listener.

Why is this so tough? Ironically, of the four basic communication skills—reading, writing, speaking, and listening—only one is not formally taught. Elementary schools focus heavily on the

---

SERVICE SNAPSHOT

P&G's Listening Paid Off

Here's a brief trip down memory lane: Procter and Gamble was one of the first companies to actively listen to its customers. In the 1960s, P&G publicized a toll-free 800 number to more actively listen to customer concerns. People staffing those phone lines were trained in active listening. The information they gathered from the customer told them that the average household's weekly laundry increased from 6.4 to 7.6 loads. At the same time, the average washing temperature dropped 15 degrees, caused by the new fabrics introduced into the market. Because of their careful listening, the company created a new product to meet the demand, one that became a hugely profitable market leader—All-Temperature Cheer.

---

first three and assume that students are picking up listening. After all, isn't listening really just a matter of sitting back and letting the talker have his or her say?

In the following pages, we will explain why listening is so much more, define some common barriers to good listening, and offer some pointers on how to become a more skillful, active listener. Highly developed listening skills are crucial to success in any relationship—including our relationships with customers. Few people are really good at listening and those who become good have a significant competitive advantage over others in the world of customer service.

THE DIFFERENCE BETWEEN LISTENING AND MERELY HEARING

Many of us confuse hearing and listening. In reality, they are two different things. The process we call *hearing* is purely physical activity by which acoustic energy in the form of sound waves is changed to mechanical and electrochemical energy that the brain can understand. All of this has little to do with listening. *Listening* refers to the psychological processes that allow us to attach meaning to the patterns of energy we "hear." All the potential problems, which typically arise from psychological processes—differences in perception, biases, our predispositions, our lack of patience—come into play in the listening process.

The **cocktail party effect** provides a good example of the difference between hearing and listening. At a cocktail party, there are usually several conversations going on simultaneously in the same room. Everyone present at the party is aware of these conversations in that they can be heard. On the other hand, we usually have to make a conscious effort to *listen* to any one of these conversations. We are physically capable of changing all or most of the acoustic energy in the room into electrochemical energy. We are much less capable of attaching meanings to all the sounds—unless we actively focus.

> Hearing is necessary for listening but is not the same thing.

WHAT CONTRIBUTES TO LISTENING?

Before we can begin to improve our listening skills, we need to understand the demands placed upon our listening capacities. These demands fall into three categories or elements of the listening process: **internal elements, environmental elements**, and **interactional elements**.

Internal Elements Affecting Listening

Listening involves the mental process of attaching meanings to words or sounds we hear. Two preconditions must be met:

1. The words or other sounds used by the message source must be received by the hearer.
2. The listener must possess a set of meanings or referents for these sounds—the words need to make sense.

LOOK INSIDE
What Are Your Listening Habits?

How often do you find yourself relying on these ten bad listening habits? Check yourself carefully on each one, and be honest (no one is grading you).

Habit	Almost always	Usually	Sometimes	Seldom	Almost never
			Frequency		
I get sidetracked by mental distractions (thoughts going on in my head)	_____	_____	_____	_____	_____
I get distracted by the customer's speech patterns, tone of voice, accent, or noises around me	_____	_____	_____	_____	_____
Although I try to recall everything a customer says, I don't take notes	_____	_____	_____	_____	_____
I reject some topics as uninteresting before hearing the customer	_____	_____	_____	_____	_____
I fake listening	_____	_____	_____	_____	_____
I jump to conclusions about a customer's meaning before he or she is finished explaining	_____	_____	_____	_____	_____
I decide that a customer is wrong before hearing everything she or he has to say	_____	_____	_____	_____	_____
I judge a customer on personal appearance and mannerisms, etc.	_____	_____	_____	_____	_____
I ignore or discount a customer's evidence when it sounds wrong	_____	_____	_____	_____	_____
I don't bother to create a comfortable place for the customer to talk	_____	_____	_____	_____	_____
				Total:	_____

How to score:
Give yourself the following scores for every frequency checked:

For every "almost always" :   2
For every "usually"   :   4
For every "sometimes"   :   6
For every "seldom"   :   8
For every "almost never"   : 10

Total score interpretation:

Below 70   : You need a lot of training in listening.
From 71 to 90   : You listen well.
Above 90   : You listen exceptionally well.

Trying to hear in a noisy environment, dealing with a static-filled phone line, and encountering people who speak too softly are examples of problems with the first precondition. These can cause a breakdown in the ability to receive the message. Overhearing someone speaking a strange foreign language or with a strong, unfamiliar accent is an obvious example of breakdowns of the second precondition. If the sounds have no referent—they don't refer to anything that makes sense to us—we cannot understand. Listening is the way we put sounds and their meanings together to create understanding.

Environmental Elements Affecting Listening

The listening process is also impacted by factors of the communication environment, which determine what we are able to listen to and what we cannot. These factors can impact our individual ability to listen and our organization's listening capacity, as well. These factors include:

- Our individual listening capacity
- The presence of noise
- The use or misuse of gatekeepers

INDIVIDUAL LISTENING CAPACITY   Our **listening capacity** can be overburdened in two ways: It can be overloaded with too much information, or it can be underutilized with too little. In both cases, listening tends to break down.

Think about how many messages clamor for your attention every day. You wake to a clock radio and advertisers want you to listen. You catch a little TV with breakfast, and newscasters, politicians, commercials try to get you to listen to what they have to say. On the way to work or school, more radio ads. At work or in classes, we have meetings and idea sharing and lectures and discussions of all types. You can spend a huge portion of your day listening—or tuning out. Why do some messages stick, while others are never heard or soon forgotten?

Thousands of messages clamor for our attention every day. We choose which ones to listen to.

Listening breakdowns happen when we exceed our listening capacity. Only a finite number of messages can be heard and responded to in any given day; only so many phone calls can be answered at one time. Only so many meetings processed or commercials pondered. Once our capacity to accomplish these tasks has been reached, we develop defensive mechanisms for coping. We develop psychological strategies for selecting what we will attend to and what we will tune out.

These selection mechanisms, although often unconscious, are normally based on our individual needs, which, of course, change from time to time. We do listen to auto ads when we are in the market for a car, for example. When our capacity for paying attention to incoming information is overloaded, the impact on our listening behavior is difficult to predict. Only one thing is for sure: We will tune out some messages.

The opposite problem, where environmental demands cause us to underutilize our listening capacity, is also widespread. Most people speak at the rate of about 120 words per minute (except for auctioneers or some disc jockeys), yet our normal capacity for listening—assigning meanings to words—is about 500 words per minute. The problem, of course, is that we listen faster than anyone can talk to us, providing ample time for our minds to wander far afield. Listening to others becomes a tedious task, forcing us to slow down our thinking to stay synchronized with, for example, the customer speaking to us. We will fill the gaps with irrelevant or off-topic thoughts.

Since we can listen faster than people can speak, we sometimes drift off.

THE PRESENCE OF NOISE   The presence of noise is another environmental element affecting listening. **Noise** refers to those sounds that are irrelevant to the conversation. It is important to note that noise may be either environmental (the sound of machinery, other conversations, buzzers, bells, etc.) or internal (a headache, our dislike of the person to whom we are listening, preoccupation with another problem, etc.). Whatever the source, noise distracts us from the business of listening.

THE USE OR MISUSE OF GATEKEEPERS   One way busy people deal with the problems of exceeded listening capacity and excessive noise is through *gatekeepers*. The term **gatekeeper** refers to one who previews incoming information to determine if it is appropriate to the needs of the person the message is aimed at. If the message appears nonessential, the gatekeeper blocks it from getting to the person. In this sense, a gatekeeper's job is to do some of our listening for us. Managers almost always have at least one gatekeeper. This may be a secretary, administrative assistant, or any other person they turn to for organizational information. In many instances, these individuals determine what needs the manager's attention and what doesn't.

Gatekeepers can be useful and necessary but can also cause us to miss or distort some messages we may need.

Unfortunately, some managers use gatekeepers to insulate them from customers and other important sources of information. One company CEO, who we will call Phil, is very uncomfortable talking with customers. He was trained as an accountant and has excellent administrative skills. He does a good job keeping records and tracking company data. But when a salesperson asks Phil to call a customer or intervene in a dispute with other employees, Phil becomes very uncomfortable. To make matters worse, his company is a small, entrepreneurial firm where every employee should be expected to wear many hats—including customer service. But Phil often delegates the tasks of listening to customers and dealing with their concerns to someone else. His use of gatekeepers (to "protect" him from those pesky customers) is a detriment to his organization's listening ability.

While gatekeeping has its benefits (such as reducing communication overload), it also poses problems. When we finally do get the information, it has been through at least two sets of interpretations, our gatekeeper's and ours. There is a pretty good likelihood that we are listening to a message that has been distorted. Also, our gatekeeper may accidentally filter out messages that we need to hear. The effect is much like the "telephone game" where players whisper a message to several others and the end report is far different from the original.

Interactional Elements Affecting Listening

In contrast to the environmental elements of the listening process, the interactional elements concern internal psychological processes that are not as easily identified. Two such psychological elements deserve careful consideration: **self-centeredness** and **self-protection**.

EFFECTS OF SELF-CENTEREDNESS UPON LISTENING   Self-centeredness refers to the degree of "vested interest" we may have in our own point of view. When a difference of opinion arises among people, our vested interest in our ideas can create a listening barrier. For example, if a salesperson feels particularly strong about selling a particular product—for whatever reasons—she

---

SERVICE SNAPSHOT

Steph Remembers Sparky

Stephanie Burge owns a used car business specializing in high-quality cars with a lot of life still in them. And Steph herself has a lot of life in her! She works tirelessly to build relationships with her repeat customers. Literally hundreds of people in her city wouldn't even bother shopping elsewhere. When they (or someone they care about) need a good car, they just go over and see Steph. They know she can be trusted to give them a good deal on a good car.

Part of her secret is she is a really good listener. She remembers people's names, the names of their family and friends, their preferences, and what they like to do. It's not unusual for past customers to drop by the lot just to chat. She and her husband, Lee, treat every customer like family.

Their conversations seem to pick up where they left off last time—even if it's been months or even years.

The "little thing" that sealed the deal for a continuing business relationship for one customer was when he stopped to look at a spiffy red sports car she had on her lot. Several years earlier, he had owned an older Mazda Miata he had named Sparky. They had no sooner begun talking about sports cars when Steph asked, "Are you thinking about a replacement for Sparky? I know you've missed that little car." She remembered Sparky! She had been listening way back then and her listening paid off in knowing her customer. And the man drove off in that little red one.

may quite literally not even hear a customer's request for a different product. She will be so personally sold on Product A that she will tune out a customer's desire to buy Product B—even when the customer may be better served with Product B. (Remember our opening story?)

It isn't hard to understand why self-centeredness occurs. When we have taken the time to formulate an idea, we usually verbalize that idea in the presence of others, like the salesman in our opening story (*phones should have cool features*). In essence, we have made a public commitment to that position (*I played games on my phone for 20 hours one weekend*), and it becomes awkward for us to change. At the same time, the people we are interacting with have also publicly committed themselves to their opinions (*I only want a simple phone for my mother*). In such cases, neither party is really listening.

Since listening is a psychological process, based on our individual needs, we think and listen from a self-centered orientation. As a result, we don't listen to *what* the other person is saying; we listen instead to how his or her views affect our position. In other words, we are "listening" through a predetermined set of biases, looking for flaws in our "opponent's" views rather than seeking common understanding. We develop a mind like a steel trap—closed.

We sometimes listen just long enough to formulate our counterargument.

Too often we find ourselves listening to other people solely for the purpose of finding the weaknesses in their positions so that we can formulate a convincing response. At that point, we stop listening and begin to plan what we'll say in response. The other person is still talking and we still hear him or her, but we are no longer listening.

Self-centered listening has a direct impact on the amount of information we receive. Since, in most cases, additional information helps make better decisions, such blocking out of relevant information cannot help but lowers the quality of our decisions and our ability to assist customers.

EFFECTS OF SELF-PROTECTION ON LISTENING   Another element affecting the listening process is self-protection. We "protect" ourselves by playing out an anticipated conversation in our own minds before the real conversation ever occurs, to make sure we don't get caught saying something stupid. We figure we know where this conversation is going so we anticipate what we expect to hear and plan our counterargument, rather than listening to the actual message. In essence, then, we are practicing by listening to ourselves listen to others.

Years ago, I heard an old joke that illustrates this notion of self-protective listening. (I am recalling this from memory, but it goes something like this. If you've heard it before, enjoy it again in light of our discussion of self-protective listening):

> *A fellow was speeding down a country road late at night and BANG! went a tire. He got out and looked but he had no jack.*
>
> *Then he said to himself. "Well, I'll just walk to the nearest farmhouse and borrow a jack." He saw a light in the distance and said, "Well, I'm in luck; the farmer's up. I'll just knock on the door and say I'm in trouble, would you please lend me a jack? And he'll say, why sure, neighbor, help yourself, but bring it back."*
>
> *He walked on a little farther and the light went out so he said to himself, "Now he's gone to bed, and he'll be annoyed because I'm bothering him so he'll probably want some money for his jack. And I'll say, all right, it isn't very neighborly but I'll give you a dollar. And he'll say, do you think you can get me out of bed in the middle of the night and then offer me a dollar? Give me five dollars or get yourself a jack somewhere else."*
>
> *By the time he got to the farmhouse, the fellow had worked himself into a lather. He turned into the gate and muttered, "Five dollars! All right, I'll give you five dollars. But not a cent more! A poor devil has an accident and all he needs is a jack. You probably won't let me have one no matter what I give you. That's the kind of guy you are."*
>
> *Which brought him to the door and he knocked angrily, loudly. The farmer stuck his head out the window above the door and hollered down, "Who's there? What do you want?" The fellow stopped pounding on the door and yelled up, "You and your stupid jack! You know what you can do with it!"*

How does this illustrate self-protectiveness? The fellow had played the scene in his mind and adjusted what he planned to say because of his fear of being hurt or embarrassed. He was being self-protective.

Serious listening problems can arise when we engage in conjecture by listening to ourselves listen to others, by anticipating what *might be said* and reacting to that instead of to what the customer is actually saying. Actively listen to your customer before you start making up a dialogue in your head.

Both of these interactional elements—self-centeredness and self-protectiveness—affect the listening process in that they tend to orient our listening behavior toward biased interpretations of messages.

These three elements of the listening process—internal, environmental, and interactional—pose potential problems requiring *active* effort. Listening must be recognized as more than something we sit back and do to kill time when we're not talking. As communication scholar Harold Janis has said, "Listening . . . is not merely hearing; it is a state of receptivity that permits understanding of what is heard and grants the listener full partnership in the communication process."[1] Are your customers full partners in your communication processes?

What can we do to improve our listening skills? A good starting point would be to apply some rather simple action tips designed to break bad habits and strengthen some good ones.

Active listening means making sure you understand your customer before you formulate a response.

LISTENING HABITS TO AVOID

Most of us didn't become poor listeners overnight; we learned how over a period of time—we develop poor listening habits. Here are some ideas for avoiding common bad habits.

Action Tip 1—Stop Talking

How is your listen–talk ratio? If you are like most people you talk a lot more than you listen and that can be a problem. You can never become a better listener till you aren't disciplined to be quiet until others have expressed their thought fully.

Action Tip 2—Prepare to Listen

Preparation to listen means you decide to set aside time and other activities so that you can focus on listening. Mentally disconnect from other matters playing on your mind. Look at the person you are listening to. Let them know you are now "open for business" to listen to their concerns.

Sometimes this preparation means going to another location where you will not be interrupted, where it's more quiet or comfortable. *Where* we listen can have an impact on *how* we listen. If your organization has physical barriers between you and customers such as a large counter or desk, consider inviting the customer to sit somewhere more conducive to talking. Executives sometimes run the risk of "hiding" behind their large desks, and coming around to stand or sit where the customer can comfortably interact will make a better listening environment.

Reduce physical barriers to prepare for better listening.

Action Tip 3—Avoid Faking Attention

Faking attention is an attempt to be polite to someone during a conversation and results in what someone called the "**wide asleep listener**." This is usually accomplished by looking directly at the speaker when you are really thinking about something else, automatically nodding responses, or even saying "yes" and "uh huh" to conversations you have mentally tuned out. When you have agreed to listen to someone, commit yourself to expending the needed effort to listen and give that conversation your active attention.

ANOTHER LOOK

Good Listeners Listen with Their Faces

The first skill that you can practice to be a good listener is *to act like a good listener*. We have spent a lot of our modern lives working at tuning out all of the information that is thrust at us. It therefore becomes important to change our physical body language from that of a deflector to that of a receiver, much like a satellite dish. Our faces contain most of the receptive equipment in our bodies, so it is only natural that we should tilt our faces toward the channel of information.

A second skill is to use the other bodily receptors besides your ears. You can be a better listener when you *look at the other person*. Your eyes pick up the nonverbal signals that all people send out when they are speaking. By looking at the speaker, your eyes will also complete the eye contact that speaker is trying to make. A speaker will work harder at sending out the information when he or she sees a receptive audience in attendance. Your eyes help complete the communication circuit that must be established between speaker and listener.

When you have established eye and face contact with your speaker, you must then *react to the speaker* by sending out nonverbal signals. Your face must move and give the range of emotions that indicate whether you are following what the speaker has to say. By moving your face to the information, you can better concentrate on what the person is saying. Your face must become an active and contoured catcher of information.

A good listener will *stop talking and use receptive language* instead. Use the *I see . . . un huh . . . oh really* words and phrases that follow and encourage your speaker's train of thought. This forces you to react to the ideas presented, rather than the person. You can then move to asking questions, instead of giving your opinion on the information being presented.

A final skill is to move your mind to *concentrate on what the speaker is saying*. You cannot fully hear a person's point of view or process information when you argue mentally or judge what he or she is saying before the speaker has completed. An open mind receives and listens to information.

If you really want to listen, you will act like a good listener. Good listeners are good catchers because they give their speakers a target and then move that target to capture the information that is being sent.

Source: Some of these ideas are adapted from the booklet put out by the Canadian Association of Student Activity Advisors (CASAA) Student Activity Sourcebook, *http://customerservicezone. com/cgi-bin/links/jump.cgi?ID=4256*

Action Tip 4—Be Patient, Defer Disagreement

Changing channels in the middle of a presentation or conversation is another unproductive habit. When something appears to be too uninteresting, too hard to comprehend, or too time consuming—or if a customer starts to tell a story you've heard before, the poor listener will tune out. Since we know there is plenty of thinking time between the speaker's thoughts, we figure we can switch back and forth between several conversations without losing any information. This assumption is often incorrect. Let them have their say before "correcting" or debating what they say.

Customers can't always communicate to you efficiently. Sometimes they don't know the terminology or exactly how to describe their problem. Be patient. Be sure they have had ample opportunity to express themselves fully before you offer additional information or respectful disagreement.

> Be patient with customers. They may not know your terminology or be less able to express ideas clearly.

Action Tip 5—Listen for More than the Facts

Much of what people communicate are feelings, impressions, and emotions; the actual facts of messages are often wrapped up in these. For example, an employee came to her manager's office, and in the course of the conversation she appeared quite upset about something. When she explained to the manager that her husband had just been terminated from his job, the manager expressed what he thought was appropriate concern and soon changed the subject. Shortly after, the employee abruptly left the office, apparently angry with the manager. He had listened to the facts of what she'd said, but completely missed her meaning.

From the manager's perspective, these were the facts:

1. Her husband was a very capable young executive who was unhappy with his present employer and had been looking around for another company.
2. This couple was young, had no children, and had few financial burdens.
3. Her husband had recently been offered another comparable position, which he turned down because it paid about the same as he was currently making.
4. Her husband had just lost his job.

In his listening process, the manager associated the new fact (4) with facts he already knew (1, 2, and 3) and concluded that there was no real serious problem. The husband would find a new and probably better job soon.

So why did the employee storm out of the office? The manager had listened only for the facts, while the employee wanted to talk about feelings and concerns she had. She wanted him to listen to what she was *not* saying—that she felt threatened by her husband's loss of the job or that she was embarrassed by his termination. What she needed was someone to share these thoughts with, and perhaps get some comfort from. Many messages convey emotion as well as information. Listening only for the facts is often not enough.

Customers almost always make buying decisions based on feelings and emotion. We don't just pay for the core product but rather seek some emotional gratification out of our purchases. Buying an automobile is rarely simply acquiring a means to transport us from point A to point B. We get gratification out of the prestige of a new car or the satisfaction of making a wise purchase. If the salesperson is listening only for the facts, he or she may miss the emotional hook that helps establish understanding—and a better relationship with the customer.

Messages often convey emotion that goes beyond the facts.

Action Tip 6—Bite Your Tongue before Interrupting

We tend to interrupt people because we get impatient. We want them to get their point across more quickly so that we can jump in and solve it. This, by the way, is a characteristic of men more frequently than women. Women have often been socialized to engage in longer, more supportive sharing of feelings, while men have often been socialized to get to the point and solve the problem.

Men tend to interrupt more frequently than women, but not always.

Interrupting in the middle of the message can damage a conversation. Yes, you may need to gain clarification of some points, but wait for an appropriate time to ask for that clarification rather than abruptly interrupting. Hold back on frequent use of questions like "What do you mean?" and "Why do you say that?" until you are sure the customer is finished. Then, if you need clarification, ask for it.

A colleague mentioned a situation where she called a business and stated her name at the beginning of the conversation. Before saying another word, the receptionist asked, "Who?" It was abrupt and unpleasant. The receptionist and her company image would have been far better served if she had waited for the caller to finish and then asked, "I'm sorry, I didn't get your name." Interruptions—especially abrupt ones—can quickly damage customer service.

POSITIVE STEPS TO BETTER LISTENING

Avoidance of poor listening behaviors is only part of the process of becoming a good listener. You also need to take some positive steps to improve your listening effectiveness. In doing so, your customer service skills can dramatically improve. Here are some proactive behaviors that lead to improvement.

Action Tip 7—Reinforce the Customer with Positive Nonverbal and Verbal Cues

Use nonverbal gestures or movements to encourage speakers to get their ideas across.

Especially in face-to-face interactions, nonverbal behaviors are critical. Appropriate responses such as good eye contact, facial expression, appearing concerned, nodding, and reinforcing to show agreement are examples of nonverbal behaviors that contribute to better listening.

ANOTHER LOOK

Do Men and Women Listen Differently?

Numerous books and studies of differences in communication between male and female communicators lay the blame on socialization. Young girls often communicate to build bonds with each other, and to be supportive and sympathetic. Boys tend to communicate in ways that assert their dominance—to compete with others, or dominate them in some way. Studies also show differences in listening behaviors.

Studies on gender difference in listening behaviors indicate that minimal responses such as nods, "yes," and "mm hum" are common features of conversation. These responses often lead to male–female miscommunication. For women, a minimal response of this type means simply that she is listening, not necessarily that she agrees with the speaker. She is expressing her supportiveness. For men, such responses are likely to be interpreted as meaning, "I agree with you."

A female speaker who receives only occasional nods from a male thinks he isn't listening. This example explains two common complaints about male–female communication: (1) women who get upset with men who never seem to listen and (2) men who think that a woman is always agreeing and then conclude, when they find the woman doesn't agree, that it's impossible to tell what a woman really thinks.

Of course, such generalizations are just that—generalizations. Some men are supportive and understanding, while some women are very competitive and eager to dominate. Gender differences across communication behaviors do, however, hold up when looking at the genders as a group.

Source: Sherron Bienvenu, Ph.D., *Management Consultant, Communication Solutions*. See more ideas on communication effectiveness, including workplace gender differences at her Web site: *www.ChinUp.net*

Verbally, we can improve communication by using "continuers" such as *Uh huh*, or *I see*, or *I can see why you'd be upset*. These types of comments tend to let the customer know that you are listening and to encourage them to fully express their thoughts.

Action Tip 8—Solicit Clarification

When customers are being unclear, it is important that we tactfully let them know it. We sometimes don't do this because:

- We think we will sound uninformed.
- We think we can figure the message out on our own—eventually.
- We don't want to take the time or expend the effort to make sure we understand.

By failing to ask for clarification, we rely too heavily on our own guesses in interpreting messages. When you ask questions about the meanings of a message, any implication that you lack knowledge will be more than made up for by your sincere desire to understand. This is flattering to others. It conveys a regard for people who speak to you. When you solicit clarification, ask open-ended questions, or use a phrase such as, "Help me understand." For example, "Help me understand. You felt that the service you received was not what you had expected." These comments open the door for further description by the customer.

> "Help me understand" is a good phrase to invite people to clarify their ideas without getting defensive.

Action Tip 9—Minimize the Number of Gatekeepers

As previously noted, gatekeeping results in our listening to someone else's version of the message. Whenever possible, avoid sending an intermediary to get the story from the source and then report back to you. Avoid requesting that someone tell his or her story to your assistant and then let that person synthesize the information for you. Get customer concerns directly from the proverbial horse's mouth. The more people the message must go through, the more likely the message will be distorted.

> Remember that the gatekeeper's version may not be exactly what the original messages source may have meant.

You'll notice this recommendation was prefaced with "whenever possible." A top company executive cannot listen to every customer directly. A manager may be handling thousands of accounts and can be overloaded with too many messages. To reduce information overload, managers should develop a clear policy on which situations need their direct personal attention and which can be satisfactorily handled by others in the organization. Problems that can be handled at lower levels in the organization should be resolved there. A customer problem requiring a decision should go only as far as the lowest-ranking person authorized to make the decision. And the best companies empower people at all levels in an organization to solve problems.

Action Tip 10—Try Counter-Attitudinal Advocacy

Counter-attitudinal advocacy (CAA) is a big term for a simple process. It means to take the other person's position—to advocate or express a point of view that runs counter to your own attitude. The objective of CAA is to reduce the degree to which a listener listens through his or her own biases. CAA forces you to listen objectively until you truly understand, rather than to listen only until you think of a response or counterargument.

Here is how CAA works: You, as a listener, simply make a commitment to *restate* and *defend* the position that is counter to your attitude, that is, opposite to your position. Say, for example, a customer feels that the company doesn't care about the environment. You could immediately tell that customer about all the environmentally friendly things the company does, but, using CAA, you hold back. Instead, you honestly try to restate to that customer exactly what you hear him or her expressing. This, of course, includes both the facts and the emotions you think the customer is conveying. Use your own words to express the idea you hear the other person saying. You may say, "You see our company as being harmful by erecting too many signs that are visually unattractive and make the neighborhood look junky." Then ask if your interpretation is accurate. If not, restate it again until agreement is reached.

What happens is this: By committing yourself to restate and defend someone else's position, you must listen more effectively to that position in order to understand what you are defending. This more accurate listening provides a basis for solving the problem. By articulating a position counter to your own, you force yourself to consider information that you may have avoided when advancing your own position. You have forced yourself to listen to ideas through someone else's biases. The end result is a better understanding of the entire situation, rather than just your position.

> Defending another person's position requires that you understand it from their perspective.

This process does not obligate you to cave in to the views of others when you honestly disagree. It simply provides one way of better understanding where those you disagree with are coming from. In some cases, disagreements evaporate when we clarify each other's position. We may recognize that we don't really disagree in principle; we are simply expressing similar ideas in different or confusing ways. At any rate, clearer understanding forms a basis for problem resolution.

Action Tip 11—Take Notes

Should you take notes when listening to a customer? There are some real advantages to doing so. Note-taking conveys that you are sincerely interested in understanding. Most customers will be flattered that you are taking their input so seriously.

Of course, when taking notes, jot down only major ideas and important facts that may help you to listen and remember more effectively. Don't try to write down everything word for word. Let the customer see you taking the notes (or tell him or her that you are doing so if you are on the phone).

Note-taking shows that you are committed to listening and understanding the customer. Few people would be offended by such a show of concern.

A FINAL THOUGHT

Most thoughtful people recognize the need for careful listening. We spend more time in listening than in any other communication activity. Of all the sources of information we have when dealing with customers, listening is the most important. No tool rivals skilled and sympathetic listening for building stronger customer relationships.

How do we motivate others to listen? A cartoon showed the boss talking to employees at a meeting, saying, "Now pay careful attention. I'll let you know at the end of the meeting who will write up the minutes." When everyone in the organization begins to listen as though they were going to have to write up the minutes, understanding will advance in a quantum leap.

If we give undivided attention to our customers, coworkers, and associates, we will see a dramatic improvement in our ability to meet customer needs and win their loyalty. Such listening improvement starts at home; it starts with ourselves.

Summary of Key Ideas

- Hearing differs from listening in that hearing is a purely physiological activity, while listening also involves the psychological processing of sounds.
- Three types of factors complicate the listening process and pose potential barriers: internal elements within the listener's mind, environmental elements surrounding the communication, and interactional elements that arise especially from listener self-centeredness and self-protection.
- Communication problems can arise from information overload or from underuse of our listening capacity.
- Interactional elements of the listening process encompass the problems of self-centeredness and self-protection.
- To be a better listener, avoid poor listening behaviors such as faking attention, changing channels, listening only for facts, responses that turn people off, impatience, and overuse of gatekeepers.
- To improve listening effectiveness, use these behaviors (in addition to avoiding those previously) listed: solicit clarification, tactfully use CAA, and minimize the number of gatekeepers.

Key Concepts

cocktail party effect	gatekeepers	listening capacity	self-centeredness
counter-attitudinal advocacy (CAA)	internal, environmental, and interactional	listening for more than the facts	self-protection
faking attention	elements of listening	noise	wide asleep listener

Reviewing the Facts

1. How do hearing and listening differ?
2. What is the "cocktail party effect"? What can you do to minimize this effect when dealing with a customer?
3. What are three major elements that complicate listening? Give customer-service related examples of each.
4. What happens when people experience communication overload? Describe at least three ways we respond. How can this be a problem in customer service?
5. What do we mean by environmental and internal "noise"? Give examples of each as they might be found in a customer service situation.

6. How do "gatekeepers" complicate the listening process? What can organizations do to minimize the number of gatekeepers between the customer and top management?
7. What are self-centeredness and self-protection as they relate to listening? Give an example of each in the context of customer service.
8. What is counter-attitudinal advocacy and how can it be used to clarify understanding? How can this be used to deal with customer issues?

Applying the Ideas: Discover Your Listening Style

1. Try a Listening Log

    Try this skill-building activity: keep a listening log for one full day. As you engage in conversations with people, analyze what you are doing. Identify the number of times you engage in the unproductive habits described in this chapter. Record these in a log. (Be honest and open. We all do these ineffective things and becoming aware of how frequently we do them can be helpful in improving our listening skills.)

    Which habits seem to pop up in your listening? What can you do to replace these habits with more productive behaviors?

    Write a one-page paper describing what you have discovered about your listening skills.

2. Calculate Your Talk–Listen Ratio

    There is no such thing as an unpopular listener. Almost everyone becomes more interesting when he or she stops talking. Pay attention to your talk–listen ratio. Are you talking a lot more than listening? Are you giving the customer at least equal time? Is this ratio appropriate for the given communication situation? (Sometimes you need to talk more, but often we talk too much and listen too little.)

    Record a conversation you have with another person—preferably a customer. Then, using a stop watch, time how much you talked and how much the other person talked. Was this talk–listen ratio appropriate for the conversation? Do you feel you talked too much? Not enough?

3. Search It Out: What Do We Know about Listening Styles?

    Use your preferred search engine to see what you can find on the Internet about differences in listening styles. Be creative about your search terms. You may want to start with phrases such as "listening styles," "male–female listening patterns," "listening to customers," and so on.

    Write a brief report about the most commonly described listening problems that are related to customer service. Be sure to document the Web site addresses you access.

Consider this Case

Storytelling Helps Listeners

Let's consider the flip side of good listening for a moment. How can we make it easier for other people to listen to us?

Some things are easier to listen to than others. If we want to be listened to, we can apply some easy tactics to be more engaging by interlacing stories into our conversations. Typically, people enjoy hearing stories or vivid descriptions because these create mental pictures in the mind. Further, storytelling is one of the most effective ways to foster relationships in an organization. Indeed, the whole area of organizational stories has become a fruitful area of research into why some companies do better than others.

Jack Welch, CEO of GE, tells about a young manager leading his first project. As a result of the young man's bad decisions, the company lost $5 million. He went to Jack Welch to apologize and resign. Instead of accepting his resignation, Welch told the embarrassed young manager that the company could not afford for him to resign because GE had just invested $5 million in his education!

Stories about people's antics—heroic or humorous—make for engaging conversation. They are often easier to listen to than other kinds of messages.

A story can be used to change the way people operate in a company. The GE story says several things: that people can make a mistake and still be valuable to the company; that experiments don't always work; and that people are more important than projects. Whatever the interpretation, messages like these free up creativity and encourage experimentation and discovery. It is a reason that Jack Welch was one of the most highly regarded CEOs in corporate America.

Probes

1. Why is it easier for most of us to listen to stories as opposed to other forms of information?
2. What can you do to use stories or vivid anecdotes and thus help others listen?

Consider this Case

The Boss's Great Idea

Mario had barely arrived at the office when his boss, Marilyn, swept into his office and in her usual brusque way said, "Hi, Mario. Good weekend? Hope so. I got this idea: We've been concerned about the way our people never seem to listen to us—or to the customers. So, I was surfing the Net and found this little chart. Let's see that we get copies to everybody and maybe they'll listen better. I gotta run. Talk with you later."

Before Mario could respond, she was gone. He smiled to himself and shook his head. "Ah, Marilyn. You always think problems can be solved with simple quick messages. Oh well, no harm looking at this. Maybe it'll get our people thinking about better listening, even if their boss isn't much of a role model," he said to himself.

He then read the chart and noticed a few poor listening characteristics in his own behaviors, although he thought of himself as a pretty good listener. Maybe this chart will provide a wake-up call for our people, he thought. The chart looked like this:

Poor Listener	Effective Listener
Tends to have his/her mind wander with slow-speaking customers	Thinks and mentally summarizes, weighs the evidence, listens between the lines to the customer's tone of voice and evidence
Tunes out if the subject is dry or he/she has heard it all before	Works to find same value in the comments—what's in it for me
Is distracted easily	Fights distractions, sees past bad communication habits, knows how to concentrate
May take intensive notes, but the more notes taken, the less value; has only one way to take notes	Has two to three ways to take notes and organize important information
Is over-stimulated, tends to seek and enter into arguments with customer	Doesn't judge until comprehension is complete
Reacts immediately to logic flaws or emotional words	Interprets emotional wording and doesn't get hung up on it to catch his or her attention
Shows no reaction, energy output	Holds eye contact and helps speaker along by showing an active body state
Judges the customer's delivery—tunes out	Judges content, skips over delivery errors
Listens for facts	Listens for central ideas

Probes

1. What should Mario do to get his employees thinking about the better listening ideas described in the chart?
2. How likely is it that people will recognize and change their behaviors on the basis of this brief message? What else could Mario do?
3. What do you think of Marilyn's listening, on the basis of this brief description? Do you know people who communicate like she did? How do you react?
4. To what extent are your own listening skills reflective of the poor or effective listener described in the chart?

Note

1. J. Harold Janis, *Writing and Organizational Communication*, 3rd ed. (New York: Macmillan, 1978), p. 492.

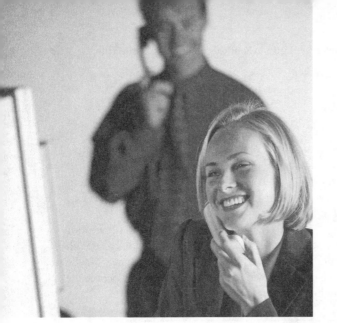

Use the Telephone Well for Good Service
Phone Responsiveness Can Enhance Customer Loyalty

Telephone, n. An invention of the devil which abrogates some of the advantages of making a disagreeable person keep his distance.

—AMBROSE BIERCE

If e-mail had been around before the telephone was invented, people would have said, "Hey, forget e-mail—with this new telephone invention I can actually talk to people"

—ANONYMOUS

After reading this chapter, you should be able to

1. Know the benefits and drawbacks of telephonic communication.

2. Identify your own telephone use attitudes as well as those of your company.

3. Apply specific action tips on what to do and say when dealing with customers on the phone.

4. Employ specific action tips to better express yourself on the phone.

5. Use specific action tips to be more efficient on the phone.

6. Recognize challenges and opportunities associated with building customer relationships with call centers.

The Way It Is . . . Frustrations of Unresponsive Telephone Use

Hearing a radio commercial for a concert, Sarah called the number to buy tickets. The number was an easy-to-remember 888 toll-free one that had the word ARTS as the last four digits. So far, so good. On the first try, the phone rang eight times before she gave up and decided to try again later. Her second attempt rang nine times and then a recorded message gave her another number to call. When Sarah dialed that number, an electronic voice put her on hold, after which another recorded voice told her to call the first number she had tried!

Hotel reservation lines, airlines, credit card companies, banks . . . virtually all companies run their customers through an electronic maze of choices that supposedly make the call more efficient, but often succeed to annoy the caller who simply wants to talk to a human being. By contrast, many consumers do repeat business with organizations where calls are answered by a real person and avoid companies whose phone service is mechanical, unresponsive, or laborious. How about you?

Wise, service-oriented companies are constantly improving phone and Net services, but many are succeeding only at angering or annoying their customers when the customer is ready to buy!

KNOW THE BENEFITS AND DRAWBACKS OF TELEPHONIC COMMUNICATION

People who answer calls from customers (often working in **call centers**) have been described as the conscripts of the Information Age: "Lined up headset-to-headset, they make pitches, take orders, and provide technical support. They get sworn at, hung up on, sometimes even thanked. But what these telephone-wielding armies really do is tell people about your business."[1] Ironically, these people are often among the lowest paid in the organization, yet they are the voice and image of the entire company to customers.

The telephone certainly can be, as the ads used to say, "The next best thing to being there." In fact, no business can long survive without a phone because, in many cases, a large percentage of their customers make first contact with the company via phone. However, there are two significant drawbacks to telephones that can almost cancel out their benefits:

1. *Many people have never learned the basics of telephone courtesy and effectiveness necessary to convey a good business image.* Employees have been using the phone since childhood but may have never polished their business telephone techniques. Everyday casual telephone usage may be totally inappropriate for business. The result can be customer dissatisfaction and a severe loss of organizational image and effectiveness. And, unfortunately, companies (other than call centers) often fail to provide sufficient phone training.
2. *People cannot see the person they are dealing with.* Thus, the phone does not permit most nonverbal communication. Without **visual cues** to reinforce or clarify a message, the listener may be easily misled or confused.

Always remember that people are operating blind when on the phone.

Phrased another way, each telephone call creates interactions where people are operating blind—without the visual feedback that helps assign meaning to spoken messages. To compensate for this lack of visual feedback, we as telephone callers create our own conclusions from what we experience—every nuance conveys subtle messages through timing, tone of voice, word choice, and interruptions. For many people, this ambiguity makes telephone use uncomfortable and even threatening. Although it is a great piece of technology, the telephone can also be frustrating. We draw conclusions from our phone interaction about the quality of the company.

An increasing number of companies now have call centers (sometimes called contact centers) where most or all phone calls are directed. But whether dealing with a call center or an individual in an organization, the way the phone call is handled has an impact on the quality of service provided.

Consider this story about one incident where a company lost a customer because it forgot (or never stopped to think about) the drawbacks to telephone communication:

SERVICE SNAPSHOT

Garth and the Auto Dealer

Garth enjoys working on old cars. A few years ago as he drove to work, he noticed a sports car in an auto dealership's lot. Sensing that such a car would do a lot for his image, Garth decided to inquire about it. He telephoned the dealership. A receptionist briskly identified the name of the dealership and, just as quickly, commanded, "Hold a minute." Fifteen seconds later, the receptionist came back on the line and asked, "Can I help ya?" Garth asked to "speak to someone in used cars, please."

"Just a minute," the receptionist replied.

After a pause, a man's voice said, "Hello?"

"I'd like a little information about the Porsche Boxster you have on your lot," Garth said.

"Ya mean the silver one?"

"Yes. Could you give me some information on that car?"

The male voice hesitated for a moment and said, "I think that's the owner's daughter's car. She's been driving it around. Let me check and see what the deal is on it."

There was a long pause. While Garth waited on hold, another male voice came on the line saying, "Hello? Hello?" to which he replied, "I'm already being helped." There was a click as the interrupter hung up without acknowledging Garth's comment.

After a few more minutes, the original salesman came back on the line and said, "Yeah, I think that's the car the boss's daughter has been driving around. If they sell it, they'll want an arm and a leg for it. I think it's a '98 model."

"Well, would you check and let me know if it's for sale?" Garth asked again, getting exasperated.

"Just a minute, I'll ask the owner," he said as he put Garth on hold again. After a few moments, the salesperson again picked up the telephone and abruptly said, "The owner says it's not for sale."

As Garth began to say, "Thanks for the information," he was cut off in mid-sentence by the click of the telephone as the man hung up.

Although this sales representative was probably not being intentionally rude, he sure came across that way. Garth was irritated to the point where he would definitely not do business with this dealership. Have you ever decided to stop doing business with a company because of their minuses on the phone? Many people have.

The next section of this chapter will discuss specific actions and behaviors that can make your phone use more professional and appropriate for customer service. We will first consider some action tips for identifying the attitudes you (and your organization) may have about telephone use. Then, you will learn action tips on when and how you can make the most of the telephone, what you should say and do, and how you can best phrase certain messages to assure better customer service.

ACTION TIPS FOR IDENTIFYING TELEPHONE USE ATTITUDES

Action Tip 1—Check Your Phone Use Attitudes

Many people have a love–hate relationship with the telephone. Of course, we all know that the telephone can be a powerful tool for sales, information gathering, and relationship building. By receiving and initiating calls, we can accomplish a lot. Yet some people are phone-shy. They are hesitant to call others and sometimes hesitant about answering incoming calls. They perceive the phone call as an intrusion on their other activities. Perhaps this attitude is reinforced by the annoyance of dinnertime telemarketers.

Many people are phone-shy—they see calls as interruptions.

Check your telephone-use attitudes using the self-evaluation that follows. It can help you understand some of your attitudes toward using the telephone. It can also help you improve your telephone techniques by showing what you may be doing wrong.

Action Tip 2—Contact and Compare Your Company

Call the general contact number of your current employer and ask a routine question such as information about office hours or products. Then call a company that you have dealt with in the past as a customer and ask a similar question. What attitude toward communicating does your company's phone use reflect? How does the other company compare?

A telephone call is often a customer's first point of contact with an organization. And as the old saying goes, you never get a second chance to make a first impression. Callers create first impressions

LOOK INSIDE

How Are Your Phone Usage Skills and Attitudes?

Circle the appropriate letter for each item:

    N = never, R = rarely, SM = sometimes, O = often, A = always.

Then read the instructions at the end of the form.

How Often Do You . . .	
1. Delay calling someone or fail to return a call?	N R SM O A
2. Answer the telephone with a curt or mechanical greeting?	N R SM O A
3. Let the phone ring, hoping the caller will give up?	N R SM O A
4. Save travel time by calling for information ("let your fingers do the walking")?	N R SM O A
5. End the conversation by summarizing what was agreed upon?	N R SM O A
6. Solicit feedback about your customer service by phone call?	N R SM O A
7. Put people on hold for more than a few seconds?	N R SM O A
8. Have someone else place your calls for you?	N R SM O A
9. Smile as you speak?	N R SM O A
10. Speak clearly and in pleasant, conversational tones?	N R SM O A

Take a moment to think about your responses. If they signal possible areas for improvement—even a minor "little thing" that you might do well to change—jot down your top three ideas or goals here:

-
-
-
-

and draw immediate conclusions about the person's (and the company's) efficiency, communication skills, friendliness, and expertise, all in the first few moments of an electronic visit. In short, your courtesy and effectiveness quickly convey unspoken but important attitudes to calling customers.

Managers should regularly check on their organization's phone skills. Have people who know how the phones should be handled call periodically and then prepare a brief report. If you are not sure exactly what to listen for, hire a phone consulting firm to gather some good data.

Telephone contact is often the first impression a customer gets of your company.

Action Tip 3—Avoid Unnecessary Call Screening

The amount of **call screening** reveals certain attitudes toward phone use. Screening means having someone answer for you, acting as your gatekeeper, as we discussed in Chapter 3. Ideally, people should be encouraged to answer their own telephone unless busy in a face-to-face conversation with a customer. Routine screening of calls by a secretary or receptionist often creates resentment in the caller. The constant use of "May I say who is calling?" is recognized as a dodge—an opportunity for the person to decide if he or she wants to talk or not. Customers get annoyed when there are too many gatekeepers. On the other hand, giving customers your direct line—and actually answering it—can speak volumes about your openness and willingness to serve.

Use call screening only when necessary, not as a way of projecting power.

ANOTHER LOOK

Oops! Accessibility Is Job #1

An administrative assistant for a chiropractic office called an insurance company to verify benefits for a patient. Although the call was important, she couldn't reach a human being, only a recording. The recording said, "Thank you for calling. Our office will be closed until two o'clock as we enjoy our Customer Appreciation Week Celebration."

Action Tip 4—Answer with Professionalism

When customers do get through to you, answer professionally. The appropriate way to answer a business call is to simply state your name or your department and your name. Example: "Customer support. This is Nancy Chin." Calling yourself Mrs., Ms., Mr., or with a title may sound a bit self-important. Example: "Accounting office, Mr. Silvia speaking." Some people use just their last name, although this can sometimes confuse callers. (A manager named Paul Waite found his last-name-only greeting often followed by a very long pause!)

Identify yourself when answering the phone.

Use of "How may I help you?" (or a similar phrase) following your name tells callers whom they are speaking to and that you are ready to converse with them. When answering another person's telephone, be sure to identify both that other person and yourself. Example: "Michelle Theron's office. This is Timo Sampson. May I help you?"

Of course, receptionists would never need to ask who is calling if *callers* would use good business etiquette. Good manners dictate that when we call people, we identify ourselves immediately. Example: "Good morning, Barry Adamson calling. Is Sharon Silverstein there?" Get in the habit of doing this and you will set a good example for others who may realize the advantage of such courtesy.

ACTION TIPS ON WHAT TO DO AND SAY

Action Tip 5—Answer Promptly and Be Prepared to Handle Calls

An answer after two rings or less conveys efficiency and a willingness to serve. When the telephone rings longer, callers get the feeling that you are unavailable and that their call is an intrusion. What is worse is that unanswered callers get the message that you think they are not important.

If your phone system goes to a message announcing a delay in answering, make that message efficient and avoid clichés. One company's answering machine promptly says, "We know your time is valuable and we want to serve you promptly. Calls will be answered in order. We sincerely apologize for this brief delay." That is a pretty good message. We too often hear the more common clichéd phrases such as "All of our representatives are currently helping other customers," which sound more like an excuse than an apology. Make your message efficient (reduce wordiness) and considerate of the caller's feelings.

Have your work area set up for comfortable and efficient telephone use. Place the telephone at a convenient spot on your desk or worktable. Keep your frequently called numbers list current and have material you may need to refer to within reach. Have your computer screen, note paper, message slips, and necessary forms handy. Use a planner system (electronic or a paper) that has room to jot down notes about your conversations. Don't scribble notes on random sheets of paper. They'll get misplaced.

Get the caller's name and number as soon as possible and summarize the conversations briefly—especially any commitments you will need to follow up. If you agree to do something for a caller, be sure to record it (in writing or on the computer) and then check it off when completed.

Action Tip 5—Use Courtesy Titles

While calling yourself Mr. or Ms. may sound stuffy, don't assume that a caller prefers to be called by his or her first name. Use proper **courtesy titles** for the people to whom you refer. If in doubt whether to use a first name, call the person by the more formal "Mr." or "Ms." If they prefer the more informal first name, they will say so. It is better to be a bit overly formal than be too familiar.

There is no downside to addressing people politely and formally.

Titles and formality can create credibility. If you refer to other professionals, refer to them formally. You'd be a bit thrown off if a medical doctor introduced himself: "Hi, I'm Larry, your brain surgeon." Even if your organization has an informal culture, don't assume that others do. If referring to a company executive, consider using a courtesy title: "I'll get this information to our marketing director, Mr. Kagel, and he'll get back to you by Monday, okay?"

ANOTHER LOOK

Hello, Your Paycheck Is Calling

By Anne M. Obarski

I challenge businesses to think that every time their phone rings, it is their paycheck calling. I also challenge businesses to look at their phone with as much respect and interest as they look at their merchandise, their marketing, and their employees; it is a reflection of their "brand." And reinforcing a brand through every customer touch point can provide the repetition necessary to inspire repeat purchasing decisions.

When you think about your phone calls that way, you are more apt to answer the phone with a little more expectation in your voice rather than disgust. You will start looking at your phone as a sales-building tool. People develop a perception about you within the first 30 seconds of a phone conversation and their final opinion of you in the last 30 seconds. Let's look at some phone tips that will boost that final opinion to one of an ongoing, positive relationship.

1. *Breathe!* Before you pick up the phone, take a deep breath. Most of us are what they call "shallow breathers." We take small breaths in and out and, therefore, sound tired when we answer the phone. The goal is to sound like you like your job and you are glad they called.

   Practice taking a very big breath and answering the phone at the top of that breath. You will continue speaking on the exhale of that breath and the caller will hear energy in your voice. You can also practice it when you are making a call and start your breath as the phone is ringing on the other end.

2. *Identify yourself.* Give your full name and function or name of your company. I answer the phone this way: "Thank you for calling Merchandise Concepts. This is Anne Obarski. How can I make it a great day for you?" Hokey, maybe; memorable, maybe; friendly, you bet. Since I have an unusual last name, this helps me say it first so that the caller doesn't have to fumble with the pronunciation.

3. *Be sincere.* We are all problem solvers in some way. People call us on the phone to have a problem answered. Whether it is to get driving directions, or hours of operation, or questions about our merchandise, they have a question and want it answered quickly, intelligently, and politely.

4. *Listen attentively.* Put everything down when you answer the phone! Easier said than done, isn't it? How many times have you been in your office answering email, talking on the phone, listening to your iPod, and sipping on a Starbucks? Me too. Shame on us. Customers don't like to be ignored, and by multitasking, we are not focused on the customer's wants and needs.

   Visualize the person, even if you don't know him or her, so that you remind yourself you are engaged in a two-way conversation. If you still have trouble listening, take notes on what the customer is saying. Use a headset, if possible, to keep your hands free. By taking notes, you can verify with them, as well as yourself, the important points of the conversation and the action items that need attention.

5. *Outcome.* If the phone call has been successful, the first 30 seconds established a positive perception about you through voice, tone, and focus. The last 30 seconds will be when callers finalize their opinion about you. You can make that a positive experience by thanking them for calling, reviewing the problem you were able to solve, and then, most importantly, thanking them for their continued business.

Source: www.businessknowhow.com/marketing/telephone-skills.htm. Downloaded and edited March 1, 2006. Anne M. Obarski is a professional speaker and trainer. For more information, visit her Web site at www.merchandiseconcepts.com/speaking.html. Used with her permission.

Action Tip 6—Thank People for Calling

"Thank you" is the most powerful phrase in human relations. Express appreciation regularly. Some companies use it as a greeting: "Thank you for calling Avis." A "thanks for calling" at the end of a conversation is also a strong customer satisfaction booster. It reassures the customer that you are interested in serving and that the call was not an intrusion.

If a caller is complaining, thanking is still useful. Remember that complainers can be our best friends. They give us feedback that can help us improve and, by virtue of the fact that they made the effort to call us, deserve our thanks. By saying "I appreciate your bringing this problem to my attention," we shift the conversation from confrontation to a problem-solving tone.

Never underestimate the power of the words thank you.

Action Tip 7—Smile

Picture the person you are talking with and treat that person as though you were face-to-face with a friend. Be pleasant, concerned, and helpful. Physically smiling somehow comes through the telephone line via your voice tones.

Keep a mirror by the telephone to remind yourself to smile. If your face looks grumpy or stressed, you are probably coming across that way to the caller. Lighten up and your cheerfulness can be contagious.

Try looking into a mirror while on the phone. A smile (or lack thereof) can communicate.

Action Tip 8—Be Sure the Conversation Is Finished before You Hang Up

If you initiated the call, take the responsibility for ending it. Use conclusion words such as "Thank you for your help" or "That is just what I needed."

If you received the call, be sure the caller is finished. In our earlier auto dealer story, Garth was about to ask the salesperson if the dealership had any other sports cars available, but was cut off before he could. It can be a good practice to simply ask, "Is there anything else I can help you with?" at the end of the call. Or, depending on your company, you might offer additional, specific services or products. Airline ticket agents will often ask if you'll "be needing help with hotel or rental car reservations" before signing off. Of course, that is an attempt to sell more, but it also provides customer convenience and an effective way to signal the end of the call.

Have a polished way to signal the end of a conversation.

Action Tip 9—Handle the Upset Caller with Tact and Skill

Here are some additional tips for recovering upset callers. First, recognize that there are two phases to handling upset or difficult people:

Step One: Understand why they are upset or difficult.

The three common root causes of anger/frustration arise from peoples' feelings that:

- They are not valued or important.
- They are helpless.
- "It" just isn't fair (whatever "it" may be).

We have all experienced these feelings at some time. Be empathic and recognize that these don't make the caller a bad person but rather a person who is having an unpleasant experience. Try to put yourself in the caller's position. Then,

Step Two: Diffuse the anger or frustration with statements or questions like:

1. *Help me to understand.* . . . This will encourage them to explain why they are upset. Don't try to defend or argue with their perceptions—they know what they feel, even if it doesn't make a lot of sense to you. Then, let them know that you empathize by saying,

2. *I can understand why you would feel that way.* Do not say "I know *exactly* what you mean" because you probably don't. Instead, convey that you have an idea of what he or she might be feeling. Then ask

3. *What would be a good solution from your point of view?* This begins to shift the conversation away from the venting of emotion toward solution seeking.

Strive to have the caller share the responsibility for finding a reasonable solution to the problem being experienced. When he has made a proposal or suggested an idea that might work, you can begin a negotiating process that can lead to a reconciliation—and cooling off—of the caller.

ACTION TIPS ON HOW TO EXPRESS YOURSELF ON THE PHONE

Action Tip 10—Keep Your Conversation Tactful and Businesslike

Nothing turns off a customer or caller like poor wording or abruptness. Have you ever had the experience where, upon telling people your name, they abruptly say, "Who?" Few things make a caller feel less appreciated. If you didn't catch the name, ask politely, "I'm sorry, I didn't get your name, sir. Would you repeat it?"

Keep your comments positive and oriented toward solving the caller's problem or concern. Don't just toss the ball back when you can't immediately help. Don't say anything that makes people or your organization look unprofessional or uncaring.[2]

Here are some other dos and don'ts:

Avoid Saying	Do Say
Who is this?	May I ask who's calling?
What's your name?	I'm sorry, but I didn't get your name *or* May I have your name?
What do you need?	How can I help you?
Speak up, I can't hear you.	I'm sorry, I can't hear you. Could you speak a little louder, please?
Well, I wasn't the one you talked to.	I'm sorry, Ms. James, someone else must have helped you earlier.
He's out to lunch.	Mr. Barringer is away from the office for about one hour. Can I ask him to call you back?
You'll need to call our billing office.	That information is available in our billing office. I'll be happy to connect you. (Or, shall I ask someone in billing to call you back?)
Sorry, I can't help you with that.	I don't have that information here. May I have someone from our quality service department call you?
There's nothing I can do about that.	I'll put that on my calendar for next Tuesday and I'll check on your request again then. Then I'll call you back.

Action Tip 11—Speak Clearly and Distinctly

Hold the telephone mouthpiece about a half inch from your lips. Whether you answer with your name, the company name, or the department name, speak clearly and distinctly. Example: Carefully say "Good morning, Primo Computer Service," "Hello, this is KJQQ radio," or "Scheduling department," followed by your name. Separate the words with tiny pauses.

ANOTHER LOOK

Use Plain Language

Some people think their ability to sling a lot of professional jargon is a way to show how smart they are. The problem is this can be annoying and confusing to customers.

It's easy to forget that our customers do not necessarily understand the jargon, acronyms, and terms that we use every day and take for granted. Using plain language involves translating our language into language that the customer can understand.

For example, a computer technician might use the term *LCD* to refer to a liquid crystal display computer monitor with other technicians, but this term may be totally foreign to most casual computer users. Some will know it, but some will not, so it's good to anticipate that not everyone will understand the term. The technician might translate it into "computer monitor," which is a more familiar term. In addition, the technician should be prepared to explain even that term in simple language. For example, "the computer monitor is a device that you look at when you use the computer." In this example, the technician would use the latter explanation only if the customer seemed to not understand so as not to insult the customer's knowledge and intelligence.

Technology terms like *smartphones*, *handhelds*, *DVDs*, and *PDAs* are fairly commonplace among some tech-savvy people but may sound like a foreign language to others. Do you know what they mean? Can you explain them to others?

Tech-world is not the only place for unfamiliar terms. A human resource professional might be comfortable using terms like a *401(k)*, *compensation*, or *spousal benefits*; but those terms may not be completely clear to an employee. So, the HR employee could replace 401(k) with *company retirement account*, *compensation* with *salary*, and *spousal benefits* with *medical insurance for your wife and children*. The idea is to focus on clarity and simplicity without being patronizing and to remember to communicate for the benefit of the customer, not yourself.

Don't let your greeting sound mechanical—it's the first time your caller hears it.

Even if you say these words a hundred times a day, resist the temptation to get lazy or to repeat the greeting in a mechanical, unfriendly manner. Remember that each caller hears your greeting just once, even though you have said it many times. Make it fresh and sincere.

Avoid eating, drinking, or chewing gum while talking to customers. Munching and slurping sounds are unpleasant and unprofessional.

Action Tip 12—Speak Naturally and Comfortably

Talk to your caller as you would to a friend. Use warm, friendly voice tones and natural spontaneous reactions. If a caller says something humorous, laugh. If his or her tone of voice suggests tension or even anger, it may be appropriate to comment on that: "You sound upset. Is there something I can do to help?"

Talk to callers like friends.

A strong, clear voice is a tremendous asset. It conveys confidence and high credibility. But even if a person is not gifted with the voice of a professional broadcaster, he or she can do things with the voice that creates and holds listener interest.

The key to holding interest is *variation* in the voice. People cannot pay attention to something that does not change. But we do perk up when speakers adjust their voice. The three things any speaker can vary are pitch, loudness, and rate.

Pitch is almost a musical quality: the place on a musical scale where the voice would be. Male speakers tend to have more trouble varying pitch than females. The problem, of course, is that too little variation in **voice pitch** sounds like a monotone. In a word, it is boring.

Another problem is that people try to force their voice into a different pitch. By artificially speaking too low or too high, we create a stage voice that sounds phony. Use your natural range, but experiment with broadening that range, too.

Some speakers do not want to risk much pitch variation. (This tends to be more common for men who may want to keep their pitch low to sound more manly.) They fear sounding silly. Failing to vary pitch is like throwing away one of your most useful tools for effective communication. Listen carefully to good radio or TV announcers, comedians, or other entertainers. You will find that they vary their pitch a lot. Try pushing your range of pitch outward a bit. Go a little higher and a little lower than you typically do, but be careful to not be so extreme as to sound sing-songy (more common in women). Pitch variation conveys personality and helps hold listener interest. Try small changes—you don't need a major makeover—and see how you come across.

Also be mindful of **loudness** and rate of loudness and rate of your speech. Some people speak very softly and that can be difficult to hear sufficient volume so that your caller can get what you are saying without straining to hear. **Rate** of speech is also important. Although this may differ in various parts of the country where the norm is to speak quickly or slower, speaking at a pace about like you hear from professional communicators such as news reporters is usually appropriate. Speaking too slowly actually leads to more problems than speaking too quickly. Slow speech gives listeners too much time between thoughts and their thoughts may wander, as we discussed in Chapter 3 on listening.

Try small adjustments in your vocal variation to improve overall tone.

Speaking too slowly can cause your caller's attention to drift.

Action Tip 13—Do Not Let "Dead Air" Happen

Broadcasters call those awkward gaps when nothing is being broadcast "**dead air**". Listeners have no idea what is going on and often change stations if the silence persists. The same can happen with a telephone call.

If you need to transfer a caller, look up some information, or read some material, *tell the caller what you are doing*. Remember, he or she cannot see you. Use statements such as these to reassure your caller that you are still with him or her:

> "I will transfer you to Jim Kovak now. He can get you that information. One moment please."

> "I understand your concern. Ms. Jessop in our billing department can best help you with that. May I put you on hold for a moment? I will see if she is in."

> "I'm reviewing your account now, Mr. Jenson. Let me just check a few figures and I can give you that information in a moment."

Putting people on hold can be annoying to callers, but you can reduce this annoyance by telling them what you are doing and why.

Always acknowledge comments audibly. Be sure to react to your caller's conversation. Since your callers can't see you and don't receive visual feedback from you, they must rely on your spoken feedback—on what you say—to determine whether you understand what is being said.

Acknowledge caller comments audibly. They can't hear you nodding your head.

By frequently saying "yes" or "I see" or "uh-huh" or "I agree," you are providing the needed feedback. Don't let caller comments go unacknowledged.

Also, use the hold button carefully. What may seem to you like a brief hold can seem awfully long to a caller. Even if your phone system plays music, callers get pretty upset after 30 seconds or so. Try watching your clock the next time you are put on hold. A minute can seem like an eternity. Keep voice contact or pick up every 15–20 seconds to let the caller know that you haven't forgotten him or her. If you anticipate a fairly long hold time, offer to call back or at least prepare the caller by saying that this will require several minutes to complete. Then give him or her the option of holding or awaiting a callback.

Action Tip 14—Keep Callers on Track

If a caller digresses into chit chat or nonessential conversation, use a bridging technique to get back on track. This often calls for some creativity, but give it a try.

> *If your caller says:* "I get really sick of this gloomy weather around here. It really gets to you after a while, don't you think?"

> *You might say:* "Well, one way we can brighten your day is to . . . get this billing problem straightened out . . . [or] get that new recliner ordered for you . . . [or] give you the information you've been wanting."

If your caller says: "How about those Buffalo Bills last week. They never looked tougher. Kelly is still the best QB in the league, don't you think?"

You might say: "They were good. I hope I can get your *bills* straightened out for you real soon . . . [or] which reminds me, we need to be looking long and deep into your financial plan . . . [or] let's tackle this order for you."

If your caller says: "I really appreciate your help with the Special Olympics last weekend. Your company is a big help."

You might say: "Well thank you, Ms. Knowaki. I hope I can help you find that widget you called about, too. Let's see. Here it is. . . ."

If your caller wants to chat on and on, take charge: "Mrs. Customer, let me summarize what you've said and then if there is anything else you need to tell me, you can fill in."

Let upset callers express themselves fully before interrupting for more information or suggestions.

If your caller is exceptionally upset, let him or her get it all out before you attempt to interrupt. An interruption will just make the caller angrier. As callers describe their anger, offer sympathetic comments that let them know that you are still listening: "I see" or "Wow, that doesn't sound like we treated you very well," or "I know how upsetting that can be."

When appropriate, bring the conversation to a pleasant but efficient close. It can be tempting to talk on with friendly people, but others may be waiting to talk to you and other work awaits. Try some of these techniques for tactfully closing a conversation even when the caller seems to want to go on:

1. *Summarize the call and what has been decided.* Say, "Let me go over what we decided to do" or "Let me summarize the process for you." Spell out what has been done: "I closed that account and transferred $1,000 to your new fund." "That is all you need to do for now. It has been taken care of."
2. *Speak in the past tense.* "As we discussed" or "That was all the information I needed" or "I'm glad that you called."
3. *Say "thank you for calling."* This is a universal clue that the conversation is over.
4. *End the call positively* by saying, "I've enjoyed talking with you, Mr. Blanko."

ACTION TIPS FOR EFFICIENT USE OF THE PHONE

Action Tip 15—When Calling Others, Ask: "Is This a Convenient Time to Talk?"

Too many callers burst into their message when the person being called may be involved in something else. If there is any possibility that the person may be busy, ask if this is a good time before you begin.

If asked that question and it really isn't a good time, let the caller know and arrange another time to talk that would be more convenient.

This tip also holds if you don't have information you may need to answer a caller's questions. Be honest and tell him so. Then arrange a callback.

Action Tip 16—Take Messages Cheerfully and Accurately

Be willing to take messages for others. Keep a notepad handy to record key words and phrases. Read the message back to the caller to be sure it is accurate. Then be sure to pass the message to the right person.

If your company uses message slips, be complete when filling them out. To avoid possible communication problems, it is especially important to:

1. *Get the full name and correct spelling.* If you don't understand it clearly, ask the caller to spell it for you. Let the caller know why you are asking for the spelling by saying something like, "I want to make sure your message is accurate. Will you spell your name?"

2. *Ask for the name of the organization if appropriate.* The best reason for this is that it may give the message receiver a hint as to the nature of the call. It can also be a way of double-checking if there is a mistake with the number.

3. *Get the full telephone number, including the area code if it's long distance.* If the caller says, "She has it," you can say politely, "I know she can get back to you even faster if I jot your number down with your message."

4. If the caller doesn't volunteer any specific message, it will save on the callback if you ask, "Is there any information you would like to leave that may be helpful to Ms. Jones when she calls you back?"

5. *Say, "Thank you," and tell the caller that you will give the person the message as soon as he or she is available.* Say this with assurance.

6. *Note the time and date the message was taken, and add your initials in case there are any questions.*

Action Tip 17—Make Your Greeting Message Efficient

Use an answering machine or voice mail to capture messages when you are not available. Keep your greeting message current and not too long or too clever. Record your message to be brief. Messages like the following usually work fine:

> *You have reached 555-1131. We cannot take your call now. Please leave a message at the tone.*
>
> *(Note: This message does not identify who you are and may provide privacy and security.)*
>
> *This is Acme Manufacturing's Warehouse. Our business hours are from 8 a.m. to 6 p.m., Monday through Friday. Please leave a message.*
>
> *Thank you for calling NuHousing, Inc.—your mobile home leader. Please leave a message and we will get back to you as soon as we can. Thank you.*

Recorded messages may also ask for specific information from callers ("*If you have your account number available, please leave it so we can respond to your request more quickly.*"). Do not, however, ask for too much. Also, assure the caller that you will return the call.

When you leave a message on another person's machine, be sure to state the following:

- Your name (spoken clearly and spelled if necessary)
- Time and day of your call
- A brief explanation of why you are calling
- Your phone number
- When you can be reached

Here are two examples:

> *This is Jarom Steadman calling. It's 7 p.m. Friday. I have a question about your new Wave Runners. Please call me at 555-3077 after 10 a.m. Saturday.*
>
> *This is Raul Sancheski—that is spelled S-A-N-C-H-E-S-K-I. I am interested in your job opening for an experienced night programmer and would like to arrange an interview. I have six years' experience with a company like yours. Please call me at 555-0819 after 6 p.m. today, Thursday the 4th. Thank you.*

Action Tip 18—Learn to Use Your Phone's Features

The wonderful world of telephone technology is constantly coming up with new features. Unfortunately, like the many people who have no idea to program a DVD recorder, many businesspeople haven't learned to use the many tricks available through their phone system.

Customer dissatisfaction with a firm's phone call handling stems from two general classes:

1. Inability of employees to use the features of telephone and voice mail systems, and
2. Shortcomings in treating customers with the highest degree of courtesy.

Misuse of phone features is awkward for both the caller and the person taking the call. Make sure you know how to use them.

Customer-focused companies respond to these concerns by providing appropriate training for all employees. Such training boosts customer satisfaction with the firm's telephone responsiveness dramatically.

The most frequently used features on even the most basic phone systems are the hold button and call transfer. While putting someone on hold seems easy enough, be careful not to be too abrupt. *Ask* customers if it'll be okay if you put them on hold for (a specific amount of time). For example, "May I put you on hold for about three minutes while I gather that information?" Ideally, you will be back on the phone in the allotted time or sooner. If you need additional time, come online and explain that: "Mr. Rissouli, I'm going to need about another minute to get your file, can you continue to hold?"

When transferring a call to another person, take a moment to explain why: "I think we can better help you if you talk directly to a service technician. Will it be okay if I transfer you to Sarah Booker, our service manager?" One question callers are likely to have when transferred is how much does the new person know about my call. Ideally, the person transferring you will have briefed the person picking up the call. Often this does not happen, however. So, if you receive a transferred call from another employee and you do not know any details about the caller's needs, be open about that. Say something like, "I'm sorry Mrs. Sycamore, but could you take a moment to bring me up-to-date on your needs." Being open about the caller's feelings can be a very nice way to reduce the annoyance of having to retell the story. "I know this can be annoying to have to start over, Mr. Brunno, but could you please help me understand how I can serve you?"

If you are uncertain about the use of your telephone system's features such as call transferring, hold, and the like, take time to read the user's guide or call the service provider. They will be happy to have a representative teach you how to use the system. After all, it is in their best interest to have you using the equipment fully—so that they have a satisfied customer.

Action Tip 19—Plan Your Outgoing Calls for Efficiency

Although small talk is sometimes useful to create a good relationship with callers, strive to make business calls concise without being curt or abrupt. This can be especially important when using portable cellular telephones because both the receiver of the call and the caller are billed for "airtime"—the time you use the cellular network. Even for local calls, charges can run 50 cents per minute or more, depending on the time of day.

When placing a business call, plan what you will say, preferably in writing. Jot down some notes that include:

1. The purpose of your call
2. A list of information you need to get or give

Be sure to identify yourself and the reason for your call early in the conversation. Businesspeople do not like playing "guess who?" or "guess what?" A good way to kick off a typical call would be to say:

"Hello. This is Tina Watson calling from Unicorn Corporation. Is Marilyn Smith in?"
Once connected with Ms. Smith, say:
   "Hello, Ms. Smith. This is Tina Watson with Unicorn Corporation. I need to get some information about your recent catalog order. Is this a good time for you to talk?"

Notice that the caller here identifies herself, previews what she needs to discuss, and also asks about the person's readiness to talk. If the person is busy and cannot give the call full attention, this provides a chance to offer to call back.

When you need to return calls to people who have called you, schedule them at times they are likely to be in. Be aware of probable lunch hours and long-distance time differences. If you do not, you are likely to play that dreaded game: telephone tag. You keep returning calls and just missing the person who is trying to call you.

Time your callbacks for efficiency. Be specific about when you plan to call a person back. Vague statements like "I'll get back to you on that" may create unrealistic expectations. The caller expects to hear from you within 15 minutes, while you meant two or three hours. Instead say, "I'll call you back between one and two this afternoon" and, of course, do it during that time frame.

> Give customers realistic callback times and meet or beat those times.

Action Tip 20—Don't Let the Telephone Interrupt an Important Live Conversation

One of the pet peeves of many customers is when their discussion with a businessperson is interrupted by a phone call. If you are talking live to someone, do not assume that the phone call is more important or should be accorded priority.

If you must take the call, always excuse yourself and, when you determine what the call is about, inform the caller that you have someone with you now and will be happy to call back in a specified time.

Consistently Work to Improve Your Telephone Communications

Good telephone skills are essential for career success in almost every field. Make it an ongoing effort to get feedback about your skill level. Take the opportunity to attend seminars or view training videos that teach new and specialized skills.

If you supervise other people, don't hesitate to critique their telephone skills. Be frank with them if some things they are doing are inconsistent with the tips in this book. Remind them of the critical importance—to the company and to their professionalism—of good telephone skills.

Be observant. Listen carefully to both the spoken and unspoken messages that may be sent to your callers. Remember that when you use the telephone, your communication channel is limited. There are no visual cues being sent—your callers can't see you. So help them "see" you in the best possible light by your use of winning telephone techniques.

CALL CENTERS: BUILDING RELATIONSHIPS ONE PHONE CALL AT A TIME

Many organizations have centralized phone answering services for most customer calls. These call centers (sometimes called **contact centers**) are a relatively new phenomenon. More than 40 years ago when customers had questions or concerns about a product or service, they would usually call the company and ask to speak to a representative. The operator would patch the caller through to an employee in customer service, who usually worked at a desk outfitted with a phone, some reference materials, a notepad, and a pen or pencil. If the rep could answer the customer's question, she would. More often than not, however, she wouldn't have all the information. She'd explain that she needed to research the issue and ask the caller to please leave his or her name and number. The customer service representative (CSR) or **call center agent** would then begin the time-consuming process of rifling through file cabinets and paper records looking for the answers. Assuming the CSR didn't lose the customer's phone number, later that day or even that week, the CSR would call back with the requested information. The times, they have changed! Such a ponderous proves would be totally unacceptable to today's customers. Well-run call centers can facilitate quicker service and better customer relationships.

What a Call Center Is

Today's call center is more than a bunch of phones, desks, and agents. Here's what the industry experts say:

> *"A call center is a department within a company or a third-party organization that handles telephone sales and service. Call centers use [automatic call distributors] to route calls to the appropriate agent."*[3]
>
> *"A call center is a physical location where calls are placed, or received, in high volume for the purpose of sales, marketing, customer service, telemarketing, technical support, or other specialized business activity. Examples include reservation centers, catalog retailers, help desks, telemarketers, and fundraisers. Call centers are generally set up as large rooms, with workstations that include a computer, a telephone set (or headset) hooked into a large telecom switch, and one or more supervisor stations."*[4]

Call centers are an integral part of many businesses and should be staffed with well-trained personnel.

At a minimum, then, a call center is a facility where CSRs handle high-volume phone traffic, whether inbound or outbound, using sophisticated telephone and computer technology. Call centers typically serve external customers by answering questions, taking orders, responding to billing concerns, or pitching products and services through telemarketing. For some industries such as financial services, catalog retailing, and travel, call centers provide the primary presale contact point with the customer. For other industries such as consumer products and utilities, call centers are the primary postsale customer care channel. Regardless of when the customer is served, however, call centers have earned their place as an integral part in a modern customer care strategy.

Was the traditional approach effective? Generally, yes. Customers' concerns were actually addressed and usually to their satisfaction. But such an operation was hardly efficient. It took lots of agents, lots of time. As the volume of calls increased, companies either added more desks, phones, and reps or took longer to get back to their callers. Life was slower then, and customers were more patient.

Since then, the pace of business has accelerated from the speed of sound to the speed of light. The current generation of consumers—the Net Generation—would never put up with, "I'll get back to you in a couple of days." Today's customers want answers now. Fortunately, for them, technology changed everything, allowing companies to improve the service they provided over the phone.

All the principles of good phone usage apply to call center operators as well as individuals who handle customer communications on the telephone. By designating specialists as call center staff, companies can more easily monitor and more intensively train the people who interface with customers over the telephones.

A FINAL THOUGHT

More and more customers are using electronic media to access businesses. Telephones, Web sites, and email usage are increasingly important to modern organizations. This chapter focused on specific ideas for better telephone use. (We'll look at the other e-media in Chapter 5.) People need to be aware of the advantages as well as the limitations of these media. Customers who have a poor experience with your company over the phone are highly unlikely to become loyal customers.

Clearly, poor telephone use can have a dramatic impact on a company's success. Whether or not a company sets up separate call centers or other staff members answer customer calls, positive attitudes and winning techniques build stronger relationships with customers and other people important to the organization. Employees who master such techniques are particularly valuable to the organization. Truly, phone skills are critical to professional success on all levels.

Summary of Key Ideas

- Understanding our own attitudes toward telephone use and courtesy can help us become more effective in dealing with customers via electronic media.
- Ineffective telephone mannerisms can lead to poor first impressions and customer dissatisfaction.
- Considering your phone use attitudes, contacting a company to see how they do, and avoiding unnecessary call screening are three ways to better understand and determine how customers may see you and your company.
- Apply action tips on what to do and say, including such things as prompt answering, using courtesy titles, thanking, smiling, and using tact and skill, especially with upset callers.
- Apply tips for efficient use of the phone such as asking if this is a good time to talk, taking messages, using efficient greetings, using all phone features, planning outgoing calls, and constantly improving skills.
- Some companies centralize most phone call functions by creating call centers. For such centers to enhance the company's reputation, they must provide excellent customer contact and responsiveness.

Key Concepts

call center (aka contact center)

call center agent
call screening

courtesy titles
dead air

visual cues (lack of)
voice pitch, rate, loudness

Reviewing the Facts

1. Compare and contrast the benefits of phone communication versus face-to-face contact with customers.
2. How do attitudes toward using the phone affect one's telephone techniques?
3. What is call screening? When is it appropriate to use it? When should it be avoided?
4. What three elements can speakers vary in their voices to better hold listener attention?
5. What is "dead air" and how can it impact customer relationships?
6. What information should people have on their answering machine messages? What should be avoided?
7. What are the two important factors required to effectively handle irate customers on the phone?
8. What are courtesy titles and why are they important?
9. How can you improve the efficiency of your call use?
10. Why is it important to not let a phone call interrupt a live conversation?
11. What are some advantages and disadvantages of call centers?

Applying the Ideas: Try Rewording for a Better Tone

Rephrase the following statements to make the wording positive and tactful. Also strive to solve the caller's concern as efficiently as possible.

1. Bill is out playing golf again. I doubt that he'll be back in the office today.
2. Sarah went to the restroom and then is going to lunch for about an hour or so.
3. Who did you say you were?
4. You say you've been trying to get through? When did you try?
5. Who are you holding for?
6. This is Bobby. What do you need?
7. Hey, sorry about that. I got backed up and couldn't call you back.
8. We don't do that kind of work here.
9. Try again after five, okay?
10. Sally used to work here but we let her go. Maybe I can help.

Applying the Ideas: Hear the Difference

1. Try this simple exercise to demonstrate how voice inflection can change the meaning of what you say. Repeat out loud the following sentence, first just using your normal voice:

"Henry didn't show up for work today."

Now restate the same sentence expressing criticism in your voice:

Next, make it sound like a secret.
Finally, turn it into a question.
Next, try saying the following sentence with the emphasis on a different word each time:

"I think Doris can do that."

Notice that when you emphasize the word "I," the unspoken message may be "I think she can do it, although maybe no one else thinks so." When you emphasize the word "think," it conveys more uncertainty.

Listen for the possible unspoken messages as you emphasize "Doris," "can," and "that."

Notice how these subtle changes in voice and emphasis can convey widely different meanings.

2. Go to the Web using your preferred search engine to locate additional articles on telephone techniques. Report on what you find regarding the changing nature of telephone use in businesses. What are the key trends? How does the use of cellular phones change the ways companies serve customers?

Consider this Case
Critique this Call

The following situation describes a fairly commonplace business telephone conversation. In the space provided at the right, critique what is going on, noting both effective and ineffective techniques used by each speaker. Then answer the probe questions at the end of this exercise.

The Story		My Critique
Dallin:	Good morning, marketing department. This is Dallin. May I help you?	
Kristine:	Hi, is this marketing? Oh good. I need to find out some information about your future seminar schedule. Let me see now . . . [pause] there are several cities where our people might want to attend. [pause] I've got a list here somewhere. I know Cleveland is one. . . .	
Dallin:	We do have seminars scheduled for Cleveland, but which programs are you interested in?	
Kristine:	I'm not real sure. My boss just asked me to get a schedule from you. Don't you have a secretary training class?	
Dallin:	Yes. In fact we have three professional secretaries' programs. One is for the new employee and the others for advanced—those with two years experience or more—and one that focuses on advanced word processing.	
Kristine:	Oh, good. Oh, here it is. I found my list of cities. The Cleveland, Buffalo, Denver, and Biloxi offices all seem interested. They said they saw a brochure about your company.	
Dallin:	Do you have one of our brochures?	
Kristine:	No, I haven't seen it.	
Dallin:	Okay. Here's what I think we should do. I will send you a brochure with the list of cities and dates for our seminars. Let's see. We will be in Cleveland, Buffalo, and Denver in the next two months, but not Biloxi. Perhaps there is a nearby city your Biloxi people could go to. I'll send you a complete list and you can handle the registration by phone or fax. Will this be satisfactory?	
Kristine:	Great. Sounds perfect. You will include pricing and everything, I assume?	
Dallin:	I sure will. And I know your people will love the seminars. They're really neat. Now, can I get your name and address? I'll get this information into the mail today. . . .	

Probes

1. What was accomplished by Dallin's greeting?
2. What did Kristine fail to do in her opening remarks?
3. What information did Kristine need to make this a successful conversation?
4. How well did Dallin handle the call?
5. What would you do differently if you were Kristine? If you were Dallin?
6. Did you notice the ways Dallin reassured the customer? Why is that important?
7. How was the overall efficiency of this call?

Consider this Case

Identify the Errors in Garth's Call

Reread the story of Garth's call to the car dealership presented on page 56. Then describe four or more telephone use problems that probably led to Garth's irritation and his decision not to do business with that dealer.

Problem 1:

Problem 2:

Problem 3:

Problem 4:

How would you use the telephone tips in this chapter to deal with these issues?

Notes

1. Alec Appelbaum, "Who's Answering the Phone?" *Gallup Management Journal*, Fall 2001, p. 18.
2. An excellent source of ideas on phrasing your conversations can be found in Robert Bacal, *Perfect Phrases for Customer Service* (McGraw-Hill, 2005).
3. Call center. *CommWeb* [Online]. Available: *www.commweb.com/encyclopedia/search?term=callcenter*.
4. "What is a call center?" *Call Center News Service* [Online] (2002, April 30). Available: *www.callcenternews.com/specials/definition.shtml*.

CHAPTER 5

Use Friendly Web Sites and Electronic Communication[1]

Customer Service in an Online Environment

The Web was made for customer service. Do it right and you not only create satisfied, loyal customers you also save serious money.

—R. Hurst

Wireless is all very well but I'd rather send a message by a boy on a pony.

—Lord Kelvin, 1898[2]

After reading this chapter, you should be able to

1. Describe the importance of Web-based customer service and the four categories of such service.

2. Acknowledge the cost advantages of **"Webifying"** customer service.

3. Recognize the key disadvantages of e-service.

4. Identify some tools and approaches organizations can use to make the most of the service potential of the Web.

5. Apply five action tips for avoiding e-service problems.

6. Utilize five action tips for evaluating and growing your e-service effectiveness.

The Way It Is . . . Why You Should Have a Web Site!

The Internet has become the place for searching and shopping. Every day millions of people access the Internet (or "Web") fully expecting it to provide information about products and services worldwide. We have come to assume that companies have a Web presence. It's gotten to the point where if you're not on the Web, you're not in business. (Okay, that is a slight overstatement, but not too far off. Perhaps small, local businesses can do without a site, but even those risk losing customers who expect to be able to find them on the Web.)

The cost of creating and maintaining a Web site continues to come down. Many companies will assist you in creating and "hosting" such sites. (See *www.GoDaddy.com*, for example.)

So, just for the sake of discussion, let's agree that "if you're not on the Web, you're not in business." But being "on the Web" is just the start. How can you maximize this powerful sales and customer service medium? This chapter looks at that question.

WHAT IS WEB-BASED CUSTOMER SERVICE?

Listening to World Wide Web gurus talk, you'd think the Internet was made for customer service. Not only is the Web a "perfect" sales channel, it's an excellent channel for pre-sale and post-sale customer support. Customers have come to assume that almost every business today has a Web site that will provide some kinds of customer service. Although the telephone is still an important way for people to contact businesses for support, Web sites, email, and instant messaging (IM) are becoming much more commonplace. Think of your own customer behaviors. Are you quick to check out a company's Web site? Do you prefer email or IM over phone use? Many people are moving in that direction as customer comfort with technology grows. Among today's younger people, the majority of whom are being raised with an unprecedented comfort with technology, the service expectations are changing dramatically, as we will discuss later in this chapter.

Let's look at some key characteristics of Web-based customer service where contact can occur in several ways and for several purposes.

Self-serve Common Answers

From the company's perspective, low interaction communication (also known as self-service) is the nirvana of online customer service. Here customers take care of themselves using **knowledge bases,** which are databases of answers to **frequently asked questions (FAQs).**

Knowledge bases may be structured or unstructured. Structured knowledge bases are organized into a question-and-answer format. Unstructured knowledge bases are repositories of customer interaction, such as email correspondence with customer service or postings on an electronic bulletin board. Such repositories are indexed by key word so that other people with similar concerns can readily find the posting.

Online knowledge bases make it possible for customers to answer their own questions. Self-learning knowledge bases constantly update themselves based on customer inquiries.

Providing such basic information is often the starting point for organizations moving some of their customer support to the Web. Historically, organizations have started by creating and hosting a static (unchanging) Web page, something like an electronic version of a marketing brochure. At a most basic level, this includes organizational contact information such as name, address, phone number, and little more. Such a page, while better than nothing, rarely satisfied customer needs.

Characteristically, FAQs include key product questions with short answers, such as:

- Are your coffee-flavored ice creams caffeine free?
- What can I do about wind noise from my mountain bike rack accessory?
- How do I use my personal digital assistant (PDA) to read my email?

Often the questions are listed at the top of the Web page and hyperlinked to the answers further down the page. (Hyperlinks are those words or phrases that you can click on to get to another place.) Questions would be sorted alphabetically or by the frequency in which they are asked. For common questions, FAQs are both efficient and effective. And for many sites, FAQs are still the norm.

The problem with such static Web pages is that, in order to get an answer, customers have to wade through a list of the top 100 or so questions hoping to find one that matches or comes close. This is kind of like forcing them to read an encyclopedia from beginning to end to satisfy their query. Again, this is relatively easy for the organization hosting the FAQs but not efficient for the self-serve customer.

Today's customer expects efficient access to answers.

More sophisticated Web sites can do multiword searches of the FAQs. Some offer a searchable, self-learning knowledge database. A knowledge database is an online repository of information—the collective wisdom regarding the product or service. And, unlike static FAQs, this knowledge base is dynamic, ever changing, and self-learning. This means that it is automatically updated based on customer inquiries. In this way, the repository evolves with each new question. Customers can search knowledge bases not just by single key words but also by phrases.

Delayed Answers

When customers can't get the answers they need from self-serve sites, they often turn to email or IM. Customer assistance reps look up answers and take turns responding to customer-initiated inquiries. While a few years ago a Web customer may have been satisfied with a 24-hour response to an email, few find this sufficient today. And, of course, the kiss of death to customer service is to not respond at all! Because email relies on one-way communication, the possibility of misunderstanding is high. This delayed communication is neither very effective nor efficient—and certainly fails to meet today's customer expectations.

Larger volumes of email result when customers are not able to find answers they need on the Web site. Rather than representing an effective customer care solution, handling a lot of email can be a symptom of an ineffective Web presence.

Email usually increases when customers are having trouble finding answers on their own.

Live Answers

High-assistance service can be provided by such options as **Web chat** or **live chat**, a costlier but often welcome addition to the customer's service options. When customers began to complain about the slow response times of email queries, several companies responded with online chat. This is an adaptation of the "chat rooms" popular with online services such as AOL (America Online). With live chat, the customer service representative communicates live (in "real time") with the customer who needs assistance. All messaging is text-based—both parties type questions and responses. Often, a complete transcript of the chat session is available to the customer for review.

Live chat requires live people available to the customer and can be costly.

A variation of chat rooms is the use of **blogs**. A blog is a log or journal maintained by a company or individual. As others participate in sharing thoughts on an ongoing basis, a blog becomes an **online forum** for discussion. Bloggers play a role in shaping a company's discussions and even public image. When many people come together in cyberspace for blogging, they are giving open, unfiltered feedback and other information. Blogs can support service efforts when people share their experiences in dealing with service issues. Sometimes, of course, a blog becomes little more than a space to complain and even degrade a company or product. A blog can, however, also be an information-sharing site—one that can help customers help each other. Savvy companies in many industries are turning to blogs as an additional option to disseminating information and service tips.

Following are a few points to keep in mind about using blogs:

- Use blogs as a real-time online conversation. If there's a conversation going on about your issue or organization, you need to be involved in the dialogue.
- Remember the 80/20 rule; 20 percent of the people in the world have great influence on how the other 80 percent think. The 20 percent are actively reading blogs.
- Understand that almost one-third of all U.S. Internet users read online forums[3] (according to respected source Forrester Research), so the potential for communicating about customer service (for good or ill) is high.
- Reach out to bloggers who follow your issues. If possible, have conference calls with them. Engage them.
- Submit posts/comments from your organization's leaders on blogs. It establishes that you are willing and able to be part of the conversation.

Self-serve Personalized Answers

Personalized service—customized real-time data about the customer's specific problem—is the ideal technology-assisted service a company can offer. For example, you just ordered the perfect gift for your mom three days before Mother's Day. You received multiple assurances that the gift would arrive before that special Sunday morning. Now you want to know where your order stands. Has it been filled? If so, where is it? Has it left the loading dock? Is it on a UPS or FedEx truck? These kinds of customer inquiries are simple for Web-enabled tracking systems. The customer enters the tracking number and seconds later knows the package's location.

ANOTHER LOOK

Social Networking Skyrockets

Blogs and chat rooms have morphed into **social networking sites (SNSs)** such as Facebook, MySpace, LinkedIn, Friendster, Tagged, and others. These link friends and associates of all ages in easy-to-use contact networks. And these are not just for young people, as some mistakenly assume. The fastest growth segment of SNS adopters is the middle-aged or older user.

The impact of such networks cannot be overemphasized for its customer service implications. Think about it: In past days, unhappy customers would tell a few or a few dozen other people about their experience. Today's social networkers can tell thousands—perhaps hundreds of thousands! Fortunately for some businesses, good news can travel fast, too.

Although current statistics on numbers of people using SNSs are difficult to find (primarily because the growth is so phenomenal), suffice to say that hundreds of millions of people are at least signed up on one or more SNSs.

Companies cannot afford to overlook the customer service potential of these networks.

Personalized self-serve solutions rely on real-time tailoring of Web content to the customer's individual needs. Web pages are dynamically adjusted (frequently changed) based on customer profiles and even customer input. For instance, when a platinum-level frequent flyer checks her itinerary on the Web, she'll see flight status, the in-flight meal menu, and an airport map showing her where the Platinum Club lounge is located in relation to her arriving gate. Economy-class flyers, on the other hand, would see only flight status. Such personalization

---

ANOTHER LOOK

Customer Service Expectations for Today's Net-Savvy Generation

A whole new class of technology-savvy young people (often called Net-geners) with considerable purchasing power is emerging. Their definition of customer service success goes beyond what has been traditionally expected of businesses.

The norms that guide Net-geners when they shop—and which they are coming to assume from businesses—are strikingly different from what customers have traditionally expected. Some examples:

- Customization: They assume companies will provide them with personalized products or services. They often demand the ability to custom-build or individualize and are rarely content with one-size-fits-all products or services. They want to make it their own.
- Scrutiny: They check out products online or with friends (often via their SNSs) before they go to the store. Eighty-three percent know what they want before going to buy a product. Shopping now involves simply picking up the product.
- Integrity: They are more conscious than ever of company reputation and readily share impressions with each other. Does this company deserve my money? Social networks spread word as do their blogs of the "your company sucks.com"-type.
- Collaboration: They want to participate with companies to make the product or service better and they expect to be able to do so via open communication channels. Unresponsive or difficult to reach companies lose credulity and Net-gener customers.
- Entertainment: They expect companies to make it fun to do business with them. Since 93 percent of kids ages 2–17 have regular access to video games, their tolerance for uninteresting media used by traditional companies won't fly.
- Speed: They want the company to serve them *now*. They assume instant response to requests (like they get when they IM with friends) and sophisticated technology that makes interaction easy. An unresponsive Web site loses the Net-gener instantly.
- Innovation: They want companies to give them the latest, hippest, trendiest products and services. The old model of slow-to-change products (such as the once-a-year model changes of automobiles, for example) is unacceptable.

These norms put a lot of pressure on businesses to get into the swim of a very fast-moving economy. To capture and keep such customers means that less responsive forms of customer service may no longer cut it.

Source: Paraphrased from Don Tapscott's excellent book, *Grown Up Digital* (New York: McGraw Hill, 2009), especially pp. 188–192.

provides tailored information for frequent flyers, engendering an almost-religious loyalty among those valuable business travelers. The Net-savvy customer expects such personalization and even the opportunity to participate with the company. For example, these customers want not only to choose from options, but to suggest additional ones.

RECOGNIZE DISADVANTAGES OF WEB-BASED E-SERVICE

E-service alone is not, and probably never will be a 100 percent, surefire strategy for handling all customer contacts. It is a helpful "platform" for several cost-effective channels—self-service Web, blogs, email, text messaging, and live chat—but e-service is not a substitute for old-fashioned phone calls and direct contact with customer care representatives. E-service, then, is "in addition"—another set of channels for communicating with customers. As such, e-service is just one more assistance approach that must be designed, implemented, and maintained. Installing an e-service solution is no small undertaking. It is costly and highly dependent on available technology.

The Internet, like most information technologies, is a moving target. The hardware used has a life cycle averaging less than five years before it becomes obsolete. Software life cycles are even shorter, with minor product updates appearing every few months and major updates every 18 months.

Finally, the rush to migrate customer service to the Web has produced its share of failed sites and frustrated customers, prompting a not necessarily undeserved reputation akin to the voice-response runaround, where the customer sits on hold listening to tinny elevator music. Poor e-service delivery can substitute one negative stereotype for another. Ignoring the human side of customer service can turn what looks like a low-cost service alternative into a costly mistake. But it doesn't have to be that way if we apply some simple action tips for better service on the Web.

APPLY FIVE ACTION TIPS FOR AVOIDING E-SERVICE PROBLEMS

While the Web offers great potential for building customer loyalty, it also can lead to frustration and failure if not done right. By putting the following actions into practice, a company can be well on its way to establishing an A-plus presence on the Web.

Action Tip 1—Be There and Be Quick

Did you ever log on to your favorite site to do a little online business only to find the site down? It's like showing up at the company during business hours only to find the doors locked. When the site is down, you are closed for business. And to make matters worse, a competitor is only a click away for your increasingly impatient customer. For customers looking for assistance (who are likely to already be frustrated), an inaccessible or slow site can be extremely annoying. Instead of a customer being able to help herself online, the situation usually escalates. Now your company has to deal with three problems: an inoperable site, a frazzled customer, and the customer's original concern.

Or, have you ever found yourself frustrated because a Web site seemed to take forever to open pages? If a page takes longer than a few seconds to load, most visitors won't stick around. With today's lightning-fast Internet connections, eight or ten seconds can seem like a lifetime. Customers today will wait only a few seconds at best.

Therefore, the first rule of successful e-service is to be there and be quick. When customers hit your company's Web page, they want it to be up. Many companies go to great effort to offer stable, **redundant servers**. (*Redundant* means having backup to ensure that if one aspect of the service goes down, others take over to keep it running.) The goal is 99.999 percent uptime and rapid page-loading times.

Customers are coming to expect personalized options in e-commerce.

Poorly managed e-service systems can result in a reputation for bad service.

Technology applications are moving targets—the rate of change is extremely fast.

Action Tip 2—Make Site Navigation Simple

Web customer service should be only one click away. Once customers connect to a home page, they should be able to get to the customer assistance page with a single click. And they shouldn't have to scour the home page to find the button, tab, or hyperlink.

Site navigation should be simple and obvious, with a consistent scheme for going from page to page. The customer should always have a way to get back to a specific page or be able to press the back button on the browser to escape. Forcing a customer to stay in a site or wade through a complex maze is counterproductive to good service.

Customers won't tolerate hard-to-navigate Web sites.

Action Tip 3—Respond Quickly

Today's video game generation expects immediate response from their game consoles, desktop computers, and sports cars. Waiting more than two to three seconds for a computer screen to refresh is unacceptable to them.

But such Web site performance is only one dimension of quick response. Even more important is quick turnaround or customer questions. Here again, the bar is rising. Whereas people were once quite satisfied with a 24-hour response time to an email, today that is way too long. If staffing prohibits quick responses, automatically generated responses should go out indicating that the customer's message was received and tell when he can expect a more detailed response. For something as dynamic as Web chat, the communication should have the pace of a live conversation. Long pauses on the order of five minutes or more may confuse the customer into thinking the chat has been abandoned. Before long, the customer is typing "Are you still there?" in the chat window.

Action Tip 4—Provide Communication Alternatives

The more high-tech the world becomes, the more some people crave high touch service or non-electronic contact of some sort. In the realm of customer care, the Internet is almost a synonym for high-tech, the opposite of high touch. At some point, customers may become frustrated with the various self-serve options or the distant communication of bits and bites. They will seek human contact. The solution may be to provide several communication alternatives such as email, Web chat, two-way interactive video, or even something as low-tech as the telephone. Some customers just need the human touch—someone to talk with—and should be given such options.

Action Tip 5—Pay Attention to Form and Function

Just because technology can give a company animations, 256 type fonts, and 16 million colors doesn't mean its Web site has to use it all. Customer care sites should be functional and visually pleasing, but they need not be elaborate or incorporate every possible bell and whistle.

SERVICE SNAPSHOT

Wilde Mats and Matting

Erika Wilde runs a Web site selling floor mats to businesses. Her site, *www.StopDirt.com*, is easily available for people needing a wide variety of industrial floor mats and matting products, including custom logo mats. When customers contact Erika's Web site to get personalized information or to describe a problem, she quickly calls them back on the phone. Her upbeat personality makes this immediate and very personalized service even better. It also helps to create "hand-holding" relationships with her customers, who are invariably impressed by the level of personal service they receive. She thus exceeds customer expectations with better information and with her bubbly telephone personality.

Just because a business sells on the Web doesn't mean that it must forego all other forms of communication. Often, the telephone can supplement e-commerce and provide the opportunity to project the human touch.

Successful sites, like modern video games, are the result of a team effort. Graphic designers, usability engineers, database administrators, content experts, and programmers all play a part. Form should support function, avoiding jazzy technology for technology's sake while remaining current with the technology expectations of today's customers. The most customer-friendly sites avoid unnecessary clutter, and instead keep the site simple and functional.

UTILIZE FIVE ACTION TIPS FOR EVALUATING AND GROWING E-SERVICE EFFECTIVENESS

The following are some action tips that can take your Web site to new levels of effectiveness and give customers a better experience.

Action Tip 6—Track Customer Traffic

The best thing about the Web may be that companies can track anything using available software. Companies can use the services of firms that specialize in "**Web analytics**"—the measurement, collection, analysis, and reporting of Internet data for purposes of understanding and optimizing Web usage. These data can show them such things as the "**click path**" the customer took to get to the site and whether the customer is a first-time visitor. (A click path is a record of all the URLs or Web addresses the customer clicked on to get to your site.) They can track service resolution and abandonment rates, average connect time, and frequent requests. If companies want to know where to spend their time to better serve customers, they should track customer paths and then use such analytic data to systematically improve the site.

Action Tip 7—Benchmark Service Levels

Web sites with successful customer care **benchmark** and compare against themselves and against their best competitors. Benchmarking means keeping careful statistics about existing service levels. These statistics can then be used to set targets for the future. Typical services monitored include site uptime, average response rate per page request, average time to respond to email inquiries, average time to respond to Web chat inquiries, and number of resolved and unresolved inquiries per day.

Action Tip 8—Teach Your Site to Learn

If the content of a Web site remains the same today as it was last month, chances are it will be able to satisfy only last month's customers. Successful e-service requires learning such things as:

- What doesn't work and what content is missing
- What click paths end in dissatisfied customers
- What new questions your customers are asking

Some commercial software electronically reviews Web activity and automatically updates a company's knowledge base with new content. Whether a company chooses to have its site "learn" via such software or whether it has the content updated by staff, adaptive, dynamic sites let customers know the organization is listening and responding to their needs.

Action Tip 9—Build an Ongoing E-Relationship

Successful human relationships require two-way communication (verbal and nonverbal). Sometimes people initiate communication or behaviors that build the relationship; sometimes they reciprocate to others. Traditional customer service, however, tends to be primarily customer-initiated

LOOK INSIDE

How Well Does Your Company Use Its Web Site?

Now that you've had a chance to explore the Internet's role in building customer loyalty, it's time to see how well your organization is doing. If you are currently working in an organization with a Web site, take a minute and complete the following survey. If you do not work in such an organization, select the Web site of a company you have visited, put yourself in the role of one of the company's leaders, and answer as many of the questions as you can.

Is your Web site static or dynamic (more than simply a posted brochure)?	Yes	No	Don't Know
Is it easy for your customers to quickly find answers on your Web site to their most FAQs?			
Is the FAQ section updated frequently based on customer input?			
Do you respond to all customer emails quickly (in less than 24 hours)?			
Can your customer's input change the content on your site automatically (i.e., do they participate in information sharing beyond the FAQs)?			
Can your customers track the status of their requests easily on your site?			
Can customers get to a human support staffer easily?			
Do you monitor how frequently customers return to your site for information?			
Is information on your site presented in easy-to-use formats (including video clips) rather than as only text?			
Is it easy for visitors to have updates sent to them automatically by email, text messages, or other media?			
Are you consistently using your Web site to capture and share useful information with your staff so that they may understand and adjust to customer concerns?			
Does your call center only handle queries that couldn't be handled automatically on your Web site?			
Do customers ever praise your company because they found your site especially helpful?			
Do you use systematic Web analytics to determine if you are making the most of your Web site's potential?			
Do you strive for consistency of messages so that answers you give your customers on the phone are the same as the ones you give them on your Web site?			

Scoring

A "Yes" answer on 10 or more items indicates that your organization's e-service health is excellent. Anything less should prompt you to reexamine some of your online customer service strategies.

and thus mostly reactive. Yet e-service offers companies additional opportunities to take the initiative—to be proactive. To build an e-relationship, companies can simply offer email notifications to customers. "Notify-on-change" puts the customer's e-mailbox to use. With each change in product, catalog, or content area, the company can automatically fire off an appropriate email to its customer base. Of course, they should be sure to get permission from customers first. "**Spamming**," the practice of sending unwanted email, can damage a relationship rather than enhance it. If customers do agree to accept notifications, the company should always give them the option with each email to have their name removed from the notification list.

Action Tip 10—End High for Better Loyalty

One common model for providing traditional in-person customer service suggests apologizing for any inconvenience (expressing caring), solving the problem (showing competence), and offering a peace token (providing comfort) such as a small gift or additional points in a customer loyalty program. This last step is designed to leave the customer on a high note, thinking positively about the company. With Web-based customer service, even though the focus is on helping the customer help himself or herself, it still makes sense to make peace.

Before customers log off from a Web site, the company should always thank them for visiting. To rebuild the goodwill (if the customer has had a problem), offer some kind of peace token—a discount on their next purchase, free shipping, or some kind of additional service coverage, if appropriate. You want them to be glad they visited your site.

Thank customers for visiting and using your Web site. This can help build goodwill and repeat usage.

A FINAL THOUGHT

Today's Web-mediated customer service offers a low-cost approach for many customer transactions. Getting answers to FAQs, checking the status of an order, or even researching the details of an invoice are easy tasks for Internet-enabled customer care service centers. The Web has made building and maintaining customer relationships simpler. We would expect that of technology. But there's the dark side—some Web sites are more complicated and difficult to navigate than a video arcade game. They can, if poorly managed, turn customers off rather than support good service.

Successful companies put considerable thought into their Web sites, blogs, messaging, and email processes. Few companies today can thrive without an electronic presence. People simply expect to be able to communicate with companies through these media. Take the opportunity to surprise customers with exceptional e-service.

Summary of Key Ideas

- The Internet has provided a new avenue for delivering customer assistance.
- Online knowledge bases make it possible for customers to answer their own questions. The best of such knowledge bases are dynamic and keep "learning" as they process customer input.
- Email provides delayed answers to customer inquiries. A rule of thumb for A-plus customer service is to acknowledge all customer email and respond to it within 24 hours or less—usually less. An instant response message acknowledging receipt of the message

is good so long as a real follow-up happens in a timely manner.
- Web chat is an adaptation of Internet chat room technology that allows customers and service representatives to carry on two-way communication. Blogs and SNSs can serve similar functions.
- Web analytics and benchmarking (comparing to others) provide data for constant improvement of your Web site's effectiveness. The target is moving!
- Web self-service has a significant cost advantage over traditional customer service channels, such as talking to

a live agent on the telephone. That said, some customers still prefer the "human touch" of a real person.

- E-services are not only cost-effective, but they can provide additional benefits such as improved customer relationships. However, poorly managed e-services can eliminate any potential cost savings and result in lost customers.

- Successful e-service delivery requires attention to several factors: Web site uptime, navigation ease, server speed, personal touch, appropriate site design, benchmarking, traffic monitoring, adaptive knowledge bases, proactive communication, and customer loyalty programs.

Key Concepts

benchmarking
blog
click path
e-service

frequently asked questions
  (FAQs)
knowledge base
live chat

online forum
redundant servers
social networking sites
  (SNSs)

spamming
Web chat
"Webifying"
Web analytics

Reviewing the Facts

1. Describe in your own words the categories of Web-enabled customer service as discussed in this chapter. What options may make sense for a business like yours (if you are currently employed)?
2. Is "webifying" customer service equally important for all types of businesses? Justify your answer.
3. Summarize the advantages and disadvantages of Web-based service.
4. Make a list of the kinds of questions you would like answered by Web analytics—by systematic evaluation of date—in order to make the most of a Web service.

5. What are some ways customer profiles could be used to provide information tailored to the individual's needs? Cite specific examples. What are the advantages of such personalized self-service?
6. What are some ways companies can make their Web sites more efficient and ever-evolving to provide better service? How have customer expectations about Web sites changed in recent years?

Applying the Ideas: Explore the World of E-Service

1. Pick three of your favorite companies or organizations, locate the home page for each of these organizations, and investigate the online customer service they provide. Do they include most e-service channels such as FAQs, email, and chat? What additional online services are provided?
2. Imagine that you have purchased a technology product. You take it home, hook it up, and find you can't get it to work properly. Select a major vendor, and connect to its customer service Web site. Perform a navigation analysis of the site. How many links did you have to follow to get your problem resolved? Were you able to "serve yourself," or did you have to contact a customer assistance representative? If you were assisted, was it easy to contact a customer assistance representative? Did you use email? Web chat? Telephone?
3. Log on to the customer service site of an established Internet retailing company (e.g., *www.amazon.com*, *www.overstock.com*, *www.proflowers.com*) and the site of a relatively new entrant to the Web (e.g., a local business such as a martial arts studio or an auto repair shop). Record how long it takes to move from Web page to Web page. (Use a

stopwatch if possible.) Send an email and see how long it takes to receive a reply. Compare the performance (speed) of the two e-service providers. Did these organizations meet your need for speed?
4. Find a business or an organization that doesn't have a customer service Web presence. Develop a plan to create Web-assisted e-service capability. Outline what steps would be necessary. You need not flesh out every detail, just the major decisions and steps involved in the organization in moving some of its customer assistance processes to the Internet.
5. A fascinating Web site is called the Wayback Machine or the Internet Archive found at *www.archive.org*. You can put in a Web address from as far back as 1996 and see how it looked back then.

   Select several popular sites or favorites you use regularly. Use the Wayback Machine to see how they have evolved and changed over the years. Then write a description of five key ways each site has changed (or failed to change). What trends can you spot? What does this say about the use of the Web for customer service?

Consider this Case

Weeding Out the Unprofitable Customer

Bruno LeBron was recently assigned as the technology officer for a midsized, business-to-business (B2B) consulting firm. His company offered other businesses help with planning locations for new stores, restaurants, and the like. While great service to clients has always been a core value of the company, Bruno was concerned that his people were spending too much time with e-service to customers or prospects who were not profitable. And, too often, they were gabbing among themselves instead of working efficiently with clients. "How can I get my people to spend time and effort only with the clients who matter?" he wondered.

Then he hit on an idea after reading an online "white paper" about business rules[4] and the Internet. That's it, he thought, I'll put certain rules into place that prevent a lot of wasted time. As he thought this idea through, he decided to have his systems people configure the call handling systems so that his employees (1) could not use electronic chat to gab with other employees internally, (2) could not deal with customers outside their assigned specialty, and (3) could handle calls only from clients and potential clients who are deemed as having high value. "That should do it," he thought. "I'll minimize the jibber-jabber [his term] and keep people focused on real clients and real problems."

Probes

1. To what extent do you think Bruno's approach will work?
2. What are some possible negative side effects of implementing such a system?
3. If you were Bruno's boss, what would you recommend?

Consider this Case

The Future of the Internet

What does the future of the Internet look like? Many people have written about what has been described as one of humanity's greatest technologies. But, time marches on and technology changes rapidly. For example, while virtually all Internet users used to enter through some portal software, such as Microsoft's Internet Explorer or Foxfire's Mozilla, people now access the Net via cell phones and other devices, making its reach even greater and its impact quite profound. When experts are asked if they think that business is exploiting the Internet's full potential, most feel it's barely scratching the surface of what we can do with this kind of communications technology. Expert Vinton Cerf, for example, says that we can see new product announcements that involve networked devices almost daily. He is expecting to see "many billions of devices using the Net to communicate with each other. This is not just for human communication, which has been tremendously valuable, or human sharing of knowledge, which has also been very valuable, but it can also be used for managing and controlling various devices."[5]

Cerf goes on to talk about how devices will be able to communicate with each other so that, for example, entertainment systems could be manageable through the network and even household and office devices can be controlled via mobile phone. Once these devices are able to communicate with each other, it means that third parties can build software that services those devices, interacts with them, and manages them. This can add a whole new dimension to customer service.

Probes

1. If, in fact, the Internet can provide many more ways that devices can communicate with each other, what are some implications for customer service?
2. What kinds of new expectations might customers hold regarding online repairs, adjustments, and new features?
3. Describe how such "futuristic" online services might possibly affect an organization you work in or are familiar with. Be creative.

Notes

1. The author acknowledges the work of Dr. Christopher G. Jones, Professor of Accounting at California State University–Northridge for developing some of the material for this chapter.
2. Referring to the telegraph (new technology in its time).
3. Data from *http://blog.lefora.com/2008/06/17/just-how-many-people-use-forums/* as of June 17, 2008.
4. An example of such a "white paper" is one by Jackson Wilson, "Business Rules and the Internet: The Good, the Bad, and the Ugly." Vendor whitepaper published February 1, 2006. See: *http://callcenter.knowledgestorm.com/search*.
5. Comments in an interview posted on *http://gmj.gallup.com/*

PART 2

LIFE: Insight

The second letter in our acronym LIFE is **I** for "insight." Customer service professionals (and hopefully that is all of us) greatly improve their ability to build customer loyalty gaining insight into two areas: (1) potential turnoffs customers may experience and (2) changing trends in dealing with customers and their needs. Attention to these concerns can head off the kinds of problems that leave the customer feeling less than satisfied or even mistreated.

The next two chapters focus on these insights and how professionals can minimize the potential damage to relationships felt when our company fails to deliver the best in service. Chapter 6 focuses on ways we can identify and deal with potential turnoffs that can reduce loyalty. Chapter 7 provides insight into emerging trends that may be changing the landscape in customer service. The idea of these chapters is to get us thinking about these issues and generate ideas for ways we can avoid damage to our loyalty efforts. So, let's consider the "insights" we need to develop to provide consistently exceptional customer service.

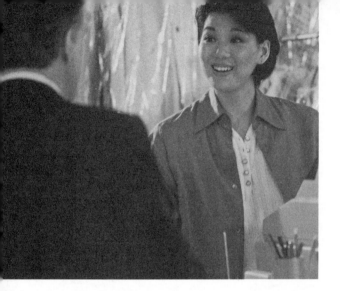

CHAPTER | **6**

Recognize and Deal with Customer Turnoffs
The Customer Keeps Score

People remember about a third of what they read, half of what people tell you, but 100 percent of what they feel. The question: How do they feel about doing business with you?

After reading this chapter, you should be able to

1. Recognize the pet peeves customers have about poor service.

2. Categorize customer turnoffs as stemming from value, systems, or people problems.

3. Understand that reducing customer turnoffs may be the best form of advertising.

4. Appreciate how great value arises from moving people beyond satisfaction in their "zone of indifference" into the category of loyal customer.

The Way It Is . . . Breakdown on the Highway

A cross-country traveler tells this story:

On a recent cross-country trip, my tire blew out on the Ohio Turnpike south of Toledo. It was 6 p.m. on Friday, the temperature hovered in the upper 90s, and traffic was heavy. The right rear tire blew like a bomb, and I limped onto the median to dodge the constant flow of rumbling semis. I called the American Automobile Association's hotline on my cell phone. I was greeted by an unsympathetic monotone who mechanically sought my membership card number, expiration date, address, home phone, complete description of my car, my mother's maiden name, and the middle name of my oldest grandchild or some such stuff. All the while I am attempting to explain to her the imminent danger of being crushed by a big rig roaring by at 80 mph.

"Exactly where are you?" she asked. I tried to explain my general location. That wasn't good enough. I'd need to give her an exact mileage marker. So I trekked up the median in 98-degree heat, screaming into the cell phone over the roar of the trucks, until I could see a mileage marker. She then told me that a tow truck would be there "in 45 minutes or less" and that I was to jump out of the car when I saw him coming to flag him down. This, apparently, so that he would know which white Lexus with a blown-out tire in the median at mileage marker 68 of the Ohio Turnpike was mine.

Fifty minutes later, I called for an update. "Any possibility that the truck will actually get here today?" I asked. A different, and more sympathetic, service rep answered this time; and after going through the membership card info all over again, he told me he would "check to see if they'd received my call!" I waited on hold for four minutes. I was not encouraged. He then, to his credit, at least apologized ("I'm sorry about the wait. The truck was called to an accident up the road.") and promised me the truck would be there in "25 minutes or less." I waited.

This story has a happier ending. The truck driver—Paul, it said on his shirt—was a very nice man. He immediately apologized and told me he was literally 50 miles away when he got the call. He then jumped to work on my tire and I was on the road again. I also had a pleasant surprise: my newly purchased car had a full-size spare tire mounted on a matching wheel. I was anticipating one of those crummy emergency donuts and a trip to the tire store before I could continue my travel. Thank you, Lexus!

Paul was a lifesaver. If I had attempted to change the tire myself, I would have lost it when discovering the special socket for the locking lug nuts. Paul knew his stuff, and I somehow felt secure in the shadow of his huge towing rig. We chatted pleasantly and he worked efficiently and, although the "45 minutes or less" turned out to be an hour and 18 minutes, I was saved as a Triple-A customer by a tow-truck operator named Paul from Toledo, Ohio.

But there were moments when AAA ran a serious risk of losing me, a customer since 1984. Paul's behavior overcame the indifferent telephone behaviors of the AAA employees. And Lexus moved me one step toward customer loyalty by providing a real spare tire.

A classic 1993 movie, Falling Down starring Michael Douglas, shows a series of customer service breakdowns that quite literally push the protagonist over the edge. In one scene, Douglas's character goes to Whammy Burger—a fast-food restaurant. There he is told that "they are no longer serving breakfast" and he'd "have to order something off of the lunch menu." When he finally receives his Whammy Burger, it bears no resemblance to the one pictured on the menu board, and instead is "a pathetic, squashed thing."

And don't get me going on airlines. If ever you have to witness a textbook case of a great industry morphing into a panoply of customer service debacles, just look at the last decade of commercial air travel. Customer turnoffs range from unfair and undecipherable fares to petty (and often arbitrary) charges for baggage, schedule changes, substandard overpriced food, and the list goes on. A once pleasurable travel option has become a veritable fountain of customer complaints.

Everyday disappointments plague many customers, even in today's so-called "service economy."

BE AWARE. BE VERY AWARE—RECOGNIZE PET PEEVES ABOUT CUSTOMER SERVICE

Try this: With a group of people—the larger the better—ask for a show of hands in response to the question, "Can you remember a poor experience you have had as a customer?" Then ask, "Can you remember a great experience you have had as a customer?" Typically, people will very quickly raise hands for the first question and take a few seconds longer to respond to the second one (if they respond at all). The point is that negative experiences—*turnoff*, as we'll call them in this chapter—stick in our mind and are quickly remembered.

Any time you gather a few people together and ask them to describe some pet peeves about their experiences as customers, you'll get an earful. Virtually all of us can recall situations where we feel we were treated poorly, or where we bought products or services that just didn't measure up.

Customer service training sessions often begin by having the group talk about specifically irritating experiences and generate a list of gripes. You may find it useful to articulate some of your own pet peeves. Take a moment to make a list of *specific* things about customer service that turn you off.

Extensive research would predict that some of these **turnoffs** may be on your list:

- Being ignored or receiving rude or indifferent service
- Having to wait too long
- Poor-quality work (especially on repair jobs) or shoddy products
- Sale items that are not in stock
- Merchandise prices not marked, forcing a price check at the cashier

LOOK INSIDE

My Pet Peeves in Customer Service

Quickly list 10 specific turnoffs you experience as a customer. What kinds of things irritate you when doing business? Think about several customer contexts: retail, repair services, restaurants, government agencies, etc. Be as specific as possible about exactly what irritates you. Perhaps cite an example if that helps you express your ideas.

1. _____
2. _____
3. _____
4. _____
5. _____
6. _____
7. _____
8. _____
9. _____
10. _____

- Dirty restaurants or restrooms (Someone once said that the cleanliness of a restroom is the key indicator of concern for customers.)
- Phone calls put on hold or forcing you to select from a long menu of choices
- Employees lacking product knowledge (and who may try to bluff the customer)
- High-pressure sales tactics
- Employees talking down to you or using confusing jargon
- Inflexibility when you make a request

Everyone has examples of irritating experiences as customers.

Do you see some of your pet peeves on this list? Most people will, although there are many other possibilities, as well.

GAINING INSIGHT: WHAT TURNS CUSTOMERS OFF?

Winning a battle requires knowing the enemy. The first tactic in our quest to win at customer service is to know what turns people off. What kinds of things can lead to a serious risk of losing a customer, associate, or employee—perhaps forever?

"What turns customers off?" An analysis of almost two thousand collected comments identified three categories of customer turnoffs that disqualify organizations from earning allegiance: value, systems, and people. The data reveal that the following 10 turnoffs accounted for 97 percent of all comments cited by the study's participants:[1]

VALUE TURNOFFS. These include such things as:

- Poor guarantee or failure to back up products
- Quality not as good as expected
- Price too high for value received

SYSTEMS TURNOFFS. These include such thing as:

- Slow service, or help not available
- Business place dirty, messy, or cluttered
- Low selection or poor availability of product
- Inconvenient location, layout, parking, or access

PEOPLE TURNOFFS. These include things such as:

- Lack of courtesy, friendliness, or attention
- Employees who lack knowledge or are not helpful
- Employee appearance or mannerisms

Follow-up interviews and further study seems to confirm that these categories provide a useful framework for identifying root causes of customer dissatisfaction. Let's look at each in more depth.

1. Value Turnoffs

A fundamental turnoff for customers is the feeling that they receive poor value from a product or service. In short, shoddy products or sloppy work can put customers through the roof.

Value can be simply defined as *quality relative to price paid*. If you purchase an inexpensive, throwaway item at a discount store—say a 79 cent pen—you may not be upset if it doesn't last very long. But buy a $79 gold fountain pen (probably called a "writing instrument" since it costs so much) that leaks in your shirt pocket and you'd be furious. If you make a major purchase of an automobile, appliance, or professional service and it quits working or fails to meet your needs, you will experience a value turnoff.

> Value is a function of a product's quality relative to its price.

The major responsibility for providing customers with appropriate value lies with the top leadership of the organization. It's the executive decision makers in a company who determine the products or services that will be sold. They define what marketers call the **value proposition**—what the company intends to exchange with its customers. In a one-person enterprise, the owner determines the quality/pricing formula, which defines value. If you run a lemonade stand, you determine how many lemons and how much sugar you will use. (Ideally, you check with your customers to see how they like it.) If you start an auto sales business, you will need to choose if you want to sell Hyundai or Lexus, Ford or Lincoln. You may opt for a new car dealership or a pre-owned car lot that specializes in low cost, basic transportation. If you offer tax preparation services, you will need to decide whether you hire clerks who input data into software programs or certified accountants who can advise clients on tax planning.

Any of these strategies can work fine but the perception of value (product quality relative to price) may be different in the eyes of your customers. If you offer tax preparation services, you will need to decide whether you hire clerks who input data into software programs or certified accountants who can advise clients on tax planning. Again, either strategy may be acceptable but the perception of value will differ.

While other people in an organization can affect value, the top leaders bear the major responsibility for ensuring an appropriate value proposition. The responsibility for minimizing value turnoffs lies with them.

2. Systems Turnoffs

Say the word *systems* and many people think of computers or phones. In the context of customer service, however, the term *systems* is broader than that. The term is used here to describe any *process, procedure, or policy used to "deliver" the product or service to the customer*. Systems are the processes we use to get value to our customer. When seen like this, systems will include such non-techy things as:

- Company location, layout, parking facilities, phone lines
- Employee training and staffing
- Record keeping (including computer systems for handling customer transactions)
- Policies regarding guarantees and product returns
- Delivery or pickup services
- Merchandise displays
- Customer follow-up procedures
- Billing and accounting processes

> Systems turnoffs have to do with any process, procedure, or policy associated with getting goods and services to customers.

The responsibility for minimizing system turnoffs lies with managers in most organizations. This is because systems changes often require spending organizational resources (e.g., for new locations, remodeling, additional staffing and training, and added delivery services), which must be authorized by managers. Nonmanagement employees can and should be involved in suggesting systems changes, however. Management can get some of its best change ideas from employees at all levels. But ultimately, a manager must initiate a systems/process change.

How important are systems? While every organization needs systems for doing business in a consistent and orderly manner, some people argue that the majority of customer service problems are caused by systems mistakes or the illogical application of systems. The converse, however, is true as well.

Business consultant Michael Gerber believes that systems may well be the most important key to business success. He cites hamburger giant McDonald's as an example. In an excerpt from a brochure advertising Gerber's "The E-Myth Seminar," Gerber describes working with a client named Murray, who was so tied up in the day-to-day work of his business that he failed to grow a successful company. Gerber calls this episode "The Day I Fell in Love with McDonald's." His description helps us better understand the importance of good systems.

> *When my meeting with Murray ended, I was exhausted. I had pages of notes, hours of conversations swirling in my head, and a long drive home. I needed a few minutes to collect my thoughts. So, I pulled into a McDonald's to grab a bite and sort out my notes.*

He goes on to talk about being confused and not knowing where to start with Murray and his company. Murray loved his product and had big dreams for the future. But Gerber felt that something was wrong, something he couldn't put his finger on. And then it hit him:

> Maybe its fate, but that day was the first time I was in a McDonald's twice in the same day. Suddenly, from the corner of my eye, I watched a lady approach the counter, and the young girl who was serving asked if she could take her order. Nothing out of the ordinary. But there was something about what happened that caught my interest. It was both what she said and her manner of saying it.

He goes on to say that he'd been to McDonald's restaurants from coast-to-coast, was served by all types of employees, and regardless of where he was or who served him, he felt comfortable, because he knew what to expect and felt in control of his experience.

> He goes on to conclude that at that moment I knew the secret of McDonald's success. Wow! What an amazing discovery. Instantly I could see that this secret can work in any business . . . The essence of the secret . . . that they have a system for everything. Regardless of who is working on a shift, the entire staff is taught the system. . . . There is no indecision. No confusion. No hesitation. No sour faces. No frustrated looks. Everything works like a well-oiled machine.

Gerber's observations illustrate the importance of effective systems in any business. It is the systems that can create comfort for both employees and customers. Knowing what to do and how to do it comes, of course, from extensive training and careful design of the delivery systems. Failure to design and train people on effective systems not only negates the usefulness of systems but can also result in customer service turnoffs.

Systems turnoffs arise from the way a company delivers its products or services. This entails a wide range of factors ranging from product selection, business location, policies and procedures, customer convenience and comfort efforts, staffing, employee training, and, of course, technology systems as well. As you can imagine, systems problems include a multitude of sins.

ANOTHER LOOK

Don't Let Your Systems Drive Your Customers Crazy!

By Ron Kaufman

Customers are often left frustrated by a company's smooth-running and standardized, but in-flexible policies. Does your company "run like clockwork"? Are your accountants pleased with how smoothly everything moves along? Are your managers content with how customers are managed throughout your system? If so, watch out! Your present methods may include policies and procedures that are convenient for the company, but utterly frustrating for your customers. . . .

In recent weeks, I have had a series of actual experiences bizarre enough to make me wonder whether anyone is listening at all! For example, there's the case of "The Conference Rate" at Hilton Hotel in Los Angeles:

I was making arrangements to attend the American Society of Training and Development Annual Conference in Los Angeles. As a frequent flyer, I have many award coupons offering a 60 percent discount from usual hotel rates. I called Hilton Hotels in California to make my reservations. The reservations clerk was infinitely helpful. First, she took my name, then my contact numbers. She confirmed the dates, my room preference, and credit card number. She asked if I was a Hilton Honors Club member, which I was not. She signed me up on the spot and then remarked: "Now that you are a Hilton Honors Club member, I can offer you an even lower rate, and an upgraded Towers room on a higher floor. A fruit basket will be waiting for you upon arrival." I was delighted. And my special discount rate was just US$85 per night.

In signing off, I said: "Thank you for your help. I am looking forward to staying at the Hilton during the conference." "The conference?" she shot back quickly. "What conference are you attending?"

I replied that I was attending the American Society for Training and Development's 50th Annual Conference at Disneyland. She said quickly: "Mr. Kaufman, if you are attending a conference during your stay, you must use our special conference rate of US$112." I laughed at her proposal and stated that I was happy with the special rate she had already confirmed on my behalf. "Oh no," she repeated. "If you are coming for a conference, you must use the special conference rate. We have a block of rooms set aside for conference participants on a lower floor. These rooms are specially reserved for the people who are attending the conference."

My protests were to no avail. She checked with her supervisor, who concurred. "I'm sorry, but that's our policy," she said without much concern. I surrendered to her insistence, listened as she cancelled my Hilton Honors Club reservation, declined to have her book me back into the same hotel at the higher conference rate, and hung up the phone in disbelief.

I called right back. I reached a different reservations clerk and made another reservation. I used my frequent flyer award coupon and the new Hilton Honors Club membership number I had received in the previous phone call. This time I kept my mouth shut about attending any conference!

I paid just US$85 when I went to Los Angeles. I enjoyed the Hilton Towers room and enjoyed the complimentary fruit basket upon arrival. No thanks to Hilton's absurd policy and customer unfriendly procedures, though.

Somewhere deep inside the marketing department of Hilton Hotels, yield management professionals have carefully calculated the maximum rate they can, and will, charge participants at an international conference. Meanwhile conference participants are also thinkers, communicators, and frequent flyers . . . real-live customers! Hilton Hotels, are you listening?

Source: Excerpted from "Don't Let Your Systems Drive Your Customers Crazy!" by consultant/trainer Ron Kaufman, found on his Web site, *www.ronkaufman.com*, 2003.

When transactions are unnecessarily complicated, inefficient, or troublesome for people as customers or employees, they experience systems turnoffs. Complaints about long lines, slow service, poor selection, untrained employees, workplace appearance, and poor signage are examples of systems problems.

Making things too complicated for customers can cause systems turnoffs.

A few years ago, Microsoft's Expedia Web travel business decided to stop requiring people to sign in before using the site. Expedia marketing VP Erik Blachford said, "When you walk into a department store, clerks don't ask for your name and password before letting you shop."[2] A common online procedure has become a systems turnoff for many customers.

Of course, the requirement to have customers register before shopping has advantages that many customers appreciate. For example, if you expect to do repeat business with the company (say, you plan to keep buying books on Amazon.com), their having your shipping information and even your credit card number provides a convenience. But customers should not be forced to do so. Companies need to think through the tradeoff between what's potentially good for the company (customer data for possible marketing, convenience in fulfilling an order, etc.) with what's good for the customer (ease of use, quick service, etc.). Turnoffs arise when company benefit outweighs customer benefit. If the company forces customers to do something solely because it benefits the company, the turnoff likelihood will be high.

Research shows that the single most frequently mentioned turnoff for many customers is slow service or having to wait inappropriately long. We live in a society that values speed and efficiency and that resents things that slow us down. As per research, slow service is the number one turnoff for many customers. One of the first frustrations people cite is slow service or having to wait.

Customers are easily turned off by inappropriately slow service.

Company systems determine the speed of service because they involve staffing, layout of the business, accessibility, efficiency of delivery, employee relations policies, and so on. The responsibility for implementing and maintaining effective systems lies with a company's management, because changes in systems almost always require spending money. A company's decision to add personnel, provide additional training, change locations, implement new delivery methods, or even rearrange the office layout will require management approval.

Employees who lack the knowledge to answer customer questions and organizations that have just one person capable of fulfilling a key function are symptoms of system failures. Telephone menus that are unnecessarily complicated (press 1 for such and such, 2 for so and so, etc.) are another common turnoff described by customers. Poor location, lack of delivery options, cluttered workplace, clumsy or repetitive paperwork requirements, lack of parking, and poor selection as a result of inadequate reordering processes are additional examples of systems problems for both customers and employees.

3. People Turnoffs

Our third category, people turnoffs, almost always arise from communication problems. Employees who fail to communicate appropriately, both verbally (with words) and nonverbally (without words), can quickly irritate a customer. Some examples of people turnoffs are:

- Employees who fail to greet or even smile at a customer
- People who give inaccurate information or convey a lack of knowledge
- Employees chatting among themselves or allowing telephone interruptions while ignoring a customer
- Behaviors that project a rude or uncaring attitude
- Sales tactics that come across as high pressure
- Work locations that appear dirty or sloppy
- Employees who are dressed inappropriately or have poor grooming
- Employees with body piercing, tattoos (although such personal choices may be appropriate for certain clientele)
- Any communicated message that causes the customer to feel uncomfortable

Communication turnoffs often result when employees are ignorant of the kinds of "messages" they are sending to customers.

Employees at all organizational levels can create people turnoffs, often unconsciously. In most cases, these turnoffs arise because people fail to understand how they come across to other people. Everyone interested in having a successful career would be wise to become constant students of communication. Even the most subtle or unconscious behaviors can communicate the wrong messages and result in lost customers.

People turnoffs make customers feel discounted. They arise when employees who represent the company project inappropriate behaviors, indifferent attitudes, or mechanical tone (as we discussed in Chapter 2). People turnoffs include such things as rudeness, poor nonverbal behaviors such as lack of eye contact, inappropriate dress and grooming, autocratic bosses, and any behaviors that convey a low level of caring or consideration for others.

Responsibility for reducing people turnoffs lies with every employee. Often people are unaware of how their behaviors communicate. Training can help raise awareness, but ultimately the individual staff member will decide how he or she will interact with customers and other employees.

Because teaching specific behaviors is often difficult, hiring people with good attitudes and interpersonal skills is especially important. Some successful employers constantly recruit people they have seen working in other customer situations. When they meet a person in another business who gives them great service, they encourage that person to join their company. One man who owns a chain of restaurants carries extra business cards to give to people he experiences in other transactions. When such a person does a great job selling him shoes or handling a billing problem, he hands them a card and asks them to contact him if they ever want to consider another job. Notice that these people may have no experience in the restaurant business, but their customer service skills are "transferrable"—they can be taught the specifics of the restaurant business. What they bring to the job are excellent service skills and attitudes.

People communicate the way they do because they have learned that behavior. Changes come slowly and only with considerable effort. The best way to change communication behavior is by raising awareness, modeling new behaviors, having people try the new behavior, and reinforcing the improvement. Companies can benefit from using scripts or scripted phrases and from clearly identifying communication taboos—certain messages, terms, and nonverbal behaviors that are unacceptable.

Responsibility for reducing people turnoffs lies with every employee—you need not be a manager or executive. Everyone, at every organizational level communicates (if not with external customers, with others in the company), and poor communication leads to turnoffs.

In fairness, some people are unaware of how their behaviors come across to others. They may be tone deaf to the ways they communicate or fail to communicate. Training can help raise awareness, but ultimately the individual staff member will decide how he or she will interact with customers and other employees.

Here is a brief description of the three turnoff categories as applied to the road-trip experience described at the beginning of the chapter:

> Companies benefit from identifying certain communication taboos—words or phrases that should be avoided.

Value Turnoffs	Systems Turnoffs	People Turnoffs
Had paid my dues for years and never used AAA's road service before. Was not sure I was getting a good deal.	Policy of saying "45 minutes or less" to me was initially reassuring, but when the deadline was not met, it was a turnoff. Required much information before allowing me to explain my problem.	Unsympathetic tone of voice, no expressions of empathy.

In the case of the Ohio Turnpike road trip, factors that initially were turnoffs (tone of voice, uncaring attitude, demands for information, and inaccurate promises about response time) were mitigated by the good service of a dedicated employee: the truck driver who was personable, friendly, and reassuring. He worked with expertise and efficiency. And personality!

And that is largely the point of this discussion. Turnoffs happen. By recognizing and categorizing them, companies can assign responsibility and attack them.

KNOW THAT REDUCING TURNOFFS IS THE BEST ADVERTISING

No company can succeed if it lets turnoffs aggravate its customers to the point where they quit doing business with it. A typical company will lose 10 to 30 percent of customers each year because it turned them off. This touches off a treadmill-like scramble to replace the lost customers with new customers—an effort- and cost-intensive process. Employee turnover—loss of internal customers—is often a result of turnoffs as well. A far more efficient process is to keep and build upon the current customer base.

As stated earlier in this book, customer and employee loyalty is like an election held every day and people vote with their feet. If dissatisfied, they walk (sometimes run) to a competitor. When customers cannot realistically switch to another company (in the case of a public utility or government agency, for example) they do anything within their power to get even, starting with complaining loudly. And if those turned-off customers are employees, they respond by producing shoddy work, undermining their supervisors, aggravating their coworkers, and creating all sorts of mischief and counterproductive activity.

Many people think that it is advertising that induces people to buy. U.S. businesses spend about $11.5 billion a year on advertising. Yet surveys show that only 25 percent of those polled say that television ad would induce them to buy. Likewise, only 15 and 13 percent respectively said that newspaper or magazine ads caused them to buy. In short, consumers have little trust in traditional advertising. Ads can create awareness, of course, but they alone rarely make people buy.

Advice or the recommendation from a friend or relative, however, scored 63 percent as a determinant of people buying a new product.[3] This confirms what people have long known: Word of mouth is still the best way to attract customers.

To sustain repeat business, a company must generate positive word of mouth by reducing the turnoffs and exceeding customer expectations. People talk to others about a service experience when it is exceptional or out of the ordinary. Bad news travels faster and further than good news. A company can have the best products available, but it fails to minimize customer turnoffs and provide a positive customer experience, few people will notice the difference between that company and its competition. We will talk a lot more about exceeding expectations in later chapters.

Customers "vote" with their feet—they'll quickly go to a competitor if your service comes up short.

Word of mouth is still the best form of advertising.

CREATE LOYAL CUSTOMERS

Thinking about customer turnoffs is particularly important when we consider that the correlation between mere customer satisfaction and loyalty is rather tenuous. Even satisfied customers may be neutral toward their relationship with a business. They may feel little or no sense of **engagement** and the littlest thing can push them over the edge toward dissatisfaction. Service levels may meet their needs adequately but fail to motivate their continuing loyalty. Just as **motivation** researchers discovered long ago, satisfied workers are not necessarily motivated workers. They may be satisfied because they don't have to work very hard or because they like fooling around with their coworkers—even though they accomplish little. Satisfied workers are not necessarily motivated workers. Likewise, satisfied customers cannot be assumed to be motivated repeat customers. Things are okay but there is little to engage the customer in the long run.

The Zone of Indifference

Actually, customers who are satisfied may be inert, not motivated to buy more or strengthen their business dealings with a company. Their satisfaction simply means the *absence of dissatisfaction*, not the motivation to become a loyal customer. A **zone of indifference** lies between the dissatisfied and the motivated (see Exhibit 6.1).

Dissatisfied — Satisfied — Motivated

EXHIBIT 6.1   The Satisfaction–Motivation Distinction.

The challenge, then, is to get customers beyond satisfaction to *motivation*. This is best done by responding to customer perceptions and expectations.

Value Service Recovery

Despite the best efforts of customer-savvy people, problems inevitably will arise. Problem situations should not be viewed as tragic, but as opportunities to further solidify customer loyalty. Anyone can give good service when customers don't have particular needs, but it is precisely when special needs or problems arise that customer skills are put to the test.

The payoff for recovering potentially lost customers is actually an *increased* likelihood that they will be loyal to you—they are more likely to be motivated according to our model. It sounds strange, but studies have shown that a customer who encounters a problem with a company—and has that problem addressed promptly and effectively—will be even more likely to remain loyal than a customer who never had a problem. Even in cases in which the customer's problem is not resolved 100 percent in his or her favor, the loyalty still increases. Just the fact that the problem was acknowledged and addressed seems to be the key variable in strengthening the customer relationship. This is a powerful argument for opening the communication channels with customers.

An old saying claims that "people don't care how much you know until they know how much you care." A genuine sense of concern for customers must be on the bedrock of any organization's customer loyalty efforts.

Showing customers that you truly care is fundamental to building loyalty.

Loyalty Comes from Customers' Awareness that Service Is Your Business

Customer turnoffs arise when companies make service something less than an integral part of their operating philosophy. Having a "service department" should be seen as a redundancy. Every department exists only to serve its customers, internal and external. Nordstrom executive Betsy Sanders says, "As long as you seek to add an extra dynamic to your business [like time, energy, and resources to isolate service as some special program] the results will be disappointing. Service begins to be meaningful when it is an internal dynamic. This dynamic develops when you recognize that service is the underpinning of your enterprise, when you truly acknowledge that without your customers, you would not exist."[4]

Service must be seen as the very essence of your business, not a side function.

Customers are quick to see the depth of a company's commitment to service. The organization that distinguishes itself in the eyes of its customers is rare. Most companies have not made enough of an impression one way or another for their customers to even think about them, much

---

ANOTHER LOOK
The Emotional Element in Service Excellence

British consultant David Freemantle emphasizes the important role of emotions in giving customers excellent service and in creating competitive advantage. Turnoffs are far more likely to occur when there is little or no emotional connection between customers and organizations. In his book *What Customers Like about You,*[5] he contends that "**emotional connectivity** is at the center of all relationships and is thus the center of excellent customer service." This connectivity occurs when people in an exchange are tuned in to the genuine feelings they have about the situation and about each other. Many customer turnoffs can be overcome when emotional connectivity is created. Among the personal techniques Freemantle recommends for maximizing such connectivity include:

- Creating a climate of warmth before the customer approaches you
- Sending out warm and positive signals to each customer
- Being sensitive to the customer's emotional state
- Encouraging customers to express their feelings
- Listening with genuine interest
- Finding something you like in each customer
- Eliminating any negative feelings you have toward a customer.

less to share these thoughts with others. That element of loyalty—recommending a company to others—is lost because of undistinguished service.

Earn Your Customer's Loyalty with Two Steps

How can we help a customer step outside the zone of indifference and become a "raving fan" of our company? Two steps can provide the essence of a sound strategy:

1. Reduce or eliminate value, systems, and people turnoffs.
2. Exceed customer expectations to create a positive awareness.

We'll focus on the first of these steps in this chapter. The first step in reducing or eliminating turnoffs is to recognize their existence. The three kinds of turnoffs described earlier (value, systems, and people) provide a useful way of categorizing and recognizing who shoulders major responsibility for each. But how can we tell if we are turning off customers?

The short answer is to put yourself in the shoes of your customers. Objectively assess the way they are treated and compare this with how other companies may be treating them. As Yogi Berra said, "You can observe a lot by just watching."

We will discuss the second step in a sound strategy in Chapters 10–12. For now, think about the importance of playing defense—of consistently taking all reasonable steps to reduce any potential customer turnoffs. This may sound like a tall order—after all, people can always find something they are unhappy with—but the two next chapters provide the rationale and tools needed to ferret out the kinds of turnoffs your customers may well be experiencing. The key ingredient (and the third letter in or LIFE acronym) is feedback. More on that in a moment, but first let's review what we have discussed in this chapter.

The simplest way to get information about potential customer turnoffs is to listen.

A FINAL THOUGHT

Repositioning customers from that reasonably satisfied "zone of indifference" into the category of motivated, loyal fans requires close analysis of what may be turning them off. Look for value, systems, and people turnoffs and determine who in the organization can best deal with each.

SERVICE SNAPSHOT

Monika's Attitude of Service

Monika works at a medium-size credit union. In her two years there, she has won repeated awards and bonuses for her effectiveness as a teller and member-services representative. Her supervisor consistently ranks Monika's work as outstanding and her opportunities in the financial service industry look rosy. When asked about her customer service "technique," she laughed and said she doesn't really have a technique; she just tries to treat people the way she'd want to be treated. She says, "I try to anticipate anything that might be annoying or uncomfortable for my customers and fix it before it becomes a problem. Sometimes that's as simple as saying 'I'm sorry you had to wait so long—we are a bit busy today.' People seem to appreciate that you acknowledge little problems."

Monika pays attention to the little things, avoiding people turnoffs as much as possible. When members (what credit unions call their customers) approach her desk, she immediately looks up and greets with a smile. If she's busy helping someone else, she still makes eye contact to acknowledge the customer and let him or her know she'll be available in a moment. She is especially good at handling transactions quickly and efficiently without rushing the customer. When asked how she prepared for her career, she stated that when she was a little girl, her favorite toy was a cash register. She loved to play store and keep Monopoly money in a special section in the cash drawer. She even used to iron her play money to keep it crisp, she laughed!

Technique aside, Monika projects a friendly, helpful attitude. She works hard to keep current on changes in systems and procedures. She knows her customers value quick, efficient service "although some of them like to chat—which is fine." She loves her job and her customers. Serving others with professionalism and skill is its own reward, she says.

Value and systems problems require management attention, but employees at all levels can and should be aware of possible people turnoffs.

The analysis of potential turnoffs must be an ongoing process, not just occasional or haphazard actions. Even the best organizations make mistakes. When (not if) we make mistakes that leave the customer unhappy, we need to view these as opportunities for fixing our values, systems, or people behaviors to solidify our relationships with customers. Often such fixing requires attention to the little things (yes we are back to that point).

Summary of Key Ideas

- Everyone has pet peeves about the ways they are served (or not served). Often, these are little things that have a cumulative effect in creating a dissatisfied or, minimally, an indifferent customer.
- Reducing turnoffs can be the best form of advertisement. It can also help move people out of the "zone of indifference" toward being motivated, loyal customers.
- Customer turnoffs can be usefully categorized into value, systems, and people problems. Value and systems problems are best addressed by company leaders; everyone can help eliminate people problems primarily through improving interpersonal skills.
- Value is a function of the apparent quality of a product or service relative to its cost.
- *Systems* refers to anything involved with getting the product or service to the customer. Systems turnoffs arise from problems with procedures, policies, technology, training, staffing, locations, facilities, and systematic actions.
- People turnoffs are almost always communication problems. Employees communicate inappropriate "messages" by their words or nonverbal actions.
- Service recovery seeks to win back customers when they have had a disappointing experience. Customers whose problems are addressed by the company will actually be more likely to do repeat business than customers who never have a problem.
- We can reduce customer turnoffs by listening actively to customer concerns. Active listening means hearing *what* people are saying, not the way they are saying it, holding your judgments, working to maintain eye contact, disciplining yourself to listen to what is being said, resisting distractions or interruptions, seeking clarification, and being receptive.
- Regularly identifying and working to reduce possible customer turnoffs can provide a basis for building customer loyalty.

Key Concepts

customer turnoffs	people turnoffs	systems	value turnoffs
emotional connectivity	satisfaction versus	turnoffs	zone of
engagement	motivation	value proposition	indifference

Reviewing the Facts

1. Look back on your own experiences as a customer and identify situations when little things have made a difference in your buying decision. Think, for example, of places you have stopped doing business with. What little things pushed you out of the zone of indifference into the dissatisfied range? Be as specific as possible and remember that often dissatisfaction comes from a series of truly small, almost insignificant turnoffs.

2. Describe in your own words the three categories of customer turnoffs. Give five specific examples of each.

3. What do we mean by a "value proposition"? What are some of the questions one should consider when defining a value proposition? Who determines what that proposition will be for a given company?

4. What can companies do to best identify potential turnoffs? How does classifying them as value, systems, and people turnoffs become useful to organizational leaders?

5. Why do customers whose problems are addressed and rectified become even more loyal? What do we mean by a "value proposition"? What are some of the questions one should consider when defining a value proposition? Who determines what that proposition will be for a given company?

6. What can companies do to best identify potential turnoffs? How does classifying them as value, systems, and people become useful to organizational leaders?

7. Why do customers whose problems are addressed and rectified become even more loyal than customers who have not had a problem? What could motivate this behavior?

Applying the Ideas: Discovering Customer Turnoffs

1. Let's go "mystery shopping." One way we can get a clearer understanding of customer turnoffs is to observe, in a systematic way, specific behaviors in places we do business. This is called "mystery shopping" or "secret shopping." It can be an excellent way to identify possible turnoffs customers may be experiencing. In this exercise, we are focusing mostly on people turnoffs.

   Assume that the behaviors described on the Sample Mystery Shopper Form (Exhibit 6.2) are important to you as a customer (and the absence of them turns you off). Make copies of that form and try a little mystery shopping. Here is how:

   a. Select a minimum of four businesses of the same type (retailers, restaurants, banks, auto dealers, etc.) to visit as a mystery shopper. Your task will be to pose as a potential shopper seeking information. You may want information about account types from banks, details on a particular computer or appliance from electronics stores, information about a particular automobile, and so forth. Then plan to visit these businesses posing as a customer.

   b. Be yourself during these visits. Don't attempt to act. Respond naturally to the employees. Maintain an open and unbiased attitude. Carefully observe what the company does well or poorly. Don't go in with a chip on your shoulder—with the attitude that you'll catch them doing something wrong—and don't overemphasize the negative. If you can't remember whether the employee did or did not do something positive, assume that he/she did.

Sample Mystery Shopper Form

Name of business: _____ Date & Time: _____

Employee's name (if available):_____ Task: [what you are shopping for]

	Did	Did Not
A. When you entered, did the employee		
1. Look up, make eye contact?	_____	_____
2. Smile with a genuine smile?	_____	_____
3. Acknowledge you with an appropriate greeting?	_____	_____
4. Make you wait too long before helping you?	_____	_____
B. While assisting you, did the employee		
5. Project a positive, helpful attitude and willingness to assist?	_____	_____
6. Pay full and undivided attention to you?	_____	_____
7. Deliver accurate and speedy, but unhurried, service?	_____	_____
8. Ask you if there is anything else he/she can do for you?	_____	_____
C. Given the opportunity to offer or introduce other products, did the employee		
9. Acknowledge or identify other things that may meet your needs?	_____	_____
10. Offer further information or introduce you to others for more info?	_____	_____
11. Ask you for your business?	_____	_____
D. When the transaction/visit was over, did the employee		
12. Thank you for coming in?	_____	_____
13. Invite you to come again?	_____	_____
14. Offer a friendly goodbye?	_____	_____
E. At any time during the transaction, did the employee		
15. Ask for your name and/or call you by name?	_____	_____
16. Make you feel like a valued customer?	_____	_____
Score one point for each "did" answer.	**Total:** _____	_____

General comments or observations: What was particularly good or bad about the shopping experience?

EXHIBIT 6.2   Sample Mystery Shopper Form.

c. Immediately after each visit, complete an evaluation form. (In real-world mystery shopping, you can and probably should modify this data-gathering form to make it more appropriate for the specific type of businesses you will be visiting.)

d. When you have gathered your data from four or more locations, compile a brief report describing what you found. Identify key turnoffs (by category), if possible. Comment on things done well and opportunities for improvement.

e. Write a brief report on what would you do to reduce possible turnoffs and improve the service if you owned this business? Prioritize the steps you would take. Be specific.

2. Search it out: Using the Web to identify turnoffs. Go to your preferred Internet search engine and search for information on what turns off customers in a particular type of business. Describe the nature of and number of sites that deal with this topic. How well do these sites identify or categorize the kinds of things that turn customers off?

See if you can categorize the most common turnoffs using our value–systems–people distinction. If you find other kinds of turnoffs that don't seem to fit into these three categories, identify a new category or discuss why they don't fit. (Recognize that some turnoffs can fit into more than one category.) Prepare a one- or two-page report summarizing the results of your search.

Consider this Case
The Auto Inspection Center

D'Arcy takes her car to a local inspection and emission station in her town. These inspections are required in her state and, generally, the process is relatively painless. The technician checks out her car while she fills out a simple form.

Last Tuesday, she decided to stop on the way to work to get this chore finished in time to get her license renewal sticker by the end of the month. "I'm in luck," she said to herself as she approached the open garage doors, "nobody in line ahead of me." The sign said to wait at the shop entrance. This she did, for several minutes. She could see three employees. Two were engaged in an apparently personal conversation; they were laughing and joking. The third person was standing off to the side of the shop smoking a cigarette. All three people glance at D'Arcy, but ignored her.

After several minutes, the fellow having a smoke came to her car and said, "You here for an inspection? You're gonna have to wait a few minutes." As he started to

walk away, D'Arcy said, "I really need to get to work." He said, "Yeah, okay. Hold your horses. I'll get you the paperwork." He then walked to the back of the shop and appeared to join the conversation with the other two employees, while he shuffled through a stack of papers that had accumulated on the greasy desk. The phone rang and he took the call, which sounded like a personal conversation that lasted several minutes. He finally turned back to D'Arcy and said, "Pull your car into the second bay."

Probes

1. How would you feel if you were D'Arcy?
2. If this inspection station was a government agency, is customer service really important? The customer really doesn't have a choice, so why expend efforts to give better service?
3. What types of turnoffs are displayed in this case?
4. If you were the manager of this facility, what might you do to reduce potential customer turnoffs?

Consider this Case
Mac's Stack It Deep, Sell It Cheap

Devon MacGregor, known to his many friends as "Mac," jokes about being true to his Scottish heritage when he opened his warehouse-style store selling odd lots and large quantities of basic household staples. Mac and his partner, Donnie Antonio, talked for many hours as they planned the new company launch. Donnie felt they would be better off setting up a more traditional retail store with attractive merchandise displays, lighting, and a

"classier" looking place. Both men had recently graduated from State University and were committed to building a successful retail store, but they needed to get agreement on the focus of their business.

"It's all about value proposition, Donnie," Mac said. "If we try to be all things to all people, we'll be competing with all the big boys. We can't be a Wal-Mart or a Target. We're little guys. We need to give people something different, and the best way to do that is to give great deals. Our customers are cost-conscious. Let's stick with our "stack it deep, sell it cheap" philosophy. After considerable discussion, Donnie came to agree and that is the direction they decided to take.

Probes

1. If Mac and Donnie stick with this value proposition, how might that affect customer service? What are the pros and cons from the customers' perspective?

2. What expectations would you have as you go to shop at their store? Be specific—what would you expect it to like?

3. How can they best stick with their value proposition? What should they avoid?

4. Is customer service in such a low-cost operation less important than it would be in a full-service retailer? Defend your answer.

5. How could Mac and Donnie best avoid customer turnoffs? Exceed customer expectations?

Notes

1. K. DeTienne and P. R. Timm, "How Well Do Businesses Predict Customer Turnoffs?: A Discrepancy Analysis," *Journal of Marketing Management*, 5(2), 1996.
2. Frank Barnako, "Expedia Drops Registration," *Info Beat*, an online newsletter sponsored by CBS Market Watch, January 4, 2000.
3. Paul R. Timm, *Building Customer and Employee Allegiance* (Utah: Communication Solutions, 2004, p. 28).
4. Betsy Sanders, *Fabled Service* (San Diego: Pfeiffer & Company, 1995, p. 9).
5. David Freemantle, *What Customers Like about You: Adding Emotional Value* (London: Nicholas Brealey Publishing Limited, 1998).

CHAPTER 7

Insight into Emerging Trends in Customer Service
A Peek into the Future

The future ain't what it used to be.

—YOGI BERRA

After reading this chapter, you should be able to

1. Gain insights into what may turn your customers off, in addition to insights about how customer expectations are changing.

2. Better understand the importance of personalization, or "one-to-one" customer service.

3. Recognize some of the social and economic shifts impacting customer service for the future.

4. Apply some of the new interactivity options for marketing to individual customers.

5. Understand that some important aspects of customer service will remain consistent.

6. Consider some new interactive marketing options.

The Way It Is (Going) . . . Oh, the Changes We Are Seeing!

"Look at that," Roland said to Mandy as they entered the coffee shop near their office for a morning latte. "Everybody in here seems to be electronically hooked up. If they aren't on cell phones, they're on the Net working on something. This is like an office away from the office. Could you imagine seeing this even 10 years ago?"

Roland is Mandy's 60-something boss and a good friend. Mandy is 30 years younger, but even she is amazed at the technology changes in the space of her career.

"I hate to sound like a Geezer, but just look back at the past 20 years or so. I remember when there were no ATMs at banks, laser printers, or cellular phones. But even more incredible, I remember when most televisions didn't even have remotes! There were no compact disks, almost no VCRs, and no video rental stores. Only restaurants had microwave ovens. Fax machines cost several thousand dollars and took five minutes to transmit a single page and were found only in very large companies. No one had a personal computer."[1] Roland shook his head as they ordered their coffee.

Then Roland said, "I had a funny experience last week when I went to Cleveland. I checked in to the hotel through a kiosk. There wasn't even a desk clerk. I sort of missed the friendly greeting of an actual human, but it did speed up the process. I talked to the manager the next day and he asked how

I liked the kiosk check-in. I told him I appreciated the speed, but kinda missed the human touch. Then he showed me how the kiosk also hooked up to 20 airlines and I could do my online check-in, change seats, and all that right there in the hotel lobby. That won me over."[2]

As they went to a table, Mandy said, "I was reading recently something written by those marketing experts Don Peppers and Martha Rogers just the other day. Let me think if I can remember their main points. Oh yeah, they talked about the astounding capabilities of microchips and how they can impact customer relationships—at the individual level. How it's now possible to create an individual 'customer feedback loop' integrating the production and service delivery processes into the research and promotion processes. The customer database allows a business to tell its customers apart and remember them—and what they want—individually. And with **mass customization** technology, more and more businesses can actually make and deliver a single, customized product or service—cost efficiently—to an individual customer. That has got to be great for the customers. Sort of the ultimate customer service."

"It sure ties in with what we have been focusing on at work—the idea of developing relationships with individual customers, differentiating one from the next, and treating each customer as a separate, identifiable participant in the commercial relationship," said Roland.

"We keep talking about how our business 'values its customers' and how they are our 'principal asset.' It seems to me like this way of interacting with customers is really important. I think people are coming to expect it," said Mandy.

"If we are serious about really centering the business around individual customers," Roland said as he sipped his coffee, "we better learn to get and respond appropriately to the feedback we get from each. People are assuming a level of customization of products and services to their individual wants, and if we don't give them that we're going the way of the VCR and TVs without remotes!"

"Amen, Roland. We better get more creative and soon," said Mandy.

Much of this book is structured around the acronym LIFE, and the I in that acronym stands for "insight." In the previous chapter, we discussed the importance of insight into what might be turning your customers off. In this chapter, we will consider insight into new directions—and new expectations—for customer service.

The term *insight* refers to an understanding based on identification of relationships and behaviors within a context or scenario. Our context is customer service and our scenario assumes changes that are rapidly becoming realities. Three particular areas of change are having significant impact on customer service and loyalty: personalization, technology, and globalization.

Customers will no longer tolerate being treated as one of a demographic category. They won't accept a "one-size-fits-all" mentality. They will demand—and get—individually specified products and services. Successful companies will adapt to these new demands. They will thrive by exceeding customer expectations in "goodness-of-fit." They will master the art of treating each customer as an individual with special needs and wants.

Technology is the engine that will allow much of this customization. But it is not the only driver of change in the coming decades. It has reshaped expectations dramatically in the last few years. (Two quick examples: Can you imagine doing business where each credit card transaction has to be swiped on a manual card reader as was common just a decade ago? Would you tolerate flying on an airline that has no ticketless computer system?)

Others argue that the future will be shaped by changing **customer demographics** and the global marketplace. Young people are becoming active consumers, while the baby boomers are creating a huge number of active 60-plus buyers. The global economy will require many businesses to be more aware of a broad range of cultures. The demands for personalization will continue to be complicated by the changing nature of customers and employees as groups. These changed demographics can and will call for innovation and responsiveness from successful companies.

How is customer service likely to be impacted by all this? Gaining insight into that question is the central theme of this chapter.

THE IMPORTANCE OF "ONE-TO-ONE" PERSONALIZATION FOR CUSTOMER SERVICE FOR THE NEW FUTURE

The ability of today's technology to make one-to-one customer relationships possible may well be a master key to better service. In the past, keeping track of customer names and addresses, sales data, and personal preferences was a complex and time-consuming process. Many people have kept such customer data on note cards in a file box. As the number of customers grew, the task became impractical. Today's computers and **point-of-sale electronic data gathering** devices, however, make it easy. We can now track individual preferences, poll customers about their needs, and customize services and products to meet those needs. Many stores are now offering discount coupons to the customer at the checkout counter. If the customer buys a six-pack of Pepsi, the scanner generates a coupon for 50 cents off on Frito-Lay potato chips. (Frito-Lay is a division of PepsiCo.) People can also get coupons emailed to them for products they buy. For example, *Just for Men* hair coloring products target their registered users and send them $1 off coupons via email. The customer can simply print the coupon and save a buck. The latest wrinkle is the hand-held mobile phone that will provide discount coupons that can be transmitted electronically to the cash register at checkout.

Media changes have made big differences in the ways organizations communicate among their own members and with the world outside. In addition to the obvious speed and efficiency advantages of today's media, there are other considerations that have an impact on customer relationships. One of the most significant trends is in the increasing ability to efficiently generate personalized, one-to-one messages tailored to the needs and wants of individuals, especially customers, coworkers, and associates.

One-to-one, individually tailored messages can now be sent to huge audiences.

Communication experts have long recognized that (1) the more we know about our message receiver(s) and (2) the more we personalize a message to the receiver's(s) wants and interests, the more effective we will be in communicating and building relationships. Customers no longer tolerate blanket approach. They expect to be communicated with as individuals. Technology applications make this easy.

We should not underestimate the power of **customized messages** in business and professional communication. In an organization's marketing function, for example, we are seeing a shift from mass marketing—sending the same messages to a large number of people in hopes that some of them will respond favorably—to individualized marketing, where we send a unique personalized message to each person. This personalization began with word processing, which gave us the ability to produce "merge" letters that include personalized sections interspersed with the generic message.

Today, mass mailers routinely take advantage of this ability to personalize sales letters, sweepstakes entry forms, and even the envelopes they are sent in. But today's media let us go far beyond what has been done to now include past buying information and personal preferences to convey a sense that we know and understand our reader.

Today's media go beyond the simple merging of names and addresses.

Successful online retailers have taken personalization to higher levels. Amazon.com, for example, routinely tracks what you buy and recommends complementary products. They tell you that "other customers who bought [what you bought] also bought . . ." Online retailers also track gift purchases you have made, making it easier to send another gift to that same recipient.

This is all pretty basic today, and companies that don't offer such service are at a disadvantage.

We are progressively moving toward one-to-one marketing that can create long-term *relationships* with customers and provide for a wide range of their needs. With mass marketing and its communication media such as mass media ads or junk mail, the goal has been to gain a larger *share of the market*. If, for example, your store accounts for 10 percent of all the men's wear sold in your town, mass marketing will try to get that up to 12 or 15 percent. The assumption is, of course, that a larger share of market means more profits. This, however, is becoming less of a sure thing. Advertising costs have increased and results have dropped. It costs more and more money to get a new customer into your business using traditional approaches.

The one-to-one marketing instead focuses on establishing an ongoing relationship with existing customers. You do this by gathering as much information about them as possible and responding to their needs. A men's wear store today may do very little mass advertising and still be very profitable by keeping close to its customers and meeting all their clothing needs. A bank or credit union may expand its services to eventually handle all their customers' financial needs. This is called getting a larger *share of the customer* (some call it "share of the wallet") and has been found to be very profitable.

One-to-one marketing builds relationships that allow businesses to earn a larger share of the customer's business.

One-to-One Opportunities with Internal Customers

The one-to-one principle holds for internal customer relationships too. Managers who keep closely attuned to their employees' preferences, talents, and wants build long-term relationships that can be mutually beneficial to the company. A fully utilized employee is the counterpart to the fully served customer. The best companies often offer "cafeteria"-style benefits programs—approaches that give their employees choices among benefits. While some employees may enjoy day-care assistance as a benefit, others with no children may opt instead for a company-provided health club membership. While some eagerly take advantage of college tuition assistance, others may select flex-time working options. The key concept, once again, is one-to-one personalization to best meet individual needs.

Managers today are increasingly aware of individual employee differences in other ways as well. With the evolution of management theory, employees are no longer seen as interchangeable parts in a company machine but rather as unique individuals. (Do you see a theme here?) Best managers get to know employees, and understand their needs and wants, just as enlightened companies do with customers. They ask for input and suggestions, thus opening the communication channels in all directions. The "top-down, boss telling employee what to do" approach works no better than the "company telling customers what they want" approach.

Two-way communication about individual needs is a key to building any effective relationship.

And, of course, on the social, friendship level, knowing about and addressing the interests, needs, and wants of friends has always been a major factor in building rapport and lifelong relationships. Interactivity—the two-way flow of information—is the key.

SOCIAL AND ECONOMIC SHIFTS IMPACTING CUSTOMER SERVICE FOR THE FUTURE

Aside from technology, service professionals need insight into other noteworthy changes affecting business and customer relationships today. On the social and economic scene, we see substantial demographic shifts. Work forces are increasingly diverse—made up of people from a wide range of economic circumstances, cultures, religions, and both genders. Today's workforce consists of more two-income families and single parents, with the associated family responsibilities this poses. We have an increasingly educated workforce and its members are less tolerant of mindless, repetitive work. Likewise, customers will not tolerate having to jump through hoops to do business with us. Employees expect to be more involved in organizational decisions, to have their input considered. These internal customers will not stand for anything less than engagement opportunities. Failing to provide such opportunities will sentence companies to the profit-killing treadmill of hiring and training new employees as the current ones slip out the back.

The parallel for external customers is increasingly evident. Customers (especially those of the "Net-generation" discussed in Chapter 4) expect to have their input considered as companies develop products and services.

The shifting social conditions of customers have stimulated demand for new and different products and services. Working couples have come to value shopping efficiency and convenience. Ethnically diverse neighborhoods have caused restaurants serving many kinds of food to flourish. Fast food and take-home cuisine have become the mainstay of some busy families. Increasingly popular meal preparation "kitchens" where customers can prepare multiple meals for future use (e.g., "My Girlfriend's Kitchen," "Dinners to Go," and Publix Super Markets "Apron's Make-Ahead Meals") are providing a service that meets the needs of busy people. This, of course, was not always the case. In past generations, homemakers (usually the wife) spent up to six hours a day on food preparations and similarly extensive amounts of time on laundry, house cleaning, and basic maintenance.

Politically, organizations face increasing government regulations, most of which reflect levels of social awareness previously not considered in the business world. Diversity of people from all backgrounds, persons with disabilities, and gender equity are expected in most companies. Likewise concern for the environment, employee health and safety, and even emotional well-being have become hallmarks of today's successful businesses. Caring companies attract and keep better employees (internal customers) and ultimately succeed in the marketplace. Most companies are aware of "green" issues: recycling and ecologically friendly packaging. In short, customers have come to expect different kinds of satisfaction. Insight into such shifting expectations is critical to ongoing service success.

Recognize Changing Demographics

The customers and employees we work with today are different in composition than they were a decade ago. Some significant sociological changes have taken place in the recent past and will continue well into the twenty-first century. Let's review some key changes that service leaders will be dealing with.

Tomorrow's customers will be more diverse. Successful companies will serve people from a wider range of cultures, belief systems, races, and ages. In the United States, a rapidly growing Hispanic population has called for greatly expanded use of Spanish language and wider offering of consumer goods appealing to that population. In other countries, global industry has attracted more nonnative employees who bring with them their cultures and consumer wants.

People are increasingly mobile. Changing jobs is commonplace and employees (internal customers) expectations are far different from a generation ago. Rarely does a worker sign on with a company out of school and remain there throughout his or her career. We are quick to change jobs if an employer fails to provide opportunities for engagement and meaningful work.

Another trend is the aging population. With the oft-discussed "baby boomer" generation (people born after World War II, between 1946 and 1962) growing older, many new services are being offered to this huge demographic consumer base. Today's 60-year-olds are far more active than in past generations. "Sixty is the new forty," proclaims the sociologist. Active, engaged "seniors" have caused many organizations to rethink their service strategies.

Ironically, marketers have been obsessed with the "golden" demographic segment of 18–49-year-olds. The growth projections for this market make that less of a sure thing. The projected growth in the U.S. 18–49 segment over the next ten years is 0.8 million, while the projected growth in the 50-plus segment over the next ten years is 22 million.[3] Companies offering services that appeal to these aging populations will likely thrive.

Finally, the male–female shifts continue with ever more women in the full-time workforce at all organizational levels. Colleges and universities now enroll more men than women. We see more single-parent households—busy workers who juggle parenting with many other activities and thus require more consumer services and conveniences. Further, females are estimated to account for some 85 percent of all buying decisions. Services with special appeal to female shoppers cannot be ignored.

All these factors put pressure on companies to be alert, innovative, and willing to change to meet changing consumer demands. There are no calm waters for businesses in the twenty-first century. The landscape is more like a white-water river, and leaders need to be alert and agile. Today's service practices may well be inappropriate for tomorrow's customer.

Use New Interactive Options Now Available

Today's communication media typically combine the power of computers to allow such one-to-one relationship building on a larger scale. These media have the following characteristics:

1. They are *individually addressable and highly adaptive* to unique needs. They permit messages to be fully tailored to each customer, not just superficially modified versions of a form letter.
2. They are *interactive*, creating two-way, not one-way communication. They make it easy for customers to give their feedback and reactions to messages.
3. They are *affordable and powerful.*
4. They make things *easier* for people.

Technology truly has made the world smaller. The cost of communicating across town and across the continents has never been lower. Internet telephone services such as Skype.com allow us to talk with people across the globe at little or no cost. To make things better, we can even conference-call over the Net. A U.S.-based Finnish professor talks regularly with his family in Helsinki, often pulling in business associates in Singapore and Ethiopia. Calls from every continent are commonplace and affordable.

Web sites can easily use video rather than just written text or pictures.

Are such media available to the typical business person or professional? More than any time in history, the answer is an unqualified yes. Even the smallest business or individual proprietorship can afford much of today's technology. We are steadily moving toward more effective one-to-one service in business and the professions, supported by electronic media that can individualize messages.

TAP INTO THE ELECTRONIC FUTURE OF MARKETING

Any insight into the future is saturated in technology, and this is certainly true with marketing. The past decades have shown dramatic changes in marketing brought about by expanding technological capabilities. A few of these capabilities are worth further mentioning:

Internet Shopping

A friend jokingly commented that "if you aren't on Google, you don't exist." A slight overstatement, of course, but a similar statement may be largely true regarding the Web. If your organization does not have a functioning Web presence, many people will question its existence. Companies of all sizes and shapes are scrambling to get a home page and dive into e-commerce. A user of the Internet from anywhere in the world can dial up this home page and receive product information, prices, instructions, and even coupons. Internet access (regularly used in about half of the homes in America) is growing rapidly and will continue to do so. Very soon it will be as common as the telephone. This is a worldwide phenomenon.

Virtual Reality Shopping

Another use of technology is growing just behind today's Net shopping. Imagine yourself at your home and the weekly chore of grocery shopping has come again. You walk over to your computer, dial up the local grocery store and start perusing the aisles—just as if you were there. In **virtual reality (VR)**, you see the grocery aisles and can maneuver your "virtual" self down the aisles. No traffic. No carts to bump into. Just you with free run of the grocery store. With your VR joystick, you reach out and put the groceries you would like into your virtual basket. When you are done with your shopping, you reach out with your virtual arm and touch the sign that says done. Within an hour the groceries are delivered to your home.

Can you imagine the customer service opportunities companies will have with this technology? With just the use of computer programs, stores could individualize every aspect according to the customer's preferences. Let's take the above example a bit further.

While you are shopping in the VR store, consider this hypothetical example. You decide you would like to buy that six-pack of Pepsi we talked about earlier. This time, instead of getting a Frito-Lay coupon, you see Greg, the "virtual" Coca-Cola stocker. He hands you a dollar-off coupon for a six-pack of Coca-Cola. All you need to do if you would like to automatically switch brands and save a dollar is reach out and take the VR coupon. That'll tick off the Pepsi people, but it's an example of the increasing competitiveness in our VR world.

Imagine one more use of VR. You are interested in moving to California. You sit down at your computer and do a search for companies who build houses in California. You find a company and email them some things you're looking for in a home. Within hours you go back to their "site" on the Internet and take a "virtual" walk through the exact home you ordered. If you don't like it, you make some changes. When your house looks exactly the way you like it, you start taking virtual tours of locations for your home. Finally, you order your custom-designed house that you have seen—but that does not exist yet!

Interactive TV

Another important technological change will be the change in television. Right now, a consumer is forced to watch what they want to watch at certain times. Soon we can expect interactive television. If you want to watch an episode of *60 Minutes*, you will be able to order it and watch it at your convenience. You will have the option to watch shows free of charge with commercials, or watch it for a very small fee without commercials. Since advertisements on television shows today generate about 25 cents in revenue per watcher per show, some experts predict the cost of watching a show would be just 25 cents or so.

Interactive television offers much more than convenience in watching television shows. Everyone with a video camera will ultimately have the opportunity to get into viewers' homes. Just as anyone now can have a home page on the Internet, anyone in the future will be able to have a television show or television commercial. As consumers, we will dial up these commercials when we need a specific product or service. For example, if you're looking for a new car, you would just have to search the database for video information on vehicles. You will be able to watch information from BMW, GM, Ford, Acura, and from all other automobile companies. You will also be able to get video information about Sally down the street who is selling her 1999 red BMW 325i convertible.

With **interactive television**, the consumers will be in control of the information they receive. The broadcaster will just make the information available. Similarly, there will be no more junk mail, no more unwanted advertisements coming into the consumer's home. The consumer will select only the companies that he or she wants to get information from—ultimately the consumer will decide which company to start a relationship with.

These are just a few of the examples of what the future holds. Few people doubt that the future will dramatically change the way we do business forever. And the keyword is, once again, personalization.

UNDERSTAND THAT SOME THINGS REMAIN CONSISTENT

Having said all we have about technological, economic, social, and organizational change, we must also acknowledge that many aspects of the customer satisfaction process remain the same. In particular, psychological and behavioral factors have changed little. Human and organizational needs remain largely the same. A basic sense of caring, concern, and competence will continue to play a critical role in building customer satisfaction and loyalty. In fact, for some, the advent of so much technology has rekindled a hunger for the old-fashioned human touch. That is one reason the Gap clothing stores (among others) display products on large tables that become easily messed up. Rearranging the table gives the clerk something to do and keeps him nearby to interact with the customer.

Even among technology-based companies, the human touch resonates with customers. People who buy computer systems online often get frustrated when they find that setting them up is more complicated than expected. This poses an opportunity for the smaller, local computer retailer who offers personalized setup, even if the price is a bit higher. Web retailers who follow up with personal phone calls also tend to build loyalty. Human contact will never be replaced by even the most sophisticated technology.

Demand for Fair Value

Likewise, the demand for fair value will always remain. People want fairness in exchanges and good value for their money. Companies that profit from inflated prices, confusing rate structures, hidden charges, and unreasonable penalties will not survive long term. Examples of what Fred Reichheld, author of *Loyalty Rules!* and *The Ultimate Question*, calls **bad profits** include those which may generate short-term income at the cost of long-term customer relationships. Some examples of "bad profits" may be

- Inflated shipping charges such as for goods bought on the Internet
- Excessive penalties for changing services (such as cell phone contracts)
- High premium prices for certain seasonal goods or popular options (air fares inflated during holiday season, high-priced accessories)
- Complex pricing schemes that dupe customers into spending more than necessary (overpriced "service contracts" or extended warranties)
- Inappropriate products sold to trusting customers
- Lack of pricing transparency creating the impression that others are getting a better deal
- Special offers to new customers that is not available to existing, loyal customers

Examples of bad profits are easy to find when companies put more emphasis on maximizing short-term revenue than on building sustained customer relationships. Bad profits are corrosive to relationships; good profits create and sustain them. In short, bad profits are those earned at the expense of customer relationships. Going beyond customers, relationships of any type will be damaged when people feel exploited or unfairly treated. By contrast, relationships are strengthened when exchanges are fair and equitable. In the future, people will increasingly demand good service relationships.

Satisfy Individual Customer Needs and Wants

You probably have heard someone describe a super salesperson as one who can sell anything to anyone—the proverbial ice cubes to an igloo inhabitant. The old conventional wisdom taught that dynamic sales skills are the ticket to success. If the salesperson could give a decent presentation of the product and dazzle the consumer with an amazing close, then the consumer would buy. That was it: transaction complete.

In our day, a new protocol is on the rise. Although presentation and closing are still important to the sales process, an even more vital element supersedes both of these—the ability to satisfy individual customer needs and wants. Today's consumers face an unprecedented number of choices. In today's global economy, consumers have hundreds of places to go to buy the very same product. What makes the customer choose which business to buy from? To what degree are choices based on quality, price, convenience, or on customer service? How do you decide where to buy clothes, groceries, automobiles, electronics, and other consumer goods? What is most important to you as a consumer? There is no mystery in the answers to these questions. A consumer will go where he or she gets the most value, the most efficient and friendly systems, and the most pleasant and personable transactions. It is that simple. For a business to understand its customers' perception of value, systems, and people, it must establish and maintain a relationship with those customers.

Today's consumers face an unprecedented number of choices. Value, systems, and people will tip the scales for one business over others.

Create Promoters

An excellent measure of the strength of relationships is with the **Net Promoter Score (NPS)**. This simple measure gathers its data from one agree–disagree statement: "I would recommend this business to my friends or colleagues." Marking that statement on a 1–10 scale shows a good indicator of relationship strength. Those who scored 1–6 would be considered detractors; 7–8 are neutral, while 9 or 10 are the company's promoters. The NPS is calculated by subtracting all the detractors from the promoters.

Such simple measures of customer satisfaction will be more commonly used in the future. Although seemingly simple, the NPS is rooted in strong psychology and is far superior to many other more cumbersome feedback measures used today. It avoids many problems associated with surveys and observational research. I predict a broad adaptation of the NPS as an almost universally accepted assessment of customer service quality.

> The NPS will become a widely accepted measure of customer loyalty.

Apply Relationship Marketing

Companies may argue they have the best quality product around at great prices. The fact is, customers have gotten used to having quality products at good prices. These things are givens. They alone cannot readily distinguish one business from the competition.

But, customers don't yet expect great service. They continue to expect less than marginal service. Why? Because that is what they've been getting in the past. They have a list of pet peeves from experiencing poor service. Can you see the enormous opportunity that exists for building a strong competitive advantage through service that truly exceeds their expectations in positive ways?

> Customers in a free-market economy expect good products at reasonable cost. This is a given. What they don't always expect is great service.

Think back to when you were a child. Do you remember a corner grocer or a candy store manager? Did he know who you were or who your parents were? A typical comment from the grocer might have been, "Hi Jarome, it's good to see you. Did you have a good vacation to the Grand Canyon?" Or from the candy store manager, "Hello Anika, last time you were here you tried the red licorice. Can I get you the same thing, or would you like to try something different?" This is relationship marketing—having a one-to-one relationship with your customers. Every company—from a Fortune 500 to a local baby-sitter—can utilize relationship marketing with just a bit of training. In fact, relationship marketing is only limited by the creativity of the people in the company.

> Relationship marketing opportunities are limited only by one's imagination.

With the use of creativity, the opportunity to exceed customers' expectations extends well beyond just calling someone by name. While that is a great start, consider additional possibilities.

Gain Customer Share; Not Market Share

Let's talk once again about the important concept of **customer share**. Progressive companies are coming to see the wisdom of focusing on share of customers rather than share of market. Consider the following two competing flower businesses:

- The owners of The Flower Bucket have worked very hard, with a mass-marketing focus, in order to get a good piece of the market. They calculated they achieved about a 20 percent *market share*. In other words, for every dollar spent on flowers in their market, The Flower Bucket gets 20 cents.
- The owners of Smell Good Flowers, on the other hand, have worked very hard to gain a relationship with every one of the top purchasers of flowers (those who buy flowers on the most consistent basis). They estimate that they have a 20 percent *customer share*. That is, for every 10 customers who buy flowers, 2 of them buy flowers from Smell Good 100 percent of the time.

Which company is better off in the long run? Remember, Smell Good Flowers focused on the customers who are frequent buyers—the top customers of the industry—those who buy the most flowers. Therefore, Smell Good enjoys much greater efficiency in their marketing—its customers are the best customers to have. They know them and they massaged their relationship to gain even more of their flower business. They win.

If a company can truly win over the top customers, its chance of survival is much better than just having a percentage of the market. Managers need to think of the present value of a customer's future business. An example illustrates what I mean: super-successful auto dealer Carl Sewell teaches his employees the importance of thinking about the present value of future business.[4] Carl owns one of the largest luxury car dealerships in the country. He has calculated that every customer has the potential of bringing his dealership $332,000 in sales. If an average car costs about $25,000, and if people buy on average 12 cars, then the total sale is $300,000. Add service and parts and each customer of Carl's dealership is worth about $332,000 in sales. The numbers are not far-fetched. In a recent television interview, Wal-Mart's CEO David Glass said that his company has calculated the lifetime cost of a single lost customer at about $215,000. Mark Grainer, chairman of the Technical Assistance Research Programs Institute (TARP), similarly estimates that a loyal supermarket customer is worth $3,800 annually. Over the course of a lifetime, this could easily add up to more than $150,000 in sales. Furthermore, a businessperson who frequently flies to different parts of the world could easily spend over $50,000 annually on air travel. This customer could be worth over $1 million in revenue for an airline! This is what we mean by present value of future business.

> Present value of future business is an estimate of the total a customer would potentially spend with you.

With these kinds of long-range dollar thinking, who wouldn't give priority to customer share rather than a market share? The customer you already have is significantly more likely to buy from you again, while ever-scrambling for new customers drains your marketing budget and energy. Remember, though, the only way to increase customer share is to build a relationship with your customer and to enhance your customer's satisfaction and loyalty.

Thanks to computer databases, even small shops are able to collect information and use it for retention of customers. For example, gift shop owners can send out reminder cards to certain customers. A reminder card may read as follows:

> Hi, Mr. Joblinski: On March 29, last year, you remembered Jenny's birthday by sending her [a gift]. Here are some other gift ideas you might consider for Jenny this year. Please call or go to our Web site to place an order. We will make sure Jenny has a beautiful gift on her special day. Thank you for your business. We look forward to hearing from you.

When Mr. Joblinski calls, he must only tell the flower shop what flowers to send. Jenny's address, telephone number, and available times for delivery are already in the computer database. Likewise, the customer's credit card number is on file and can easily be confirmed and used.

Think how you could exceed expectations with these kinds of techniques. Why not do as a gift catalog company has using its database? The company implemented a new program that offers the following services: They will

1. Store and fulfill your orders of gifts to your friends and relatives up to 15 months in advance.
2. Deliver the gift on the day specified. The customer will never again miss any important date.
3. Bill the customer's credit card only when the gifts are sent. Send an invoice to the customer for each gift charged to the account within five working days.
4. Send a reminder postcard to the customer before the gift is sent out explaining whom the gift is going to and what the gift is. (So when the recipient says thank you, the customer knows what he or she is talking about.)
5. Send all customers an updated catalog that will have all of the previous year's names preprinted on the order sheet. The customer can add any new names to the bottom.
6. Provide a 24-hour telephone number and Web site access for any changes or updates the customer may have.

With the use of a database, the information needed to do all this is stored easily; and the catalog store employees most likely have less work than they did before the service was implemented. An additional benefit: The managers can see almost exactly what their sales revenue will be in the near future, thus helping financial planning for the company.

Special Service for Best Customers

Hertz Car Rental knew they had problems when people were getting upset about having to wait in long lines to get their rental cars. Many businesspeople travel in very tight schedules and need to have a car quickly. Hertz knew that unless they took action quickly, they would lose many of their most valuable and frequent renters. Hertz launched a special service—the #1 Gold Club—for those who needed their rental cars quickly. The #1 Gold Club members can call ahead of time to reserve a car. When the member gets off the plane, a shuttle is waiting for the customer at the curb to take him or her to the car. The shuttle driver can welcome him or her by name and explain the shuttle trip is just two minutes. The shuttle drops the customer off at the reserved car. The engine is running, the trunk lid is open, and today's issue of the *Wall Street Journal* is on the front seat. The member gets in the car and drives to the gate, where he or she shows his or her driver's license and #1 Gold Card. No lines. No hassle.

The successes of this approach led other auto rental companies to offer similar accommodations. Frequent travelers often get streamlined service on airlines (with special lines for first class and frequent flyers as well as special security lines), and frequent hotel guests get upgrades and special features. What can your company do to offer special consideration to your very best customers? The future "gold card" customer will expect something more.

To add an interactive dimension to this service, the company includes two short questions on the customer order form. They ask customers what they would like to see included in their catalog service in the future and what are some additional products they would like to have in company's gift catalog. Bingo! Customer preferences and expectations are revealed.

Insights into these ever-changing expectations are critical to maintain competitiveness and service success.

A FINAL THOUGHT

Insight. That is the key word as we seek to stay abreast of ever-changing customer service realities. The future looks exciting for people and organizations willing to change to stay competitive. Changes are often driven by technology although some organizations may choose to minimize technological innovation. They may decide to keep doing things the old-fashioned, down-home way as they do now. That's an alternative strategy that may appeal to people who don't care much for all this new-fangled techy-stuff. In some business contexts, low-tech may be fine. But for most organizations, embracing technological capabilities is a logical choice. Having the insight necessary to decipher customer wants and needs should be a high priority for service professionals.

Companies will need to give some hard thought to their **value proposition**. What exactly do they want to offer customers? It is possible to do business the old ways, to run the mom 'n pop store or restaurant just as it's been run in the past decades. But even among staunch traditionalists, customer demand for change may become a clamor. Even in Ye Olde Gift Shoppe with the 1890s theme, customers expect to be able to use their credit cards and probably even look at inventory online. Unless the shop has another gimmick, they will face a lot of pressure to upgrade to current customer demands.

Some customers are concerned about the impact of technology on privacy and the potential for intrusion into personal lives. For example, a few years ago a failed promotion offered free computers to people so long as the company can gather infinite data about every click of the mouse made on that computer. In a sense, those customers would have been selling their privacy for the price of a PC. Customers may resist some of the techniques we've discussed but would be open to friendly, informal personalization found in local, neighborhood stores or shops.

Whatever strategy your company employs, from highly sophisticated intelligent system databases to keeping mental notes on customer behaviors and preferences, one-to-one customer service and relationship building must stand as its cornerstone. This is the future of customer service.

Summary of Key Ideas

- Insight—the ability to monitor and understand an ever-changing customer service landscape is critical to success.
- Future success in customer service will depend on companies' abilities to adjust to various changes (many of which involve technology shifts). Some such shifts will dramatically change the nature of products or services offered. Others will call for adjustments in marketing and service delivery approaches.
- Companies can, using technology, personalize products or services to individual customers rather than marketing to demographic groups. While personal service has always been possible, technology makes it feasible on a wide scale and with large customer bases.
- Demographic changes will also impact the future of customer service. Successful businesses will need to be cognizant of changes in customer expectations and needs as dictated by the buying power of rising ethnic groups, age categories, and genders.

Key Concepts

bad profits	customer demographics	Net Promoter Score (NPS)	value proposition
customized messages	interactive television	point-of-sale electronic	VR shopping
customer share	mass customization	data gathering	

Reviewing the Facts

1. Some breakthrough products and services have literally changed the world. The automobile, the telephone, the Internet, and countless other inventions have historically shifted the ways people live and work. But shifts in ways of doing business have also had dramatic impact on lives throughout history. Self-service shopping, online sales, overnight shipping, 24/7 business hours, and globalization of services, such as call centers, are other examples. Look back through history and list three other major shifts you are aware of. For each, describe three or more ways these shifts impact customer service.

2. Among the most important determinants of customer satisfaction is the availability of feedback. We gain clearer insight into what customers want and don't want by systematically processing all types of feedback. Describe five ways today's organizations and individuals can sharpen their insights with useful feedback.

3. Describe one or more examples of how businesses you know are using one-to-one communication to build a stronger relationship with you. (Note: Often these are little things done to build rapport and loyalty.)

Applying the Ideas: What Changes Might Affect Your Customers

1. How are changing customer demographics affecting your business? Select a business and write a paper describing at least three demographic changes that are impacting or will soon impact its effectiveness. How might the business react to these pressures?

2. Log on to the Internet and search for information related to the notion of personalized services or "one-to-one" marketing and service. What are companies doing to take advantage of such personalization? Write a brief report on what you find.

3. Log on to the Internet and see what you can find about demographic shifts that may affect customer service. Write a brief report that answers these questions: What are the most significant shifts in your country, state, or local region? What do online sources suggest about adjusting to such demographic changes?

Consider this Case

Back from the Future

Many of you readers will have never seen a telegram, but most are familiar with the history. In 2006, Western Union delivered its last telegram. The telegraph industry's life was taken definitively and brutally by technological change. For more than 150 years, the telegram stood for immediacy and importance. It was an icon for urgency.

But now, Western Union has closed down its telegraph service around the world. Email, instant messaging, and faxes are the new technologies the telegram could not survive. So, Western Union has reconfigured itself into a business primarily dedicated to wiring money.

The shift from teletype and telegram to the new technologies represents one aspect of what some business consultants term a "paradigm shift"—a discontinuity in the otherwise steady march of business progress. There are many more examples of a lesser scale. Think about the music business. Some people alive today can remember the advent of radio and TV. Many have seen the evolution from vinyl records to 8-track tapes, to cassettes, to CDs, and now to MP3 and I-pods. Once thriving music stores have shut down or converted to vintage shops specializing in those odd antiquities—records!

The future of "video" stores doesn't look promising. Having made the transition from videotape movies to DVDs, they continue to face the competition of other delivery systems that allow home viewers access to movies without leaving the comfort of their homes such as on-demand movies through cable and satellite systems.

Looking further back in history, the automobile was another discontinuity, one that radically transformed both the economy and society. When the automobile first appeared, it seemed to be merely a horseless version of the well-known carriage. No one could have predicted the consequences of the automobile's introduction. Who would have imagined that a noisy, smelly, unreliable machine would eventually be responsible for the creation of suburbs; the fractionalization of families; and the growth of supermarkets, malls, and the interstate highway system? For that matter, who among us pictured the day when automobiles routinely included more electronics than the early spacecraft, or when on-board electronic communication systems can call for help or open an accidentally locked door?

Probes

1. How has technology shifted in your adult lifetime? What other examples reflect these kinds of paradigm shifts in recent years?
2. What future shifts do you envision? Be creative in describing possibilities.

Consider this Case

Welcome to an Exceptional Hotel

On his way back to his home in San Francisco from a business trip, Michael decided to stop for the night in a little hotel overlooking the Pacific. When he arrived at the reception desk, quickly a well-dressed woman appeared and welcomed him to the hotel. Within three minutes from the greeting, he was ushered into his room by the bellboy. The room was decorated with plush carpeting, white-on-white bedding, natural cedar walls, and a stone fireplace. The fireplace grate had oak logs, rolled paper, and matches waiting to be used.

After changing in his room, Michael walked to the restaurant. The hotel receptionist had made him reservations for the restaurant at the time of his check-in. Michael was immediately shown to his table upon arrival—even though others without reservations were waiting. When he got back to his room that night, the pillows were plumped up, the bed was turned down and there was a fire blazing in the fireplace. On the night stand was a glass of brandy and a card that read, "Welcome to your first stay at Venetia. I hope it has been enjoyable. If there is anything I can do for you, day or night, please don't hesitate to call. Kathi."

In the morning Michael woke up to the smell of coffee. When he went into the bathroom he found a perking coffee pot. A card by the pot read, "Your brand of coffee. Enjoy! K." Michael had been asked the night before at the restaurant which brand of coffee he preferred. Now it was bubbling in his room. Michael heard a polite knock on the door. When he opened the door, he saw the *New York Times* lying on the mat. When Michael had checked in, the reservationist had asked him what paper he preferred. Now his preferred paper was at his room for him to read.

Michael explains the service at the hotel has been exactly the same every time he has gone back. But after the first visit, he was never asked his preferences again.

Probes

1. How is this a great example of relationship-based customer service? How does it differ from the customer experience at other hotels you are familiar with?

2. By "learning" his preferences, the hotel management was able to manipulate a common experience into one that was very personal for Michael. What else might a hotel do? Be creative in brainstorming possibilities.

Source: Adapted from a story told in Gerber, M. E., *The E Myth Revisited* (New York: HarperCollins Publishers, Inc., 1995), pp. 188–192.

Notes

1. Don Peppers and Martha Rogers, *The One-to-One Future* (New York: Currency-Doubleday, 1993, p. 14).

2. Discussed in Susan Stellin, "Self-Service Sleeping," *Fast Company*, July/August 2006, p. 106.

3. *Source*: Southeastern Institute of Research, Inc. Boomer Project, 2006, *www.boomerproject.com*

4. C. Sewell and P. B. Brown, *Customers for Life* (New York: Pocket Books, 1990, p. 162).

PART 3

LIFE: Feedback

The third letter in our acronym LIFE is **F** for "feedback." Customer service professionals (and hopefully that is all of us) greatly improve the ability to build customer loyalty when we receive information on how we are doing currently. Without feedback, we can never improve our service.

Although most people give lip service to the idea that they want your feedback, many are less than 100 percent sincere about this, especially when the feedback is negative. We are all prone to emotional reactions to feedback we receive. Sometimes we welcome and appreciate it, especially when it validates something we did well. Sometimes feedback is embarrassing, uncomfortable, and even hurtful when it tells us we are not being effective. Human nature causes us to prefer the positive feedback, of course. But the negative feedback—especially well-intentioned criticism—can be particularly valuable. The trick is to develop a fairly thick skin and to not overly personalize criticism we receive. A complaining customer can be our best friend.

People who provide feedback are not always tactful or sensitive. Sometimes they blast us with both barrels and don't even try to soften their tone. Our job requires some maturity and wisdom to sort out the bits of useful advice from the sometime less-than-tactful delivery of complaints.

The next two chapters focus on how service professionals can benefit from feedback to build greater customer loyalty. Chapter 8 discusses how to get and use feedback. Chapter 9 ties these ideas in with the related process of recovering lost customers, a source of significant profit to any organization. Winning back customers who may have defected is almost always a worthwhile (although often avoided) activity for enhancing a company's bottom line.

The idea of these chapters is to get us thinking about feedback and recovery. Using these ideas can significantly boost our loyalty efforts.

CHAPTER 8

Get Customer Feedback
The Customer Can Be Our Coach

[People] who provide unsolicited negative feedback are advocates for a company. Most managers view these suggestions as intrusive and insulting indications that management doesn't know what they're doing, or that the customer or employee is hypercritical or "difficult." But in fact, taking the time to give this kind of feedback means that person really cares about the company and wants it to shine.

—ISABEL WALCOTT HILBORN, EXPERT IN STRATEGIC MARKETING

After reading this chapter, you should be able to

1. Reinforce why feedback is so important.

2. Understand that feedback receptiveness is a crucial characteristic of successful people and companies.

3. Recognize the varying levels of importance that companies place on customer feedback.

4. Identify seven ways feedback cards can lose their effectiveness.

5. Identify behaviors that reinforce rather than challenge customer feedback.

6. Act on complaints in productive ways.

7. Apply four ways to proactively seek out feedback information.

The Way It Is . . . Pop's Café Takes Feedback Seriously

Andre's favorite eatery is Pop's Café. Located a few blocks from his downtown office, Pop's has the best home cooking, complete with fresh-baked biscuits. The owner of the restaurant (yup, his nickname is actually Pop) personally greets each customer, and the food is delicious. One day, as Andre paid for his meal, Pop asked if everything was okay. Andre half-jokingly mentioned that the biscuits weren't as warm as usual. The owner immediately handed his money back.

"Oh no, Pop, I can't take my money back—the biscuits were okay," said Andre as he tried to pay him, "the meal was fine, just not quite as great as it usually is." But Pop would hear nothing of this and refused to accept payment. Andre continues to be a regular customer and frequently introduces his friends and business associates to Pop's.

A restaurant owner's demonstration that he wants only 100 percent satisfied customers strengthened Andre's allegiance to Pop's Café. Pop really wants feedback—positive or negative. And when he got some negative feedback (in this case a mild complaint), he acted on it immediately.

Hearing and addressing customer complaints is a crucial tactic in building customer satisfaction and loyalty. Organizations have several options for collecting customer feedback, some of which are more effective than others. We'll look at some of these options in this chapter, but the prerequisite to choosing a method is that companies must genuinely want to receive feedback, even when it may be uncomfortable. The best companies jump at opportunities to hear from their customers—especially the complaining ones.

WHY FEEDBACK IS SO IMPORTANT

At its most basic level, feedback is crucial to any kind of improvement. While positive feedback is nice—we all love a compliment—it's usually the *negative* feedback that helps us the most. Despite people saying "I always welcome your feedback," most of us, as individuals and companies, need to work to overcome the "feedback hurts" mentality. Of course, it isn't always pleasant to hear negative comments about what we are doing. Sometimes our feelings get hurt, our ego is wounded, or the feedback strikes us as, well, stupid. That said, let's consider a shift in our perspective.

Feedback Is a Form of Coaching

Try this: Think about feedback as a form of *coaching*. When we work with a coach, he or she is constantly giving us negative feedback—and we appreciate it. A golf coach, for example, will correct the way you hold or swing the club and you're delighted to get the negative feedback. In fact, you pay for all these "complaints."

We know we need feedback (which often takes the form of complaints) to improve our performance. It makes us better at what we are learning to do. Customer service skills are all about constant learning and the customers are our coaches.

Complaints Are Valuable Feedback

Dissatisfaction happens. What we choose to do about it can make all the difference in creating customer and employee loyalty. To do something about dissatisfaction, we need to know when it is happening—we need to get the silently dissatisfied customer to speak up by creating open communication channels.

Open communication occurs best when people feel that their opinions are valued and that they will be rewarded (or at least not punished) for expressing them. Companies earn customer loyalty by participating in dialogue. Dialoguing can be greatly enhanced with an easy-to-use feedback system.

Most people find expressing a complaint to be an unpleasant experience. It's uncomfortable and a bit intimidating. Most people want to maintain cordial relationships and fear that complaining will upset others. Our job, then, is to let people know that we are sincerely open to their comments—negative or positive. The following text shows a few ways to make this process more effective.

Getting Input at the Point of Contact

Most companies (even the reluctant-compliant ones) have some sort of formal feedback system, ostensibly to gather data that could make service better. The easiest system allows customers to fill out a feedback card. The way the cards are designed and what companies do with them when received will have a major impact on whether customers will use them. In too many cases, businesses make such cards available but are half-hearted at best about getting them, and even less enthusiastic about doing something based on the feedback received.

Collecting feedback cards can show historical trends and even measure customer loyalty rates, if well designed. But the information they provide is often too little, too late, and too broad-brush.

ANOTHER LOOK

Tracking Your Net Promoter Score

Managers have long sought easy-to-gather data that can indicate how well they are doing with customers. In a recent book, *The Ultimate Question*,[1] Bain & Company consultant Fred Reichheld summarizes years of research and teaches a technique for evaluating loyalty and long-term organizational success.

In short, Reichheld teaches that the most critical question one can ask customers is, "How likely is it that you would recommend this company to a friend or colleague?" Having customers respond to that question on a 10-point scale ranging from 1 (not at all likely) to 10 (extremely likely) determines if that customer is a detractor, passive, or a promoter.

With this one question, customers can be sorted into three categories: If they check 9 or 10 on the scale, they are *promoters*—customers who are loyal and enthusiastic; if they check 7 or 8, they are *passives*—customers who are satisfied but unenthusiastic; and if they check 6 or below, they are *detractors* who are unhappy but perhaps trapped in a bad relationship. From these data, we calculate a **Net Promoter Score (NPS)**.

Managers can calculate the NPS by applying the formula $P - D = NPS$, where P and D are the percentage of promoters and detractors. The (not at all simple) challenge for organizations is to improve their growth by managing improvements in their NPSs.

NPS can be a valuable indicator of the overall customer service an organization is giving. If a manager were to measure just one indicator, this may be the most robust number.

The time to gain specific, useful insights from an unhappy customer is at the point of contact and at the time of the problem. For a rapidly growing number of people, the Internet (or, within many companies, an intranet) provides the easiest way to give feedback. Some people prefer direct communication with an organization's employees, or communication by telephone or letters. Creating a climate in which people will give real-time, on-the-spot feedback is almost always more effective than printed customer-feedback cards, telephone follow-ups, or focus-group sessions.

COMMITMENT TO FEEDBACK VARIES

Companies (and people) have differing levels of commitment to feedback gathering, as shown in Exhibit 8.1. While most of us will accept it from a coach or consultant, we may be less eager to open ourselves up to broader input.

Some companies get feedback reluctantly. They know they should do it but their heart isn't in it. These companies, called **reluctant-compliant** companies, may offer customers a "feedback

EXHIBIT 8.1   Feedback Commitment Levels.

card" but the effort is half-hearted. They neither encourage customer feedback nor enthusiastically act on the information received. They do little to make it easy for customers.

The second level of feedback commitment is **active listener**. These companies are genuinely open to hearing from customers—using the term *hearing* to refer to any form of input, not just spoken words. They make it quite easy and they respond, thus reinforcing the customer's willingness to share perceptions with them.

The third level of feedback commitment involves taking customer comments and measuring and tracking them. These companies apply **metrics-conscious** techniques—they quantify as much data as possible and use that data to make organizational decisions. They keep score over extended periods and refer to these data regularly to motivate employees, correct weaknesses, and generally look for better ways to meet customer service objectives. So, where is your company?

What Statistics Reveal about Feedback

Surveys by the U.S. Office of Consumer Affairs reinforce the importance of actively soliciting feedback. They also reveal some interesting facts:

- One customer in four is dissatisfied with some aspect of a typical transaction.
- Only 5 percent of dissatisfied customers complain to the company. The vast silent majority would rather switch than fight. They take their business elsewhere.
- A dissatisfied customer, on average, will tell 12 other people about a company that provided poor service.

Let's translate those statistics: If 25 percent of your customers are unhappy with some aspect of your company's service but only 5 percent of that 25 percent bother to complain (yet each unhappy customer tells a dozen others), the impact can be devastating. For simplicity, let's say a company serves 100 customers a day. Twenty-five of them are dissatisfied, but the company hears only one or two complaints. That may sound good to management until they realize that the 23 quiet ones are likely to tell 276 other people about the unsatisfactory service!

The ripple effects can be devastating. Only by being open to complaints or concerns can companies turn this lemon into lemonade. Hearing customer and employee complaints is the first and most crucial step in fixing problems and maintaining allegiance. You really must *want* to hear people, and you really must make it easy for people to give you feedback. Avoiding feedback is, as someone once said, like being an ostrich. An ostrich can bury its head, but he always leaves the other end exposed.

Although this may sound counterintuitive, enlightened companies can and should increase the number of complainers they hear from. Handling complaints from two or three dissatisfied people can save 30 or 40 possible defections. And these complaints can teach the company what it needs to know to improve.

The best news of all is that customers who have their complaints handled well are very likely to do business with the company again. The willingness of an unhappy customer to consider doing business with you again jumps from as low as 10 percent to about 80 percent if his or her concerns are addressed. This seems to be the case even if their complaints were not resolved in their favor.[2] You may not be able to totally fix the problem (e.g., if customers complain about slow service, you cannot give them back their time) but they will give you credit for trying (perhaps by giving them a small token acknowledging the inconvenience). This point is worth repeating since it provides an overall rationale for getting and responding to customer feedback.

Customers whose complaints are heard and acted upon are more likely to continue being loyal to you than those who do not have a complaint of the first place—even if you cannot fully fix their complaint.

When an organization creates a dialoguing process with customers and employees, those who participate can become the company's best friends—even when complaining. To make the most of such dialoguing, you need to

- Make it easy for people to voice complaints (as well as compliments, suggestions, and questions).
- Act on input quickly and efficiently.

REINFORCE, DON'T CHALLENGE THE CUSTOMER

You create a good feedback climate by reinforcing customer behaviors, not by challenging them. The natural tendency is to react to complaints with some defensiveness. Instead, we should react with encouragement. Suppose you call an auto dealership service manager to tell him of a funny noise coming from your car after it had just been serviced. Instead of asking a bunch of questions about the kind of noise, or, worse yet, implying in some way that the noise may be your fault, he immediately says, "That's not good. We better get that fixed for you." You didn't have to explain, justify, or diagnose (although later he tactfully asked for some additional details about the nature of the noise). You told him of your complaint, and he immediately projected an attitude of "Let's get this fixed for you."

A quick response that acknowledges the customer's problem and conveys a willingness to work toward solutions will go a long way toward building loyalty.

Be Sensitive to Your First Reactions

The first comments out of your mouth when a customer begins to complain will largely determine the quality and quantity of feedback you will get. Like the auto-service guy, make those first comments positive and helpful.

Avoid acting defensively and making unnecessary demands for details. Accept the fact that the complaint is legitimate because it *is* real to the customer. Don't justify, or even try to explain, your reaction until you hear the whole story.

In face-to-face situations, maintain eye contact and use nonverbal behaviors that show your interest in hearing it all. Be careful of facial expressions that may convey skepticism, boredom, or anything that may discount the customer's concerns. If your contact is by phone, avoid dead air or prolonged silences, as discussed in Chapter 4.

Avoid any comments that would be construed as challenging the customer. If you suspect that the problem may be caused by customer misuse of the product, wait until the whole complaint is

---

ANOTHER LOOK

Seven Deadly Sins of Feedback Cards

Too often, companies use feedback cards as an easy way to get customer insights and, perhaps, as an alternative to having to deal with customers face to face. (This is a typical approach of reluctant-compliance described above). Here are seven ways such cards fall short of being effective:

1. Customers strongly tend to fill out a card only when they are extremely upset or extremely happy. Customer experiences in the larger gray area in between will seldom generate enough interest to give us usable feedback.
2. The card is not readily available. Sometimes customers have to ask for a card—and they generally won't, unless they are particularly upset (see 1, above).
3. Some cards have too many questions and use check boxes or rating scales that may be irrelevant to the customer's current concern. If the restaurant service was too slow, customers don't want to have to answer a bunch of questions about food temperature, ambiance, cleanliness, and so on.
4. Some cards are too open-ended. They may be essentially a blank form that invites customer comments. This requires a lot of work from the customer, who may find it difficult to express the problem in writing.
5. Customers may not know what to do with the card when it is completed. Some cards fail to have prepaid postage or even an address, thus requiring the customer to deposit it in a designated box. Or, worse yet, some cards require the customer to put postage on it before mailing!
6. The card fails to reassure customers that you really want this feedback, encourage people to complete it, and thank customers who use it.
7. The card mixes marketing surveys with customer service questions. In addition to scales for rating service, the card may ask for information about how the customer found the business, age or income demographics, postal code information, and so on. While such data may be useful for marketing, it should not be a part of a feedback card.

expressed and then ask some tactful questions about how the product was used. The issue is *not* whether the customer or the company is "right." The productive attitude is one of cooperation and problem solving.

ACT ON COMPLAINTS IN PRODUCTIVE WAYS

As previously discussed, you create a good feedback climate by reinforcing customer behaviors, not by challenging them. If customers fear a debate or argument every time they voice a concern, they will quit giving feedback. Now, what can we do to act on customer complaints? Here are some ideas.

First, look at the ways you open the door to receiving feedback. With appropriate feedback receptiveness, companies accomplish this first important step—they show customers and employees that they are serious about receiving feedback and establishing a dialogue. The second step, then, is to respond to feedback quickly and in constructive ways.

Timing is critical when you get customer or employee input. Early recovery is far easier than letting a bad situation fester and then trying to fix it. Act on complaints quickly, tactfully, and efficiently using a three-step process of (1) feeling empathy, (2) resolving the problem, and (3) offering something more to exceed what the customer anticipates.

Efficiency of responses is easily monitored by the ALS. In both the customer and employee versions, a built-in clock provides metrics that indicate how long it takes to respond and close out a dialogue. Managers can quickly determine the status of any input and, if necessary, provide resources needed to make response times acceptable. Nothing impresses people as significantly as quick follow-up.

The following are some tips for responding once input is received.

Feel the Customer's Pain

Recognize that upset customers are likely to be disappointed, angry, frustrated, or even in pain—and they blame you to some extent. Typically, they want you to do some or all of the following:

- Treat them with respect and empathy.
- Listen to their concerns, understand their problems, and take them seriously.

SERVICE SNAPSHOT

How to Kill off Feedback

The following text that appears on a Web page shows how *not* to solicit feedback. Under the "Customer Feedback/Feature Request Area" we find this (note: the company's name has been changed):[3]

> *Customer Feedback/Feature Request Area*
> *Tell us what's on your mind (good or bad!)*

Thank you for your interest in giving X-corporation feedback for the current as well as future versions of our products. It is with your suggestions and comments that we can continue to work to produce products which meet the needs of our end users.

> **** You Will Receive No Response with This Form ****

This form is for feedback/feature request submissions only. Please do not submit sales questions, support questions, or email unsubscribe requests to this form as you will not receive a response.

In addition, please review the Top Customer Questions [on our Web page] as we have noticed that many feedback submissions are regarding one or more of those issues.

> *I understand that I will not receive a response to my feedback and would like to continue to fill the feedback form.*

Probes

1. How would you feel about giving feedback that the company will not respond to?
2. Does this feedback page make you want to do business with X-corporation?

ANOTHER LOOK

The Allegiance Technologies™ Active Listening System

Allegiance Technologies has developed a Web-based "active listening system" (ALS) that provides an exceptional turn-key customer and employee dialoguing tool. After you read this, take a few moments to go to *www.Allegiance.com* and look at the system's demo.

Allegiance Technologies gathers four kinds of customer input: complaints, compliments, questions, and suggestions. This input is directed to the client company, while the complaining customer can remain anonymous if he or she wishes to. The system also provides measures of customer loyalty and satisfaction before and after the company responds to the feedback. The person filing a complaint is also asked what he or she would like to see the company do to remedy the situation. In this way, the customer or employee is drawn into a dialogue and enjoys engagement with the company. The feeling of engagement goes a long way toward earning allegiance and building confidence in management. Allegiance Technologies sells three versions of the ALS—one for customers, one for employees, and one for partners. All three versions follow the same general format. Client organizations subscribe to the hosted service, which is modestly priced—less expensive than the cost of developing a similar in-house system.

By having a neutral third party acting as a conduit between the customer (or employee) and the organization, frank and open communication can be achieved. Any feedback can be submitted anonymously; the person giving the feedback need only provide an email address to Allegiance, not to the client company. This anonymity feature makes the system especially useful for employees who may fear retaliation. (It can be useful for government-mandated processes for facilitating whistle-blowing on company misdeeds.)

Customers or employees who do not have Web access can submit feedback by telephone, at kiosks, or in person. Designated representatives then enter the comments in the system.

- Compensate them or provide restitution for the unsatisfactory product or service.
- Share their sense of urgency; get the problems handled quickly.
- Avoid further inconveniences.
- Punish someone for the problem (sometimes).
- Assure them the problem will not happen again.

Respond to complaints with **empathy**. This means considering how you would feel if you were this customer. Express this understanding with comments such as, "I'm sorry you were disappointed" and "I can see why that would upset you."

Do All You Can to Resolve the Problem

An acceptable solution to a problem may be perceived differently by different people. It is often a good tactic to simply ask the complaining person what he or she would regard as an appropriate solution. Often, the person will request something perfectly reasonable and perhaps even less drastic than the company would be willing to do. Do what is requested, and the problem is resolved.

OTHER PROACTIVE WAYS TO GET FEEDBACK

The best way to fish for feedback as an everyday activity is with *naïve* listening. **Naïve listening** is more of an attitude than a strategy. As its name implies, this kind of listening conveys that you don't know—that is, you are naïve—about what customers want. Your task is to get them to explain it to you. Create an atmosphere where you and your people are cheerfully receptive to customer comments, even—*especially*—comments that might not be pleasant to hear. Then provide multiple channels for them to tell you what's on their minds. In prompting customers to share what they're thinking, use open-ended questions to get the most information.

Open-ended questions cannot be answered with a simple yes, no, or other simple response but instead encourage a considered, meaningful response. For example, restaurant servers who

ANOTHER LOOK

Encouraging Continuous Feedback

To generate an ongoing flow of good feedback, apply these simple tips:

- Avoid being defensive. Listen—don't explain or justify. Learn to withhold your response. While someone criticizes you is not the time to explain or justify your actions, even if you feel the criticism is unwarranted or stems from a misunderstanding. Listen now, explain later. Being defensive stifles your customer's feedback. It tells others you are more interested in justifying yourself than in understanding what they are saying.
- Ask for more information, especially for specifics. This is a good opportunity to obtain more information. Honest questions will support and encourage the continued flow of feedback. For example, say, "That's very helpful. Tell me more. Is there anything else I should know about that?"

- Express an honest reaction. You certainly have a right to express your feelings about the feedback received. You may well say, "I'm a little surprised (or frustrated or disappointed) you had that experience, but you may have a point," or "I'm not sure what to say. I never even thought of that, but I will from now on." Be careful to not sound like you are judging the person. Accept his or her perceptions at face value.
- Thank the person for providing feedback. Let him or her know that you realize how risky giving feedback can be, and express your appreciation for the efforts.

Using these kinds of communication behaviors gives you the opportunity to avoid turning off future feedback that could be valuable to you.

---

ask an open-ended question like, "How else can I make your dinner enjoyable?" will get a broader range of responses than one who asks the more common, "Do you need anything else?" ("No.") or "Is everything okay?" ("Yes.").

In addition to being open to customer-initiated feedback, companies should also reach out for feedback. This is commonly done via

- Focus groups
- Explorer groups
- Customer surveys
- Mystery shoppers

Try Focus Groups

Focus groups have long been used for marketing research, and they can play an important role in understanding customer and employee perceptions and expectations as well. Although some marketing consultants may disagree, there's no great mystery to how focus groups work, and any intelligent person could run one effectively.

Here is the procedure for creating and getting the most from a focus group:

- Select a sample of your customers or employees to join with you in the focus-group session. Don't just pick people you know or customers you like. You may, however, want to be sure they are among your better customers by qualifying them according to their influence or how much they spend with you.
- Formally invite the customers or employees to participate, telling them when and where the focus group will meet, as well as how long the session will take. Let them know the reason: that you are attempting to better understand their needs and how you can better be of service to them.
- Limit your focus group to not fewer than five or more than a dozen people. Ask customers to confirm their attendance, but expect that some will not show up. Fifteen confirmed reservations will generally get you 12 actual participants. Follow up with phone calls to confirm attendance.

- Reward focus-group participants. Tell those invited that you will give them something for their participation. Retail stores may give focus-group participants a certificate, a free dinner, or even cash. In marketing research, it's not uncommon to pay people $50 or more for a one- or two-hour session.

When running the focus groups:

- Set the stage by having someone from top management moderate the group.
- Create an open atmosphere where participants will feel comfortable giving you all kinds of feedback. Be polite, open, encouraging, and receptive.
- Avoid cutting people off when they're making a critical comment, and do not, above all, be defensive of the way you're doing things now, when in the eyes of the customer it's not working.
- Keep any follow-up questions open-ended. Don't interrogate or imply judgment of a participant's comments.
- Acknowledge compliments that group members may express, and thank the contributor for the compliment. Then make a statement such as, "We're happy to hear that we are doing things you like. Our major purpose here is to identify ways we can do a better job in meeting your needs. How can we do even better?"
- Limit the group to a predetermined amount of time—typically a one-hour or 90-minute (maximum) session works best. Focus-group sessions that are any longer than that will not sustain people's interest.
- Tape-record the entire focus-group session and transcribe key notes for review. As you analyze the results of the group session, look for key words that might tip you off to what customers are looking for.
- At the end of the focus-group session, of course, be sure to thank the participants for all of their input—and give them their pay.

The critical key to successful focus groups is the careful analysis of the information you receive. It is almost always necessary to transcribe, word-for-word, the entire discussion and to read this transcription carefully—several times. This can be laborious but the careful processing of the raw data can lead to important insights about customer/employee perceptions that might never come out in other feedback sessions. Continually adjusting to exceed what customers anticipate is the focus of the remainder of this book. The following chapters will show a series of powerful ways to apply an A-plus strategy for earning customer and employee allegiance.

Use Explorer Groups

Explorer groups go to other businesses to see how they do things. When you hear about a great idea another business is using, send out an explorer group to scope it out. One retailer known for exceptional service encourages employees to take a company van and rush to the scene of a great service idea used by another company. They take notes and discuss possible implementation in their store. Explorer groups need not be sent only to direct competitors; often totally unrelated businesses have great ideas you can use.

Another way to gather great data is to "explore" how your own organization is serving customers by being a "customer." Call the company and listen to the impression created by the person answering the phone. Is this what your customer is hearing? How do you like it? Then visit other locations or areas in your own organization and see how you are treated.

Explorer groups are forms of **observational research**, which is most effective when carefully planned. Before going exploring, decide what you are looking for. Limit the exploration. For example, if you are looking for better ideas on merchandise display, focus on that rather than other factors such as employee behaviors. If you are interested in how a competitor handles training classes for its customers, check out the classes, not pricing strategies or other factors.

Exploring can be fun for your employees. Many will enjoy being "sent on a mission" to gather ideas and insights. Listen carefully to their observations and thoughts about implementing these in your organization.

Use Customer Surveys

How do we find out whether our customers are satisfied? The best way is to ask them! **Customer surveys** are systematic ways of asking a series of questions to determine what the respondents—and, if the sample is random, many of your customers—think. A **random sample** means that any customer has an equal chance of being selected for surveying. A **stratified random sample** means that a certain category of customers has been selected and that anyone in that category has an equal chance of being surveyed. For example, a bank may decide to survey higher net-worth customers—say those with more than $300,000 in assets—to gather their impressions about service. Assuming it is impractical to survey every one of the people in that demographic, they will seek to randomly select a sample of people who fit that description. If proper selection techniques and statistical analysis are used, the sample should accurately represent the thinking of all people in that category.

When you conduct a customer satisfaction survey, what you ask the customers is important. How, when, and how often you ask these questions are also important. However, the most important thing about conducting a customer satisfaction survey is what you do with their answers.

THE MECHANICS OF ASKING FOR CUSTOMER SURVEY INPUT There are many techniques for asking your customers whether or not they are satisfied with your company, your products, and the service they received. Among the choices are:

- Face-to-face interviews as they are about to walk out of your store or office.
- Telephone surveys calling customers at home or work.
- Mail questionnaires they complete and send back to you or email surveys they respond to online. (Be careful to not violate spam laws and keep the survey brief and easy to complete.)
- Written surveys handed to customers with a mail-back envelope or a drop box.
- Internet-based surveys that invite customers to go to a Web site to complete a brief form. Typically, companies give some incentive (such as a future discount) to people who take the time to complete the survey.

WHEN TO CONDUCT A CUSTOMER SATISFACTION SURVEY The best time to conduct a customer satisfaction survey is when customers have recently completed a transaction with you and the experience is fresh in their minds. If you wait to conduct a survey, customer responses may be less accurate. They may have forgotten some of the details, color their answers because of confusion with other visits, or even confuse you with some other company.

WHAT TO ASK IN A CUSTOMER SATISFACTION SURVEY One school of thought advocates that you only need to ask a single question in a customer satisfaction survey: "Will you buy from me again?" While this minimalist approach is a tempting way to reduce your survey to this supposed "essence," you miss a lot of valuable information and you can be easily misled. Just as with the use of simple yes-no (versus open-ended) questions, it is too easy for customers to answer yes to the "Will you buy from me again?" question whether they mean it or not. You want to ask other questions in a customer satisfaction survey to get closer to the expected behavior and to collect information about what to change and what to keep doing.

You may well decide to ask the basic customer satisfaction questions:

- How satisfied are you with the purchase you made (of a product or service)?
- How satisfied are you with the service you received?
- How satisfied are you with our company overall?

And ask the customer "loyalty questions":

- How likely are you to buy from us again?
- How likely are you to recommend our product/service to others?
- How likely are you to recommend our company to others?

If you give the respondent choices to mark in response to these questions, be certain that you cover all possible choices. The specific design of survey questions goes beyond the scope of this book. However, the KISS (keep-it-simple-surveyors) principle is a good guideline. One useful tip is to not ask questions at all. Instead, give customers a series of statements followed by agree–disagree scales. For example:

Please circle the number that best reflects your degree of agreement with the following statements: 1= strongly disagree, 2 = disagree, 3 = neither agree nor disagree, 4 = agree, 5 = strongly agree

1.	**The business office is conveniently located.**	**1 2 3 4 5**
2.	**The tellers in the bank are generally friendly.**	**1 2 3 4 5**
3.	**The manager is readily available if I need to speak with him or her.**	**1 2 3 4 5**
4.	**Product prices are fair.**	**1 2 3 4 5**

Be sure that each survey statement deals with only one variable. For example, avoid saying "the business office is attractive and well staffed" because it may be one or the other but not both. Likewise, "process of company products and services are excellent" may confuse a respondent who thinks product price is fine, but services are too high.

Using this technique for the "big three" loyalty questions, you might ask people to agree or disagree (again using the 5-point scale) with these statements:

- *I am generally satisfied with_____ company.*
- *I intend to continue doing business with_____ company as the need arises.*
- *I would recommend_____ company to others.*

If you did no more surveying than these three items, you could develop a fairly reliable indicator of where you stand with regard to customer loyalty.

You may, of course, also want to drill down with more pointed questions about what customers like and don't like. If you suspect, for example, that waiting time is a potential turnoff for your customers, ask about it. Use "I feel that I am served promptly" followed by agree–disagree scales. Likewise, any potential turnoff that you get wind of (whether regarding value, systems, or people) may be worth looking into more deeply.

HOW OFTEN SHOULD YOU CONDUCT A SURVEY?   The best answer is "often enough to get the most information, but not so often as to annoy the customer." In real terms, the frequency with which you conduct a customer satisfaction survey depends on how often you interact with your customers. If you sell automobiles and your customers are likely to buy every three to five years, it would be inappropriate to ask them each year what they thought of their last buying experience. Conversely, if your customers buy from you daily—commuters on a rapid transit system—surveying them once a year would miss important changes in their attitudes that may be driven by seasonal events.

WHAT TO DO WITH ANSWERS FROM A SURVEY   Regardless of *how* you ask customers for their feedback, *what* you ask them in the customer satisfaction survey, and *when* you survey them, the most important part of the process is what you do with their answers. Gathering data only to ignore it is a waste of organizational time and energy.

Minimally, you need to compile the answers from different customers and look for trends. You may want to look for differences by location and/or product. And if the survey reveals weak areas, you need to act on the information you gathered. Use the information to prioritize tasks. Work first on things customers are unhappy with. Fix the things the customers have complained about. In addition, investigate their suggestions to improve the company and products in those areas that mean the most to your customers.

Most importantly, give them feedback showing how their responses are appreciated and are being acted upon. That feedback can be individual responses to the customers if appropriate, or it can simply be fixing the things that they tell you need to be fixed. Use your company newsletter or other forms of communication to express appreciation for feedback and to show how customer input is being used to improve the company for the benefit of customers.

Use "Mystery Shoppers"

Mystery shoppers (sometimes called secret shoppers) are hired evaluators who visit or contact companies posing as customers to assess how they are treated. Typically, a mystery shopper works as a contract worker for an independent research agency. The agency is hired by retail firms, restaurants, and similar businesses to provide an objective evaluation of their customer service and possibly other aspects of the business.

Mystery shopping has become a big business with many firms offering these services. If you Google "mystery shoppers," you will get more than 2 million hits. Many are for firms offering mystery shopping services, and many are advertising for people to do the shopping. Yes, you actually can get paid for shopping.

Mystery shoppers can help companies know what their customers experience and can inform companies about things that need improving. Armed with the right information, businesses can make necessary improvements. Shopper findings are used in developing employee training materials, for improving business operations, for improving product quality, and to compare one location to another.

The reports from mystery shoppers are also used to point out positive things. Shopper findings are used to help identify store locations and employees due rewards for outstanding customer service or cleanliness. Secret shoppers are sometimes even allowed to reward employees on the spot for meeting certain criteria. It can be fulfilling for a shopper to hand an employee a certificate for a paid day off for doing a great job!

One challenge faced by mystery shopping is the problem of reliability. Although firms train shoppers extensively, subjective elements enter into the evaluations made. One shopper may rate a characteristic as a 5, while another may see the same characteristic as a 3. Who is right? And how does a manager convey critical comments to employees if it's pretty much one person's word against another? The shopper may report a rude clerk, but the clerk denies it. Who is right?

Enter the latest advancement in mystery shopping: use of digital video. Several firms now offer hidden camera visits by evaluators that tape the actual experience in living color. One such firm, Human Touch Consulting (*www.HumanTouchConsulting.com*), visits thousands of businesses (including many fast-food restaurants) to gather video footage. Actually, it is no longer "video" per se, but images that are digitally recorded and stored on a computer. The evaluations are streamed via the Internet back to the client organization within 48 hours of the mystery shop. The action is filmed through a camera lens mounted in a button on the evaluator's shirt. The evaluator has a tiny computer tape under his or her clothing that records both visual images and sound.

The beauty of such technology is that the camera never lies. Nor is it subject to subjective judgment of the shopper. Once shot, the video can be edited and sent to a client organization within a few days, all via the Internet. Managers in the restaurants can then sit down with employees and invite them to view the tape. The manager can simply ask, "How do you think you did with that customer?" and sit back and listen. The employee gets the benefit of exceptionally clear, robust data—feedback that he or she may use to improve service skills.

The video shopper can also pan the dining room, parking lot, and counter area to give an unbiased assessment of cleanliness, the lack of which is a huge turnoff in the restaurant business. In short, this approach gives managers and employees exceptionally detailed and useful feedback.

A FINAL THOUGHT

Capturing and using feedback is critical to success. Managers can benefit from maintaining a **complaint log** to capture ideas from customers and others. The shortest pencil is better than the longest memory. So, get in the habit of jotting down descriptions of feedback received (especially complaints) and the actions taken to resolve them. Use the complaint log as a part of regular staff meetings, where you can discuss how the situation has been handled or brainstorm other ways it could be done.

You can tally such information manually or use a technology product such as the Allegiance ALS. As a minimum, encourage all employees and managers to keep a feedback "file." This may be something as simple as a file folder where they collect notes or comments. Look at these files periodically to learn from the feedback received.

Summary of Key Ideas

- Many people dislike negative feedback. It can be embarrassing or hurtful. It is human nature to try to avoid it.
- Feedback is a form of coaching that can teach us to be better at what we do. A complaining customer can be our best friend.
- Companies have varying levels of commitment to feedback: reluctant-compliant (they get it because they feel obligated to), active listener (they are open and receptive), and metric-conscious (they systematically process and measure it over time).
- For some organizations, *increasing* the number of complaints heard may be an effective strategy. If the amount of feedback received is low, something may be blocking customers from speaking out.
- Feedback cards are a relatively unproductive way of getting customer input, although they are better than nothing. The design of the card will impact the quality and quantity of feedback received.

- How we react to customer complaints will determine whether we get additional "coaching." Our first reaction is important. Avoid putting the customer on the defensive, instead of simply accepting the criticism.
- Four ways to proactively seek out feedback are focus groups, explorer groups, customer surveys, and mystery shoppers.
- Customer surveys work best when the instrument is carefully designed and administered to a random sample (or a stratified random sample) of customers. Repeated administration of surveys is useful so long as the customer is not inconvenienced.
- Focus groups gather unstructured observations and opinions from customers or potential customers. Explorer groups evaluate the ways other companies do things.
- Mystery shoppers use observational research techniques to reflect the kinds of experiences your customers have when doing business with you. The latest approach to this uses hidden video to gather particularly robust data.

Key Concepts

active listener	explorer groups	naïve listening	random sample
complaint log	focus groups	Net Promoter	reluctant-compliant
customer surveys	metrics-conscious	Score (NPS)	stratified random
empathy	mystery shoppers	observational research	sample

Reviewing the Facts

1. Describe in your own words the reasons many companies fail to get enough negative feedback.
2. How can organizations become more open to feedback? What kinds of employee training would help? What would you tell your employees about feedback importance if you were the boss?
3. Explain the concept of Net Promoter Score. Why is this score important? How can managers use this number to improve service?
4. Describe the three levels of feedback commitment. Select three companies or organizations you are familiar with and describe which level they seem to be using.
5. Describe the relative advantages and disadvantages of focus groups. How can they be useful? How could they go wrong?
6. What are some advantages of explorer groups? How could they go wrong?
7. Summarize the most important factors in creating a valid survey. What are some ways that surveys can go wrong? How can data potentially be distorted?
8. What are the rules of thumb on how often customers should be surveyed?
9. What are mystery shoppers and how can such feedback processes provide useful data? What should managers avoid when employing this feedback technique?

Applying the Ideas: Getting Customer Feedback

1. Suppose that you own a retail shop. Design a feedback card that could be used to gather useful feedback. Describe how you would implement this system. Who would get the cards? How might you encourage customers to use it? What would you seek to avoid?
2. Focus on an organization you now work in. This could be a business, church or civic group, student organization, or even a class. Write a brief paper describing the feedback receptiveness in this organization. Do the leaders seem eager and willing to get feedback? Have they put mechanisms in place to gather feedback? Are they reluctant-compliant, active listeners, or metric-conscious?
3. Select a company or organization for which you can survey a sample of customers. (You might want to use your college class as an organization.) Create a simple NPS ballot and ask at least 10 customers to complete it. Calculate the NPS. How do you think this score compares with other similar organizations? Justify your answer.
4. Plan and conduct a focus group for an organization. Describe how you prepare it, invite the right participants, conduct the session, and process results. How did it go? What did you learn? What would you do differently next time?
5. Go to the Internet and look at the Web site for Allegiance Technologies (*www.Allegiance.com*). Look through the description of their active listening system and report on its capabilities. Then Google (or use a similar search engine) "customer feedback systems" and see what you find. How do these systems compare? Based on this research, which system would you choose for your organization?
6. Visit the Web site for Human Touch Consulting, the firm that offers digital video evaluations of company experiences (*www.HumanTouchConsulting.com*). Write a brief paper describing the advantages and disadvantages of this approach. Search online for other companies that offer similar services and compare them.

Consider this Case

Getting Feedback at Bill's New Restaurant

"Was everything okay?" The restaurant server asked it routinely, without much vocal inflection. It came across as a required line employees were taught to say. Reggie gave the expected reply: "Okay." The server walked away, having performed her customer service duty, and Reggie left the restaurant reasonably satisfied, but not the slightest bit motivated to return anytime soon. Asked by a friend how he likes that restaurant, he gave the same response: "It's okay."

Bill Buckner recently purchased the Garden of Eat'n Family Restaurant where Reggie just had lunch.

Bill overheard the conversation and realized that the "standard question" his server asked wasn't really a very effective way of getting customer feedback. He had been thinking a lot recently about how he could "position" his restaurant in the minds of customers. To do so, he realized he really needed to know what people thought of the service and what they would like to see in future visits. But first, he needs to be sure there are future visits.

Probes

1. How effective is the standard feedback question? How could this be phrased differently to get better information from customers?

2. If you were Bill, what steps would you take to get better feedback? Describe specific actions he should take, based on the ideas in this chapter.

Consider this Case

Fear of Feedback[4]

The biggest obstacle to knowing what customers really think about us is fear. We fear they'll tell us our product or service stinks, that we're horrible people, and that we should never have set foot on earth.

Danica, a marketing manager for a midsized technology firm, read this opening paragraph and nodded. That's the truth! she thought. We have got to get more proactive about getting and using good feedback. Too many of my people are afraid of feedback. They seem to be tuning out that type of painful feedback—and we need it if we are ever going to grow this business.

Danica was a good amateur golfer and she knew the value of coaching. Her game had improved dramatically since she had hired a coach, Roy, a rather crusty fellow who was quick to point out when she was doing something wrong. Sometimes Roy could be annoying—such a stickler for detail—but he had helped her improve her game to a single digit handicap. Danica thought, maybe I need to look at feedback from customers in the same way: occasionally painful, but almost always useful.

The article she was reading described an Australian beer company, Blowfly, that has integrated customer feedback into its company's decision-making process by asking customer "shareholders" to determine marketing plans, product names, street-team strategies, and operational decisions usually made by executive committees. In many ways, Blowfly has turned ownership of the company over to customers. This has caused so much positive word of mouth that the company—even before it was a year old—landed a hefty North American distribution deal with hip grocer Trader Joe's.

Another example described toy retailer Build-a-Bear Workshop [that] sends out weekly surveys to its database of 6 million customers asking them to rate their recent store experience, including the cleanliness of the bathrooms! Company founder Maxine Clark attributes her company's success—it has grown to 113 stores in five years doing $200 million in revenue—to its intense focus on gathering customer feedback.

Wow, she thought. That's what I want to see happen in my company. We have to get more proactive about gathering customer feedback. Waiting for it to arrive on its own is fraught with peril. To know what customers are thinking, we must ask.

Probes

1. How does this case reinforce the ideas in this chapter? How is feedback like coaching?

2. Assuming that most of Danica's customers communicate with the company only via the Internet or phone, what steps can she take to enhance feedback-gathering? Be specific about a plan of action.

Notes

1. Fred Reichheld, *The Ultimate Question* (Boston: Harvard Business School Press, 2006, p. 21).

2. Ibid.

3. *http://www.dataviz.com/eforms/feedback/generalfeedback.html*. Downloaded March 3, 2006.

4. Some material in paragraphs 4 and 5 were excerpted from Ben McConnell and Jackie Huba. *Fight the Fear: The 10 Golden Rules of Customer Feedback* appearing in *MarketingProfs.com*, March 2004.

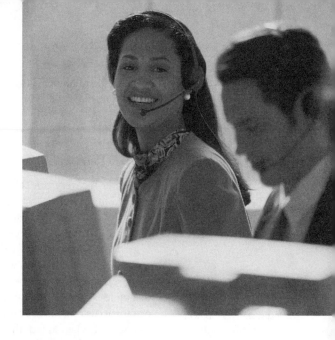

CHAPTER 9

Recover the Potentially Lost Customer

Here's an Opportunity for You

Those who enter to buy, support me. Those who come to flatter, please me. Those who complain, teach me how I may please others so that more will come. Those only hurt me who are displeased but do not complain. They refuse me permission to correct my errors and thus improve my service.

—RETAILING PIONEER MARSHALL FIELD

*British Airways calculates that **customer retention** efforts return $2 for every dollar invested. In fact, British Airways finds that "Recovered" customers give the airline more of their business.*

After reading this chapter, you should be able to

1. Understand the case for customer recovery.
2. Maintain healthy attitudes about customer recovery.
3. Apply techniques that develop your customer recovery skills.
4. Handle a nasty complaint letter or email.
5. Develop skills to convey the appropriate tone when dealing with customers.
6. Understand the distinction between assertive and aggressive behavior.

The Way It Is . . . the Importance of Customer Recovery[1]

An average company will lose half its customers every five years. Such turnover hurts profitability and the brand. A satisfied customer will tell four or five others about a pleasant customer experience. Deliver a poor experience, and 7 to 13 others will hear about it. Another study's scary statistic: Unhappy customers will continue to voice their dissatisfaction for up to 23 years.

No company can afford to have its brand dissed in the marketplace for two decades. No company can also afford to lose half its customers every five years, although that's the average across most industries. Yet despite the unprofitable implications of customer dissatisfaction, surprisingly little attention is paid to customer retention. About 80 percent of marketing budgets are devoted to acquiring customers, even though it costs three to five times more to replace than to keep a customer.

131

"That's unfortunate. **Customer recovery**—the effort to satisfy unhappy customers to reduce defection—must be a core element of customer equity strategies," believes Nick Wrenden, author of *FusionBranding: How to Forge Your Brand for the Future*.

UNDERSTAND THE CASE FOR CUSTOMER RECOVERY

Customer recovery can substantially impact profitability. Studies indicate that money and effort invested in recovering lost customers comes back to the company many times over. British Airways calculates that customer retention efforts return $2 for every dollar invested. In fact, British Airways finds that "recovered" customers give the airline *more* of their business after they have been won back.

Many companies miss a huge opportunity when they fail to aggressively seek to recover lost customers. The problem starts with the fact that many companies don't even know how many customers they are losing. Service expert Jill Griffin of loyaltysolutions.com sites a nationwide study that found that up to 50 percent of marketing and sales managers could not identify their company's percentage of annual customer loss. Those who thought they did know their firm's defection rates said it averages 7–8 percent, when in fact, the average company loses 20 percent or more of its customers every year.

Another national study showed that 43 percent of sales managers and 47 percent of marketing managers said they did not conduct **defection interviews** thus depriving their companies of insight about root causes of defection. And even when companies do interview departing customers, they may not get the real reasons. Studies show that newly departed customers are often reluctant to tell why they left. They may be embarrassed to explain why they're leaving. Instead they will give an easy reason for defection, like "I am moving," or "I don't need the products anymore." It's often better to wait a month or two to get the real facts.

A study by Paramus, from New Jersey–based Marketing Metrics, found firms have a much better chance of winning business from lost customers than from new prospects. The research found the average firm has a 60–70 percent probability of successfully selling again to "active" customers, 20–40 percent probability of successfully selling to lost customers, and only a 5–20 percent probability of making a successful sale to new prospects.

If you win the customer back, they enter a second life with you. This **"second life cycle"** (the recovered customer) can differ greatly from the "first life cycle" of the same customer in at least four ways:

1. The recovered customer is already familiar with the products and services you offer. You don't have to teach him about what you can do.
2. You are likely to have more data about the likes and dislikes of this particular customer than about any first-time customer and can offer a more targeted service.
3. The customer may feel flattered by your efforts to win her back. This can often lead to sales greater than that generated by newly recruited first-time customers.
4. The length of the "prospect phase" and the "new customer phase" would arguably be shorter in the second life cycle than in the first one. The customer will become acclimated to doing business with you more quickly.

We talked in Chapter 6 about the importance of reducing turnoffs. These efforts are worthwhile, but reality tells us that we cannot predict with certainty every possible customer complaint. In short, dissatisfaction happens. What we choose to do about it can go a long way toward creating customer loyalty. It's not always easy, but saving customers can be enormously profitable. Effective complaint handling begins with the right attitudes coupled with the skills we'll discuss in this chapter.

MAINTAIN HEALTHY ATTITUDES ABOUT CUSTOMER RECOVERY

The best attitudes for service provider stem from the desire for a win-win relationship with the customer. Both parties want to feel good about the business transacted. This is not necessarily a "customer-is-always-right" attitude.

Companies that do not aggressively work to recover lost customers miss a huge opportunity.

Customer recovery isn't always easy, but it is tremendously profitable.

The issue is not whether the customer or the company is right. The attitude is one of cooperation and problem solving that won a loyal customer.

In addition to a problem-solving rather than blame-setting attitude, service recovery is best handled when seen as an **attitude of opportunity** rather than a painful chore. Granted, most of us would prefer not to hear about customers' dissatisfaction. That's human nature. But given that dissatisfaction does occur, an attitude of accepting the opportunity and challenge can be useful. Customer complaints are opportunities to cement relationships. The vast majority of such relationships are worth saving, although occasionally—I stress *occasionally*—we need to let go of the **chronic complainer**, as we'll discuss later in this chapter.

An attitude of opportunity begins with an understanding that complaints are triggers for improvement. There can be no positive change without negative (corrective) feedback. And much of corrective feedback comes to us disguised as complaints.

No one likes to hear complaints, but they are truly opportunities for possible change, not reasons for defensiveness. Carefully track the number of complaints and resolution. More important, complaints must be relayed to the appropriate organizational areas to minimize re-occurrences. Remember that a rising number of complaints is usually a sign of success, not failure. Often, complaining customers are the ones most committed to a brand. British Airways found that 87 percent of customers who complained did not defect.

Defensiveness is the enemy of improvement. To succeed at customer service, we need to work very hard to reduce defensiveness and focus on how the dissatisfied customer can be our best friend!

> "The customer is always right" may not be a good motto. Better to think about win-win relationships, not who is right and who is wrong.

> Defensiveness against feedback is the enemy of improvement.

ANOTHER LOOK
Action Ideas to Deal with Difficult Customers

Upset customers are liable to have strong feelings when you, your product, or service lets them down and they'll probably want to "dump" these feeling on you. Deal with the feelings before trying concentrating [only] on solving the problem.

Here are five action ideas that deal with the customers' human needs:

1. **Don't let them get to you**. Customers may make disparaging and emotional remarks—don't rise to the bait. They are upset and may say things they don't mean. Cut them some slack. Concentrate on listening nondefensively and actively. Don't acknowledge their out-of-line comments.
2. **Listen–listen–listen**. At the risk of beating this horse too much, apply the ideas on listening discussed in Chapter 3. Look and sound like you're listening. The customer wants to know that you care and that you're interested in their problem.
3. **Stop saying sorry**. "Sorry" is an overused word; everyone says it when something goes wrong and it has lost its value. How often have you heard—"Sorry about that, give me the details and I'll sort this out for you." Far better to say, "I apologize for . . ." And if you really need to use the *sorry* word, make sure to include it as part of a full sentence: "I'm sorry you haven't received that information as promised

Mr. Smith." (It's also good practice to use the customer's name in a difficult situation.)

4. **Empathize**. Empathy isn't about agreement, only acceptance of what the customer is saying and feeling, Basically the message is, "I understand how you feel." Obviously this has to be a genuine response; the customer will realize if you're insincere and they'll feel patronized.

   Examples of empathy response would be— "I can understand that you're angry," or "I see what you mean." Again, these responses need to be genuine.
5. **Build rapport**. Sometimes it's useful to add another phrase to the empathy response, including yourself in the picture. "I can understand how you feel, I don't like it either when I'm kept waiting." This has the effect of getting on the customer's side and builds rapport. Some customer service people get concerned with this response as they believe it'll lead to—"Why don't you do something about it then." The majority of people won't respond this way if they realize that you're a reasonable and caring person.

   If they do, then continue empathizing and tell the customer what you'll do about the situation. "I'll report this to my manager" or "I'll do my best to ensure it doesn't happen in the future."

LOOK INSIDE

What Are Your Feelings about Dealing with Difficult Customers?

Below is a list of words that may describe the ways you feel about dealing with upset customers. Select the five that best describe your general feelings. When you have finished this chapter, review these words to see if you have some better ideas on how to deal with these emotions. Discuss your results in a small group, asking for others' feedback on how to deal with the feelings you have.

afraid	confident	foolish	relieved
angry	confused	frustrated	sad
anxious	contented	glad	silly
apathetic	distraught	hesitant	uncomfortable
bored	eager	humiliated	uneasy
calm	ecstatic	joyful	wishful
cautious	elated	nervous	
comfortable	excited	proud	

My top five:

1. _____
2. _____
3. _____
4. _____
5. _____

Probes

1. How can you reframe these feelings—change the negative into potential positive—when adopting an attitude of opportunity?
2. To what extent are these feelings irrational or unreasonable? Is it possible that some may reflect fears or discomfort that you could learn to manage? Give an example of what you might do.

DEVELOP YOUR RECOVERY SKILLS

Customer service is easy when nothing goes wrong. However, a study by the Technical Assistance Research Program (TARP) estimates that approximately one in every four purchases results in some form of customer problem experience.[2] Yes, about 25 percent of customers are less than fully satisfied with some aspect of a given transaction. This doesn't mean the customer is spitting mad. It may simply mean that some aspect of the transaction was less than ideal from the customer's perspective.

Only about 5 percent of unhappy customers complain to the company.

Only about 5 percent of unhappy customers actually complain to someone in the company. The rest are more likely to simply grumble to others. Do the math: if 25 out of 100 customers are less than fully satisfied but only 5 actually tell anyone in the company, we have another 20 people who may, instead, tell other people. You can see how this sort of talk can be devastating to a company.

Employees often underestimate the negative ripple effects caused by even one unhappy customer. To reduce the impact of such ripples, we need to develop **recovery skills**. As the name implies, we try to recover the potentially lost customer. We can best do this by applying the following ideas:

Feel Their Pain

The first step in developing recovery skills is to recognize that upset customers are likely to be disappointed, angry, frustrated, or even in pain, and they blame you to some extent. Typically, they want you to do some or all of the following:

- Listen to their concerns and take them seriously
- Understand their problem and the reason they are upset
- Share their sense of urgency; get their problem handled quickly

- Compensate them or provide restitution for their dissatisfaction or inconvenience
- Eliminate further inconvenience
- Treat them with respect and empathy
- See that someone is punished for the problem (sometimes)
- Assure them the problem will not happen again (to them or others)

You may not need to do all of these things in every situation, but typically the upset customer requires several of them. Feel their pain.

Do All You Can to Resolve the Problem

Be certain that you have a clear understanding of the customer's concerns or needs. Ask appropriate questions to clarify exactly what the problem is, but don't interrogate. Phrases such as "Help me understand" or "Can you tell me exactly what happened" convey a sense that you are genuinely interested in helping.

Ask for clarification of customer concerns but don't interrogate.

Once the nature of the problem is clear, move to fix it as expeditiously as possible. Customers appreciate any efforts you expended to solve their problem quickly. If a product needs to be replaced, do it now. If something needs to be repaired (or repaired again), give a high priority to scheduling such repairs. If a delivery has to be rescheduled, do it immediately and confirm it with the customer.

Share the customer's sense of urgency. People will appreciate anything you can do, especially if you can do it quickly.

Go Beyond: Offer "Symbolic Atonement"

Although this sounds like a religious term, we are really talking about something more down-to-earth. *Symbolic atonement* simply means giving something to the customer to make up for the problem they have had. Often it cannot fully repair the damage, but it symbolically indicates that you are trying. It's the "something extra" you give to appease the customer and help win him back.

This atonement is called symbolic because, in some cases, you cannot fully repay the customer. For example, if a person complains about having to wait 15 minutes on hold, you cannot give her back those 15 minutes. But you can give some token that recognizes her inconvenience. You cannot fully repay a customer who has to take time and energy to return a faulty product, but you can give him something to express your appreciation that he went to the trouble.

Give the upset customer some symbolic repayment for their problem.

What other kinds of things can we do to make up for customer problems? Chapters 10 through 12 of this book will deal in much more depth with this topic. Meanwhile, to give you a little idea of what I mean, here are a few possible ideas that could be seen as going the extra mile in the eyes of a complaining customer.

- *Offer to pick up or deliver the goods to be replaced or repaired.* Auto companies got a lot of mileage out of offering to pick up recalled cars for product defects rather than have customs bring them in.
- *Give a gift of merchandise to repay for the inconvenience.* The gift may be small, but the thought will be appreciated. Things like a free dessert for the restaurant customer who endures slow service or extra copies of a print job to offset a minor delay are examples. It's the thought that counts.
- *Reimburse for costs of returning merchandise such as parking fees, etc.* Mail-order retailers often pay all return postage fees to reduce customer annoyance and inconvenience.
- *Acknowledge the customer's inconvenience and thank him or her for giving you the opportunity to try to make it right.* A sincere apology can go a long way. Make the wording of the apology sincere and personal. Say "I'm sorry you had to wait," rather than "The company regrets the delay." Empathy can be expressed with statements like, "I know how aggravating it can be to . . ." or "I hate when that happens, and I'm sorry you had to go through . . ."

> If you don't have the authority to do what's needed to save the customer, become his or her advocate. Go to bat for the customer with your boss.

- *Follow up to see that the problem was handled.* Don't assume the customer's difficulty has been fixed unless you handled it yourself and have checked with the customer to see that the fix held up.

You may not have the authority to do all of these things (although many of these cost practically nothing). But you can go to bat for the customer with your boss. Just being the customer's advocate can help reduce much of the problem. If all goes well, you should feel a genuine sense of satisfaction after handling an unhappy or irate customer.

Look Back and Learn from Each Situation

When the customer situation has cooled, you may want to review it with an eye toward improving your skills. Think where you used your recovery skills, and ask questions like these:

- What was the nature of the customer's complaint? Was it generated primarily by value, systems, or people?
- How did the customer see the problem? Who was to blame; what irritated the customer most; why was he or she angry or frustrated?

SERVICE SNAPSHOT

MarkingProfs.com Recovers a Lost Customer

A few years ago I subscribed to an online newsletter called Marketing Profs. After several months of use, I decided it wasn't particularly useful to the research I was doing at that time. I noticed that I was being billed a small monthly charge on my credit card, but didn't think much about it until I recently tried to log in. When the system wouldn't let me in, I emailed the publisher. To my amazement, I received a prompt, friendly, and personal reply. Here is my original email and their response:

My Original Message:

From: *drtimm@aol.com*

Sent: Sun, 12 Feb 2006   20:12:38 -0600

To: *support@marketingprofs.com*

Subject: Question/Comment from General Website Form

I am unable to access this site despite being billed every month. It's been a while since I tried, but I need it now.

I received the following response *within an hour* from their "Customer Service Samurai":

From: *support@marketingprofs.com*

To: *drtimm@aol.com*

Subject: MarketingProfs access

Date: Sun, 12 Feb 2006 20:57:22 -0600

Hi, Paul—

It looks like you hit the "unsubscribe" link in one of our emails many moons ago. That removed you from our member list, but back then, it didn't actually stop your monthly Premium billing. I'm not sure how that could have happened.

I wish I could reverse all of those charges, but our credit card system won't let me issue credits on transactions that are more than 90 days old. Here's what I'm going to do for you instead:

1. I'm reinstating your membership. Your password is still xxxyzz.
2. I'm canceling your monthly Premium status so that the billing will stop.
3. I'm upgrading you to a Premium Plus member (normally $199/year).

Now you will have access to ALL of our Premium content on the website, including our virtual seminars. You'll start receiving the newsletter again, as well as announcements about upcoming seminars. Our next one is on Thursday, and it's about search engine optimization.

Read about that seminar here:

http://www.marketingprofs.com/newprem/library/default.asp

Your Premium Plus membership is good through February 12, 2007. I hope this arrangement is satisfactory, and I'm very sorry about the glitch with your old membership.

Contact me directly if there's anything else I can do for you!

Regards,

Shelley Ryan
Customer Service Samurai
www.MarketingProfs.com
Premium hotline @ (888) 572–7934

Needless to say, MarketingProfs did everything right. They responded promptly, explained and solved the problem, and offered symbolic atonement in the form of the Premium Plus membership. Well done, Shelley.

- How did you see the problem? Was the customer partially to blame? What did you say to the customer that helped the situation?
- What did you say that seemed to aggravate the situation?
- How did you show your concern to the customer?
- What would you do differently?
- Do you think this customer will do business with you again? Why or why not?

Making careful notes of your responses to these questions can build your confidence and professionalism.

Understand What Happens If the Customer Is Still Not Satisfied

Often you can creatively recover an unhappy customer, but this is not a perfect world and people are not always rational, so sometimes you too get upset. Working with customers involves what organizational researchers call **emotional labor**. This term means we sometimes need to do things that we don't much feel like. For example, our job may call for us to be upbeat and pleasant even when we don't feel that way (and we all have our less-than-chirpy days). Professionalism requires that we do everything possible to avoid letting out our anger or frustrations on customers.

The key things to remember are:

- *If you try your best to satisfy the customer, you have done all that you can do.*
- *Don't take it personally.* Upset people often say things they don't really mean. They are blowing off steam, venting frustration. If the problem was really your fault, resolve to learn from the experience and do better next time. If you had no control over the situation, do what you can, but don't bat your head against the wall.
- *Don't rehash the experience with your coworkers or in your own mind.* What's done is done. Recounting the experience with others probably won't make their day any better, and rehashing it to yourself will just make you mad. You may, however, want to ask another person how they would have handled the situation.

Building service skills is an ongoing professional activity. Looking back on both positive and negative experiences can be very fruitful in providing guidance for future actions. Learn from your successes and your failures.

ANOTHER LOOK

Customer Complaints and Types of Customers

Typical companies are likely to face at least five types of complainers. Each type is motivated by different beliefs, attitudes, and needs. Consider the following definitions of the types of complainers, how one might respond to them, and the danger of not handling complaints effectively.

The Meek Customer. Generally, will not complain.

Response: Must work hard at soliciting comments and complaints and act appropriately to resolve complaints.

The Aggressive Customer. Opposite of the Meek Customer. Readily complains, often loudly and at length.

Response: Listen completely, ask, "what else?" Agree that a problem exists and indicate what will be done to resolve it and when.

Danger: Being aggressive in return. The Aggressive Customer does not respond well to excuses or reasons why the product or service was unsatisfactory.

The High-Roller Customer. Expects the absolute best and is willing to pay for it. Likely to complain in a reasonable manner, unless a hybrid of the Aggressive Customer.

Response: Is interested in results and what you are going to do to recover the customer service breakdown. Always listen respectfully and actively and question carefully to fully determine cause. Ask: "what else?" and correct the situation. Like the Aggressive Customer, the High-Roller Customer is not interested in excuses.

(continued)

The Rip-Off Customer. The goal is not to get the complaint satisfied but rather to win by getting something the customer is not entitled to receive. A constant and repetitive "not good enough" response to efforts to satisfy this customer is a sure indicator of a rip-off artist.

Response: Remain unfailingly objective. Use accurate quantified data to back up your response. Be sure the adjustment is in keeping with what the organization would normally do under the circumstances. Consider asking, "What can I do to make things right?" after the first "not good enough."

The Chronic Complainer Customer. Is never satisfied; there is always something wrong. This customer's mission is to whine. Yet, he is your customer, and as frustrating as this customer can be, he cannot be dismissed.

Response: Extraordinary patience is required. One must listen carefully and completely and never let one's anger get aroused. A sympathetic ear, a sincere apology, and an honest effort to correct the situation are likely to be the most productive. Unlike the Rip-Off Customer, most Chronic Complainer Customers will accept and appreciate your efforts to make things right. This customer wants an apology and appreciates it when you listen. Tends to be a good customer (in spite of his constant complaining) and will tell others about your positive response to his complaints. [For further thoughts and another viewpoint on the Chronic Complainer, see the following discussion.]

Source: Some of these ideas are adapted from Allen F. Wysocki, Karl W. Kepner, and Michelle W. Glasser, "Customer Complaints and Types of Customers," University of Florida Extension, Institute of Food and Agricultural Sciences; see: *http://edis.ifas.ufl.edu/pdffiles/HR/HR00500.pdf*. Accessed February 16, 2006.

HANDLE THE OCCASIONAL CUSTOMER FROM HELL

"Stubbornness is the energy of fools," says a German proverb. Sometimes we need to draw the line between upset customers with legitimate problems and excessively chronic complainers who consume our time with unreasonable demands—the dreaded "customer from hell." These folks can create emotional *hard* labor for us!

Here are some action tips for dealing with these challenging people:

Action Tip 1—Be Sure This Really Is a Chronic Complainer

Step one in dealing with such people is to be sure you've got a chronic complainer. When you've tried the normal recovery approaches and nothing seems to work, look for the following telltale signs of the CC:

- They always look for someone to blame. In their world, accidents don't happen: someone is always at fault, and it's probably you.
- They never admit any degree of fault or responsibility. They see themselves as blameless and victims of the incompetence or malice of others.
- They have strong ideas about what others should do. They love to define other people's duties. If you hear a complaint phrased exclusively in terms of what other people always, never, must, or must not do, you may be talking to a chronic complainer.
- They complain at length. While normal complainers pause for breath every now and then, chronics seem to be able to inhale while saying the words, "and another thing . . ."

Action Tip 2—Know What to Do with This Guy (or Gal)

When you are certain that you are faced with that occasional chronic complainer (they really are quite rare, fortunately), try these techniques:

- Actively listen to identify the legitimate grievance beneath the endless griping. Rephrase the complainer's main points in your own words, even if you have to interrupt to do so. Say something like, "Excuse me, but do I understand you to say that the package didn't arrive on time and you feel frustrated and annoyed?"
- Establish the facts to reduce the complainer's tendency to exaggerate or overgeneralize. If he says he "tried calling all day but as usual you tried to avoid me," establish the actual number of times he called and when.
- Resist the temptation to apologize, although that may seem to be the natural thing to do. Since the main thing the complainer is trying to do is fix blame—not solve problems—your apology will be seen as an open invitation to further blaming. Instead, ask questions like,

"Would an extended warranty solve your problem?" or "When would be the best time for me to call you back with that information?"

- Force the complainer to pose solutions to the problem, especially if he doesn't seem to like your ideas. Also, try putting a time limit on the conversation by saying something like "I have to talk with someone in 10 minutes. What sort of action plan can we work out in that time?" The object of this is to get him away from whining and into a problem-solving mode.

Action Tip 3—Take a Break, Cool Off, Reflect

High-stress customer contact employees need breaks. Emotional labor is very hard work. Its difficulty is not limited to just handling complaints. Card dealers in Las Vegas casinos receive frequent breaks because managers recognize the stress they face. They serve people who may become very emotional (high or low) and need to keep a sharp edge so that they don't become emotionally drained, thus affecting their work accuracy. Representatives who handle complaints and knotty problems may get great satisfaction out of helping people, but they do so at a fairly high emotional price.

Take a break after particularly challenging encounters. Allow yourself to cool off—to detach from the episode—and to think back on what happened with an eye to learning from it. Don't beat yourself up for what happened—that serves no useful purpose. But do learn from it.

HANDLE A NASTY COMPLAINT LETTER OR EMAIL

Today's customers don't write letters very often, but when they do it reflects a significant effort. Perhaps because they are fairly rare, a letter carries considerable impact. Letters provide a graphic and tangible reminder of a customer's dissatisfaction and have a nasty habit of appearing in your personnel file. So, it makes sense to respond to them and to document what you've done.

Email complaints are becoming increasingly common. Email has become the medium of choice for many customers. It is quick and easy, although it still requires writing—an activity that is not all that easy for many people. So we need to respect the effort expended and respond.

Respect the time and effort the complaining customer exerted.

This notwithstanding, many written messages go unanswered! You have probably had that experience yourself. Letters seem to evaporate and emails to companies have a tendency to fall into a cyber world black hole. And when they do, the unhappy customer gets much more aggravated.

So, RULE NUMBER ONE for letters and email complaints is: *answer them!*

If you choose to respond to a letter or email with a phone call (this may positively surprise your customer), be certain to have the original message in front of you and to refer to the specific points as written. If you answer a letter/email with a letter/email of your own, be certain that your message conveys an attitude of problem solving, projects goodwill, and exhibits professionalism.

Be an effective writer by applying the same human relations skills you would use in a face-to-face encounter. Specifically, be especially sensitive to people's feelings, interests, wants, and needs. Failure to do so creates unnecessary strains on a relationship. The fact that a letter or email is a hard copy of a conversation makes it especially important that it be tactful. A poorly written document will come back to haunt you.

ANOTHER LOOK
Just How Hard Can It Be?

By Sherron Bienenu, Executive Consultant

How hard can it be to answer an email, to say thank you, to simply *respond*?

Are you on the receiving end of "dead air"? Is your email box empty (well, except for spam)? Do you feed "black holes" with your work? Read and commiserate with me.

Are you guilty? *Please* read—for the sake of your career.

Just How Hard Can It Be?
A noted female author emailed me to inquire about presentation coaching before her national tour. I responded immediately. She agreed to an arrangement and suggested dates. Then, she didn't answer my next email. OR the one after that. I had apparently dropped all my work down a black

(continued)

hole. How hard would it have been to write, "Thanks, but I've decided to do something else"?

A woman I met at a networking luncheon emailed me about my training programs. I replied immediately with several options, including suggestions about other trainers. I spent about half an hour researching her question and crafting my response. She didn't bother to acknowledge receiving the information. How hard would it have been to say "thanks"?

Let's count the keystrokes:

1. Reply
2. t
3. h
4. a
5. n
6. k
7. s
8. Send

Now, how hard is that?

Don't get me started on how long it often takes to receive thank-you notes after shipping wedding gifts or giving birthday presents or hosting dinner parties—or how many people never acknowledge what you did for them at all.

A manager with the Human Resources Department of a large, national telecommunications company called to say that they had a "communications problem." They hired me to conduct an extensive communications audit. At the end of the process, I submitted a report that included several recommendations, but the first two (and significantly largest) were:

1. Return your phone calls.
2. Answer your emails.

Really.

I could go on and on. Okay, I will go on and on. My husband and I took my mother to special buffet brunch at Marriott Hotel on Mother's Day—her choice. Brunch was, well, adequate. On the way out, there were three staff people at the door with no other guests around. I said, "Thank you." None of the three even acknowledged us. First of all, they should have been the ones to express their appreciation. If they were a bit classier, something like "Thank you for choosing the Marriott for your Mother's Day celebration" would have been appropriate. Being ignored was not. How hard would it have been to thank us?

Another one of my pet peeves: The retail clerk who never meets your eyes but takes your money, hands over a receipt, and then mutters, "There you go." How much effort goes into an additional "thanks"? One small syllable. I often find myself saying thank you to them, to which they too

often say "no problem." Gee, I didn't realize I had potentially been a problem.

One last story really disappoints me. A former colleague and mentor (whom I have often used as a role model and positive example in books and speeches) wrote to ask me about suggestions for improving the business communications program at his university. Over several emails and a telephone conversation, we discussed one or two visits and maybe a speaking engagement. Then all conversation stopped. No return call or email. Nothing. How hard would it have been to tell me that they decided to make other plans, to pursue other options? He's not my role model any longer. And I checked his Web site. He didn't die.

Second questions: Why the lack of common courtesy? I used to say "raised by wolves," but that's not fair to wolves. A colleague was lamenting the tacky professional dress of job applicants and cried, "Where are their mothers?" Ah, but in some cases, their mothers have no manners, either.

So How Do People Learn?

Learn by watching. Do not, however, use "watching" as an excuse ("No one sends thank-you notes anymore!"). Watch the right people, the successful people, and the people who make you feel good about yourself when you are with them. They are usually the people who respond to you, acknowledge you, give you credit, and thank you.

I hear other excuses coming: "She makes me feel inferior because she does everything well," and "he makes me uncomfortable because he remembers so much about me." Did you ever consider that they do their homework to learn about you or work a little harder to do things well?

Yes, it takes hard work to produce great work. It takes some effort to initiate a small act of kindness. It takes a *little* effort to remember a birthday and send a free e-card. It takes very *little* effort to answer an email. It takes almost *no effort at all* to say those two little words: "Thank you."

If you have been cheering my viewpoint throughout this column, then you probably do respond and do say thank you. Please understand that knowing you and doing business with you is a pleasure—for everyone. We all appreciate the time you take and the work you do. It makes us feel good that you are conscientious about your relationships. We will work harder for you because you treat us right. Thank you.

Source: Sherron Bienvenu, PhD, Communication Solutions Newsletter, June 2005. See *www.ChinUp.net*. Reprinted with permission.

USE HUMAN RELATIONS SKILLS TO CONVEY APPROPRIATE TONE

Let's consider a few principles of human relations with an eye toward how these might apply in phrasing messages to unhappy customers. The first and perhaps most basic principle concerns the other person's self-interest.

People Are Strongly Interested in Themselves

It is the nature of the human being—and all other known creatures, for that matter—to be concerned with and motivated by their own personal needs, wants, and interests. This self-centeredness, or egocentricity, is normal and is not particularly harmful unless carried to the extreme, where it overwhelms any caring about others. People are often socially conditioned to not say it out loud, but there is constant background music in everyone's mind that says "what's in this for me?"

> Every person's primary motivation is self-interest.

When people speak or write, they reflect this egocentricity in their language. Every fifth word written or spoken by a human being is "I" or one of its derivations—*me, mine, my, we, ours, us*.

The point here is that service providers can turn this egocentricity into an advantage if they recognize the customer's needs. Effective communicators learn to express concern and appreciation for the views of others in all their messages.

> You can turn a person's natural egocentricity into an advantage by recognizing his or her needs.

People Prefer Receiver-Centered Messages

One important way to reflect consideration for another person is by phrasing your message in terms of that person's viewpoint. Expressing the appropriate viewpoint involves much more than just selecting certain keywords. A genuine receiver viewpoint causes the tone of a letter or email to reflect a sincere interest in the other person. Self-centered writers and talkers think of themselves first. Receiver-oriented writers think of and convey their messages in terms of what the message receiver wants or needs.

> The receiver-oriented communicator thinks of the other person first.

One "red flag" that you should look for are the words *I, me, my*, or the plural *we, us, our* found in abundance in your messages. Second or third person (*you*, or the impersonal, *one*) often conveys more receiver interest and objectivity.

Please don't conclude that you should try to eliminate the use of "I" and its variations. To do so may be impossible in some cases. In other cases, your efforts may result in rather tortured syntax and excessive wordiness. Besides, the use of *I, we*, or *me* does not always indicate a self-centered viewpoint. For example, the person who says, "I hope you will be happy with this product," is not really violating a receiver viewpoint even though the sentence begins with the word "I." The overall tone and sense of caring for the other person is far more important than simply avoiding the use of first-person pronouns.

Look at the following sample sentences and see the difference in the tone of the **receiver-oriented** version compared to the "**I-centered**" one:

I-Centered	Receiver Viewpoint
We require that you sign the sales slip before we charge this purchase to your account.	For your protection, we charge your account only after you have signed the sales slip.
I have been a sales professional for 22 years.	My 22 years' experience as a sales professional provides a strong background in understanding customer concerns.
I am sending your report back to you for an update.	So that you may update this report to the most current version, it is being returned to you.
I'd like to show you this life insurance plan.	As a young father, you'll be interested in a life insurance plan tailored to families with small children and a limited budget.
I need you to fill out the application form and get it back to me.	As soon as you can complete the application form, we can get you.

Phrasing ideas in terms of the receiver's viewpoint conveys an interest in the other person and recognizes a principle of good human relations.

PEOPLE WANT TO BE TREATED AS INDIVIDUALS

We can improve the tone of communication by phrasing our information as though talking to individuals, rather than groups. A personally addressed business letter, for example, singles out a reader for individual attention. Such a letter conveys a more sincere regard for the specific person than one addressed to "Dear Customer" or "Dear Fellow Employee."

Avoid the "**blanket tone**"—attempting to talk to people as a group rather than as individuals.

When a message makes a person feel lost in the crowd, the blanket tone is responsible. For example, consider the blanket tone in the excerpts below:

Blanket Tone	More Personal Tone
When a thousand requests are received from prospective customers, we feel pleased. These requests show that our product is well received.	A copy of the booklet you requested is being sent to you today. Thank you for requesting it.
The cooperation of our charge customers in paying their accounts is appreciated. By paying on time, they allow us to give better service.	I certainly appreciate your paying the account. Your prompt payment allows us to give you better service and keep prices down.

Strive to express ideas in terms of the individual's benefit. One way to do this is through direct address, or "this means you!" statements. Each day we see examples of this approach in television and radio commercials. The announcer "personally" addresses each of the several million people who may be listening and attempts to make each one feel that he or she is spoken to as an individual. Direct address shows your receivers how your message applies to them and how it can meet their individual needs in some way.

PEOPLE WANT POSITIVE INFORMATION

Positive language often conveys more information than negative language. It also tends to be more upbeat with a more pleasant tone. Rather than telling a person what is *not* or what you *cannot* do, focus on the positive—what *is* or what you *can* do. If you say, "I *cannot* give cash refunds on sale merchandise," it conveys only negative information. It does not say what you can do; it only rules out one of the possibilities. On the other hand, the positive statement "I can arrange to have the product exchanged for another model that may better your needs" conveys more specific and positive information.

Positive language also has a more pleasant ring to the ear. Yet many common negative phrases still creep up in customer service, such as:

We *regret* to inform you that we cannot . . .

We have received your *claim* . . . [*claim* has a negative connotation for most people]

Your *failure* to maintain the servicing schedule . . .

We *regret* that we cannot permit . . .

To illustrate the difference in tone between positive and negative word choices, here is an example: A corporate executive wrote to a local civic group that asked if they could use the company's meeting facilities. To soften the refusal, however, the executive decided to let the group use a conference room, which might be somewhat small for its purpose, but was probably better than no room at all. Unfortunately, the executive was not sensitive to the effects of **negative wording**. She wrote:

We regret to inform you that we cannot permit you to use our company training room for your meeting, because the Beardstown Ladies' Investment Club asked for it first. This group has a standing date to use our place the third Thursday of every month. We can, however, let you use our conference room, but it seats only 25.

A review of the message clearly brings out the negative words (*regret, cannot, seats only 25*) first, while the otherwise positive message (you can use the conference room) is drowned out.

A more positive way of addressing the same situation would be this tactful response:

Although the Beardstown Ladies' Investment Club has already reserved our company training room for Thursday, we would like to suggest that you use our conference room, which seats 25.

No negative words appear in this version. Both approaches yield the primary message of denying the request and offering an alternative, but the **positive wording** does the better job of building and holding goodwill for the company.

Let's look at some examples of negative and positive sentences. Note the tone of each. (The negative words are in italics.)

Negative Wording	Positive Wording
• You *failed* to give us the part number of the muffler you ordered.	• So that we may get you the muffler you want, will you please check your part number on the enclosed card?
• We *regret* to inform you that we must *deny* your request for credit.	• For the time being, we can serve you only on a cash basis.
• You were *wrong* in your conclusion, for paragraph three of our agreement clearly states . . .	• You will agree after reading paragraph three of our agreement that . . .
• We *cannot* deliver your order until next Wednesday.	• We can deliver your order on Wednesday.
• You are *not* allowed to park in the employee lot but must use designated visitor spots.	• You are welcome to park in our visitor's lot.

SERVICE SNAPSHOT

Let's Treat Our Guests Like Criminals

The following notice was placed in the information folder at an Atlanta motel. Talk about negative wording!

[PRICE LIST, IF ITEMS ARE STOLEN FROM THE ROOM!!!!!!!]

25 INCH TV = $275.00

REMOTE CONTROL = $7.00

COFFEE MAKER = $25.00

RADIO ALARM CLOCKS = $17.00

HAIR DRYERS = $22.00

ICE BUCKET = $6.00

IRON = $28.00

IRONING BOARD = $25.00

BLANKETS = $25.00

BEDSPREADS—King = $75.00 Queen = $65.00 Full = $55.00

SHEETS—King = $18.00 Queen = $15.00 Full = $13.00

MICRO/FRIDGE = $290.00

PHONE = $30.00

INTERNET CORDS = $7.00

Probes

1. What negative message does this convey to guests?
2. Don't you think $275 for a cheap TV is a little high?:)

PEOPLE DON'T LIKE ABRASIVE PEOPLE

Assertive behavior and abrasiveness are different. To be assertive is to be pleasantly direct.

If you tend to have a somewhat abrasive personality, it can hurt the tone of your messages. **Abrasiveness** refers to an irritating manner or tone that sounds pushy or critical. To determine if you tend to have an abrasive personality, you might ask yourself questions such as these:

The abrasive personality will tend to communicate in a manner that can be irritating to others. Try to recognize in yourself whether you have a strong need to control or dominate other people or a tendency to have a knee-jerk reaction to things others may say. If you suspect that you do, it would be important for you to make an extra effort to soften the tone of your communications.

Keep in mind that there is a major difference between being abrasive and being assertive. Assertiveness simply means that you express your feelings and observations in a normally phrased manner that is nonthreatening to other people. For example, instead of saying to someone, "You don't make any sense," the assertive person would say, "I'm having a difficult time understanding what you're saying." Or rather than saying, "Deadbeats like you burn me up," the assertive person might say, "People who consistently make late payments cause us a lot of extra work and lost revenue." Few people get offended by the assertive individual. Indeed, one definition of assertiveness is "being pleasantly direct."

Assertiveness means being pleasantly direct.

UNDERSTAND THAT ASSERTIVE BEHAVIOR IS NOT AGGRESSIVE BEHAVIOR

Many people confuse assertiveness with aggressiveness. Aggressive behaviors differ in the following ways:

1. *Aggressors communicate from a position of superiority.* Aggressive people feel that they know best or must get their way at almost any cost. They see communication situations as win-lose, meaning that they either get their way or they have lost. And if they lose, someone else won! The idea of compromise or a decision whereby all parties benefit or win is foreign to them.
2. *Aggressors can be indirect, manipulative, or underhanded.* The aggressive communicator may not be the guy or gal with the big mouth. Sometimes aggressive people use tricks and manipulation such as false emotion or acting false roles designed to get their way.
3. *Aggressors set themselves up for retaliation.* Aggressive communicators eventually face adversaries. By being less than authentic, they spin webs of deception that get more and more confusing. Like habitual liars, they eventually lose track of what they told whom.
4. *Aggressors use a lot of judgmental or emotionally charged terms for emphasis.* The aggressive communicator thinks that strong language is clear but fails to see how it can create barriers to understanding. Emotional language almost always generates emotionally worded responses.

LOOK INSIDE

Do You Have an Abrasive Personality?

- Are you often critical of others? When you supervise others, do you speak of "straightening them out" or "whipping them into shape"?
- Do you have a strong need to be in control? Must you have almost everything cleared with you?
- Are you quick to rise to the attack, to challenge, to say no?

- Do you have a strong need to debate with others? Do your discussions often become arguments?
- Do you regard yourself as more competent than your peers? Does your behavior let others know that?
- Do you have a "short fuse" that causes you to lose your temper?

People with assertive behaviors avoid these problems by being honest and authentic. They are based on beliefs such as the following:

1. *One should have high self-respect for one's own ideas and abilities.* Assertive communicators know that they are valuable. Their time, talents, and efforts are to be respected. They take a back seat to no one, although they do recognize and respect other people's different abilities.

2. *It is important to respect other people.* They see people as having a wide range of experiences and know that we can all learn something from another person. They know that organizational titles or social status do not guarantee people a right to the best ideas. People need people and can gain much from others.

3. *Win-win solutions can be found for many problems.* The purpose of communication is to create understanding, not to beat out another person. Conflicts or challenges need not be couched in win-lose terms. A fresh perspective or creative twist can often be found to create solutions that leave no one as a loser.

4. *Consensus is best created by direct and honest expression of points of view.* The assertive person wins by influencing, listening, and negotiating, not by manipulating.

5. *Honest, open relationships eliminate the desire for retaliation or distrust.* Communication does not get tangled in a web of game playing. Openness begets openness. People are more comfortable with assertive communicators. They can be trusted.

6. *Emotionally charged language is seldom effective.* Using strong, judgmental words hampers the resolution of problems or the creation of understanding. Neutral, descriptive terms are better. They will not turn listeners off.

Rather than relying on assertive and aggressive communication, some people are simply passive. They communicate ineffectively because they do not really care much—they are *apathetic.* They have chosen to stay out of a particular discussion. Do not confuse passiveness with assertiveness.

ANOTHER LOOK

Calming Hostile Customers

A hostile, angry reaction usually follows a certain pattern if it is handled skillfully. This pattern is called the **hostility curve**, illustrated in Figure 9.1. It is important to thoroughly understand each step of the hostility curve:

1. Most persons are reasonable much of the time. They function at a *rational level.* At this level, you can reason with them about things.

2. When irritations pile up or a specific incident provokes a person, he or she will *take off*, blowing off steam, possibly becoming abusive, and in general expressing a lot of hostility. Once the person leaves the rational level, there is no use trying to get the person to be "reasonable."

3. This taking-off stage cannot last forever. If not provoked any further, the hostile person just runs out of steam and begins to *slow down.* He or she may feel embarrassed for making a scene.

4. At this point, you can say something *supportive*, such as, "Things can be awfully frustrating when you're under so much pressure" or "I know this has been an upsetting experience for you." In addition, you must be supportive in your nonverbal behavior. Being supportive does not necessarily mean agreeing, but it does mean letting the other person know that you understand his or her feelings.

5. Your supportive comments will usually help the hostile person *cool off.* He or she can come back down to the rational level.

6. Once the person has returned to the rational level, you can begin to *problem solve* with him or her about what caused the anger. Persons are in a mood to problem solve when they are rational, not when they are at the top of the hostility curve.

Probes

1. Why is it important to help an upset customer cool off before trying to solve the problem?

2. How can you best help him or her through the hostility curve? What specific things could you say? What should you avoid saying or doing?

(continued)

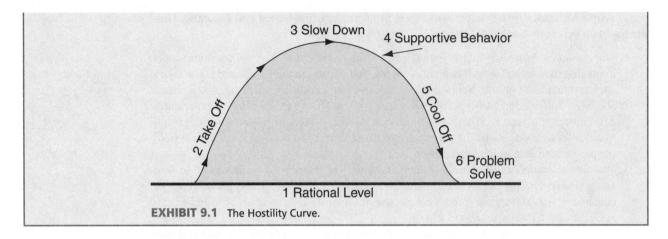

EXHIBIT 9.1 The Hostility Curve.

A FINAL THOUGHT

Customer complaints are opportunities for building customer loyalty. Sure, complainers can be annoying, but they can also be your best friends. They can point out ways to improve and strengthen your business like no one else will. That's valuable intelligence for the competitive battlefield. Use it to recover the potentially lost customer, and, in doing so, improve your business and your career success.

Summary of Key Ideas

- Customer retention requires positive attitudes toward problem solving but not necessarily an oversimplified "customer is always right" mind-set.
- The key issue in customer disputes is not who is right or wrong, but rather how all parties can cooperate to solve the customer's concerns.
- A customer complaint is an opportunity to cement a relationship and create customer loyalty.
- Recovery skills are necessary to career success and will be regularly used in business.
- The key skills in recovery involve feeling the customer's "pain," doing all you can to resolve the problem, and then going the extra step via "symbolic atonement."
- After doing your best to deal with a customer problem, it is useful to review the episode and learn from it.
- The best way to handle the occasional chronic complainer is to understand his or her motives and then get the person to propose an acceptable solution.
- Effective communication uses human relations principles such as receiver self-interest, receiver-centeredness, individual treatment, and positive information.
- Abrasiveness is a drawback to customer relations, while assertiveness leads to better problem resolution.

Key Concepts

abrasiveness
aggressive behavior
assertive behavior
attitude of opportunity
blanket tone

chronic complainers
customer recovery
customer retention
defection interviews
emotional labor

hostility curve
positive and negative
 wording
receiver-oriented and
 I-centered messages

recovery skills
second life cycle
symbolic atonement

Reviewing the Facts

1. In customer disputes, who is right or wrong is not the key issue. What overriding issue is more important?
2. What are the three important steps needed to recover the potentially lost customer?
3. What are some of the telltale signs of a chronic complainer? What special customer service techniques can be used when you are faced with a chronic complainer?

4. What are the three F's, and how can they be used to disarm the upset customer? What are some specific phrases you can use?

5. What human relations principles can we apply to improve our written communication?

6. Compare and contrast assertive versus aggressive behavior.

Applying the Ideas: Defusing and Recovering the Unhappy Customer

Read the following case. Then get another person to role-play the part of the unhappy customer. Practice responding to his or her concerns in a constructive manner that could lead to recovering this customer. If possible, videotape your role-play and review the tape to identify nonverbal and verbal behaviors.

Before you get into this activity, look carefully at the language used to describe the situation. What problems do you see concerning the tone? How could you express the viewpoint of the two parties in more constructive terms? When role-playing, work through the "hostility curve" in Figure 9.1.

Consider this Case

A Hot Traveler and a Hot Motel Manager

The Motel Manager's Story

A fellow from a city several hundred miles away has just checked into your motel. He gives the impression that he is a big-shot government worker. After a short visit to his room, he storms into your office, claiming his air conditioner is faulty. You have recently spent $275 to repair the unit in his room. You are certain that he must have banged it with his fist and that he is responsible for the trouble with the unit. You are not about to let him push you around.

The Traveler's Story

You have just settled into a rather dumpy motel. It is mid-August, and the temperature is 109 degrees. You flip on the switch to the air conditioner; there is a buzz, a hum, and smoke starts to pour out of the vents of the air conditioner. After several bangs with your fist, the smoke vanishes, but the air conditioner will not work. You are hot and tired, and wish you had selected a better motel. At that point, you storm into the motel manager's office and inform him that he runs a cheap, dumpy, and poorly-cared-for motel. You demand that he rush immediately to your room and repair your air conditioner.

Consider this Case

American Express Delta SkyMiles Credit Card

The following letter was sent to American Express corporate offices.* Read the letter and evaluate it in terms of the feedback it gives to AmEx. Then suggest a plan of action for a reply.

Subject: Why My Wife And I Plan To Discontinue Our Skymiles Platinum Cards

We thought it may be of some interest to you to know why we plan to drop our cards after many years. As frequent flyers (Platinum level on Delta) we use our AmEx cards extensively, but no longer feel it is a good value.

The most significant reason is that the "benefit" of getting your companion ticket is far more of a hassle than it is worth. My wife,

Marleen, tried to use this certificate a few weeks ago and quickly found that

1. The restriction on the classes of service eligible was so strict that we could get virtually no flights even though booking many months in advance. (We were not trying to get to an exotic location—a simple Salt Lake City to JFK was all we sought. The only option was to connect through Atlanta on the way home despite several available non-stop flights a day between these Delta hubs.)

2. When Marleen finally agreed to the less convenient flights, she was then told that she would have to go to the Salt Lake City airport within 24 hours of booking to get the ticket. Delta has

closed virtually all its in-city ticket offices and this run to the airport would have meant a 2-hour round trip plus time, parking, and waiting in line. This to save a few hundred dollars—and to take advantage of the best benefit of our $130 annual fee ($260 for us both, of course).

3. While trying to arrange these flights, the AmEx reps were amazingly unhelpful—consistently passed the buck back to Delta and projected a low level of caring. Booking the transaction took more than an hour—and still resulted in a poor flight schedule and the aforementioned half-day trip to the airport.

4. Although SkyMiles are nice—we get zillions of them anyway since we each fly to Europe 3–4 times a year and make many additional flights. Besides, these "award miles" are very tough to spend as well—but that's not your fault. That is part of Delta's relentless efforts to make air travel worse and worse.

5. Alternative credit cards provide much better return with far less hassle. We are leaning toward another card which gives up to 3 percent cash back and has no fee. Since my wife and I bill about $30,000 a year each—this cash back deal looks good! And we can actually *use* cash, as contrasted to the companion ticket.

So, the question for us is, "Why should we pay $130 in annual fees to get benefits we cannot use and uncaring service?"

If you have any interest in keeping us as customers and/or have a better deal, we'd like to hear about it. Otherwise, we will say sayonara when renewal time comes about. And, I will suggest dropping the SkyMiles cards to my clients and friends as well.

I realize that not all these problems are caused by you. Delta Airlines' customer accommodations have been abysmal. But, you folks need to sweeten the deal. Customers have alternatives and your offering is no longer competitive, in my opinion.

We hope to hear from you, but won't hold our breath. I can be reached at the above address or via email at Claude@ooooooo.com

Sincerely,

Dr. Claude Barnes
Dr. Marleen Tobin-Barnes

P.S.: We offer such feedback to companies we care about. If we didn't like AmEx, we would just dump you. But you used to be pretty good.

Probes

1. What particular problems does this case pose? Do you want to keep these customers?
2. Assume you have some authority to provide this customer with a better deal. What might that look like?
3. What media would you use to respond to this letter? Why?
4. Outline the message you would give back to this customer.

—————
*Note this is a real letter. Only the names have been changed.

Notes

1. Some material in the opening paragraphs was excerpted from Nick Wrenden, "How to Recover Lost Customers," May 5, 2003. See *http://www.smartbiz.com/article/articleprint/ 112/-1/7*.

2. TARP research is cited in J. R. Shannon, "The Components Customer Service: A New Taxonomy," *Journal of Customer Service in Marking & Management*, 2(1), 1996, p. 6.

PART 4

LIFE: Expectations

The fourth letter in our acronym LIFE is **E** for "expectations." Understanding the role of expectations in creating and maintaining customer relationships is crucial to service success. Psychological theory supports the notion that customers whose expectations are exceeded in some positive ways may feel some need or desire to give back—to strengthen their relationship with the person or organization that seems to be giving them more than anticipated.

The next three chapters focus on ways we can exceed customer expectations. Chapter 10 discusses the concept of value and ideas for creating an enhanced sense of value for customers. Since virtually all products and services today have an informational component—some information accompanies them or are critical to the product—Chapter 11 deals with ideas for exceeding expectations in the realm of information. Chapter 12 addresses opportunities for exceeding expectations in convenience and timing—an area that is often cited as a turnoff when customer needs are not met.

When you have studied these chapters, you will be better equipped to create "A-plus service"—customer service that surprises and delights customers. This is a critical key to creating customer loyalty.

CHAPTER **10**

Exceed Expectations with Value

Build Customer Loyalty with A-Plus Perceptions of Value

Napoleon's habit of giving medals to troops instead of extra money gave him the value of saving money, but also gave them prestige. All sorts of honors provide the same sort of value, both in terms of self-image and also the effect on others. An empty value is no longer an empty value if it affects things.

—EDWARD DE BONO

After reading this chapter, you should be able to

1. Define what constitutes A-plus value in the minds of customers.

2. Understand intrinsic and associated value which can affect a customer's loyalty to you or your company.

3. Apply seven categories of actions to enhance the customer's perception of value.

The Way It Is . . . Finding Value in Unusual Places

A few years ago a *Wall Street Journal* article sang the praises of the public toilets in Suwon, South Korea. The city is so proud of its exceptional toilet facilities that it gives weekly tours to show them off to tourists. The public restroom is inside a building with the sloping wooden roof of a traditional Korean pavilion. Guests are invited to try out its heated toilet seats, examine the sinks, and take pictures . . . Violin music plays in the background, and small paintings of the Korean countryside hang on the walls . . . The facilities have bouquets of flowers (both fake and genuine), automatic faucets, sliding stall doors for the disabled, and solar-powered heat. Speakers pipe in Vivaldi's "Four Seasons," Korean palace music, or recordings of chirping birds.[1]

The perception of value is highly subjective, but people seem to know value when they experience it. While long-term durability or utility is often seen as the ultimate value, companies generally cannot wait the many years needed for their customers to recognize that long-term value. What companies can do is focus on creating an enhanced *sense* or *perception* of customer value, just as the city of Suwon did with its exceptional toilet facilities.

DEFINE A-PLUS VALUE: WHAT IT IS

Poor value is a major source of customer turnoffs, along with ineffective systems and inappropriate people skills. On the other hand, exceptional value or, more accurately, exceptional *perceptions of value* is one way to create customer loyalty. We can build customer allegiance by giving them something that exceeds what they anticipate (what I call A-plus service)—an enhanced *perception* of value.

A basic definition of value is the perception of quality relative to cost.

Marketing scholars define **perceived value** as a "subjective perception of the tradeoff between multiple benefits and sacrifices, relative to competition. . . . This definition highlights not only the benefits gained, but also the sacrifices or investments that a customer makes to gain the benefits. The difference may be positive, resulting in customer perceived value, or negative, resulting in customer perceived worthlessness."[2]

Several key ideas stand out in that definition. First, value is *perceived*. This means that it is individual and personalized. What you may find to be valuable may be worthless to me, and vice versa. Second, value arises from some tradeoff between the benefits gained and the costs (sacrifices or investments) expended.

A more simplified definition of perception of value is a person's sense of the quality of a product or service (benefits it provides to us) relative to its *cost*. For example, if you purchased a cheap throw-away product, say, an inexpensive disposable camera that cost less than $10, and the picture quality was not quite up to studio quality, you probably would not be overly upset. The camera's quality, relative to its cost, is what you anticipated—you expected snapshots, not professional portraits. If, however, you spent $900 for a deluxe camera with many professional features, you would have high expectations for the quality of the pictures the camera would produce. If the pictures were no better than those produced by a cheap camera, you'd have a right to be upset. You would have a *diminished* perception of the camera's value.

Likewise, if you gave a kid a few dollars to mow your lawn and he didn't get it exactly right, you'd chalk it up to a learning experience. Your perception of value would be satisfactory—you got what you paid for, and probably what you expected. But if you hired an expensive lawn-care professional and the work wasn't up to snuff, your perception of value would likely be reduced or diminished because you didn't get what you expected, considering what you paid. You expect to get what you pay for; and the more you pay, the more you expect.

Recognize the Cost of Diminished Perceptions of Value

The history of commerce is filled with examples of how once-valuable goods diminished in value. At one time, whale oil was a valuable commodity, telegraph service was a vital service, and brick-size mobile phones were all the rage. The markets changed and the old became worthless. Sometimes even good companies let their quality slip, and customers eventually catch on to the quality deficit. A company's failure to perceive and then respond to customers' diminished perceptions of value (the opposite of A-plus) can destroy a company.

One historical example: In the 1980s and early 1990s, Volkswagen Corporation of America saw its sales drop by 90 percent—from its 1970 high of over half a million cars to less than 50,000 in 1993. What happened?

Much of VW's competitive advantage in subcompact cars evaporated when competitors (especially the Japanese manufacturers) engaged in extended conversations with their customers and used feedback received to develop appealing features. While VW engineers knew the "right" way to position a steering wheel, Japanese compacts offered adjustable tilt wheels. While VW was certain that its radios were "just fine," competitors responded to customer desires for multi-speaker stereo sound. Little automotive details like cup holders and power locks—features not really central to the core product of reliable transportation—provided a competitive advantage to companies that listened to their customers. VW didn't listen to its customers nearly enough. As a result, customers began to perceive VW as offering less value. By the early 1990s, Volkswagen of America was fighting for its life. Fortunately, VW learned from this experience and has produced a remarkable turnaround. By the late 1990s, the company had regained its traditional position as one of the most innovative and successful auto manufacturers, and the company is now solid. But it almost didn't make it after having paid a terrible price for its indifference to customer wants.

A *USA Today* "test drive" article[3] reviewing Nissan's lowest priced automobile illustrates how value expectations have risen. While, ostensibly, an automobile's primary function is to transport people from one place to another, we have all come to expect something more. The article on the new Versa model car was fairly balanced once you got past the first few paragraphs (designed to hook the reader, no doubt), which bemoaned the "riot of creaks from the instrument panel" and "the back seat that was as uncomfortably firm as a park bench," among the other negative comments. These criticisms surface despite Nissan's U.S. general manager asserting that the Versa is "one of our most trouble-free cars." Even the writer acknowledges later in the article a number of positive characteristics for this intentionally stripped down model.

The challenge for the Versa is probably not competing with other low-cost new cars but rather with comparably priced but better-equipped used cars. About a third of the article focused on what it calls "things of importance, rather than indulgence, that you sacrifice" on this vehicle. These "things of importance" are power windows, power locks, power mirrors, and the like. What are today being described as important were not long ago regarded as luxuries. Basic transportation is not enough; the expectation bar has been raised and anything lacking these kinds of features is seen as lacking in sufficient value.

Companies need to be aware of the constantly rising value bar. People demand and expect good value. The snake oil salesman may sell some product in the short-run, transaction-based business. But the likelihood of an ongoing relationship with customers who receive poor value is nil. Good value is a minimum; enhanced value is a competitive advantage.

ANOTHER LOOK

Of Wine and Corks and Perceived Value

Wine makers know that screw cap bottles are better and cheaper than the traditional cork. Yet it is impossible to change to such caps. It may be because buyers would equate screw caps with inferior wine. It may be because the whole event of wine drinking requires the cork.

How can this perception of value be changed? Marketing expert Edward deBono wrote about this challenge and explored some possible options. Among them were

- Make the screw caps look more expensive. Perhaps make them enameled or decorate them so they become collector's items.
- Sell exactly the same wine at two prices: £12 with the usual cork and £10 with a screw cap. (People would now set out to convince themselves that the cork was not that important a part of the event of wine drinking.)
- Initiate an education campaign to show that corks could go bad and could leak, whereas screw caps could not. This would be less effective than either of the other two approaches—making screw caps either dearer or cheaper—but could be combined with either.
- de Bono concludes that "it is almost impossible to delete or block a perception pattern. Another pattern needs to be set up to lead values in a different direction."

Source: Adapted from Edward de Bono, "Perceived Value: When considering value, perception can be as important as reality." See *http://www.thinkingmanagers.com/management/perceived-value.php*; downloaded March 20, 2006.

CREATE AN ENHANCED SENSE OF INTRINSIC AND ASSOCIATED VALUE

Perception of value is based on how customers view both intrinsic and extrinsic or associated factors. Understanding these factors is the starting point for creating A-plus value experiences for your customers.

Intrinsic Value of the Product Itself

Intrinsic value arises from the core product or service itself. Does it meet customer needs—do what it's supposed to do? This form of product value may not be immediately evident in some cases. We may assume a product is adequate because it seems to work, but the true extent of its value—especially its durability—may not be clear for some time. For example, a truck buyer may not fully appreciate the value until the truck has a hundred-thousand care-free miles on it. Similarly, the intrinsic value of a legal document an attorney prepared may not be fully evident until it holds up in court. The intrinsic value of a house-painting job becomes apparent only when it still looks great years later.

The first-time car buyer may be delighted with his very basic transportation (think teenager getting his first set of wheels), but this delight diminishes as the buyer comes to expect more (like power windows or locks). One man reported that he was very disillusioned with a new car because it didn't have an outside temperature indicator like his last one did. This rather insignificant (in the bigger scheme of things) feature was so annoying that the man traded the car in shortly after purchase.

In customer service training sessions your author asks participants to describe products or services that have exceeded their expectations in terms of intrinsic value. People often respond by mentioning unusually reliable products like John Deer lawn tractors, Sony TVs, Kirby vacuum cleaners, certain appliances, Craftsman® tools, and the like. Companies are also publicizing their intrinsic value. Toyota once ran a series of television commercials featuring a driver stepping out of a 10-year-old truck perched on top of a mountain. The actor looks into the camera and announces that he has over 300,000 miles on his truck. Implication: buy a new truck and it'll exceed your expectations for long-term value. More recently, Ford and Chevy are trumpeting the longevity of their trucks in advertisements, even seeking testimonial stories from long-term owners. We can all think of products with high intrinsic value that have lasted a long time and earned our brand allegiance.

Value takes on another dimension for intangible products or services. With these products, accuracy and attention to detail of the service provider may be the hallmark of value. A public utility, cable provider, or financial institution that gives customers consistently accurate, easy-to-read statements may be giving A-plus service. A repair shop that fixes things quickly and correctly at a reasonable cost will have a favorable perception of intrinsic value. The company that makes it easy for customers to contact it and then responds quickly to fix any errors or problems will also be perceived by customers as high in value.

The opposite conditions create immediate and often lasting negative perceptions of value. Electrical blackouts, phone service interruptions, and cable TV quality problems project a sense of poor reliability that can have negative repercussions on whole industries. An example: The phones stopped working at the national reservation center of LOT Polish Airlines in New York a few years ago. The airline called the phone company's problem line at 9 a.m. *Eleven hours* later, after the reservations center had closed for the day, repair technicians arrived. Before all was fixed, the center was without phone service for 33 hours. Without phones, LOT was essentially out of business, and an eleven-hour response time was, needless to say, inexcusable. The intrinsic value of the telephone company was clearly lacking.

Another often-cited example of a catastrophic example of service failures is when Jet Blue Airlines held nine planes full of passengers on the tarmac at JFK Airport for six or more hours during an ice storm in early 2007. Although other airlines experienced similar "hostage passenger" situations, the Jet Blue case got the most publicity and directly resulted in the dismissal of the company's CEO and founder.

There is a personal side to these kinds of service disasters in addition to that suffered by the customers. As the *New York Times* reported, "The founder and chief executive of JetBlue Airways, his voice cracking at times, called himself 'humiliated and mortified' by a huge breakdown in the airline's operations that has dragged on for nearly a week, and promised that in the future JetBlue would pay penalties to customers if they were stranded on a plane for too long."[4]

Stories of poor intrinsic value can be dramatic and destructive to customer relationships, but what about the advantages of excellent intrinsic value?

Credit card companies offer varying degrees of service. Associates I have talked with favor the American Express Card and Discover Private Issue. They perceive higher intrinsic value in these products for two reasons: They give airline miles or cash back, and when the customer needs to call either of these, they can speak to a live person almost immediately. Other cards linger in the wallet because, when customers have a problem, these companies force them through a maze of telephone switching that is annoying and time-consuming. Access to a live-person contact enhances the perception of intrinsic value.

Still another example of intrinsic value is the personal touch provided by some banks to their key clients (whether individuals or corporations). Each client is assigned a personal banker—a bank executive who is willing to meet personally with the client to oversee his or her financial needs. The status of having a personal banker is premium value for many people.

Associated Value

Associated (or extrinsic) value goes beyond the core product. It is associated with the product, but it is not essential to it. Associated value involves more than whether an automobile starts and drives reliably or the degree to which an Internet service provider stays up and running. It encompasses the entire customer experience with the company.

Remember that value is *perceptual.* Since perception, by definition, is different for different individuals, some people may be turned on by a company's extrinsic value efforts, while others may regard them as nothing more than what is expected, or, worse, as unnecessary fluff.

Companies need to create conditions that improve the likelihood of customers seeing extrinsic or associated value favorably. Some ways companies seek to enhance these perceptions include:

- Packaging
- Guarantees and warranties
- Goodness of product fit
- Memorability of product experience
- Uniqueness and shared values
- Company credibility
- Add-ons

In the remainder of this chapter, we will look at examples of how each of these extrinsic-value enhancers can create an A-plus situation for customers and increase the likelihood of loyalty.

SEVEN WAYS TO ENHANCE THE PERCEPTION OF VALUE

We can build customer loyalty with the creative application of the following techniques for enhancing the perception of value. These approaches, of course, may vary in effectiveness, but companies serious about customer loyalty would be wise to consider each as part of an ongoing process of offering A-plus value.

Build A-Plus Value with Packaging

Imagine going to a hardware store to buy a power drill. There you find a stack of the particular model you want. All but one of these is in its original package. What is the likelihood that you would select the one without a box? Zero, right? You will undoubtedly buy one in a box even knowing that you'll throw the box away when you get home. The box—the package—enhances the perception of value.

Packaging can enhance the perceived value of a product—or service.

Vik Wool of Iceland

While doing consulting work in Iceland, Arnie shopped for some Icelandic wool gifts for his daughters. After receiving adequate but nondescript service in several shops, he found one store in Reykjavik called Vik Wool that had particularly friendly employees and a nice selection of knitted gloves. Arnie selected two pairs and a few other small items. When the clerk rang up the goods, she wrapped each gift in a small, hand-knit sack tied with a ribbon. The little sacks were made of knitting remnants from their factory. The packaging of these inexpensive gifts far exceeded what he had anticipated. Other stores set the expectation with generic plastic bags; Vik Wool exceeds customer expectations of value with the beautiful knitted wool sacks.

A business associate occasionally passes along books he thinks will be useful. Sometimes, he simply hands off a copy of a recommended book. On a few occasions, he enhanced the value of his gift by writing a friendly note in the book or by gift wrapping it. The core product is the same (it's the same book!), but the gift-wrapped packaging and personalization enhance its perceived value.

This illustrates the "little things" principle we talked about in Part 1 of this book. Tiny differences make the extrinsic value of the product greater.

If your business sells intangibles, don't overlook possible packaging. If anything, packaging enhancements can be even more powerful when they are completely unexpected. But how do we package an intangible? Here are a few examples.

A successful insurance sales representative gives his clients their policies in an attractive leather portfolio, which can be used to store other important papers. He goes a step further by engraving the client's name on the portfolio. His clients keep the leather binder for many years—the associated value of his product lives on.

If your customers receive only documents in exchange for their money (often the only tangible product associated with a service such as life insurance), give some thought to packaging these papers in an attractive or useful manner. Or add some tangible items that might relate to your services. A cellular phone company sent its best customers a road-travel gift set. It included a thermos, Starbucks coffee, and some snacks. Financial and educational institutions often give tokens of appreciation that tie in with their intangible products. For example, schools give leather notebook folders, USB jump drives, or writing instruments of various types.

Upscale department stores or boutiques have long known the value of attractive gift wrapping. Customers love it—especially customers like your author who is all thumbs when it comes to wrapping gifts. But any organization can enhance its packaging and thus increase the customer's perception of value.

Build A-Plus Value with Guarantees or Warranties

Would you be likely to see a product with a lifetime warranty as having higher value than a similar product with only a 30-day warranty? Most people do. Jack, a producer of videotape training programs, used to tell customers that these tapes were unconditionally guaranteed for 30 days. If they felt the programs did not meet their needs, they could return the videos within 30 days and get a full refund. Then he began to think about enhancing this sense of value and changed that guarantee to *forever*. If the customer ever felt the product did not meet his or her needs, it could be returned for a full refund.

Long-term or lifetime warrantees have a higher perceived value than short-term ones.

Jack found that, with the unlimited guarantee period, the percentage of goods returned was unchanged. In fact, with the 30-day guarantee, he may have actually been encouraging refund requests by setting a target date. The customer who had the product for 25 days or so may have felt some urgency to make a decision—and sometimes that decision was to send the product back. A lifetime guarantee eliminates the motivation to act now, thus reducing the likelihood the customer will return the product.

If your product has good intrinsic value, the return rates for short-term guarantees versus long-term or lifetime guarantees will be virtually equal.

Nordstrom's department stores have earned a tremendous amount of good publicity from their no-questions-asked, unconditional return policy. The oft-repeated (old) story of the fellow who returned a set of tires to Nordstrom's (a store that doesn't sell tires!) has had incredible positive ripple effects. The tale has become legend and, when written about in Tom Peters and Robert Waterman's 1982 best seller *In Search of Excellence*, caught the eye of millions of readers, many of whom are exactly the kind of customers Nordstrom's caters to. The cost of granting the request of one unreasonable customer bought incalculable advertising. Ironically, in some countries, government regulation forbids lifetime guarantees! The American catalog company Lands' End has a simple and reassuring motto for shoppers: *Guaranteed. Period.* Some short-sighted competitors in Germany took Lands' End to court. They claimed this guarantee was unfair advertising and got the court to agree that this guarantee policy was "economically unfeasible" and therefore amounted to unfair competition.

That is a classic case of thinking small and not understanding the value of A-plus service. Lands' End responded to the court ruling with a set of ads in German newspapers and magazines poking fun at the ban. One ad pictured a common housefly with the caption "one-day guarantee." Another showed a washing machine, guaranteed six months. Other companies facing similar bans (Zippo lighters, Tupperware, etc.) have dropped their lifetime guarantees but are benefited from the publicity. Zippo ran ads in British papers proclaiming, "A guarantee so good the Germans banned it."[5]

Your company can quibble over guarantees or it can take advantage of A-plus value perceptions by being generous and open. Consider as a cost of doing business the occasional customer who takes unfair advantage of a generous guarantee. Pleasantly surprise the large majority of your customers by offering generous guarantee terms. Go beyond what the customer anticipates and reap the reward of customer loyalty.

Build A-Plus Value with Goodness of Product Fit

Goodness of product fit means thinking one-size-fits-*one*. Personalization, not classification into demographic groups, permits real relationship building. The danger of categorizing individuals is illustrated by a letter to the editor of *Fortune,* written by a 13-year-old girl who "often enjoys reading [the] magazine." She was responding to an article called "Girl Power!" in which the magazine described what girls her age were "into." The young lady's articulate response explained that she was not at all like the profile offered in the article. She also criticized *Seventeen, YM, Teen,* and the other magazines that think "much the way you do: that girls can be broken down into a demographic group, that our minds consist of very little more than boys, shopping, makeup, boys, clothes, and shopping."

She goes on to say, "My request to you is that if you are going to say things like this, don't. There is no movie that all girls like, there is no way we all like to dress; there is no music we all like to listen to. It's never fair to make generalizations about any group of people, be it teenage girls or middle-aged business people. Sorry to break it to you, but I am not a demographic group and I don't like your stereotypes, and that is Girl Power!"[6]

Taking the concept of goodness of fit to new levels, *mass customization* is all the rage in manufacturing. Companies are creating products just the way the customer wants them. Some clothing manufacturers can custom-make jeans to the exact measurements of individual customers. Lands' End, for example, has a feature called My Virtual Model™ on its Web site so that customers can input body dimensions and see how clothing items look on a model (*www.LandsEnd.com*). The Internet is a popular medium for custom orders. Ford Motor Co. lets buyers "build your own Ford" from a palette of options,[7] while Golf to Fit crafts custom golf clubs based on questionnaire responses. The average person can buy custom clothing at an affordable price, made-to-order music CDs, even personalized vitamins on the Net. Many economists believe that if you don't mass customize, you're going to lose business in today's marketplace.

Think of customers as individuals, not demographic groups, to enhance value through "goodness of product fit."

When companies offer menus of product characteristics for customers to select from, they can create **industrial intimacy**. This "intimacy" comes from better understanding the specific needs and personal wants of customers. Ultimately, the key is to focus on what is important to the customer and, so long as this still permits the company to make a profit, give customers exactly what they want.

Customer-relationship management, enabled by technology, gives businesses almost unlimited opportunities to personalize products for their customers. CRM software crunches an enormous amount of data and gives specific recommendations for personalizing customer contacts. Here is a hypothetical example.

Suppose that you are in a financial services business, like a consumer bank or credit union. If your organization is using CRM software, customers who call or visit your office would deal with a person who knows a great deal about them. If George Customer calls your office with a question about his mortgage, your employee would key in the customer's account number. The **intelligent systems** (sophisticated computer programs that diagnose patterns of data) would display a series of dialogues your employee could use—word for word—to explain customer options and perhaps sell additional products.

The software system gathers and digests mountains of data about the individual customer and about people like him (demographic data). The system may have information about cars he owns, their price range, and the ages of the cars. It may also factor in data about George such as the fact that he is 55 years old, he is recently divorced, his kids are grown, his mortgage is almost paid off, his Buick is four years old, and he recently changed jobs after receiving a substantial payout from his previous employer. If you were a financial institution, wouldn't you want to know this?

All this data can suggest additional products appropriate to George, thus helping build a stronger relationship. Companies provide A-plus value by offering products that fit perfectly with this customer's needs. This can be a significant win-win situation.

One large mortgage company that uses such a CRM system has had tremendous success in increasing the close rate for additional products. Previously, 4 percent of customers contacting the company purchased additional products. After implementing the system, which provides explicit prompts for customer representatives, the close rate jumped to 38 percent.[8]

The benefit of such additional sales is obvious, but the customer-service element is equally important. This marriage of technology and customer data can build relationships, industrial intimacy, and ultimately enhance customer allegiance.

It is worth noting that CRM uses various approaches to collect data. Some customers, however, balk at being forced to give companies a lot of personal information. Supermarket preferred-shopper programs, which reward customers with discounts when they allow the store to scan their coded card, are meeting resistance from people who don't want to carry a special card or who resent the deep discounts available only to those who sign up. But companies should be careful to not throw out the baby with the bathwater. Some form of CRM that helps tailor products to individual customers can be very helpful in creating A-plus value.

Sophisticated customer-contact-management products are becoming less expensive and more readily available. Even small businesses can learn more than ever about customer needs, wants, and preferences by gathering appropriate personal data. CRM systems reflect the most advanced form of technology-enhanced relationship-building. But even manual systems that make notes of customer preferences can move companies toward enhanced customer value.

To provide A-plus value, your company may need to be implementing such one-to-one customer service. People don't want to be treated like pieces of demographic data. People have unique, individual needs and wants. A-plus value is personalized value. It involves doing all you can to be sure the products or services you offer fit the needs of the individual customer, not just some large demographic group.

Build A-Plus Value with Memorable Experiences

A highlight of many a kid's birthday celebrations has been a trip to a Chuck E Cheese restaurant. These pizza emporiums are something else; they go beyond the traditional description of a restaurant. The food is adequate, but the experience is, well, something kids go nuts over. It's a carnival atmosphere, with all kinds of exciting sights and sounds. Providing customers with an *experience* may well be the highest level of economic value.

In today's developed countries, consumers have most of the tangible goods they *need*. (Maybe not all they *want*, but what they need.) People who have benefitted from economic good fortune have about all the luxury cars, quality clothes, flat-screen TVs, and trendy coffees they can handle. (Arguably, today's middle-class folks in Western cultures live better than royalty in years past.) Even in times of temporary economic downturns, people today are using discretionary income to enjoy experiences such as entertainment, travel, cruises, spas, and wellness or retreat centers.

Smart companies are connecting with their customers through experiences. An experience occurs when the company's core products are used as props to engage individual customers in a way that creates a **memorable experience** or event. Examples of events include live entertainment at restaurants and coffee-shop chats at bookstores. Sporting events and competitions may place the company's products in the background, but the customer receives value from the event itself. Ties to the company are likely to follow. An upscale coffee shop is not just a place to get a beverage—it has become, for some people, an office/meeting place. Denise Wymore, who is a marketing consultant and author, wrote her latest book entirely at a Wi-Fi–friendly Starbucks. Says Denise:

> When I ask audiences who Starbucks targets—people don't say "coffee drinkers." Starbucks serves coffee to be sure. But they don't target coffee drinkers. They target me. I'm writing this in a Starbucks right now. I have a bottle of water (no coffee) and a chocolate dipped macaroon. Yum. I bought the water because the chalkboard sign behind the cashier said that the proceeds will go to help children in third-world countries get clean water. I support that.[9]

(We'll talk more about adding value with shared values, such as supporting clean water, in a moment.)

A word of caution, however: When creating extrinsic A-plus value using customer experiences, don't let the core product go bad. Planet Hollywood was a red-hot restaurant chain in the mid-1990s, only to crash when people realized that the glitzy experience of possible celebrity spotting was not worth eating the substandard food. The company largely forgot about its core product—the food. Experiences can enhance the sense of value so long as the core product maintains its good quality.

Even the best of associated value cannot make up for a poor core product.

Build A-Plus Value with Uniqueness and Shared Values

An enhanced sense of value can stem from a company being perceived as unique or novel. Much of this uniqueness arises from the personality or culture of your organization. Ben and Jerry's ice-cream business projects a sense of culture based on the liberal political values of its founders and its sense of civic responsibility to Vermont. (The ice-cream-plant tours are the most-popular tourist attraction in the state.) Their theme was consistent throughout the history of the company (until it was sold to a large food conglomerate) and had been the subject of books, articles, and television magazine shows.

Southwest Airlines, an airline that has maintained good customer relationships despite turmoil in its industry, continues to convey a charming quirkiness that reflects its founder, Herb Kelleher. The airline started as a scrappy little outfit and has grown into an aviation powerhouse in part because it customers like the people who work there. SWA hires people based on their upbeat attitudes. The interview process and new-employee orientation is uniquely tailored to help people fit the corporate culture. New employees engage in a scavenger hunt to find answers to company-orientation questions, for example. It is noteworthy that SWA is the one of only a few U.S. airlines to be continually profitable in the early years of this century. Upstart competitor JetBlue has similarly created a cult of fans with its customer-friendly features. (Jet Blue CEO David Neeleman once worked for Southwest and learned much from that experience.) Ben and Jerry's, SWA, Home Depot, numerous hi-tech firms, and many other companies offer their internal customers—their employees—A-plus value by inviting participation in their uniqueness and shared values. JetBlue reservations clerks work out of their homes (allowing flex-time hours) in part to honor the corporate commitment to valuing family-friendly, work–life balance. North Carolina–based SAS software offers a huge range of perks to employees (fitness centers, day care, health clinic, discounted country club, to name a few) that reduces employee turnover to low single digits in an industry where 20 percent or more of workers leave similar companies every year.

Customers will often go out of their way to support companies that share their **values**. Talk-show hosts such as Rush Limbaugh, Sean Hannity, and the late news commentator Paul Harvey have been credited with launching many popular brands because listeners who share their views feel they are getting enhanced value from companies that agree with them. Of course, the flip side to this is that customers who don't agree with the tie-in may deflect. In 2009, many companies received huge government "bailouts" that some consumers felt were unnecessary or unfair. Some customers declared they would not do business with companies that took taxpayer handouts.

> Customers gain a sense of increased value when companies or corporate sponsors support their shared values.

Political, church, civic, alumni, and charitable groups often band together to promote or support certain organizations. This bonding may range from partnering with credit-card companies to have the organization's logo on the cards, to cell phones with a hockey-team logo, to the purchase of Girl Scout cookies. The opportunity to share in an affiliation, an interest, or a cause can be an enhanced sense of value for customers and employees. On a more local basis, customers become loyal to companies that make them feel comfortable. They patronize organizations that reflect their values and preferences. A small, local bookstore with friendly, helpful employees, a comfortable atmosphere, and, perhaps, book recommendations from its staff can compete against the large book retailers. Even the enormous pricing advantage of the world's big-box discount stores cannot compete with the highly personalized camaraderie of shared values offered when well-run local businesses offer A-plus value. People do and will pay a premium for exceptional extrinsic value. The "little guy" can compete against the low-price providers if he offers something they cannot offer, some higher value.

Build A-Plus Value with Credibility

Customers also feel they are receiving extra value when dealing with companies that have exceptional **credibility**. A critical dimension of value is the *degree to which customers trust* a company or organization. Failure to follow through on commitments and other deceptive practices can (and should) damage a company. Of course, sometimes this too is perceptual. You may feel you explained a policy or guarantee to the customer adequately but he interpreted it differently. You think you communicated openly but she sees your limitations as unnecessary fine-print nitpicking. Keep pricing and restrictions simple and understandable for customers.

> Communicate clearly with customers to enhance your credibility.

While many industries are simplifying and bundling services for flat or simplified fees, the airlines are doing a poor job in this area. Their myriad of restrictions and their enormous fare discrepancies damage credibility. On any given flight, you will find passengers who have paid up to ten times as much as another passenger for the same service: transportation from point A to point B. You may be delighted with your $300 fare, while the guy next to you paid $1,000 or more, depending on when the ticket was booked and a lot of other factors. In short, the airlines' fare systems are unintelligible to their customers and foster a lack of trust. Better transparency and more understandable fares would boost the industry's credibility.

> Complicated fares and the perception of inequity among passengers hurt the credibility of airlines.

Speaking of airlines, they would do well to *avoid frequent-flyer-type fiascos*. Yes, such programs have been successful from a marketing perspective, but they have also been the source of many customer frustrations. Too often, frequent-flyer programs are confusing and are perceived as untrustworthy. While enticing passengers to fly the same airline, the promised rewards come only with a lot of strings attached. Customers who accumulate miles too often find the promised free tickets or service-class upgrades are simply not available. Further, the number of miles required for free travel is subject to the airline's discretion. One man recently paid 65,000 miles for a single coach ticket from Salt Lake City to Maui. Gone are the days when 25,000–50,000 miles got you a first-class ticket almost anywhere. The reward value had degraded.

Don't let the perceived value of loyalty incentives degrade.

What the airlines also do not freely tell is that each flight has only a few award-travel seats. They don't mention blackout dates, upgrades that cannot be offered from a certain class of tickets, and a lot of other limitations. In short, they shoot their corporate credibility in the foot with lavish promises that are too often not delivered. In fact, seats available for reward travel average about 6 percent—six seats out of a hundred. The glut of frequent-flyer points held by people has led to less value per point. An estimated 60 percent of all frequent-flyer miles are "earned" by people who don't even fly—they get them for using credit cards.[10] The airlines made a deal with the devil with their tie-ins with credit card companies and now face the need to reduce the number of seats available since such seats generate no revenue for the airline.

People have tried to redeem frequent-flyer seats by booking months in advance, only to be told that the flight was sold out. A quick check on the Web showed many empty seats on that flight. This does not help credibility. Airlines insist that they are not trying to make it hard to redeem miles for tickets, but with planes carrying record numbers of passengers, the demand for free seats far exceeds the space available. Be open and credible with pricing and restrictions or risk damaged credibility and missed opportunity to create an enhanced sense of value.

What can your business learn from the airlines? Consider the pitfalls of frequent-customer programs carefully. A company's credibility can be damaged by making inflated offers it cannot fulfill.

Following up on commitments made is also crucial to building trust with customers. A few years ago, Marcy purchased a rather pricey six-month-old used car from a dealership that touted itself as a no-dicker, full-service auto consortium. Among the many frustrations she experienced, she was given just one key to the car and promised that they would get her another because they had lost the backup. After repeated phone calls, she finally gave up, took the car to another dealership and bought the key—along with several other missing parts like the CD-changer cartridge and all the owner's manuals. She had to go to the right dealership in another city and buy the parts that were missing from her car! The aggravation of getting anything out of the original dealership became more than she could handle.

That dealership may think it "won" since Marcy quit pestering them. But the price they paid in damaged credibility returned to bite them. She takes every opportunity to tell other

---

ANOTHER LOOK

How Much Are Frequent-Flyer Miles Worth?

Traditionally, one frequent-flyer mile has been worth about 2 cents assuming that the passenger travels coach class within the continental United States (available at 25,000 miles on average) and that the average ticket price is $500. So: $500 ticket ÷ 25,000 miles = $.02 per point. One must also consider the "hassle factor" in redeeming airline miles, which may outweigh the reward. Recently, airline fares have dropped to $300 and $350 due to the rise of competitive discount airlines. Likewise, the average value of frequent flyer miles has dropped from $.02 to $1.2. Although airline fares are now believed to be increasing yet again, the value of frequent-flyer miles will remain constant due to the increased "hassle factor," which increased and stabilized in recent years.

Passengers are increasingly feeling like hostages, while the value of their hard-earned miles drops.

Source: http://wiki.smartertravel.com/index.php/Value_of_Frequent_Flyer_Miles

people (including students she teaches in her large university classes) about this poor value experience. Incidentally, that dealership went out of business.

There can be no A-plus value without credibility.

The solutions to the kinds of problems described above are to not offer incentives you cannot provide or to make good on your word. Those are the only choices.

On a more positive note, we all prefer to do business with people we can trust. A scrupulously honest handyman who fixes things around a client's house earns the right to a house key so that he can work while the client travels. He can be trusted to do good work at a fair price. Trust is a powerful form of A-plus value. It is fundamental to building loyalty.

Build A-Plus Value with Add-ons

One of the simplest ways to surprise customers or employees is to give them something unexpected—or sell them something else they may need. When a shoe-store clerk gives you a shoehorn with a pair of new shoes or when he asks if you'd like to try padded inserts or a pair of lifetime-guarantee socks, he is using this A-plus value approach. Sometimes add-ons are sold, sometimes given away. Both can be effective. A clerk at a supermarket hands customers a few chocolate kisses with the receipt, an unexpected thank-you. The hotel check-in desk has a basket of complimentary apples or a plate of freshly baked cookies. The paint-store salesperson checks to be sure buyers have caulking, sandpaper, and perhaps a drop cloth.

Add-ons may be given away or sold. Either type can have high perceived value.

Employees who receive unexpected tangible rewards experience A-plus relationships. A surprise free lunch, a few movie tickets, flowers, impromptu celebrations, and the like all build employee allegiance. SAS Corporation in North Carolina (which I mentioned above) started their extensive array of perks with a tradition of passing out M&M candies on Wednesdays. The folks who work at a Ryder truck rental location enjoy Friday afternoon barbeques. Add-ons need not be expensive. The little things principle certainly applies.

The best kinds of free add-ons are those with high perceived value and low cost to the business. For example, gas stations that give away a free car wash with fill-up are offering something that costs them a few cents (water and soap—not counting, of course, the cost of the equipment), but their customers receive a service with a perceived value of four or five dollars (often the price is printed on the coupon). Free popcorn or drinks given away with video rentals cost three or four cents but have a much higher perceived value. (Really high, when compared to the price of movie-theater popcorn!)

Obviously, this A-plus opportunity area ties in closely with its marketing counterpart, add-on sales. Marketers have long recognized the value of trying to sell current customers something else so long as they are already buying. This can backfire if it's too pushy, but most customers will not resent low-key inquiries about the need for other products. The hardware salesperson who checks with the customer to be sure he has the right tools is not going to be resented. And the company may well sell some additional products.

A very creative add-on came out of a customer service seminar a few years ago. A woman attending the session owned several quick-lube shops. When people bought a full-service oil change, she did what her competitors had been doing. She checked all fluids, washed windows, checked tire pressure, and vacuumed the car's interior. But then she had this add-on idea: She ran a CD head-cleaning disk through the customer's sound system. We all know that cleaning the CD tape player this way makes for better sound, but most people never get around to it. After running the cleaning disk, she inserted a preprinted card into the CD player noting that the heads had been cleaned courtesy of her company. This add-on cost practically nothing (truly a "little thing"), but provided a clear and distinctive A-plus for her customers.

Central to the philosophy of add-ons is the belief that you cannot give away more than you eventually receive. That is a tough concept for people to accept. But, at some philosophical level, you need to be comfortable with the belief that what goes around comes around. In fact, that is fundamental to all the A-plus loyalty-building tactics. You really will benefit from generosity. Take the leap of faith and reap the rewards of greater customer and employee loyalty.

ANOTHER LOOK

Personal Touch Service Versus the Big Box Store

Many small merchants lose sleep over loss of business to the "big box" stores—large retailers with massive buying power that attract customers with generally lower prices. So, what can the smaller business do to combat the Wal-Marts, K-Marts, Target, Home Depot, Lowes, and the like? Here are some suggestions based on exceeding customer expectations in the perception of value:

1. Offer personalization—individual attention to the customer. Create a shopper service, or "selection consultants" who assist customers with a level of individualized attention and service beyond what retail associates could offer.
2. Take personalization a step further by inviting customers to call ahead with specific details—height, weight, favorite colors, hobbies and interests, and even the amount they are willing to spend. When they arrive at the store or business, you can have prepared a custom-specified selection of merchandise to choose from.
3. If the customer already knows exactly what they want to purchase, give customers the convenience of calling your sales associates ahead of time, and have the merchandise waiting for them at the front of your store for quick pick-up.
4. E-mail "holiday idea lists" to your former customers which feature the hot items of the holiday season, or mine your customer database for buying trends, and provide specialized lists of items that might interest them.
5. Provide a shuttle service for seniors or disabled customers.
6. Offer special preparation or handling of merchandise. For example, offer to unwrap and iron a new shirt the customer purchases (most people dislike the hassle of all those pins and cardboard). A ready-to-wear shirt has higher perception of value for many customers.
7. Promote special hours to shop for preferred customers. Make this an invitation-only event (e.g., men's night at a jewelry or women's clothing store around Valentine's Day) and give these customers added comfort of shopping.
8. Devise systems for getting to know your customers as individuals. Then get creative about personalization options that the big-box retailers can't offer.

Smaller businesses have numerous opportunities to exceed customer expectation with value the big guys can't offer. Lower prices can be offset by other forms of value.

A-Plus Value and Your Employees

The principles for creating A-plus value not only work for customers but also apply to employees—internal customers. Companies with strong employee allegiance regularly use these kinds of ideas to surprise their people—to exceed their expectations with little things.

Virtually every type of A-plus value can be applied to employee relations with powerful results. Employees who receive small tokens of appreciation respond as positively as do other types of customers. Employees who enjoy the shared experience of working in a good company, who appreciate the credibility of the organization, who recognize the company's efforts to fit people to the best job for them, and who are offered unexpected value will be loyal to the company. Loyal, long-term employees make economic good sense.

Get all members of the organization thinking about ways to utilize little things to create A-plus value. The payoff in customer and employee allegiance can be enormous.

A FINAL THOUGHT

Products and services have intrinsic and extrinsic, associated value. Exceeding customer expectations with an enhanced sense of value can be a powerful way of tipping the balance in favor of your company (or you as an individual). A key term is *perception*. At some level, customers will sense that you are offering something more when you give A-plus value.

It's the little things that mean a great deal. You need not give away the business. Simply adding some of the characteristics we discussed in this chapter can provide that value-enhancing customer experience that leads to loyalty and repeat buying.

Summary of Key Ideas

- A customer's perception of value includes a product or service's internal (core) value and external or associated value. Often the associated value includes how the overall buying experience feels.
- An enhanced perception of value is likely to increase a customer's likelihood to be loyal to the company.
- While the intrinsic (core) value of a product must be satisfactory, the extrinsic (or associated) value can go a long way toward exceeding customer expectations. The kinds of things that enhance this sense of value are often little things—subtle factors that distinguish one company from another.
- Seven categories of actions that can enhance the customer's perception of value include packaging, guarantees (warrantees), goodness of product fit, "memorability" of product experience, uniqueness and shared values, company credibility, and add-ons.
- Smaller businesses can compete with the big guys by offering additional personalization—an important form of value.
- The credibility of an organization (or individual) will be impacted by its willingness to be open, honest, and trustworthy. Some manipulative attempts at buying customer loyalty (such as with frequent-user points) can lead to disappointment or a decrease in trust. A-plus value requires credibility.

Key Concepts

credibility	goodness of product fit	intrinsic value	perceived value
extrinsic (or associated) value	industrial intimacy	memorable experience	shared values
	intelligent systems		

Reviewing the Facts

1. What is the difference between intrinsic and extrinsic value? Give three examples of each from three different kinds of businesses.
2. Describe a brief example of each of the seven tactics for enhancing the customers' perception of value described in this chapter. Try to use examples other than the ones mentioned in the text. Be creative in describing what companies could do.
3. How might a company selling intangible products or services use packaging to enhance the perception of value? Come up with one or more ideas for a public utility, a bank, an insurance agency, and a government office.

4. Some people argue that experiences are the highest form of value. Defend or oppose that general position. Use examples of your own experiences, as appropriate.
5. How can smaller companies use A-plus value to better compete against large companies that have a pricing advantage? Select a small business and describe some things it could do to compete successfully. Be specific.
6. Create a list of possible add-ons for each of the following kinds of businesses. Remember that the best add-ons have a high perceived value and relatively low cost to the company. Be realistic about what these companies might be able to do to give or sell customers A-plus value.

An appliance store	A Web-based retailer of floor mats
A man's shoe store	A sporting goods store
A bank	An auto tire shop
A motel	A dentist's office
A massage therapist	A coffee shop

Applying the Ideas: Creating A-Plus Value

1. Identify three companies you do business with because you appreciate their values. Identify what values you find attractive and describe how the companies are supportive of those values. Write a brief paper summarizing these points.

2. Imagine that you are planning to open a restaurant in your home town. Write a one-paragraph description of what that restaurant will be like and describe at least five ways you would intend to exceed customer expectations in the area of value.

3. Visit at least three different businesses of the same type. For example, go to three different banks, shoe stores, office equipment retailers, auto repair shops, and so on. Write a brief paper comparing each of these similar businesses in the light of their application of the A-plus ideas we discussed in this chapter. How successful was each at enhancing their sense of value? Which (if any) of the techniques we discussed did they employ? What would you suggest they do to further their efforts to exceed customer expectations with value?

4. What do companies do to provide A-plus value for their employees? Use your Internet searching skills to discover at least five innovative ways companies enhance value for their employees.

Look for tactics that go beyond the typical compensation or benefits packages. In what creative ways do companies surprise their employees by giving A-plus value? (Hint: a good place to start may be at the *Fortune* magazine site, where they publish articles on "The Best Companies to Work For" annually.) (See, for example: *http://money.cnn.com/magazines/fortune/fortune_archive/2006/01/23/8366990/index.htm*)

Write a brief commentary on how you would react if your company were to offer such A-plus incentives. Would they be likely to make you more loyal? If you are not currently employed, how would you respond if your school offered special value incentives?

Consider this Case

Big Companies Buy Small Brands with Big Values

Even in challenging economic times, consumers have shown they are willing to pay a premium for "natural" products, organic foods, green-friendly products, and the like that carry a cost premium. Such values-oriented companies make customers feel good, and big marketers want a piece of this profitable trend.

In 2000, the large agribusiness conglomerate Unilever bought the flavorful Ben & Jerry's ice cream company. Today, the company ads remind customers of shared values when they promote family farms, a dairy source for Ben & Jerry's ice creams. Colgate bought 84 percent of Tom's of Maine, the all-natural personal care brand based in Kennebunk, Maine. Tom's was a small company with a social responsibility message. French cosmetics giant L'Oreal bought London-based retailer The Body Shop, a personal care chain known for its avoidance of animal testing and its support for human and animal rights causes. Large companies recognize the added value the customer of these formerly small companies received.

Many customers today appreciate the notion that what's good for you and good for the planet is the ultimate win-win. Being a consumer of companies that share your values can make you feel selfless.

Probes

1. What are some causes that you believe deeply in?
2. What companies or organizations support those similar beliefs?
3. To what extent do you feel more inclined to do business with these supportive organizations? What factors influence your loyalty to them as a customer (external or internal)?
4. Are there companies you will always try to avoid because of some extrinsic value perceptions such as disagreement with their policy stands, etc.? Could they win you back?

Consider this Case

Perceptions of Value and the "Cult of Mac"

A group of MBA students were asked to research what companies do to create an enhanced perception of value. They chose to look at Apple Computers and entitled their report, *How Apple instills the "Cult of Mac" into their company*. They found these six points of the Apple strategy:

1. *Make innovative products.* Apple makes design and innovation an obsession and customers know their products are groundbreaking. Think of the impact of iPods and iPhones, for example.
2. *Keep the product line relatively simple.* Whereas competitors such as HP and Dell offer hundreds of models of computers, Apple offers less than 20. Don't offer so many choices that customers can't make a decision.
3. *Create truly memorable ads.* No one understood what an MP3 player was until the first iPod

commercial. "One thousand songs in your pocket." Make it really simple to understand for the masses.

4. *Find an enemy.* Think different. And clearly identify those outside your cult. Create a "you and me against the world" with your customers.

5. *Offer surprises* to keep your customers guessing, and surprised, with new products. Exceed expectations: don't work to meet them.

6. *Put on a show.* Apple never passes up an opportunity to "wow" an audience, including preparing presentations months in advance. Allow your customers to contribute to your "snowball" effect by mesmerizing them.

Probes

1. In what ways do each of these strategy points reflects principles discussed in this chapter? Describe each using chapter terminology.

2. Select another type of business you are familiar with and describe how that organization might apply these same strategy points.

Notes

1. Michael Schuman and Hae Won Choi, "Suwon's Restrooms, Once the Pits, Are Flush with Tourists," *Wall Street Journal*, November 26, 1999, p. A-1.

2. Hanna Komulainen, Tuija Mainela, Jaana Tähtinen and Pauliina Ulkuniemi, "Exploring Customer Perceived Value in a Technology Intensive Service Innovation," University of Oulu, Department of Marketing, Oulu, Finland, Proceedings of the 20th Annual IMP Conference, September 2–4, 2004, Copenhagen, Denmark.

3. James R. Healy, "Base Versa Sings Like a Bird: Cheap, Cheap, Cheap," *USA Today*, February 27, 2009, p. 5B.

4. Jeff Bailey, "JetBlue's C.E.O. Is 'Mortified' after Fliers Are Stranded," February 19, 2007.

5. "Lands' End Guarantee Verboten in Germany," Salt Lake City, *Deseret News* (AP), September 25, 1999, p. B-1.

6. Brittany Martin, in "Letters to Fortune," *Fortune*, January 12, 1998, p. 19.

7. Build your own Ford can be found at: *http://www58. forddirect.fordvehicles.com/FordVehicles.jsp?target=Config& partner=fv*

8. Interview with Randall Myers, Senior Knowledge Engineer, Sterling Wentworth Corporation, Salt Lake City, October 2004.

9. Based on personal conversation with Denise Wymore, marketing consultant. Denise wrote her book, *Tatoos: The Ultimate Proof of a Successful Brand* (2006) entirely at her local Starbucks coffee shop. See: *www.denisewymore.com.*

10. *www.frequentflyer.com.au/press/theage20Mar05.htm*

CHAPTER 11

Exceed Customer Expectations with Information
Make Instructions Simple

*The Internet is the most important single development
in the history of human communication since the invention
of call waiting.*

—DAVE BARRY

After reading this chapter, you should be able to

1. Understand what A-plus information is.

2. Know five ways of producing A-plus information.

3. Recognize informational barriers to customer entry in e-commerce.

4. Select informational media carefully.

5. Use techniques to enhance message clarity.

6. Create and support user groups.

7. Pay special attention to A-plus information in e-commerce.

8. Evaluate your A-plus information efforts.

The Way It Is . . . Auto Dealer's Informational Surprise

When Thomas bought an Acura automobile a few years ago, he received what I call **A-plus information**—the dealership exceeded what the customer anticipated in the area of information. Based on his purchasing experience with dozens of cars, Thomas anticipated that the sales person would tell him to read the owner's manual in the glove box to figure out how to use the various accessories and features of the car. Instead, the Acura sales rep spent about 20 minutes with Thomas—after the sale—showing him how each of the car's features worked, where to check and add oil, how to find and use the jack, spare tire, and tool kit, and how to maintain the car's finish. The sales rep then programmed the radio to Thomas's favorite stations. In short, he gave Thomas the detailed information he needed to make the most of his purchase, and he gave that information using an unexpected medium: personal instruction. This far exceeded any previous experience Thomas had had with auto dealerships.

Another A-plus information experience happened a few years ago when a teenage young man had knee surgery. After the surgery, he was referred to a physiotherapist. His parents anticipated that the therapist would show him how to exercise the knees to aid in recovery. She did this, but also added some small touches that exceeded the anticipated. She photocopied pictures of each exercise, wrote his name on the pages in large red letters, taught him each exercise, gave him her home phone number, and encouraged him to call with any questions. She even called him the next day to see how he was doing. Little things? Sure they were. But the composite of these little things went beyond what the parent had anticipated and created an A-plus experience.

The "dot-com" e-tailers are learning about the importance of A-plus information—some doing better than others. A friend's recent online purchase through an online merchant resulted in an unsatisfactory exchange of information. The company sent a message saying the order would be shipped within three to four days; however, the order did not arrive as promised. When the customer inquired about when she could expect the merchandise ordered, she was again provided with inaccurate information—information that promised shipment that did not happen. A few days later, the customer found the product she ordered—valued at several hundred dollars—on her doorstep, having been left out in the rain all night. All this because the company failed to give correct and timely information.

A recent experience with another dot-com merchant also failed badly in the information area. While the company's Web page touted special next-day delivery service at no extra charge, the merchandise ordered on Monday still had not arrived on Friday. The customer's email to the company went unanswered. He finally called and was told that part of his order had been shipped and the back-ordered portion would be shipped in two days. A day later, he received the following email message addressed to "Dear Valued Customer" (shown exactly as he received it):

The following item(s) within your order #WO3690775 have been updated, and now have the following status:

SKU # IN-2027	-Processing;
SKU # TQ-1010	-Shipped;
SKU # VS-1135	-Shipped;
SKU # UE-1003	-Shipped;

Does this make any sense to you? The company's message uses internal jargon and numbers that mean nothing to the customer. Customers don't refer to products ordered by SKU numbers, and the status report of "processing" tells nothing. The opportunity to provide A-plus customers with useful information is obviously a foreign concept to this company. For that matter, communicating with any clarity also seems to be a low priority.

SERVICE SNAPSHOT

ProFlowers.com

In fairness, some e-tailers are getting it right. Online florist ProFlowers.com for example, tells the customer when the ordered flowers were picked up from the distributor, when they were delivered, and even who accepted the delivery. In doing so, ProFlowers is creating the standard in the young and quickly evolving online business world. Customers are quickly coming to expect that e-tailers will send immediate acknowledgments telling the precise status of order, the shipping date, and costs. Companies that fail to meet this level of service will soon be left in the e-trade dust.

Joanna's recent experience with ProFlowers reinforced her loyalty. A Christmas wreath order for her sister in Iowa was scheduled for delivery on December 15. ProFlowers called her on the 12th and left a voice message asking her to contact them on their toll-free line. When Joanna did, they apologized profusely for a failure to get the order faxed to their Iowa distributor and advised her that the shipment would be one day late. They then waived the shipping charge.

Probes

1. How does this description of ProFlowers compare with other online retailers you have worked with? Did they seem to be better or less effective?
2. How does ProFlowers use the idea of A-plus information to exceed customer expectations?

UNDERSTAND WHAT A-PLUS INFORMATION IS

A company delivers A-plus information—that is, exceeds expectations—by communicating in ways that are more timely, clear, interesting, or creative than its customers anticipate.

Every product, service, or purchasing experience has an informational component. If you buy a can of soup, its label is likely to include nutritional data, preparation tips, and recipes. Vehicles, tools, appliances, and electronic equipment have detailed owner's manuals. Lawn care services are likely to tell you how often to water or fertilize your grass. Athletic equipment comes with exercise guides or perhaps with a video or DVD showing how to get the best results from the product. Customers have come to expect to receive such information.

> Virtually every product has an informational component—something communicated to the customer.

Special Informational Demands of E-commerce

For e-commerce, timely information on the status of customer orders is especially important to retention and loyalty. Online customers may feel left in a vacuum if the company does not communicate efficiently, clearly, and in a timely manner.

One ingenious application of timeliness is provided by Domino's Pizza. The company that pioneered the idea of pizza delivery some 40 years ago continues to be on the cutting edge of customer convenience—and information. Introduced in 2008, "Pizza Tracker" now lets customers literally track their pizza from the moment they place the order until it leaves the store en route to them. What's more, Domino's vows that its online tracking system—for phone or online orders—is accurate to within 40 seconds. "We're filling that black box of uncertainty—'Has my pizza been forgotten?'—with information and entertainment," says Chris McGlothlin, technology chief at Domino's.[1] Pizza Tracker is fun to watch. Its colorful graphics and chatty, conversational tone really do keep the customer informed. Although some critics grouse that "I guess they'll sell a ton of pizzas to people with no social life who are sitting in front of computers."[2]

The U.S. insurance industry seems to be making an effort to improve on customer responsiveness. According to recent data,[3]

- Responsiveness to inquiries improved to where only 19 percent of queries were left unanswered, down from 36 percent in a year earlier.
- For those that did respond to user inquiries, 30 percent of surveyed firms provided a response after two days; and 54 percent provided a response within one day.
- Fourteen percent provided a response in less than an hour; 26 percent provided a response in one to four hours; 16 percent between one and two days.
- Most companies acknowledge receipt of an inquiry quickly. Eighty-one percent of surveyed insurers utilize some form of rapid acknowledgment such as email autoresponders; 16 percent issued an acknowledgment within two hours, and only 3 percent didn't acknowledge inquiries at all.

Any way you slice and dice these statistics, companies have a significant opportunity for improvement. Companies that improve upon response times and quality of information given will be likely to please their customers.

As Woody Allen once said, "eighty percent of all success is just showing up." Being available and responsive to customers is a precondition to giving A-plus information. While it is encouraging that some companies are getting better at that, too many still fail to provide even the most basic information in a timely manner to customers.

> Customers increasingly expect prompt responses to their inquiries.

As e-commerce becomes more sophisticated, companies will continue to find ways to respond in more timely and effective ways. Such responsiveness will become the expectation and companies that fail to meet or exceed that expectation will suffer customer dissatisfaction.

Information handling provides an opportunity for surprising customers. A-plus information happens when customers receive timely, clearer, or more useful information than they anticipated. The same applies to employee communication, of course. When workers feel well informed and involved in their company, loyalty increases.

KNOW HOW TO PRODUCE A-PLUS INFORMATION

Let's look not at some specific ways to create an A-plus information experience for customers and employees. This chapter will get you thinking about several categories of A-plus information ideas, including **informational hand-holding**, **media selection**, **message clarity**, **information accessibility**, and **user groups**. There may, however, be other variations that you can creatively apply.

Provide Informational Hand-holding

As discussed above, the explosive growth of electronic commerce provides a golden opportunity to exceed what customers anticipate with A-plus information. The young and rapidly changing e-commerce world offers a wide range of service levels as many companies work to figure out how to do it well. Customers are just beginning to develop loyalties to certain e-tailers and are bookmarking select Web sites on their computers. Until customers feel completely comfortable about the information they receive on the Net, they are likely to examine merchandise on the Net and then purchase it offline at brick-and-mortar retailers. Although improving, customers still say they aren't filling electronic shopping carts because they don't get enough hand-holding on the Net. We can assume that people are getting increasingly comfortable with e-commerce but there will always be a substantial number who prefer the kinds of information they get from human contact. Getting useful, reassuring information into the heads of customers should be an important part of the development of any e-commerce efforts.

Opportunities to improve customer hand-holding aren't just for electronic commerce. Better organizations of all types are increasingly sensitive to customer discomfort and are doing things to reduce it. Companies that have personal guides, personal shoppers, and private bankers are doing additional hand-holding. Companies that have exceptionally friendly receptionists or folks at the door who greet and keep customers informed of matters of interest to them are doing hand-holding. Managers who maintain legitimate open-door policies and are receptive to employee concerns are doing additional hand-holding for their internal customers. Company leaders who give customers their home phone numbers and invite them to call if they have problems of concerns are doing hand-holding, too.

ANOTHER LOOK

Barriers to Customer Entry

Some e-commerce experts contend that Web sites turn away more business than they realize. Typical barriers they routinely put in front of potential customers:

Barrier 1: Requiring too much Information from Visitors

Many sites require an exorbitant amount of information to register users at all. People are increasingly reticent to disclose personal information and Web sites that require too much lose customers.

Barrier 2: Make Users Repeat Themselves Often

Once you've asked users a question once, you should always know the answer. The more often a customer needs to repeat himself, the dumber your Web site seems.

Barrier 3: Make Users Enter Order Numbers, Promotion Codes, or other Obscure Pieces of Information

Sometimes sites have ads for special discounts on the home page which require the user enter a promotional code during the checkout process. Sometimes there is no way to copy and paste long codes into the correct box during checkout. That's a frustrating annoyance customers should not have to experience.

Probes

1. Describe situations where you have faced similar inconveniences on the Web.
2. How does this article relate to A-plus information? What are some opportunity areas you might use?

Look carefully at your company. Are you providing informational opportunities that make customers and employees comfortable and confident as they do business with you?

Select Informational Media Carefully

When providing customers with information, consider various media options—written documents, DVDs, online helps, and the like. Media should be chosen on the basis of communication effectiveness, not just efficiency. Let me explain.

Communication efficiency is a simple ratio of the costs of communicating relative to the number of people reached by the message. If a message is extremely simple (a no-parking sign, or widely distributed memo announcing a price change on a particular product, a simple cooking tip or recipe), we can get away with an efficient medium such as a flyer, label, or simple instruction sheet. But, as soon as we go beyond such simple messages, communication effectiveness becomes more important.

Communication *effectiveness* is different from communication efficiency. **Communication effectiveness** is achieved when the message is

- *received* by the right people (and not others),
- *understood*,
- *remembered* for a reasonable amount of time, and
- *used*.

Effective media are seldom simple or cheap. The greatest effectiveness is typically achieved when people talk face-to-face. This one-to-one communication is, of course, much more expensive (far less efficient) than an instruction sheet or owner's manual. But if the message is crucial to the customer's satisfaction with the product, it can be well worth the extra cost. The Acura dealer described earlier apparently believed in paying the price for personalized, face-to-face communication when he taught his customer about the features of his new car.

We can attribute much misunderstanding to overemphasizing efficiency when we should focus on effectiveness. Sometimes it doesn't pay to be efficient. The cheap, easy way to transfer information (e.g., the email from the e-merchant who identified products only by SKU numbers) doesn't do the job.

Creative companies surprise their customers by breaking away from the usual and by using a variety of media for various messages. Chevrolet, for example, has gone beyond the owner's manual when they provided an audiotape to teach customers how to use the features of their car or truck. Some companies provide DVDs to teach customers how to assemble or use a product. Online help and telephone hotlines (if well designed and responsive) have saved many a frustrated consumer.

Many organizations now have online help services with **frequently asked questions (FAQs)**. The best ones use several levels of FAQs. Some questions address the basic needs of prospects and newer customers. Other FAQs are for experienced customers who know their way around the company's products and services.

In the early days of personal computers, documentation (the instruction manual) was notoriously bad. It was hard to read and often grammatically incorrect. Today's computer or software buyer wouldn't stand for that for a minute. The informational bar has been raised considerably. What passed for the norm in the 1980s would be totally unacceptable in today's plug-and-play world. For that matter, what has passed for plug-and-play a few years ago is no longer acceptable. One reason Apple has grabbed such a huge percentage of online music sales is because iPods are so easy to use. Even the least technologically sophisticated consumer seems to be able to figure out how to load an iPod.

Employee communication also poses opportunities for exceeding expectations with information. The best companies to work for typically use active, multifaceted employee communication and training efforts. People are unlikely to feel allegiance to companies that

Communication efficiency is a simple ratio between the cost of sending a message and the number of people "reached."

When conveying important information, sometimes it doesn't pay to be efficient.

treat them like hired hands. Great companies hire the whole man or woman. They provide extensive training and information that create high levels of employee engagement.

Progressive companies are constantly looking for media options that allow them to provide A-plus products and services to their customers.

The best companies typically use active, multiple media employee communication and training, thus exceeding their employees' expectations.

USE TECHNIQUES THAT ENHANCE MESSAGE CLARITY

Regardless of the media used, information must be clear and understandable. Intelligent companies seek clarity by presenting their messages with short, clear sentences, a logical sequence of information, and enough repetition to effectively teach the message receiver. They also test messages with similar readers, getting their feedback, before publishing final versions.

Audit of Your Company's Writing

How clear are the messages you are sending customers? Many organizations assume they are doing just fine but, in reality, could benefit from having a professional business communication expert do an audit of their written documents, telephone scripts, and presentations. My colleague, Dr. Sherron Bienvenu of Emory University, has completed consulting projects for companies who recognized that their written documents were not of the quality they wanted. (By the way—we often have blind spots. The message may make perfect sense to us because we understand the lingo and the products, while the same messages leave less informed customers scratching their heads.)

Her auditing approach was straightforward. She analyzed a sample of the letters and memos sent to the client's customers and quickly recognized some patterns that could be improved upon. Among the problems she found are some you too may be experiencing in your documents:

1. *Abrupt tone.* While most readers appreciate business writers getting directly to the point, many of these letters were too abrupt.
2. Use of *clichés or jargon.* Clichés are overused, stale phrases; **jargon** is specialized language the company may well understand but the customer may not. If you are not sure whether the customer will know the meaning of a term, use a simpler, clearer description.
3. Use of *stock numbers or abbreviations.* In many cases, the reader may not understand or recognize these.
4. *Failure to express appreciation.* The most powerful phrase in any relationship is probably *thank-you.* Instead of telling a reader that her order cannot be shipped as planned, start the message with a thank-you for ordering, or thank-you for her patience.
5. *Failure to offer an alternative* to solve a problem. Don't just tell readers what you cannot do; tell them what you can do. Take the initiative to solve the customer's problem if at all possible.
6. *Failure to provide a reasonable explanation.* Don't say "it's against our policy" and think that that does it. Take a moment to explain why the policy is as it is—in terms the reader can understand (even if they may be disappointed).

As any author would testify, we can constantly improve the wording of almost anything we write or say. Companies are wise to periodically look at their messages and be willing to edit and reedit messages. This is critical to ongoing improvement and the opportunity to create A-plus information.

Frequently review your company's written materials to be certain they communicate clearly and with appropriate tone.

Use Some Redundancy

People don't always get your messages immediately. For example, you get better results by presenting information verbally (with words) and graphically (with pictures or diagrams). Likewise, an owner's manual with a supplemental DVD, reference chart, online help program, or telephone hotline will improve the likelihood of customer satisfaction with your product. Such redundant media are keys to understanding.

Make Key Information Easily Accessible with Graphics and Icons

Sometimes you can create A-plus information by simply providing clear signs. I consulted with a hospital that had a rather unusual floor plan. What appeared to be the main entrance opened onto a large foyer area with a reception desk. But, because the local folks knew that just about everyone came in through the emergency room entry, this reception area was not staffed. People unfamiliar with the hospital would come in this front door and have no idea where to go. When the hospital learned of this confusion, they improved the signs and added some color-coded strips on the floor to lead to various departments.

> Sometimes something as simple as better signs or color-coded lines can surprise the customer with A-plus information.

Signs can have marketing and employee benefits as well. One example comes from the pharmacy department in a large retail store. Pharmacy employees faced the large burden of stocking all those little bottles, jars, and boxes in perfectly straight rows in aisle after aisle. Every time a customer picked something up to read the label, the display needed to be straightened or the products turned to faces front. It was a lot of work. So, the store began replacing traditional shelves with a system of bins. Instead of facing a shelf of aspirin bottles, say, the shopper saw a blowup of the aspirin bottle's label. Under that blowup was the bin, into which the aspirin bottles had been dumped.

The enlarged sign provided A-plus information and solved the problem of stocking—a clerk could just roll a trolley of merchandise to the aisle, open the bin, dump in the goods, and move on. No more straight lines.

Shoppers liked it better, too. Instead of facing a row of bottles with tiny print, they saw a large, easy-to-read version of the label. It was much easier on the eyes, especially for elderly shoppers.

CREATE AND SUPPORT CUSTOMER USER GROUPS AND CLASSES

Organizations that bring groups of customers together for **user's groups** are also offering A-plus information. Such groups are naturals for craft shops, computer stores, financial institutions, and the like and may also work in other arenas. Examples are food stores that offer cooking classes, credit unions that sponsors free classes on investments, budgeting, and personal finance, or auto repair shops that offer classes on auto maintenance.

One of my clients was a medium-sized tire shop and auto repair business. While brainstorming ideas for giving A-plus information, the employees decided to offer auto maintenance classes, specifically aimed at their female customers. Through some creative advertising and frequent mention of the classes to customers, they got a pretty good turnout. The classes covered tips for tire care, guided tours of a car's exhaust system (with a mechanic showing the parts on a car on a lift), and even a session on maintaining auto paint and upholstery. The groups were small at first but grew as customers became aware that the classes ran every other Tuesday evening at 7 p.m. And you can bet those who attended the classes were loyal customers.

Motorcycle manufacturer Harley Davidson brings A-plus service to its customers via its Harley Owners Group (HOG). Started in 1983 in an attempt to stem slipping sales, HOG grew from 33,000 members to about 700,000 today.

Harley found that people were giving up riding because they didn't have anyone to ride with. HOG brings Harley riders together for rides or to swap tips. "It gives a person a way into a subculture," says Mike Keefe, HOG's director. In a recent *Investor's Business Daily* story, Keefe describes spending eight days riding and camping out with other Harley owners. "In the mornings, I'm standing in line with six other naked men waiting to use a cold shower. You can't get much closer to a customer than that."[4]

Incidentally, Harley buyers get a one-year HOG membership free with bike purchase. After that, it costs $40 a year. It's common for Harley executives and administrative workers to take part in HOG activities, thus fostering open communication with customers. This is an excellent example of A-plus information sharing.

Utah Community Credit Union recently launched an excellent Web site aimed at teaching young people how to better manage money. The site, *www.BeMoneySmart.org*, has friendly talking characters that show youth how to handle money and win awards for saving and for good grades. Although UCCU gets no direct income from the site, it creates much goodwill, exceeds its members' expectations, and supports its vision of people helping people with financial matters. (By way of disclosure—your author serves on the Board of Directors for Utah Community Credit Union, although he had little to do with their innovative BeMoneySmart program.)

Internal customers—employees—can also gain great benefit from user groups. Repair technicians, for example, can be encouraged to create "**communities of practice**" where they can share tips and ideas. Cross-departmental cooperation can be enhanced by getting to know each other and each other's functions in the company. Often such groups meet informally over lunch or a few beers after work. Enlightened companies encourage and promote such information-sharing activities.

> Wise companies support information sharing among employees with such things as communities of practice.

Businesses should try to increase the level of interaction with their customers and employees using any available media. If a business values its customer relationships, it will want to interact with those customers at every conceivable opportunity. Such interactivity can occur in a wide variety of ways.

PAY SPECIAL ATTENTION TO A-PLUS INFORMATION IN E-COMMERCE

As discussed earlier, e-commerce faces some special challenges and opportunities in providing A-plus information. Two critical actions are to make customer support easily accessible and to honor the customer feedback loop.

Make Customer Support Accessible

One of the greatest challenges of business today is providing timely, effective support to customers who have questions. E-commerce is especially vulnerable to complaints of lack of support. Electronic commerce relies heavily on email for communicating with customers—sometimes too heavily.

A Web site developer describes a commonly heard complaint about e-commerce: "Companies by design are leaving their phone numbers off because they don't want to spend money on having someone stand by and answer the phone. . . . Their feeling seems to be that companies ought to be able to answer questions on the Web. Indeed, a substantial number of companies don't provide an email address and/or phone numbers for customers to ask questions. In many cases, this is shortsighted. Offering customers the option of talking live to a company representative can create the opportunity for 'high touch' service to supplement the high tech."

One Web site that sells a fairly mundane product (floor mats) is StopDirt.com. Erika Wilde, the business owner, encourages phone calls—and even initiates some calls to follow up on customer satisfaction. Because Erika is pleasant and fun to talk with, she solidifies her customer's loyalty with such personal touch communication. This relationship-building has, over the years, created strong repeat business and more than a few friendships.

Honor the Customer Feedback Loop

A related and all-too-common complaint of e-commerce customers is the lack of responsiveness when they do contact the company with a problem. Have you experienced this? Too often, our requests seem to drop into a black hole somewhere and we get no response at all.

A survey by e-tailer trade group Shop.org showed that about a quarter of shoppers never received a response to an email request for assistance. "It's retailing 101: Don't ignore your customers," says Mary Helen Gillespie, president of E-BuyersGuide.com. "Plus, it's not just bad business, it's extremely rude even by today's standards."[5] Answer your email!

Making your company more accessible to your customers is an excellent way to exceed customer expectations and surprise with service that's better than anticipated. But if you offer help lines, be sure they are adequately staffed with knowledgeable people.

EVALUATE YOUR A-PLUS INFORMATION EFFORTS

By measuring the effectiveness of information provided, customers can assess a company's effectiveness at creating A-plus service. Two key measures are logging common questions and auditing communication effectiveness.

Logging Common Questions (FAQs)

Maintaining a current FAQ page can be challenging, but can provide your customers with A-plus information.

Develop a system for keeping track of common customer questions. If several people are asking the same questions or experiencing similar confusion, you have an information problem.

This advice applies to all companies, not just the technologically sophisticated ones. The smallest shop can make notes of recurring customer concerns and encourage all employees to share their experiences. However this information is gathered, managers need to make it worthwhile for employees to record and pass on the customer's feedback. Offer employees incentives for listing and reporting customer comments. Invite customers to tell you what they are thinking either in writing or orally. Writing inhibits many comments because it is cumbersome for many people to take the time to write. Teach your employees to make notes of customer responses, preferably in front of customers so that they know they are being heard.

Audit Your Company's Communication

Consider auditing your company's communication with customers.

A **communication audit** is a process for determining the quantity and quality of information flowing through the company as well as that coming into the organization from outside stakeholders. Often done with the help of a communication consultant, an audit uses multiple approaches to objectively pinpoint communication roadblocks, identify overload problems, and assess the effectiveness of the company's formal and informal communication networks.

Such audits can range from relatively informal observation to gathering information with interviews, to content analysis of the documents you give customers. Put yourself in the shoes of your customer and ask, "Does this information exceed my expectations?" Be consistently alert to messages that may confuse customers. As we discussed earlier, consider using a communication specialist to analyze the content and clarity of messages your company sends customers and employees.

For internal customers, remember that internal communication effectiveness reveals a great deal about the status of employee relations. Employees who feel free to communicate and who see that their input is being considered are far more likely to be loyal to the company than are those who feel outside the communication loop. A primary variable in employee motivation is the feeling that their input is being heard. The same principle holds for external customers, of course.

A FINAL THOUGHT

Overall, giving customers and employees clear, appropriate, easy-to-use A-plus information is a powerful way to build loyalty. Look carefully at the quality, quantity, and usability of the messages conveyed in all company interactions. Then find ways to exceed customer expectation—ways to surprise people with even better, clearer, more timely, and more interesting information. Put on your creativity hat. Listen for unmet information needs and encourage customers and employees to suggest ways to provide A-plus information. The payoff can be substantial in building customer and employee allegiance.

Summary of Key Ideas

- Be aware that ignoring communications from customers (external and internal) will damage goodwill. Take the time necessary to answer emails and letters. It is really not that hard.
- Be sensitive to the impact of various informational media. Consider both communication efficiency and effectiveness. Be willing to pay the necessary price for true effectiveness when it can enhance communication quality.
- Seek A-plus opportunities by breaking away from the "normal" and by using a variety of media for various messages. Be creative in building customer relationships via good communication.
- Consider creating and supporting customer user groups (such as the HOGs), communities of practice, classes, or online advice (such as BeMoneySmart.net).
- Provide responsive and easy-to-use support and answer inquiries from all customers. Honor the feedback loop.
- Keep track of FAQs and audit routine information your company shares with customers. This can reveal opportunities for improving message content and tone.

Key Concepts

A-plus information
communication audit
communication
   effectiveness

communication efficiency
communities of practice
frequently asked
   questions (FAQs)

information
   accessibility
informational
   hand-holding

jargon
media selection
message clarity
user groups

Reviewing the Facts

1. Why is it potentially important for organizations to provide better-than-expected information to customers?
2. When considering various ways to exceed expectations (A-plus information), what customer benefits can we attempt to provide?
3. What are communication *media*? Which of such media do companies typically use to communicate with their customers? To employees?
4. Explain the difference between communication efficiency and communication effectiveness. Give an example that depicts each.
5. The Internet and e-commerce provide several challenges to providing A-plus information. What are some of these challenges?
6. How can e-commerce be used to supplement other forms of information and potentially build greater customer loyalty?

Applying the Ideas: How Does Information Affect Your Customers

1. The author states that virtually all products have "an informational component." To what extent do you agree or disagree with this statement? Has it always been this way? What products do you buy that have more information today than they had in the past? Give specific examples.
2. Select five consumer products you use and examine the information that is provided with them. Write a paragraph for each product, describing the product and all associated information. (Example, as mentioned early in the chapter, a can of soup has certain information provided on its label—preparation instructions, nutritional information, perhaps recipes, etc.) Then brainstorm other possibilities that could be associated with that product. How could the company provide other information that would enhance the buyer's experience? Let your imagination go and be creative.
3. Identify a product you are familiar with that goes beyond what a customer might expect with regard to information. If similar products use only written materials, look for one that supplements its written materials with some other media. Describe the relative effectiveness of this approach. How could the company take the idea of A-plus information even further? Be creative.
4. Use your favorite search engine to find information about what companies are doing to exceed customer expectations in information. Select an industry you are interested in (such as automobiles, video games, sporting goods, hospitality, motorcycles, collectables). Visit three sites and describe what they offer. Evaluate the relative creativity and effectiveness of these sites. To what extent do they exceed your expectations?

Consider this Case

Bumble and bumble Exceed Expectations with School for Stylists

Hair care companies everywhere spend a bundle on ads in trendy fashion magazines and in television advertising campaigns. But one niche player, Bumble and bumble, has a different strategy—they provide their customers (salon owners) with in-salon workshops. As an added service, they offer hair care lessons and business education to salon owners and stylists through Bumble and bumble University, its self-styled center for the craft, culture, and commerce of hairdressing.

Executives at Bumble recognize their true customer—the salon owners and stylists. They are the people who recommend products to the end-user, the hair-care product consumer. Bumble exceeds expectations with the kinds of information that empowers the stylists with knowledge. And in the process they make them well-informed, passionate, raving fans for the Bumble brand. Foregoing a large advertising budget,

B&b seeks to work with only the narrow band of the best salons in the industry to create a very deep, integrated relationship.

Bumble and bumble University (Bb.U.) delivers a curriculum that is "extremely exciting, challenging, and inspiring," according to Jack Ray, a Raleigh salon owner: "It's a real honor to be working with the same people that are behind the scenes of the fashion shows in Milan, Paris, and New York."[6]

Probes

1. How does Bumble and bumble illustrate the principle of A-plus information?
2. How can this approach be a win-win for customers and company alike?
3. What possible applications can you think of for similar businesses?

Consider this Case

The Nontechy Solution

Monika specifically timed her visit to the Sociology Department for a quiet day before winter classes began. As a 19-year-old student at a well-regarded private university, Monika was gathering information about various majors and sociology sounded interesting. She had completed most of her general education courses and had a 3.8 grade-point average.

It was 10 a.m. when she respectfully entered the department office. A middle-aged woman was typing something into a computer and did not look up. After about 30 seconds of standing at the receptionist's desk, Monika cleared her throat and, asked "Can I get some information about majoring in Sociology?"

The woman never even looked up. Instead, she pointed to a bulletin board and resumed typing. Feeling chastened, Monika apologized for interrupting her, and went to the bulletin board, feeling awkward and a bit embarrassed. On the board, she found pages that had been clipped from the university catalog (which she had already read) and a few pictures of professors in the

department, but little additional information. After her rude reception, she decided to not even ask for an appointment with an academic advisor. "I guess they aren't really interested in attracting students into their program," she said to herself. She left and never again returned to that office.

Probes

1. In what ways did this department miss an opportunity to create a positive relationship with a potential customer?
2. If you were the department chair and had observed this situation, what would you do? (Assume that the success of the department depends on attracting good students.)
3. How could the department move toward exceeding student expectations regarding the information it provides? Come up with some creative ideas.

Notes

1. Bruce Horovitz, "Where's Your Domino's Pizza? Track It Online," *USA Today*, January 30, 2008.

2. Christopher Muller, restaurant expert at the University of Central Florida, who's less than enthusiastic about pizza-tracking technology.

3. Sean Michael Kerner, "Insurance Companies Score Online Customer Respect," March 28, 2005. Source: *http://www.clickz.com/stats/sectors/professional/article.php/3493201*

4. Mike Angell, "By Focusing on Customers, Firms Can Boost Shareholder Value," *Investor's Business Daily*, October 11, 2002, p. A-4.

5. Quoted in Frank Barnako, *Internet Daily* (sponsored by CBS MarketWatch), September 10, 1999.

6. Excerpts from news release by Samuel Cole Salon, "New York State of Mind: Jack Ray to Provide Bumble and Bumble Training in His Raleigh Salons," *http://www.pr.com/press-release/48671*, August 15, 2007.

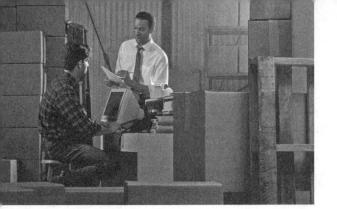

Exceed Customer Expectations with Convenience *and Timing*

Make Things Easier for Customers

"Don't you worry 'bout a thing" (the six key words your customers want to hear)

—A UPS STORE RADIO COMMERCIAL

After reading this chapter, you should be able to

1. Understand what A-plus convenience is.

2. Identify and site examples of ways to improve speed of service and ease of doing business.

3. Avoid the problem of over-promising and under-delivering service.

4. Show customers how you value their time.

5. Explain how past examples of increasing speed and convenience have allowed for major advances in customer service.

6. Understand the concept of "virtual waiting" and how you can use this to exceed customer expectations.

7. Identify examples of improvement in customer ease of use and **once-and-done service**.

8. Consider possible **ancillary services** that could help create an A-plus experience for customers.

9. Describe the potential advantages of simplifying products for better customer service.

The Way It Is . . . A Little Extra Convenience

Marcia was a regular customer at the Perimeter Center Publix Supermarket in Atlanta. During the busy Christmas holiday season, she discovered a delicious, low-fat eggnog. But after trying it, she came back for more only to discover the store was out of stock.

A chat with the dairy section employee brought promises that more would be coming in soon. But when she returned to the store a day later, the product was again out of stock. This time the employee said, "More is coming in tomorrow and I'll set some aside for you." When she returned the next day, the delivery truck had been late and again, she got no eggnog.

This time the employee offered her A-plus convenience. He apologized and told her that as soon as the delivery comes in, he will set some aside for her and deliver it to her home on his way home from work! And he did.

Home delivery! What a concept. A generation ago, home delivery of milk and other products was commonplace. In the early twenty-first century, it may be making a comeback. Online grocery delivery services, at-home auto oil changes and glass replacement, and a number of other services are reintroducing consumers to a level of convenience not often found in today's business world. Companies are recognizing the opportunities to exceed customer expectations with greater convenience.

Enhancing speed and convenience for customers is a critical tactic. E-commerce sites live and die by their speed and responsiveness. Traditional businesses build great loyalty among customers who value the ways they respect their time and try to provide easy, timely transactions.

UNDERSTAND WHAT A-PLUS CONVENIENCE IS

Customer convenience arises from speed of service and ease of doing business. Organizations that strive for efficient, easy-to-use services capture customer loyalty.

Let's look first at the first component, speed. Surpassing what the customer anticipates about speed may be one of the simplest yet most powerful ways of building customer loyalty. The ubiquitous convenience store personifies key elements that can be applied to other businesses. C-stores allow parking at the door, reasonable selection, and quick out-the-door-in-a-minute service. Some now offer credit card scanning machines that allow the customer to pay almost instantly with a tap of their card. Pay-at-the-pump gas dispensing is now everywhere and makes things quick and easy for customers and store employees alike. Likewise, quick delivery of products ordered online has made the old line in many commercials, "Please allow four to six weeks for delivery" to sound like something from the Dark Ages. We want it NOW!

The reason people like businesses that offer convenience is simple: people today value time, perhaps more than ever before. Unfortunately, aside from convenience stores, many companies are far too casual about wasting customers' time. They often don't even recognize when they are taking longer than the customer expects. They are so wrapped up in their own internal systems—the ways they do things—that they don't even consider the possibility that they are eating up a lot of the customers' time and patience.

We live in a world of commerce where we expect nearly instant gratification. We see things on the Web, order them, and fully expect that they will arrive on our doorstep in a day or two. When they do, we are likely to reorder; if they fail to make the promised deadline, we are likely to be disappointed and will quit shopping with that company in favor of one that hustles a bit more.

Despite this, many companies still fall into the trap of **over-promising and under-delivering**. They make vague or unfulfilled commitments involving their customers' time. A few examples:

> Many companies over-promise and under-deliver when it comes to speed of service. They simply take longer than the customer has been led to expect.

- A major computer distributor in Europe tells the customer that their mainframe will be restored to service "soon." The customer thought that "soon" meant 20 minutes or so; to the technician, who better understood the complexity of the problem, "soon" meant about eight hours.
- Some phone or cable companies routinely tell customers that they will be at their home to install service "between 7:30 a.m. and 5 p.m." on a given date. Is the customer expected to sit around all day waiting for the installation?
- A medical clinic's most common complaint was that patients had to wait too long for the doctor. Customers felt that doctors had little regard for the value of their time. The result was a negative spiral where patients showed up later than the appointment time figuring that the doctor would be late. The clinic then scheduled even more slack into the system and the situation got worse.
- An online business makes a big deal of offering to ship products overnight so the customer will have them the next day (at no extra charge, according to company promotions). But when a customer's merchandise doesn't show up for five days, the opportunity to give A-plus convenience is long gone. So is that customer's loyalty.

On a more positive note, a number of businesses are built on the simple promise of giving **A-plus speed and convenience**. Federal Express promises package delivery "by 10:30 a.m.," while it knows it can have the package there by 9:30 or 9:45. Customers are routinely surprised because most businesses fail to meet their own deadlines, thus showing disrespect for the customer's time. Likewise, when I worked for Xerox Corporation, we used a similar practice. When customers called for a technician to fix their copy machine, we promised that someone would be at their office by 2 o'clock when we knew the rep would be there by 1:30 or so. This never failed to pleasantly surprise clients.

> Consistently beating a time deadline provides customers with A-plus speed and convenience.

The Disney amusement parks create A-plus speed by having signs showing how long it will take to get on the "Space Mountain" ride from a given point in a queue. They have actually scheduled in a little fat. The lines inevitably move more quickly and customers are pleasantly surprised. Restaurants that tell patrons a table will be available in 15 minutes and then seat them in 10 will be far more popular than one promising 15 minutes and delivering 18- or 20-minute seating.

HOW TO PRODUCE A-PLUS CONVENIENCE

We can exceed customer expectations and provide A-plus convenience and speed by applying or adjusting actions that convey to customers that the company (1) seriously values the customers' time, (2) makes things easier for customers, (3) produces "once-and-done" service, (4) makes doing business with the company easy, and (5) offers ancillary services that make the customer's life easier.

As with any A-plus tactic, companies need to be ever-vigilant to ways of improving systems and behaviors that can enhance convenience. If you don't offer better and better convenience, your competition will. Customers are screaming for it, and you need to provide it. So, let's look at some key actions we can consider.

> Customers are constantly demanding enhanced convenience.

GIVE SERIOUS REGARD TO CUSTOMER TIME AND CONVENIENCE

Time is a valuable commodity to your customers. When we disregard it or fail to share our customer's sense of urgency, we discount our customer. Few things are more frustrating than waiting for something that seems to take longer than necessary. In fact, of all the pet peeves identified in my research and described by seminar participants, slow service is at or near the top of everyone's list.

Speed is easier to work with than convenience. In fact, the nice thing about creating A-plus speed is that you have a lot of control. You can clearly create the expectation by telling customers how long things will take. Once the customer anticipates a particular time period, you can simply beat it.

> Customers often don't know how long things take. You need to advise them and, in so doing, set the expectation.

Make sure customers get a realistic perception of how long things take. I heard from a nurse in a hospital client of a situation where a patient was sent to the blood lab for a blood test. The phlebotomist drew the blood sample and took it behind a curtain to be sent off for analysis. Upon returning to the patient, the patient asked what the results of the test were. The lab technician laughed and explained that the test was to be done at another facility and results would not be ready until the next day. The point: customers don't always know how long things take. You need to tell them.

Too many businesses fall for the temptation to promise quicker service and hope for the best. They hate to deliver unpleasant news, so, instead, offer a time that sounds good even when it cannot be realistically delivered. In doing so, they miss a significant opportunity to under-promise and over-deliver. It is better to give a realistic time you can beat rather than a pie-in-the-sky estimate you cannot meet.

ANOTHER LOOK

Managing Queues

An increasing number of organizations are using **queue management systems (QMS)** to manage queues (or lines, as we say in the United States). What may have once been limited to a bakery or butcher shop, where customers took a number, has now expanded to electronic versions applied in businesses from banks to bus stations to auto parts stores.

Modern QMSs can allow a service center to manage long lines without the customers physically standing in a line. A customer wanting for a particular service presses a switch in the printer interface box and receives a receipt with a "queue number." The customer can then sit in the seating area or continue to shop while waiting for his/her turn without having to stay in a physical line. After serving the previous customer, the service employee presses a switch and notifies the QMS that it is free. The QMS display then calls the next number on the queue.

A simple system like this makes waiting more comfortable and fair. Customers know they are being served in the order they arrived and can occupy themselves with other things while waiting, if they wish.

In addition to considering customers' time, companies need to think about time's cousin: customer convenience. Offering A-plus convenience is one of the most powerful ways to build loyalty. This is illustrated by two kinds of businesses: pizza and auto lubrication.

The most popular restaurant food in America is pizza. In the late 1950s, when pizza was gaining widespread popularity across the country, it was served just like any other restaurant entrée. People ordered their pizza, waited 15 or 20 minutes for it to be baked, and ate it at the restaurant. Then came the convenience pioneers like Domino's. Early in the life of this pizza chain, it made the strategic decision to not have eat-in restaurants; to focus exclusively on takeout (what Europeans call "take away") and on delivery service.

The strategy was a hit. People came to associate Domino's with the 30-minute delivery guarantee and in turn Domino's and its competitors taught Americans a new way of buying restaurant food. Since then, countless pizza chains and independent restaurants have followed that model. Today, meals prepared outside the home account for nearly half the U.S. food dollar spending. The Food Marketing Institute says that "Americans want to spend no more than 15 minutes preparing a meal. . . . Today's shoppers want their food and they want it now." Seven out of ten households buy "home meal replacements" (otherwise known as takeouts) at least once a month.[1]

Of course, the choices now go far beyond pizza or restaurant meals alone. Supermarkets and delis provide a wide range of prepared meals that need nothing more than heating and eating. Food producers are packaging ingredients together to prepare complete meals without having to buy each ingredient separately. Shredded potatoes, chopped peppers, onions, and diced ham are provided in separate plastic bags within a box describing the meal. Pizza crusts are sold with packets of topping, while prepared sandwiches are packaged with chips and cookie to make an instant box lunch. All these efforts are attempts to meet customer needs for convenience.

Products packaged together allow the convenience of not having to shop for separate ingredients.

Another classic convenience breakthrough is the stand-alone automobile oil change business which emerged in the late 1970s and 1980s. Before companies like Jiffy Lube, Q-Lube, and Minute Man, auto owners needing an oil change typically took their car to a dealership or service station. They dropped it off, caught a ride to work, returned after work, and picked up their car. It could easily be an all-day deal and was pretty inconvenient. Then came the quick lube shop.

Today, auto owners go to a Jiffy Lube or similar shop, have a cup of coffee in a customer lounge while a team of technicians pounces on their car, changes the oil, checks the tires and all fluids, vacuums the inside, and so on. The whole process takes 10 or 15 minutes. This is A-plus convenience.

The fastest-growing age-group on earth, according to United Nations research, is people above 60. In the United States alone, people over 65 will rise to 20 percent of the population within ten years. That's a lot of people.

Older customers have special needs and provide special opportunities to exceed expectations with added convenience. Researchers at prestigious universities such as the Massachusetts Institute of Technology are actively studying the effects of aging and changes in people's abilities as they get older. Some very simple changes businesses are making to provide convenience to these customers are to make packages easier to open and provide instructions in print easy to read. Some restaurants offer special parking spaces for "senior citizens" and easier physical access, including ramps for wheelchairs.

The MIT research includes the development of a suit of clothing that can make anyone feel old. The navy-blue jumpsuit is laced with braces and elastic bands that teach young engineers how to design products for people in their 70s to use.[2]

While service providers may not be necessarily involved in designing products, the empathy for older customers can lead to positive ways of surprising them with thoughtful touches that add convenience to their shopping experience.

CONSIDER THE USE OF VIRTUAL WAITING TECHNIQUES

A breakthrough article published by the Cornell University Hotel and Restaurant School[3] summarizes some creative and effective ways to apply "**virtual waiting.**"

Waiting can cause customer dissatisfaction that impacts the intent to be a repeat buyer. Although waiting can be an expected part of some services such as elegant dining, it is, for most customers, an annoyance to be minimized or avoided. So, what can companies do to reduce waiting time for customers? And if waiting times cannot be avoided, what can companies do to minimize their unpleasantness?

Hospitality management scholars Duncan Dickson, Robert C. Ford, and Bruce Laval suggest three possible strategies:

1. Manage the reality of the actual wait through the use of techniques that better match capacity with customer demand.
2. Manage the perception of the wait by responding to how customers perceive the wait.
3. Make the wait invisible through developing virtual queues, which allow customers to participate in other activities while they wait for an appointed time at their desired activity.[4]

Match Capacity to Demand

Companies can quickly determine their busiest times and slower times. The first step to reduce undue waiting is to plan for peak-time loads with adequate staffing. Supermarkets that open additional checkout lines in the early evening when customers are shopping after work are doing such capacity management. Likewise, organizations that hire additional employees to handle holiday or seasonal demand and tax services who gear up for longer hours during tax season are adjusting to meet customer demand.

On the other side of the coin, companies can beef up low demand periods by enticing customers to come in when business is slow. Restaurants that offer "early bird" dinner specials, bars that have special happy-hour prices, and resorts that offer off-season rates are examples of ways companies try to even out the demand and thus minimize customer inconvenience and waiting times.

Respond to How Customers Perceive the Wait

A good way to make waiting less unpleasant is to be distracted. Think about what we all do to break boredom. We listen to a headset while jogging. We read a book or magazine when stuck in a doctor's office or at the bus station. Some folks are contented to simply "people watch" while at an airport or in busy mall.

Companies can help provide for customer distraction. While waiting in a line at an amusement park, we are likely to see cartoon characters or a marching band go by. While in line at my local post office, I can view stamp collections or watch the Discovery channel playing on a mounted TV set. I've seen office waiting rooms with elaborate fish tanks or soothing fountains. All such things can help reduce the annoyance of waiting times.

Make Things Easier for Customers

Another way businesses provide A-plus service is by taking the hassle out of cumbersome systems. Unnecessary paperwork is an area where many companies can improve. Smart companies regularly look at the forms or applications customers need to complete and determine if these are all really necessary. They check for redundancy or requests for unnecessary information that may be making the paperwork process more difficult than it needs to be. Some of the better mortgage or consumer loan companies make the application process streamlined by pre-completing parts of the paperwork. For example, a credit union mortgage department I recently worked with downloaded all relevant credit and account information from my account before giving me forms to complete. I needed to fill out only a few lines.

Continuously check for unnecessary redundancy. Don't require customers to do anything repetitive or unneeded.

Likewise, a used auto dealership I bought from had all the information about the car preprinted on the sales documents. The sales rep slipped a few forms into his computer printer and the otherwise complicated paperwork was reduced to a matter of a few signatures. This provided a surprising convenience for the buyer and moved the sales process along more efficiently.

By contrast, I recently had the unpleasant experience of filling out some forms for a health care provider. Too often, a new patient at a doctor's office is required to fill out a stack of forms, each time reentering their name, address, phone number, social security number, and such. Page after page of forms, all requiring the same information! It gets annoying. Input the data one time and cut the repetition.

Repetitious or unnecessary paperwork is annoying. Make life easier for your customer by simplifying forms, applications, and so on.

Look at your organization to determine if you are requiring repetitive busywork from your customers, then A-plus them by eliminating it. Contact management systems and computerized records can easily gather and store a great deal of customer information, making it unnecessary for repetitive work. Check into the use of these.

CREATE ONCE-AND-DONE SERVICE

"That's not my department," may be one of the least-favorite phrases for customers. Likewise, having to repeatedly tell a story to person after person while seeking a solution drives people nuts. Strive for once-and-done service. Make it easy for customers to get everything they need and any problem solved at a single place or through one person authorized to take "ownership" of the customer's issue.

Try to solve customer transaction problems in one easy step—not by passing the customer off to others.

The Ritz-Carlton Hotels are well known for their simple employee position that they are "ladies and gentlemen serving ladies and gentlemen." When a hotel guest asks any employee for something, that employee "owns" that request or problem until it is fulfilled or solved. If a guest asks a maid where he can get a copy of a foreign language newspaper, the maid will either get the paper for him or find out where the guest can get it. The maid is empowered to take the time to run to a news stand if that will get the guest what he wants. It's once-and-done service. And it blows customers away. Employees are given a substantial annual budget they can spend on their customers with no questions asked. The chain won the prestigious Malcolm Baldridge Quality Award in part because of such an exceptional service philosophy.

At the heart of once-and-done service is employee willingness and ability to take responsibility for meeting needs and reducing customer inconvenience. Strong companies hire people with initiative and empower them to do whatever the customer needs.

Make Doing Business Easy

A *Wall Street Journal* article revealed a "secret weapon" used by discount retailers to "once again trounce traditional department stores." "Was it sophisticated pricing, the latest in-store design, or cutting-edge inventory management? Actually, after twenty years of growing discounter dominance, a simpler explanation rolls into view: the shopping cart."

The article goes on to say that the impact of something as simple as a shopping cart is significant. A marketing research firm found that "the average shopper with a cart buys 7.2 items, while the customer without a cart buys 6.1." "As old-fashioned as they seem, carts are perfectly suited for the way people shop today: They're pressed for time and buy more in fewer trips. Mothers struggling to corral children love them. The growing ranks of senior citizens lean on carts for support and appreciate not having to carry their purchases."[5]

Shopping malls are beginning to recognize the importance of making shopping easier. Worried about competition from point-and-click e-commerce, developers are working to cluster similar stores together so customers can comparison shop.

The traditional mall was designed to be difficult to navigate. Retailers wanted people to wander through the malls to increase exposure to other stores. The more the customer walks, the greater the chance he or she will find something else to buy. But e-commerce is changing this too. People want to compare prices and selection at similar stores and they don't want to have to walk far to do it. (After all, they can do it very easily online.) Many frustrated, time-pressed shoppers have already defected from malls to big-box discounters (Wal-Mart, K-Mart, Target, Home Depot) where they can get everything they need in one place.

> Simple things like shopping carts and convenient store location can enhance customer loyalty.

OFFER ANCILLARY SERVICES

Loblaw's Supermarkets, Canada's largest chain, offers an ever-growing range of ancillary services to its shoppers. A recent innovation at a new Toronto store is a complete women-only fitness club equipped with saunas, tanning beds, a day-care center, and offering everything from treadmills to Tae-Bo classes, just steps from the cauliflower. The *Wall Street Journal* reports that "Like many grocery-store chains, Loblaw rents store space to dry cleaners, liquor stores, coffee shops, and has in-house pharmacies and banking centers. But few chains carry the concept as far as Loblaw does. [T]he chain has started offering video-game and cell-phone sales outlets in some of its stores. In addition, it began leasing space to the Club Monoco Inc. clothing store chain and teaching community cooking lessons in stores."[6] Such ancillary services create A-plus convenience for the chain's customers, while providing one-stop shopping for almost every need.

One of the wildly popular ancillary services offered by Starbucks (and competing) coffee shops is wireless Internet connections. Many a student and business person spend hours (and dollars) at such shops while working via a Wi-Fi connection.

SIMPLIFY THE PRODUCT

The running joke about people being unable to program a video player indicates the constant need to simplify products for exceptional ease of use—and convenience. The computer industry has made quantum leaps with plug-and-play technology, but still has a long way to go. Apple has made a dramatic impact on personal entertainment products with their popular iPod products that had exceptional ease of use.

> Simplification of products sold can improve customer convenience and win loyalty.

On a more mundane level, product packaging is responding to the customer's desire for convenience. A Kellogg cereal, Special-K plus, is packaged in a resealable box that looks like a half-gallon milk carton. It contains the same amount of cereal as larger more cumbersome boxes but

LOOK INSIDE

Measure Your A-Plus Convenience Efforts

As with any measurement, the critical element is to get into the customer's point of view. Try using mystery shoppers to go through what your customers must. This will help you evaluate the speed and convenience they experience.

Mystery shopping is a process whereby companies send researchers who act like customers to gather information about the customer experience. After visiting a business, "shoppers" should be able to tell you answers to these kinds of questions:

1. *How long do customer contacts take?* Use a stopwatch to calculate average times for a variety of types of transactions. Chart these times after any changes are made in procedures or policies.

    (Remember, however, it may not be the absolute amount of time but rather the customer's perception of time that is important. You can better measure this if you ask a customer how long he or she had to wait for a service and compare this time with the actual time observed. Customers will typically report a longer time than is actual. A wait of one minute may seem like two or three to the customer.)

    Be careful, however, to not rush a customer when more leisurely, personalized service may be the standard you seek. A gourmet restaurant does not push its customer to chow down and get moving. Likewise, some stores seem to savor their customer contact time.

    For example, Kiehl's is a little 148-year-old New York company that makes and sells hair- and skin-care products for men and women. While competitors push product out of the door, Kiehl's philosophy of business is different. They intentionally keep their business small to preserve their brand of customer service (which includes actresses Winona Ryder and Sarah Jessica Parker). At the Kiehl's store, the staff is famous for spending a half hour with one customer. While a long line waits, the employee grills customer after customer about skin- and hair-care characteristics and then disgorges detailed information about the products.[7]

2. *How easy is your telephone system?* A persistent pet peeve is the clumsy telephone system. Call your own company to hear for yourself how well or poorly your phone menus are. Check, especially, the following questions:
   - Can you get to a live person at any time? Does the caller know how to do that?
   - Are you requesting too much information from customers before they get to speak with someone? (Do you really need their account number, for example?)
   - Do you offer too many choices (more than four, typically, would be too many) for customers to remember?

3. *Do you currently offer delivery, immediate faxing, instantaneous email responses, or the like?* If not, would such options be possibilities your company could consider?

4. *Do you know what kinds of conveniences your competitors are offering?* If not, send an explorer group to visit them and see what they are doing.

stores in less space and is easy to pour. Premeasured products and portion-size packages are examples of achieving additional convenience through packaging.

One other illustration of a simplified product is the Jitter Bug phone™ marketed to people who want a cell phone that simply makes phone calls. It has no built-in camera or music player, no video games, no hi-tech gizmos. It is a simple phone with easy-to-read large keys and a simple, straightforward billing plan. And it is selling very well, especially among seniors. The product advertises widely in *AARP Magazine* (for retired persons) and fills a significant need. Sometime less is more in the eyes of the customer.

SERVICE SNAPSHOT

Mickey D's Speed Measurement

In a recent visit to my friendly neighborhood McDonald's, I noticed a small digital readout on the cash register—facing the customer. It displayed the "average service time" in seconds. On that day, it told me that the average customer order was filled in 72 seconds. I was impressed.

A FINAL THOUGHT

Customers are easily surprised by efficient service that goes beyond what they anticipate. Likewise, they appreciate anything that can make life more convenient for them. This need has spun off some pretty innovative time-savers such as drive-in mortuaries, quickie-wedding chapels, and the like. While those examples may carry the principle further than most of us want to go, they do reflect the almost universal desire for efficient, timely service with a minimum of inconvenience.

Beverage refills without having to ask provide a convenience that is easy to give and is much appreciated by customers.

And don't forget the "little things" principle. The little things can make big differences. I saw an example of this during the busy Christmas season when a package shipping store sent a greeting card to all its customers and included with it shipping forms so the customer could fill it out in advance when bringing in a package to ship. Another little thing that is a pet peeve of mine is when restaurant servers make customers wait for their check or for beverage refills instead of just providing them. My favorite servers anticipate my needs and meet them promptly.

Summary of Key Ideas

- Customer convenience arises from speed of service and ease of doing business. These provide excellent opportunities for exceeding expectations and building customer loyalty.
- Many companies fall into the trap of over-promising (making vague or unrealistic commitments involving their customers' time).
- Companies that meet or beat their deadlines often gain customer loyalty.
- Time is valuable to customers; disregarding this or failing to share the customer's sense of urgency creates frustration and dissatisfaction.
- Attention to details in such things as managing queues (waiting lines) can reduce the unpleasantness of having to wait for service.

- "Virtual waiting techniques" allow customers to do something else while waiting for service.
- "Once-and-done" service reduces the need for the customer to experience unnecessary repetition and delays.
- Ancillary services that complement the company's main products can provide added convenience for customers.
- Sometimes products are simply too complicated—offer more features than some customers want. **Simplified products** and services may be seen as an A-plus convenience.
- Organizations are wise to measure customer wait time and other forms of inconvenience on a regular basis.

Key Concepts

ancillary services
A-plus speed and
    convenience

once-and-done service
over-promising,
    under-delivering

queue management
    systems (QMS)

simplified products
virtual waiting

Reviewing the Facts

1. This chapter makes the case for providing efficient service, assuming that customers today are increasingly concerned about time. What evidence do you have that people are more concerned about time than in the past?

2. What companies and industries have done a good job of providing increasingly timely and/or convenient service? Describe five such businesses—preferably ones that have innovated in recent years.

3. How does the idea of A-plus convenience overlap with A-plus information? Value?
4. What are some downsides to quick service? Describe situations under which speed of service is not important to a customer. Are there, however, aspects within slow-serve situations that still require timely service? Describe some.

5. Explain in your own words the three strategies to exceed customer expectations with regard to speed and convenience.
6. What is "virtual waiting"? Describe several ways this could be applied to a business you are familiar with.

Applying the Ideas: Giving A-plus Convenience

1. This chapter talks about three strategies for dealing with customer wait times. These are (1) manage the reality, (2) manage the perception, and (3) make the wait invisible. Assume that you are a service consultant for a company or organization you are familiar with. Write a brief recommendation report describing how it could apply each of these three strategies to create A-plus convenience. Be specific about exactly what you would recommend.
2. Suppose you are considering starting an appliance repair business. What are some convenience services you could possibly apply to exceed customer expectations? Be creative. Brainstorm as many ideas as possible.
3. Of all the businesses you deal with, which ones do the best job of giving A-plus convenience/speed? Which do the worst job? How could the poor performers do better?

4. Select a business you are familiar with that does not currently use virtual waiting techniques. Explain how it could do so.
5. Do a comparison of five Web sites from the same industry. Specifically, make a list of three to five timing factors you would like to evaluate on each site. For example, how long does it take the home page to open? How quickly do other pages open? How quickly does it process an order? How quickly do you get a response to a question? Use a stopwatch and see how responsive the site is. Write a brief report of your findings including a table comparing the sites.

Consider this Case

"Service" at the Donut Shop

Early one morning, Harry found himself hungry, alone, and lost in the land of no customer service as he stumbled into a donut shop. It was a rainy, gray morning and he was tired. Cars were parked at odd angles because the lines on the lot had long ago faded. The parking lot was dirty and the trashcans overflowed.

Inside were disorganized lines of people, most wearing parkas, waiting to buy donuts. There appeared to be no systematic way of serving customers. The bold ones stepped up and demanded service, while the more timid (or courteous) hoped for attention from the clerk. Harry waited for about seven minutes as the two clerks repeatedly took orders, disappeared into the back room, reappeared, and took peoples' money. All along Harry observed the uncleared, coffee-stained counter where he soon would sit to eat his donut. It hadn't been cleared recently, and it apparently wasn't going to be cleared now. Customers groaned, as the advertised two-for-one sale didn't apply if customer ordered donuts of different prices, the clerks explained with bored, unsmiling expressions.

Harry noticed a middle-aged woman (could she be the manager?) sitting on a crate just outside the back door smoking a cigarette and reading a tabloid newspaper. She seemed oblivious to the dismal scene in the shop.

Harry finally reached the head of the line and came face to face with a 17-year-old girl who had been condemned to serve him. Something in her 17-year-old face told him that all was not well in the service economy. Harry asked her how she liked her job.

She looked him straight in the eye and said, "It sucks!"

Probes

1. Assume you are the owner of this donut shop. What would you do? What specific behaviors would you seek to change?
2. Focus on the problems of slow service. What could be done, specifically, to improve this?
3. To what extent might the slow service be a source of employee irritation and dissatisfaction?

Consider this Case

Waiting for the Doctor

As a young and ambitious physician, Rebecca Stacie was constantly looking for ways to improve office efficiency. She had recently decided to work as a sole practitioner in her own medical clinic specializing in internal medicine. Within a few months, word had gotten around about how helpful and thorough she was—she seemed to be more caring and more willing to take time with patients.

But her popularity had a downside. As her patient load increased, she began to hear grumbling from her patients about the long wait times. One rather outspoken elderly patient had told her point-blank that she was fed up with all the waiting. "You schedule me for 9 a.m. and I get here a few minutes early. Then I sit in the waiting room for 20 minutes or more. Then your nurse calls me into an exam room and I get to sit there for another half hour. I show you the courtesy of being here on time and I'd appreciate it if you'd show similar respect for my time, doctor."

Dr. Stacie apologized and said she would work on being more punctual, although it was very difficult to judge how long each patient visit would take. When she asked her office staff if they were hearing more complaints, they said they were. "And the problem is taking on a new look," said her office nurse. "Patients are showing up later and later. They don't even apologize. They typically say they know they'll be waiting and the doc will be late, so why should they try to get to their appointment on time." Of course, the tardy patients tie up everyone else and the problem gets worse for everyone.

Probes

1. If you were managing Dr. Stacie's office, what actions could you take to try to A-plus patients with timely services? Be specific.
2. How might you manage the patient's expectations more effectively?
3. Could Dr. Stacie use any other techniques discussed in this chapter? How?

Notes

1. Jane Bennett Clarke, "Washed, Cooked and Priced to Go," *Kiplinger's Personal Finance*, January 2000, p. 135.
2. Bray, Hiawatha (Boston Globe Staff), "Aging, the New Frontier," *Salt Lake Tribune*, April 7, 2009, p. C2.
3. Duncan Dickson, Robert C. Ford, and Bruce Laval, "Managing Real and Virtual Waits in Hospital and Service Organizations," *Cornell Hotel and Restaurant Administration Quarterly*, February 2005, pp. 52–68.
4. Ibid., p. 52.
5. Joseph B. Cahill, "The Secret Weapon of Big Discounters: Lowly Shopping Carts," *Wall Street Journal*, November 24, 1999, p. 1.
6. Joel A. Baglole, "Loblaw's Supermarkets Add Fitness Clubs to Offerings," *Wall Street Journal*, December 27, 1999, p. B4.
7. Hilary Stout, "The Ad Budget: Zero. The Buzz: Deafening," *Wall Street Journal European Edition*, December 30, 1999, p. 4.

PART 5

Living Life

This book has been structured around the acronym LIFE. We discussed the importance of "little things"—attention to details to give better service. We also explored some of the "insights" necessary to tune in to possible customer turnoffs and the ever-changing service environment. The concept of "feedback" is the F in our acronym and we talked about its usefulness in providing controls and ideas for improvement. "Expectations" is the E in LIFE and we spent several chapters elaborating on ways we can exceed customer expectations to strengthen relationships and loyalty.

In the remaining chapters, we focus on some additional ways to apply the ideas developed with the LIFE acronym. In Chapter 13, we address the challenges posed by "emotional labor" as we serve customers. Closely associated is the area of stress management and organizing tasks to reduce unproductive stress. In Chapter 14, we wrap up with discussion of the significant challenge of actually getting people involved in the kinds of things needed to create and implement an ongoing strategy for providing exceptional customer service.

CHAPTER 13

Dealing with Emotional Labor
Managing Time and Tasks to Reduce Stress

Being in control of your life and having realistic expectations about your day-to-day challenges are the keys to stress management, which is perhaps the most important ingredient to living a happy, healthy, and rewarding life.

—MARILU HENNER

Tension is who you think you should be. Relaxation is who you are.

—CHINESE PROVERB

After reading this chapter, you should be able to

1. Recognize that working with customers requires the exertion of "emotional labor," which can be stressful.

2. Identify the kinds of **working conditions** most likely to lead to unproductive stress.

3. Apply five key skills for better time and task management.

4. Become more effective at delegating.

The Way It Is: Customer Service Work Can Be Stressful

Emotional labor is the term researchers use to describe labor that involves managing emotions so that they are consistent with organizational or occupational display rules, regardless of whether they are discrepant with internal feelings.[1] In the context of customer service, this means that it can be hard work to project upbeat, positive emotions at all times as is often required by customer-contact jobs.

The term *emotional labor* was first defined by the sociologist Arlie Hochschild as the "management of feeling to create a publicly observable facial and bodily display."[2] This "display" takes the form of verbal and nonverbal communication as discussed elsewhere in this book. According to Hochschild, jobs involving emotional labor are defined as those that:

- require face-to-face or voice-to-voice contact with the public;
- require the worker to produce an emotional state in another person;
- allow the employees to exercise a degree of control over their emotional activities.

Clearly, these functions are typical of customer service jobs. We establish contact and try to create positive emotions in our customers, and we almost always have discretion in how we project our emotions to others.

Giving great customer service can be stressful and demanding, especially when our personal emotional state is out of sync with customers'. Everyone has bad days or gets into emotional funks now and then. To make things tougher, we may find ourselves dealing with people who are upset, unhappy, and even irrational at times. We may find ourselves pressured by too much work and too little time. We may feel stressed by the boredom of repetitive tasks and unappreciative bosses.

But then again, all jobs have their stress-producing characteristics. In fact, the less control we have over our daily activities, the greater the stress levels. Studies have shown that low-control positions such as receptionists, toll takers, and so on are quite stressful. Stress isn't just for air traffic controllers or police officers. We all face it.

So, what exactly can we do to succeed at emotional labor, deal with pressures, and still exhibit professionalism and effectiveness at work? In this chapter, we will look at these issues, much of which can be accomplished by using what for many is the best tool: time and task management techniques.

WORKING WITH CUSTOMERS CAN BE STRESSFUL, BUT NOT ALL STRESS IS BAD

The term *stress* has a negative connotation to most people, but, in reality, it is neither good nor bad. Stress is defined as "a mental or emotional disquieting response to a difficult condition or situation." It may be thought of as a state of mental or emotional imbalance caused by a perceived difference between a person's capabilities and what is expected of that person.

Of course, the kind of job stress that gets the most press is the one which is detrimental to performance or which can lead to bad physical responses ranging from nervousness to hives to high blood pressure, to strokes and heart attacks. These are bad things. But sometimes stress is a positive; it is exactly what we need to motivate ourselves. If we face a tight deadline, stress can push us toward completion. If we face a new challenge, stress will be a natural accompaniment that may keep us mentally sharp. So, eliminating stress isn't really the goal. Limiting it or managing it is a more realistic response. A good starting point is to understand where worker stress comes from.

Stress is not necessarily bad, but can become a problem if excessive or unmanaged.

What Are the Causes of Job Stress?[3]

Unproductive job stress results from some combination of **worker characteristics** and *working conditions*. According to one school of thought, differences in individual characteristics such as personality and coping style are most important in predicting whether certain job conditions will result in stress. In other words, what is stressful for one person may not be a problem for someone else. This viewpoint leads to prevention strategies that focus on workers and ways to help them cope with demanding job conditions. Much of this chapter will discuss ways we can organize our time and tasks to manage stress.

Although the importance of individual differences cannot be ignored, certain working conditions that are stressful to most people should be examined as well.

Stress arises from both working conditions and worker characteristics.

Working Conditions that May Lead to Stress

The following conditions are often causes of undue stress for employees. If you are a manager or supervisor, you should be aware of these and seek ways to minimize their detrimental effects. If you are a nonmanagement employee, you should give feedback to management just as customers must give feedback to companies. If you are experiencing unproductive stress because of these kinds of conditions, communicate your concern to your supervisor. Don't convey it as whining or complaining, but rather explain how current work conditions are counterproductive to the organization. It is very difficult to give great service if you do not receive appropriate support

---

SERVICE SNAPSHOT

Team-building Interventions[4]

Emotional labor can become particularly, well, laborious when employees face tedious job tasks, job insecurity or inflexible work schedules.

To address such issues, psychologist David M. DeJoy, PhD, a professor of health promotion and behavior at the University of Georgia, conducted a study on healthy work organization in a retail company. DeJoy and his colleagues surveyed employees at 21 stores—all part of the same company—to identify employees' concerns about issues such as their work schedules. (Note that scheduling can often relate to the amount of control employees have—an element of emotional labor.) From there, the researchers formed a team

of 8 to 12 employees at each store to develop store-specific ways to respond to those concerns. These responses included programs geared to enhance employer and employee communication skills, improve morale, manage conflict, and solve problems related to, for example, customer-service issues.

According to self-reports from employees and employers, these efforts led to better communication as well as improved employee satisfaction with work schedules, job content, and feelings of increased involvement in workplace decisions, said DeJoy. Using teams to address employee concerns had some positive effects on store sales and employee turnover.

---

from your organization. Good working conditions are truly a win-win-win for the company, you, and the customers. Open the communication channels and explore ideas for improving work conditions to reduce the burden of emotional labor.

NONSTOP ACTION Stress arises from heavy workload, infrequent rest breaks, long work hours, and shift work. It also stems from hectic and routine tasks that have little inherent meaning, do not utilize workers' skills, and provide little sense of control. No one can continuously give good customer service without taking breaks. For example, dealers at the gaming tables in Las Vegas get breaks as often as every 20 minutes. To stay sharp and remain responsive to customer needs, service people need to stay fresh. Effective managers are aware of the psychological pressures placed on customer-contact people.

MANAGEMENT STYLE Employees feel increased stress from managers who fail to allow participation by workers in decision making, from ineffective communication in the organization, or from lack of family-friendly policies. People in customer service positions should be encouraged to participate in generating ideas for improving customer experiences, for example. Such participation supports the feeling of engagement in their jobs and pays off with good ideas, as well.

INTERPERSONAL RELATIONSHIPS A poor social environment and lack of support or help from coworkers and supervisors can create unproductive stress for service employees. Poor social environment may arise when people distrust each other, argue frequently, engage in inappropriate humor or harassment, or treat each other with disrespect. One measure of a good place to work—and of high employee engagement—is work conditions where people can become friends.[5]

UNCLEAR WORK ROLES Conflicting or uncertain job expectations, too much responsibility, or too many "hats to wear" can generate stress. Service employees should have clear instructions on how to handle most problems they may encounter—and the authority to improvise when a new situation comes up. This can be tricky. Companies need an appropriate number of rules or standard procedures, but must also allow some leeway for individual discretion. Some successful companies allow extensive employee leeway.

However, new hire orientations now provide this card along with a full handbook of other more specific rules and legal regulations, as the way Nordstrom operates has evolved.

ANOTHER LOOK

Nordstrom Kept It Simple

Striking an appropriate balance between a sufficient number of rules and allowing employee's discretion has long been a challenge for companies. For many years, new employees at famed retailer Nordstrom were given a copy of the famous "**Nordstrom's Employee Handbook**," which was not a book at all. It was a single 5- × 8-inch gray card containing 75 words:[6] **Welcome to Nordstrom**

We're glad to have you with our Company. Our number one goal is to provide outstanding customer service. Set both your personal and professional goals high. We have great confidence in your ability to achieve them.

Nordstrom Rules: Rule #1: Use good judgment in all situations. There will be no additional rules.

Please feel free to ask your department manager, store manager, or division general manager any question at any time.

CAREER CONCERNS   Especially in times of economic downturn, stress can arise from job insecurity. People worried about cutbacks or layoffs inevitably experience anxiety. But even for people in secure positions, a lack of opportunity for growth, advancement, or promotion can cause stress. Employees never want to feel that their jobs are dead ends or that they are at the whims of uncontrollable forces. And, uncertainty associated with frequent and rapid change (a fairly common condition in today's workplace) can likewise create undue stress.

POOR WORK ENVIRONMENT   Stress can arise from unpleasant or dangerous physical conditions such as crowding, noise, air pollution, or from ergonomic problems such as awkward placement of equipment. A workplace needs to feel fundamentally safe. No worker should be exposed to danger or to repetitive movement problems like carpel tunnel from excessive keyboarding. Ergonomically friendly equipment and a generally pleasant work atmosphere can minimize these kinds of problems.

Companies lacking in a good work environment can suffer from what consultant John Graham called "tired company syndrome."[7] A tired company is marked by a dated look and feel, excessive caution and hesitance to change, a propensity to look to the past, being behind the technology curve, and a tendency to smother new ideas. These are stifling places to work. Employee stress is a natural outgrowth of such an environment.

FIVE KEY SKILLS FOR BETTER TIME AND TASK MANAGEMENT

Having discussed some working condition associated with stress, let's now turn to worker characteristics—ways we, as individuals, can better manage the everyday stress we face as service providers. We begin with talking about how we can reduce stress by getting more of the right things accomplished, every day. Mastering time and task management skills will not only reduce stress but also make life more happy and satisfying—and make your career more successful.

Think about times when you have had a really good day. Most people tend to be satisfied and motivated when they are being productive—when they are accomplishing things that are important. Time and task management result in productivity. Productivity is the key to career success. In challenging and competitive times, companies will always look to the productive employee to accomplish needed work and assure the organization's viability. If companies downsize, the jobs of the most productive employees are the most secure. When companies decide to promote employees, those with a track record for accomplishing important tasks in the organization are the ones considered for advancement.

Personal productivity is both satisfying to us as employees and adds greater job security.

Below are five time and task management skills that will make you more valuable to your company, more effective as a professional, and more productive in your personal life. The key skills you will learn are how to:

1. Target your efforts on the most important tasks
2. Be a goal getter, not just a goal setter
3. Do the constructive things first
4. Avoid time-wasters
5. Effectively delegate (even if you are not the boss)

Key Skill 1. Target Your Efforts on the Most Important Tasks

Productivity soars when people get the most out of their time and effort. To maximize productivity, you must know the underlying value of the tasks you do. Productivity is the process of using our limited time and resources to accomplish work that is valuable (and not get sidetracked by the trivial and unimportant).

> Focusing your activities on what is most valuable is a first key to better time management.

To focus on the valuable, you need to understand your company's mission and core objectives and you also need to clarify your *own **core values***. If your job calls for serving customers and if giving exceptional service is truly a core value of the company, you will gain the greatest satisfaction from work that does just that—serves customers.

A core value is a description of what you (or your company's leaders) see as most desirable—most worthwhile. The clearer the values, the better people can reduce the need to make time-consuming, arbitrary, and uncomfortable choices. Value-consistent behavior is spontaneously right. With clear values as anchors, you can make quicker, better decisions about the use of your time and efforts.

> Take the time to carefully clarify your core values and to understand the core values of your company.

Take the advice of top management gurus and psychologists. Make value clarification a high priority. Seek to understand your company's values as well as your personal ones. This is a critical first step to improving your productivity and professionalism.

A good way to articulate the values that will guide your personal productivity is to first name the value. Use one word or a short phrase to identify the concept. For example, you might identify values called *service excellence, sales professionalism, health and vigor, learning, financial security, leadership, personal effectiveness, balance,* and so on.

Once you have given the value a name, describe in a few phrases what it will be like when this value becomes a reality in your life. Use the present tense in your description as though you have already achieved agreement with the value.

The following are examples of how three core values (two job related, one personal) might be clarified. Your wording must be your own, but these illustrate the process.

Company value: Excellent customer service
Description of this value:
I work to satisfy the needs of each customer. I give top priority to solving customer problems and work to do so efficiently and in a friendly manner. I make it fun for customers to do business with us. I reward loyal customers with special incentives.

Name of the value: Sales professionalism
Description of this value:
I keep a positive attitude about selling as a profession. I read sales publications and apply new ideas. I set challenging sales goals and focus my daily efforts to meet these goals and satisfy customer needs. I use my sales skills to help my customers make good decisions about the products that meet their needs. I am honest in all my dealings and stay close to my customers after the sale.

NAME OF THE VALUE: HEALTH AND VIGOR
DESCRIPTION/DEFINITION OF THIS VALUE:
I exercise regularly and avoid harmful habits. I maintain appropriate weight. I get regular medical and dental checkups. I maintain vigor by daily planning, goal setting, and rewarding myself for accomplishments. I jog, play racquetball, swim, play golf, and do fun things with my family to let off steam. I view life as being fun and full of opportunity.

Naming and describing values provide criteria for evaluating the tasks you face. Work first on tasks that support your values. Other tasks may be unproductive time-wasters.

Key Skill 2. Be a Goal Getter, Not Just a Goal Setter

Setting goals is good. Getting goals is better. And the way to get your goals is to avoid squandering precious time on activities that add little or nothing to your pursuit. Goals should arise from your values. If you have described clear values, goals are easy to set. But be sure that each goal meets six criteria: Be sure it is

- ✓ WRITTEN. An unwritten goal is only a wish.
- ✓ CONCRETE AND SPECIFIC. Clear goals motivate; fuzzy ones do not.
- ✓ REALISTIC. Action targets should stretch us, but not beyond what is reasonable.
- ✓ MEASURABLE. Find ways to count actions (e.g., miles run, hours spent with kids, or items sold) or describe accomplishment (I feel confident when speaking).
- ✓ TIED TO A DEADLINE. A deadline creates constructive urgency.
- ✓ VALUE-ANCHORED. Value-based goals create direction in the mind. Goals that do not support your values are useless.

An example of a goal related to your value of *excellent customer service* might be: "Send handwritten thank-you notes to 100 top customers by March 15." A sales goal may be "Formally interview 12 current clients this quarter to determine their satisfaction with current products and possible needs for additional products." A goal relating to your value of *health and vigor* might be: "Jog 50+ miles in April."

Once you have articulated your goals, re-read your written goals frequently to reinforce and remind you of which tasks are important and productive—for you.

Look at your goals regularly to keep on track.

Key Skill 3. Do the Constructive Things First

You can better focus on constructive activities with daily planning. Use a planner system for recording your plan of action and for tracking key information. Some people use a computer or PDA (personal data assistant) or the data-keeping ability built into today's "smart phones." While such technology is popular and useful to many people, it is not necessary—many people still prefer an old-fashioned day planner or even a calendar. Use whatever is most comfortable for you, but regardless of the planner system you use, be sure it allows you to do four things:

- List and assign priorities to tasks for each day.
- Record notes and follow-up information.
- Display your goals and values. (If frequently reviewed, you will pull them into your everyday activities.)
- File frequently referred-to information, especially addresses, phone numbers, email addresses, important dates, customer preferences, and so on.

To dramatically increase your productivity, spend 10 minutes or so planning before you jump into the day's activities. Set your objectives for the day; re-read your value statements and get yourself mentally prepared for the coming day. People who use a planner system report as much as a 25 percent boost in their productivity by doing things in logical sequence. Here is a simple process for making the most of your planning:

Step 1. Develop a Priority Task List for Each Day

List all the key tasks you need to accomplish that day. Don't be concerned with the importance of the items just yet; get in the habit of listing every task you can think of. (Don't include routine tasks like brushing your teeth or going to work; make this a list of discretionary tasks—things you need to do to make your day successful.)

Step 2. Assign a Priority to Each Item to Indicate Its Importance

Put the letter "A" next to items that *must be done*. The A priority identifies tasks that are *important*—constructive because they are required by your job or because they move you toward your goals—and they must be done soon. Assign A-priorities to only the top few tasks for each day. Remember that these priorities are determined by your core values. If building customer loyalty is a core value, list specific tasks that will be consistent with that value. For example, you might make it a priority task to read a chapter from a good book on the topic, to study results from a feedback survey, to rearrange a merchandise display, to review written information you give customers, and so on. (There are plenty of such tasks suggested throughout this book.)

Use the letter "B" to indicate items you *should do*. These are worth spending time on but are not as critical as the A tasks or they may not yet be facing a deadline. The letter "C" is used for *could do* items. These are worth listing, and, if you get the As and Bs all done, worth doing.

Assign a * (star) if an unexpected but urgent task pops up during the day and you add it to your task list. Be sure that these starred tasks are *both urgent and important!* If that is the case, drop whatever else you are doing to get that task completed. Use the star rarely. Sometimes a surprise task that demands your immediate attention isn't really that *important*. Judge the action's importance just as you would a planned item. If its completion is critical to your job or your goals, then do it. If not, assign a lesser priority. Learn to discriminate between the important and the merely urgent.

> Tasks that pop up and seem urgent may not be important. Don't be overly reactive to the urgent—unless it is also important in light of your goals and values.

Step 3. Check Off Tasks as Completed or Changed

When you complete a task listed in your planner, reward yourself with one of these completion symbols (starting with the one that feels the best):

- ☑ *The task has been completed.* Use red to remind yourself of how productive you are.
- → *The task is rescheduled.* Use this when a meeting has been postponed, an appointment changed, or an activity could not be done today but needs to be done in the future. IMPORTANT: Any time you use the arrow, reschedule the task to another day (and, of course, write it on the new date in your planner or PDA). The arrow earns you the right to forget about that task for now. It will come up automatically on the new schedule.
- ○ *A task that has been delegated* to someone else. Put a circle next to the delegated task. Write the initials of the person you assigned the job to inside it. When the task is completed by that person, check it off.
- ☒ *A task that has been deleted.* You changed your mind about its importance or other circumstances changed. You have no need to reschedule this as you would with an arrowed task.

Make your priority planning work by sticking to your plan. Do not look at your A tasks and say, "I really don't feel like doing that. I'll just peek at some of these B tasks and do one of them first." If you do this instead of finishing an A, *a task you said is most important*, you defeat the purpose of planning. A good definition of a productive day is one in which you accomplished the A tasks on your list.

> A good definition of a productive day is one in which you accomplished your A-level tasks.

Your planner system should have a place for scheduling appointments and recording notes. The schedule section is self-explanatory. The notes section is used to jot down commitments you have made with others, telephone calls, ideas, thoughts, or any other bit of information that may come in handy. Use the note section instead of jotting notes on scraps of paper or post-its. Keep all your notes in one place and avoid scribbling on the back of an envelope, where the message is sure to get misplaced.

With daily planning, you avoid doing less productive things by answering the question, "What *is the best possible use of my time right now?*" Look to your priority task list for the answer.

Regularly ask, "What's the best possible use of my time right now?"

Key Skill 4. Foster Teamwork

Few of us work alone, in a vacuum. Our efforts have impact on others. Teamwork with others leads to better time and task management by reducing unproductive wheel-spinning. Four conditions are necessary for effective employee–boss teamwork: accessibility, supportiveness, reliability, and loyalty.

- Be accessible to exchange information

  You and your coworkers, boss, and others should feel comfortable exchanging information freely. For trust to grow, you must respect each other's ideas, even when you do not agree with them. Open the communication channels and keep each other informed. Encourage discussion of customer contact situations—those that went well and those that were not so successful. Take credit for good calls and accept the blame for mistakes. Learn from each other.

- Be supportive of others

  Build trust by being attentive and available physically, mentally, and emotionally, especially when one of you is under unusual pressure. Offer the boss help in any way you can and she or he will be likely to do the same for you. Offer to pitch in to help solve a difficult customer problem.

- Be consistently reliable

  Be predictable in handling work with good judgment and thoroughness. Be reliable in meeting deadlines and doing work of high quality. If a customer needs follow-up, be certain that you complete that follow-up.

- Be loyal while maintaining independence

  Two-way loyalty builds trust. Trust is destroyed if either party fears that information shared might be used to the advantage of one at the expense of the other. Accept the fact that sometimes you need to argue forcefully for your position. Do it tactfully, but firmly. Agree to disagree but do not let honest differences damage trust.

Key Skill 5. Avoid Time Wasters

Time wasters are huge stress producers. When we don't feel we are accomplishing things that need to be doing but are, rather, circling in unproductive behaviors, the stress builds up. Six major time wasters are interruptions or fragmented work, unproductive communication, clutter and paperwork, procrastination, **perfection paralysis**, and self-overload. Here are some tips for dealing with each:

TIME WASTER 1:	Interruptions or fragmented work
SOLUTION 1:	Assertively decline to be interrupted. Be pleasant but direct. If someone asks, "Have a minute?" say, "I really don't. I'm in the middle of fixing a customer problem right now. Could I get back to you in about 20 minutes?" If you are regularly interrupted from your own work by people you supervise, try this: Scheduling time when you *can be interrupted.* Use an "open door" time each day to show people when they can "interrupt" you. If a person pops in at another time, ask them to see you during your designated time.

TIME WASTER 2:	Unproductive communication
SOLUTION 1:	Choose the right media. Media are the methods and channels by which we communicate. Choose the most productive ones. Do not write a letter when a phone call will do. Don't email when a personal visit is needed to deal with a sensitive issue (even if the visit takes longer). A bit more time spent now may settle a problem, while exchanging emails will not. Consider the difference between **synchronous** and **asynchronous** media. Synchronistic media allow both parties in a communication to interact or answer each other's questions at the same time, as when communicating face to face or through telephone.
	Asynchronous media let only one person communicate at a time such as when you send an email or letter and then wait for the response. Instant messaging is asynchronic but generally gets a quick reply and is therefore somewhere between these other media.
SOLUTION 2:	Allow for feedback. When instructing people, encourage them to ask questions or get clarification. A few extra moments spent when giving instructions can save hours of fixing problems later. When explaining something complex to customers, check to be sure they understand what you plan to do or what they need to do next. Ask, in a nonjudgmental way, if they understand. Example: "Do you feel comfortable in using these advanced features?"
SOLUTION 3:	Keep other people (including your boss) appraised of your priorities. A five-minute planning discussion each day can clear the air and let others know what you are focusing on and assure that your work will be productive. If you can't get to see the boss personally, use a brief note to advise her of what you plan to do. For example:

Dear Ms. Shaker,

Here is what I am planning for today. My first priority is to research the Murphy billing problem. I'll call the customer back and get that straightened out. When I finish that, I'll review the customer feedback summary for April and write up the job description for the new service rep positions (etc.).

   If these priorities are not what you need me to be doing, please let me know. If I do not hear from you, I will assume that I'm on the right track.

—*Kim*

TIME WASTER 3:	Clutter, paperwork, and overloaded computer files
SOLUTION 1:	Handle each paper or each email only once. Learn to make decisions, and do not postpone actions on each email, letter, memo, or document (or the electronic equivalent) you receive. Use the RAFT approach—and do it NOW!

- R—refer it to someone else
- A—act on it—immediately (do what it requests or respond)
- F—file it for future reference
- T—trash it (don't let junk accumulate)

Be careful when saving or filing stuff. Often people save things they will never again use, thus creating clutter. In fact, studies show that 95 percent of the stuff in files for more than one year will *never* be used. De-junk your files (especially the ones in your computer), "tossing" whatever you can. Keep only those information required by law or policy, and get rid of the rest.

SOLUTION 2:	Clean up and organize your work area. Toss the distracting junk. Aim for a clear desk or minimalist workspace. Put frequently used supplies close by without cluttering. Keep customer contact areas clean and attractive, not cluttered with past work.
SOLUTION 3:	Reduce reading material bulk by clipping or ripping articles from magazines. Most of a magazine is irrelevant; tear out what you want and trash the rest. Also, minimize the number of electronic files you print. Unsubscribe to electronic newsletters that don't give you value. If the topics are not useful to you on the job, don't get sucked into reading them at work.
SOLUTION 4:	As a general rule for better efficiency: don't put things *down*, put them *away*. It takes only a second to put things in their proper place. Failing to do so makes a one-step process into a two-step process. First we put the tool or piece of merchandise or whatever down somewhere, then we later have to put it where it belongs. Make this a one-step process.
TIME WASTER 4:	Procrastination (I'll get to this one later. Just kidding)
SOLUTION 1:	Understand why you procrastinate. Psychologists identify three reasons for procrastination:

- fear of failure,
- fear of success, or
- the desire to rebel

Determine which reason you are using. Then do whatever is necessary to overcome it. Fears are best handled by pushing yourself through them— by stepping outside the comfort zone to try new things. If you have a particularly thorny customer problem, handle it first. Then the rest of the day will be a piece of cake. If you are procrastinating as your form of rebelling, try to identify your psychological payoff. What do you get for your rebellion? Is it really worth it?

SOLUTION 2:	Use your daily priority task list. Do the worst task first. Get it over with and enjoy the rest of the day. Make dreaded tasks into games. Compete against others or against your previous results. Try to beat your last effort.
SOLUTION 3:	Just tough it out. (Sorry, but ultimately it may come down to that.)
TIME WASTER 5:	Perfection paralysis. Some things just don't have to be perfect, and striving for perfection could waste a lot of time. Granted, I'd prefer a perfectionist brain surgeon or copy editor, but many daily tasks can get away with "close enough."
SOLUTION 1:	Use a "**ready-fire-aim!**" philosophy:

- ✓ Think through your idea (get *ready*),
- ✓ Try it (*fire!*),
- ✓ Observe and correct the results as needed (*aim*).

Wal-Mart founder Sam Walton encouraged this approach. He constantly challenged his people to try new customer service ideas, not just mull them over. Get yourself *doing something* and then adjust as necessary.

SOLUTION 2:	Recognize that virtually all ideas, products, and processes go through polishing and editing. Quality can always be improved, so don't hold back on doing something while waiting for it to be perfect. Ready-fire-aim!

TIME WASTER 6:   Self-overload

SOLUTION 1:   Use your energy to accomplish your goal-directed, value-based activities. If a task does not add value to your life or career, simply don't do it. Be vigilant about fending off tasks that are inconsistent with what is really important—those tasks that move you toward accomplishing your professional or personal goals.

SOLUTION 2:   Accept your limitations. No one can accomplish everything or hit peak performance every day. Assume you will have some down times when you will not be as productive as you'd like. If you wasted a chunk of time, so be it. It's gone and there is nothing you can do about it now. But you can regroup and decide to use better task management techniques from this point on.

EFFECTIVELY DELEGATE (EVEN IF YOU ARE NOT THE BOSS)

Having described five tactics for better time and task management, we must consider one more—perhaps the most powerful one—**delegation**. If you can delegate work, you excuse yourself from doing it! What could be more efficient?

You need not be a boss to delegate work. In fact, you *should* delegate a task whenever someone else can do it more *efficiently*, more *cheaply*, or *better* than you can. Better time management and stress reduction call for better delegation. Recognize its potential, understand why you may hesitate to delegate, and know what can go wrong and how to reduce its failures.

Delegation is crucial to better time management.

Again, you don't have to be a boss to delegate. Example: When you take your car to a car wash (instead of going home, dragging out the bucket and hose, and washing it yourself) you are delegating. Getting someone else to wash the car buys you some valuable time. You also delegate when you ask your spouse to pick up bread and milk on the way home from work, or when you ask a coworker to drop off a package at the post office on his lunch hour. You are delegating when you forward a customer communication to someone who can handle it better than you can.

For supervisors, delegation is crucial. Supervision is, by definition, accomplishing work with and through the efforts of others. If you try to do all the work alone, you are not supervising. Although it may seem easier to do a job yourself, delegating and teaching someone else is, in the long run, a key to improving your productivity. An old saying goes, "Lazy parents pick up after their children." Teaching kids to do for themselves (i.e., delegating work to them) is good for you, and good for them.

Simply stated, the more you can delegate, the more time you have to accomplish other activities. Nevertheless, people may hesitate to delegate for a number of reasons:

- LACK OF CONFIDENCE IN OTHERS. The delegated job may not get done exactly as you would like—or may not get done at all. Having a few experiences where a delegated task dropped between the cracks can make you gun-shy. Your best approach to overcoming this is to *increase* delegating until you learn people's capacity for accomplishing tasks. Also let go of the notion that there is only one *right* way to do a task. Others' ideas may be just fine, although different from yours.
- I-CAN-DO-IT-MYSELF REASONING. You probably *can* do anything you ask others to do but that's not the important issue. The real question is whether you *should*. Is doing it yourself the most productive use of your time? If not, delegate.
- FEAR OF NOT GETTING RECOGNITION. You will get full credit for your productivity regardless of who actually does the work. Leaders know that productive people do not work alone. They accomplish important work in the most efficient ways, and that almost always involves the efforts of others. The talent to delegate is highly valued.

- LACK OF TIME OR SKILLS NEEDED TO EXPLAIN DELEGATED WORK. Sometimes it seems to take more time to delegate than to do the work yourself. From a short-range viewpoint that may be true. But if the delegated job is one that will need to be done over and over, your choice is to spend time now to teach others, or to keep on spending time doing the task yourself— forever. With delegation, you buy freedom.

To be effective at delegating, be willing to do the following:

- Entrust others with responsibilities.
- Give others the freedom and authority to carry out delegated tasks.
- Spend the time to teach people.

With delegation, you *multiply your* productivity. Without delegation, you are limited to accomplishing only what you can do before exhaustion sets in.

Learn to overcome the reasons people hesitate to delegate.

How Delegation Can Go Wrong

Having sung the praises of delegation as a stress-reducing, time management technique, we still need to recognize the reality that delegation can sometimes go wrong. Here are the most common mistakes that can cause delegation to fail.

- FAILURE TO KEEP THE COMMUNICATION CHANNELS OPEN.
- SOLUTION: Let people know that they can ask you for clarifying instructions or check on how they are doing. Give helpful feedback about delegated jobs.
- FAILURE TO ALLOW FOR MISTAKES.
- SOLUTION: Don't make people feel inadequate with harsh criticism of honest mistakes. Let people learn from the inevitable—and forgiven—mistakes.
- FAILURE TO FOLLOW UP A DELEGATED TASK.
- SOLUTION: Convey a sense of continued interest; keep up-to-date on the progress of a delegated job.
- FAILURE TO DELEGATE ENOUGH AUTHORITY TO COMPLETE THE TASK.
- SOLUTION: Tell people who may be affected by the delegated task that you have given your person authority to do it. For example, if you ask someone to interview other workers to research a problem, be sure those employees know that the interviews are authorized. Announce delegated tasks.

A FINAL THOUGHT

Customer-contact work involves elements of **emotional labor**. We are sometimes required to behave in ways inconsistent with how we may feel. This can produce stress. All jobs create some stress, and some of that stress can be useful. The challenge workers face is not to *eliminate* stress (that would be both impossible and undesirable) but to *manage* it. Among the most effective techniques for keeping stress within reasonable bounds is time management—or, more accurately, time and task management.

We can better handle daily pressures by clarifying which of the many tasks we face are most valuable and by attacking these tasks based on their priority. Priorities are determined by our personal values—what activities we decide are important. Taking time and expending the effort to clarify our personal values and set appropriate goals can be very useful in keeping us on track. Making these processes a regular part of our daily lives can pay huge dividends.

We can also reduce undue stress by using the power of delegation. Doing so often requires recognizing forces that cause us to hesitate in delegating. Ideally, we should seek to delegate any tasks that can better be done by someone else. This frees us up to focus on tasks rooted in our personal values. Accomplishing such tasks gives us the greatest joy.

Any professional involved in customer-contact work (and that is just about all of us) can benefit from better managing unproductive stress.

Summary of Key Ideas

- Customer contact work involves "emotional labor." The job requires that we manage our emotions and often behave (perform) in ways that are not always an accurate reflection of what we are feeling at the time. This disconnect between feelings and behaviors can cause stress.
- Learning to manage stress levels begins with an awareness that all stress is not bad. Some stress can be a constructive motivator but excessive unproductive stress can lead to health consequences and ineffective work unless we learn to manage it.

- Individual worker characteristics and working conditions are the two factors we have to work with when trying to manage stress. Our personal characteristics include tactics for managing time and task pressures.
- Using value clarification, goal setting, and time management techniques can allow us to deal with many stressors.
- Delegation is one of the most powerful tools we have for dealing with work pressures. All people can delegate, even if they are not in formal leadership positions.

Key Concepts

core values

delegation

emotional labor

perfection

paralysis

priority task list

ready-fire-aim approach

synchronous versus
asynchronous media

worker
characteristics

working conditions

Reviewing the Facts

1. Which of the two general causes of stress, worker characteristics and working conditions, is the most significant in your job? How can you control or manage it?
2. What are core values and how can you use these to better manage your time?
3. Describe the A-B-C prioritizing approach covered in this chapter. Give an example of each you face today.

4. Why do people often fail to use the power of delegation? What can you do to improve you delegation ability?
5. What is perfection paralysis? Give an example from your own experience.
6. What are the positive and negative effects of the "ready-fire-aim" approach described in this chapter? When might it be appropriate in your work? When should it be avoided?

Applying the Ideas: Understanding Your Personal Values

1. Work through the value-clarification activity described below. Spend some time thinking about, articulating, and clarifying your personal values.

VALUE CLARIFICATION ACTIVITY: DETERMINE WHERE YOU STAND

Step 1: Review the list of possible values below. (This list is provided to stimulate thinking and, of course, is not exhaustive.) Look at each and think about the degree to which it seems important to you. Put a +, −, or 0 beside each to indicate three categories: values you personally **endorse** (mark these with a +), those you personally **reject** (mark these with a −), and those that are **neutral** to you—you are neither for nor against them (mark these with a 0). There are no right or wrong answers. Your best answer is your most honest response.

    Many of the values listed may sound good to you. Force yourself to make some choices. *Do not endorse a value unless you*

would be willing to dedicate a significant amount of your time and energy to it.

I value . . .

career success	emergency preparedness	health & vigor
total honesty	athletic excellence	keeping good records
religious activity	pride in my city	being a leader
social correctness	musical excellence	mentoring others
open-mindedness	awareness of my heritage	intellectual growth
individualism	projecting good image	trust in God
winning	honoring ancestors	tolerance of others

family success	ability to build things	being witty, clever
law abiding	thrift, frugality	financial security
loyalty	wealth	artistic sensitivity
an orderly life	keeping all commitments	being a team player
life balance	knowing right people	self-sufficiency
many friends	productivity	dressing for success
having many skills	service to less fortunate	accuracy of work
discipline	fame in my profession	skill to influence
passion for work	caring for others	being socially active, attractive
grooming fame	concern for animals romance	attention to detail, environmentalism
kindness	rigorous thinking	political activity
negotiation skills	leadership skill	sexual attractiveness

Step 2: Look back over your endorsed and rejected values and rank the top four you endorse most vigorously and the top four you reject most vigorously.

- My top four endorsed values:
  1.
  2.
  3.
  4.
- My top four rejected values:
  1.
  2.
  3.
  4.

Review your list and **circle** any values that seem to conflict with your actions—either things you value but don't do much about, or things you do but don't really value.

Step 3: Now some tough questions. Do you honestly spend a major portion of your time working to be consistent with your most important values? Do you spend time and effort working on values you actually *reject*? Do you often find yourself tangled up in activities that have little or no relationship to your values?

2. Having completed the above activity, look at your top four espoused values. To what extent are you spending your time, resources, and energy on these? Then list value-aligning activities that are likely to be congruent with those values. Note: take your time on this activity. Write first impressions and then return to the lists several times over a period of several days. Your ideas may change or clarify.

3. As a skill-building activity, try using the time management system described in this chapter. Use a daily planner or adopt a notebook that will allow you to list and prioritize tasks. Assign A, B, or C priorities for each key task. Then use the completion symbols when each task is disposed of. Use this system for a full week. Then write a brief paper describing how your productivity was affected.

Consider this Case

Brigit Goes Bananas

"No one ever said that waiting on customers all day would be a picnic," Brigit's boss said, "but you have to keep your cool. I want you to figure out how you can best meet your job requirements without all the theatrics. You cannot hide in the ladies room or sneak away for long breaks. That's not fair to the other staff. No, Brigit, you have got to get a handle on this job or else . . ." She shrugged her shoulders, patted Brigit on the back, and left.

It all began a few days ago when Brigit, who had been working for the local gas and electric company for about six months, was asked to help out in the billing office. This is where local residents who chose to pay their bills in person or who had billing questions came. The pressure on these workers had increased after the recent increases in rate. Customers were complaining about the rate hikes and often took it out on employees.

Brigit liked most of the people she worked with and the pay was pretty good. Overall, she didn't want to quit. But dealing with one person every few minutes, almost all of whom griped about paying their bill, was really grinding on her. Of course this work in the billing office was supposed to be only temporary. She would go back to other duties in a few days after the end-of-month crush. Maybe she could just call in sick.

Probes

1. What would you tell Brigit if you were her immediate supervisor?
2. Where might Brigit go for some ideas on how to better deal with the stress of upset customers?
3. How can Brigit apply ideas from this chapter to deal with her job situation?

Consider this Case

If Only I Had More Time

"Boss, I just don't have time to do all this," Baron complained. "I get working on something and then I discover two other things that need to be done and it never seems to end."

"Give me an example," Harriett, his boss, said.

"Okay. This morning I realized that I needed to finish the Burgin Report that I have been writing for a couple of days. I sat at my desk and looked at it but was drawing a total blank. So I went to the break room for a cup of coffee. While I was there, I got talking with Sarah (she was whining about her relationship problems, as usual) and then I remembered that I hadn't sent one of my clients a birthday card. I would be in deep water if I don't do that. So I rather abruptly left Sarah in the middle of her tale of woes and went back to my desk where I keep a stash of cards. While looking for a card, I found a file I had been looking for last week. I set the file aside on top of my printer—trying to stay focused here—and sorted through the greeting cards but none of them worked for my client. So, I ran down to the card shop over in the mall. Ran into an old girlfriend there, but I didn't talk for long. When I got back, I discovered that I was out of stamps, so I had to make another trip to the post office."

"So far, you haven't been getting much done, have you?" Harriett asked.

"Nope. But I realized at this point that I needed to redouble my efforts and focus. So I closed my office door, cleared everything off my desk—piling most stuff on the floor—and started typing some changes into the Burgin report. But then, my computer froze up! I couldn't save or anything—it simply would not reboot. So I pulled the plug, and you know what that does to a computer. I called IT support but got their answering machine. I was dead in the water. Again."

"What did you do then?"

"I gave up! Decided to take an early lunch and come back to it when I'm fresh. But then I ran into Bill Brady at lunch and he was telling me about the new side business he is launching. Man, he comes up with some cool ideas. He wants me to work with him in my spare time. 'Spare time'—there's a laugh."

Probe

1. Assume that this description is fairly typical of Baron's workdays. What advice would you give him to improve his time management?

Notes

1. As sited in Wikipedia. *http://en.wikipedia.org/wiki/Emotional_labor*. Downloaded March 27, 2009.
2. Hochschild, A. R. (1983). *The Managed Heart: Commercialization of Human Feeling*. Berkeley, CA: University of California Press.
3. See: *http://www.athealth.com/Consumer/disorders/workstress.html*. Downloaded April 21, 2006.
4. Some of these ideas on team building were adapted from Melissa Dittmann, "Building a Mentally Healthy Work Force," *Monitor on Psychology*, 36(1), January 2005. See: *http://www.apa.org/monitor/jan05/workforce.html*.
5. A widely used measure of employment engagement called the Q12 was developed by the Gallup polling organization. It found that a positive response to the statement, "I have a best friend at work" relates very strongly to high worker engagement. Friends are important.
6. *Lessons of the Nordstrom Way*, eCustomerServiceWorld.com.
7. See: John Graham, The Graham Lowe Group, Inc., consulting firm. *http://www.grahamlowe.ca/news/archives/2004_02.html*.

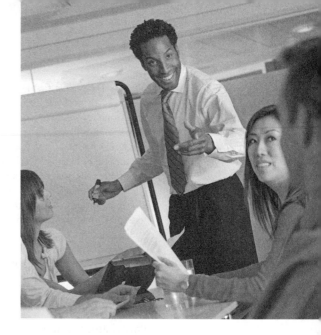

CHAPTER | **14**

Get Employees to Give Great Service
Roles of the Supervisor, Manager, or Leader

If you want a good indication of the quality of your management, ask your customers how they are being treated by your employees.

—KEN BLANCHARD

If you put fences around people, you get sheep.

—FORMER 3M CEO WILLIAM MCKNIGHT

After reading this chapter, you should be able to

1. Articulate a clear vision for customer service in your organization.

2. Organize processes, people, and resources to achieve the vision.

3. Lead and motivate employees.

4. Create and sustain an effective work culture.

5. Continuously harvest A-plus ideas.

6. Control the processes and help employees set contributing goals.

7. Empower and engage employees.

8. Tie the **reward system** to appropriate actions.

The Way It Is . . . Britany Moves to Management

Britany Howard had been with her company for almost two years and was, by all measures, an excellent employee. She had joined CostSavers[1] shortly after graduating from the local university where she had been a history major. Britany had excellent people skills and a strong work ethic—she was, in fact, outstanding. And so it seemed a logical move for her to take on management responsibilities. CostSavers' regional executives needed a person to take the lead role at its newest location, soon to be opened in Rosemont.

When Britany was asked to accept the new position, she was shocked. That evening she told her father, "I'm only 23 and they want to give me all that responsibility? I wonder if I can do that." Her dad, an experienced manager himself, told her, "management isn't for everyone, Brit. I've seen companies routinely move their best workers into management positions and then have this 'promotion' turn out badly. I know you can do it, but remember that it's different from what you have been doing."

205

During her first few weeks as the new manager, Britany read several management books. What struck her most was the realization that some very effective service employees succeed because of their personality, sensitivity, or some other skills that they really can't "manage" others into doing. "Wow, that sounds like me," she said to herself. "I've been good at what I do with customers, but I don't even realize what makes me successful. I guess I just go on my instinct or intuition. I doubt that I can teach others to be like me." The books called this **tacit knowledge**—knowledge that people have inside them but that they can't really explain or share.

In talking further with her father, Britany came to realize that the critical element in managing is to accomplish work through the efforts of others. She realized that she needed to shift her perception of what work is important. She needed to multiply her efforts by getting others to be productive. She could no longer go it alone, despite her great service skills. She had to focus on various key skills to direct and motivate the actions of her subordinates.

"That's why managers make the big bucks," her father joked.

"Yeah—that is a little trickier than what I've been doing," Britany mused.

This chapter is about ways managers can enlist the cooperation of others to accomplish organizational goals—to achieve excellence in customer service. Let's look at some of the basic functions as they relate to successful management.

ARTICULATE A VISION: WHAT MANAGERS SHOULD DO FIRST

Many experts advocate that a first step in developing a customer-driven strategy is to articulate a theme. This theme should be succinct, clear, and descriptive of the organization's uniqueness. Managers should gather ideas from customers and potential customers by asking them a few key questions, such as: "What five things do you want when doing business with us?" and look carefully at the language they use.

Similarly, managers should ask employees, "If you were our customer, what five things would you like to get from a company like ours?" and "What do you think our customers want?" and jot down their responses.

As you gather perceptions from customers and employees, managers will be likely to notice some terms coming up over and over again. Perhaps people will mention speedy service, cleanliness, friendliness, or personalized attention. These are good words to articulate in a customer service theme.

When drafting a theme for the organization, managers should remember to:

- Use participation and input from customers and employees, which is very important. The customers can best tell you what they're looking for in an organization like yours, and the employees' participation will ensure that they will accept and, hopefully, live by the intention of the theme.
- Write several rough drafts of the theme; avoid being too quick to come up with the finished version. Phrase the final version in 10 words or fewer.
- If possible, try to make the theme into an acronym, where the first letters of each word form a word in themselves.

The organization's theme should describe its uniqueness—its unique **service proposition**. This proposition should answer the question, "What distinctive service does this organization offer customers?" When the company has identified this, everyone in the organization should choose roughly the same words to describe this distinctiveness. A simple way to verify this is to ask employees to describe the organization's theme. Especially invite an employee who's been with the organization for 10 days or less to identify the theme. If the theme has been prominently displayed and is easily remembered, it will always be at the top of the mind for employees. That is the hallmark of a successful theme.

LOOK INSIDE

What's Your Organization's Vision?

If you are currently working in an organization, try this: Interview at least five managers and employees (more if you can reasonably get to them) asking them to finish this statement in 15 words or less:

- The vision of this organization can best be stated as _____

(If you are not currently employed, try this with your school. Ask students, faculty, and administrators if they can state the vision of the school in 15 words.) Then answer the following questions:

1. To what extent do you get general agreement?
2. Does the degree of agreement seem to be higher among higher ranking managers/administrators?
3. If you were a top executive in this company, what would you do about this?

(Note: Typically, agreement on the company's **vision statement** rarely exceeds 40 percent, even among top executives!)

What good does it do just to be able to repeat such a phrase? The answer is that it's a start. Repeating some words may seem meaningless at first, but most organizations fall far short even of that level of agreement. Focusing your people on a common theme can be well worth the effort.

A theme is not necessarily forever. As an organization changes directions, as markets or economic conditions change, a theme may be modified. Some organizations may want to use a theme statement for a limited period of time much the way advertisers use a slogan for only a few years. Modifying the theme should not, however, be done without careful thought. Consistency of direction is in itself valuable.

Important: By having employees participate in clarifying a theme, they will feel more committed to it. This has been shown time and again since the earliest studies in human relations: participation enhances buy-in. Besides, frontline people know the customers best and can give great ideas on how to better serve them. Never overlook the ideas of this group of experts. The employees on the firing line have the best ideas. Use them.

Managers, first and foremost, must set—and sell others on—the vision for great customer service.

A clear vision of the importance of customer loyalty should be at the core of every manager's beliefs. Increasingly, more companies are recognizing the value of customer loyalty as a predictor of future success against their competitors. The rationale is simple. The more loyal customers you have, the harder it is for your competitor to pick away your business. The first task of effective managers is to express the importance and vision. This vision must describe what the organization means for customers. Avoid "to be the best widget producer in the world," unless you can phrase that in terms of customer needs. Perhaps, "To produce and distribute the highest quality widgets that best meet our customer needs."

PLAN A STRATEGY FOR CUSTOMER LOYALTY

Planning a strategy involves looking ahead to what must be done to maintain and improve performance, to solve problems, and to develop employee competence. To plan, a manager sets objectives in each area that are to be pursued each week, each month, and each year. Having articulated a clear vision, the manager then thinks through such questions as:

- What specific actions have to be taken to reach our objectives and how can the company get employees to do them?
- How will these activities be carried out? What tools or technology will be needed?
- Who (which individuals, departments, or teams) will do the work? When will these activities take place?
- What resources will the company need to provide?

LOOK INSIDE

Ask Some Potentially Disquieting Questions

A starting point for determining how strongly managers (and employees) accept the vision of customer importance may be to answer questions like the ones below. A positive response to one or more of these may not be devastating, but if a manager answers yes to most of them, the organization will likely face an uphill task in substantially improving customer service. Companies need to walk the talk, not just have good intentions.

Answer yes or no to the following questions. Does your company, organization, or department . . .

1. Pay frontline, customer-contact people a low, flat wage?
2. Rarely if ever try accessing your own company via call centers, Web sites, or help desks to assess the friendliness of such technology?
3. Offer customer-contact people little or no training in the fundamental behaviors associated with customer service?
4. Offer no special incentives to employees for taking special care of the customer?
5. Punish or reprimand employees for giving poor customer service but take good service for granted?
6. Place greater emphasis on winning new customers than retaining ones it already has?
7. Offer no awards or recognition for non–customer-contact people's efforts to serve customers?
8. Initiate special customer service programs or campaigns that last for a few weeks or months but are soon forgotten?
9. Rarely, if ever, devote time to listening to customers and helping them solve problems?
10. Make no consistent effort to measure service quality as perceived by customers?
11. Make no attempt to hold employees at all levels accountable for and rewarded on the basis of service?
12. Fail to empower employees, instead holding them to careful application of company rules without exception?

Most managers would answer "yes" to several of the above questions. That, in itself, is not an indicator of poor service policies, but it could point to some potential problem areas. And the process of asking lots of penetrating questions can be a valuable management activity.

Most managers would admit to some failures to "walk the talk" of good service-producing leadership.

Such planning involves getting lots of input from customers and employees, and acting on the input received. Managers need to have an open mind, realizing that they do not have all the answers; much can be learned from others.

Many organizations use practices that are counterproductive to good service. They may not realize that they have drifted away from supporting their good intentions, but they often have.

ORGANIZING PROCESSES, PEOPLE, AND RESOURCES TO ACHIEVE THE VISION

The management function of organizing involves arranging the work sequence and assigning areas of responsibility and authority. Having decided the objectives and activities of each individual or work unit, the manager must:

- Assign specific responsibilities to employees.
- Give employees the supporting authority to fulfill their responsibilities.
- Work to reduce potential problems caused by systems (staffing, training, work layout, etc.). Remember that systems involve anything having to do with the delivery of products or services to the customer. Constantly organizing and improving systems is a major service leadership responsibility.

Assigning work must be accompanied by granting authority to carry out that work.

As a manager assigns work, he or she must also grant authority to carry out that work. In the best service organizations, employees at all levels have considerable latitude to creatively serve customers and solve their problems or concerns.

Granting authority is difficult for some managers. Employees will not always use it well—they'll make mistakes, perhaps costly ones. But to err on the side of giving the customer too much is often a golden opportunity to provide A-plus service. Managers must learn to let go of hard and fast rules and allow people to take initiative to serve customers exceptionally well.

Many companies with exceptional reputations for customer loyalty give their employees unusually broad authority. A service-leading hotel, for example, tells employees they can make an adjustment for a customer without getting management approval so long as the decision does not cost more than $2,000. That is a substantial authority.

LEAD AND MOTIVATE EMPLOYEES

The management functions of motivating, commanding, and coordinating are often summed up in the term *leading*. The manager leads by enabling the organization to achieve its objectives. To do this, he or she:

- Shows the direction employees must go
- Generates the energy (motivation) that stimulates subordinates to action
- Provides the needed resources (tools, technology, training, budgets, and so on)

Modern management emphasizes the **motivation** aspects of this function. An organization's leaders set the tone for motivation throughout. Motivation can be simply defined as "providing motives for action." Leaders provide motives or reasons why people should act in particular ways by setting an example and using the reward system. (We'll talk more about reward systems in a moment.)

CREATE AND SUSTAIN AN EFFECTIVE WORK CULTURE

A company's culture is shaped by its shared sense of vision, value systems, heroes, rites, and rituals. When a company's **organizational culture** is clear and unambiguous, it serves as unspoken guidelines for employee behavior.

ANOTHER LOOK

Hire People with Emotional Intelligence

Employees can learn a company's product lines or services, but their abilities to interact well with others are innate and enduring. Stated another way, companies can teach some skills but not others.

In the mid-1990s, the term **emotional intelligence** (EI) emerged to describe characteristics that we tend to call people skills. The essential elements in EI are

- Self-awareness (the understanding of one's own motives and actions)
- Self-management (the ability to control impulses)
- Self-motivation (the ability to stimulate action toward desired outcomes)
- Empathy (the ability to see a situation from another person's perspective)
- Social skills (the ability to adapt communication to situational needs)

Customer service can obviously benefit from these characteristics. But are these teachable? Most would argue that the answer is probably not. Traits as fundamental as warmth and friendliness cannot be trained. If this is true, a company can avoid the futility of trying to train someone to be empathetic or to use a "natural smile" by hiring the right type of person in the first place. Why not hire people who have high emotional intelligence?

But hiring people with good EI isn't enough. Companies must also trust their employees to react to situations appropriately to meet customer needs. Employees must be allowed to use their EI skills to create customer loyalty.

Probes

1. To what extent do you agree with the idea that personality traits such as those defining emotional intelligence cannot be trained?
2. What kinds of steps should managers take to assure that they are hiring people with good EI?
3. How can managers best display trust in their employees allowing them to use their good EI on behalf of customers?

210 Part 5 · Living Life

Organizational culture is the firm's self-identity or shared mindset. It identifies the company in the mind of its customers. Think, for example, what mindset comes to mind when you consider brands such as Google, Harley Davidson motorcycles, Ben and Jerry's ice cream, Chick Fil-A, or Apple computers. Organizations like these project a shared mindset that is appealing to their customers.

Culture arises from the stories employees tell, the ways people dress and behave, the little rituals that make employees feel a part of the company—and the way they treat their customers. Internal customers (employees) see the culture reinforced with things like birthday celebrations, Friday afternoon popcorn, or informal gatherings around the coffee pot. Likewise the things people discuss and admire—the stories people repeat—become part of the folklore of the company and reinforce its culture. If your people enjoy talking about that crazy time Harry drove all the way to a customer's house on a stormy Friday night, they are reinforcing cultural values. If your people talk about the time Bess diffused that really upset customer and made him her best friend, they are reinforcing cultural values. One oft-repeated story is about the Nordstrom manager who accepted a return of some tires the customer was unhappy with—even though Nordstrom never sold tires! That rather odd decision by a manager many years ago set the shared vision for customers: Nordstrom will always take back unsatisfactory merchandise. This has been a pillar underlying Nordstom's vision: It shouts that customers can trust Nordstrom.

Management can impact the culture by consistently looking for things to celebrate or actions to instantly reward. Some sales-oriented companies use rather silly sales "skits"—dressing up in ridiculous costumes and acting out "sales successes" to get the service reps fired up about selling. At the end of a successful initiative, they celebrate with food, entertainment, and prizes. These kinds of things make an organization's culture vibrant and alive. In short, they can make a company a fun place to work.

By contrast, I recall going to a fast-food restaurant at lunchtime. I stood in the line and, upon reaching the clerk, smiled and said hello asking how he was doing. He totally ignored my smile and my greeting and, instead, deadpanned: "For hear to go?" I ordered and looked around. Virtually none of the young people in the restaurant were smiling. And I soon saw why: their adult manager had no trace of a smile on her face either. She was grimly *working*. No time for frivolity. The whole atmosphere of that restaurant was poisoned by its shear absence of joy.

An organization's culture can have a dramatic impact on employee behavior, and managers do much to shape the culture.

ANOTHER LOOK

How Can Managers Reinfore a Service Culture?

"Culture" stems from the agreed-upon values of an organization. These values are learned and reinforced with such things as shared language ("A-plus service" "process excellence"), material symbols (uniforms, office layout, furnishings), rituals (Friday afternoon popcorn, celebrations), and stories (repeated narrative that illustrates behaviors supporting the culture.)

Managers cannot "create" a culture but they can influence it. Actions such as an undeviating focus on the corporate vision and frequent reference to heroes (recognition of people who have done outstanding things) strengthen the culture. Rites and rituals such as open-door policies, parties, picnics, Friday dress-down days, employees decorating their own workspace, after-work socializing, and so on can all sustain a positive culture.

When a culture is built around customer-centered values, the company is well on its way to creating loyalty. As employees internalize the shared values—make them their own—managers find the need to supervise greatly reduced. Employees will act in ways that support the organization's vision.

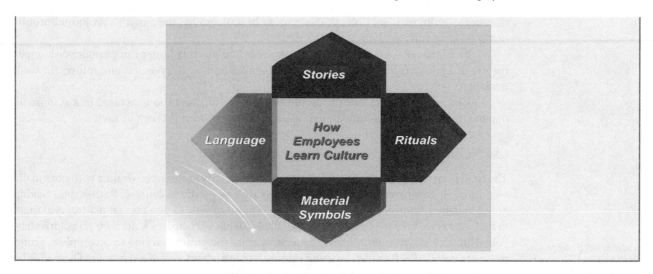

CONTINUOUSLY HARVEST A-PLUS IDEAS

Building customer loyalty is a team sport. No one person can anticipate all customer needs or come up with every possible idea for exceeding expectations. Employees at every level should feel a part of the team, having their input valued. For A-plus to work, it must have a constant flow of new ideas. Employees at all levels in an organization can and will come up with good ideas. Managers should get their people to meet regularly to discuss creative ways for handling customer needs and surprising them with an unanticipated plus. Two ways to harvest creative ideas are through the use of brainstorming and nominal group processes (NGPs).

Managers can harvest A-plus ideas using brainstorming and the nominal group process.

Use Brainstorming When You Need Creative Ideas

The term ***brainstorming*** has become synonymous with any kind of creative thinking, but that misuses the word. Brainstorming is a specific technique using explicit rules for idea-generation and development. This approach requires a communication climate in which free expression of all kinds of ideas is valued and encouraged—no matter how offbeat or bizarre they may seem. This climate should be loosely structured, friendly, and highly tolerant of humor. Strict application of four basic rules makes brainstorming a powerful process for creative idea-generation:

- *Don't criticize any ideas.* No comments; no grunts or groans; no thumbs down gestures. Just let it come out and be recorded. This is harder than it sounds.
- *No idea is too wild.* What sounds bizarre or offbeat may contain a germ of an idea that could work. This can also liberate the creative juices.
- *Quantity* of ideas generated is important. Push to get as many ideas without regard to whether or not they make any sense at this point. More is better.
- Seize opportunities to *hitchhike*—add to or amplify on ideas suggested by others. One technique for this is to require that people repeat the other person's idea and then add to it or take it in another direction.

The rules of brainstorming are easier to state than to obey—especially the second one. Unless great care is taken, nonverbal cues can be interpreted as evaluations of ideas, and that can discourage additional "wild ideas." When using brainstorming, the participants should prominently post the rules as a constant reminder.

The climate of a brainstorming session set by the meeting leader can promote or hamper the use of brainstorming. A climate that encourages humor, irreverence, and informality will work best.

After brainstorming, a team should process the information generated in a systematic manner to see which ideas could be applied. Here is one process that can be useful.

Use Nominal Group Process When Appropriate

The **NGP** is an idea-processing technique that is particularly useful when dealing with potentially emotional or controversial ideas (as highly creative suggestions can be). Rather than having group members immediately speak up with their point of view (a process that may *commit* them to that view since they've voiced it publicly), the NGP has participants write their ideas, privately. Following a clear description or restatement of what the group is trying to accomplish, group members spend 10–20 minutes writing promising ideas about possible solutions. These may be ideas triggered by brainstorming or from other sources.

The nominal group process provides a systematic way for processing ideas.

When the group gets back together, each participant describes one idea from his or her list, which is written on a flip chart in full view of the group. Ideas are recorded but not discussed at this point. This round robin listing of ideas continues until the members have no further ideas. People may then clarify or amplify on an idea, as necessary. Then a silent vote is taken where participants rank order the ideas. The steps of the process, once again, are:

1. Silently generate solution ideas in writing. (Or, listing of ideas from brainstorming sessions.)
2. Record (usually on large flip charts or a white board) the ideas in round robin fashion—get one idea from person A, then one from person B, and so on until all have given their first idea, Then repeat the process.
3. Discuss the merits of each idea. Get clarification if necessary.
4. Vote on the ideas by ranking them. (Several votes may be needed before the group accepts a final solution or priority list of actions to take.)

The ongoing use of groups or teams to generate A-plus ideas can be one of the most powerful rituals a company can engage in. Managers serious about maximizing customer loyalty should be doing this.

CONTROL THE PROCESSES

The management function called **controlling** involves comparing actual results to expected or planned-for results so as to identify any deviation from plan. Typically, any deviation from the plan calls for adjusting motivation attempts, reviewing the reward systems, replanning of activities to close the gap, or changing the objectives to be more realistic.

The key to effective controlling is to measure, specifically, what you want to achieve. If, for example, quick access to your call center is a key feature of your service efforts, measure customer waiting times. If ease-of-use of your Web page is important, poll customers about their experiences in navigating your site. If attractive merchandise display is important, check it often. If restaurant and restroom cleanliness are priorities, clean them early and often.

Getting good ideas from customers or others does little good if you don't implement them.

Of course, getting the input from customers does little good if you don't follow through on implementing ideas for improvement. We often see managers who get their employees to say they are going to do something, only to have that action drop through the cracks when people get busy with other tasks. Management consultant David Ulrich says the "the importance of feedback is not in the data—it's in the follow-up." He explains that 10 percent of people will actually make changes based on feedback (including correction from their manager). But this number jumps to between 40 and 60 percent for people who will change how they do things if the feedback is followed up. Simply a brief call from the manager asking how the change is going can dramatically increase the likelihood that employees will improve.[2]

For controlling to be effective, managers should focus on the kinds of "measurables" that make a difference. If, for example, you want to encourage your frontline employees to always ask customers if they would like to try a new product, measure how often the employees actually do that. If you calculate a positive relationship between employee appearance and customer loyalty, measure the degree to which employees meet agreed-upon appearance criteria. Measure specific behaviors, not idealized outcomes or attitudes. "Giving good service" is a rather vague outcome—it means different things to different people. "Ask the customer if there is anything else they need" is a behavior—you can observe it. Focus on vital behaviors—those specific actions that can be observed and that make a difference.

The importance of feedback is not in the data but in the follow-up.

Help Employees Set Contributing Goals

The controlling function in management may look at big-picture data or more focused behaviors that seem to affect the bottom line. What managers focus on tends to improve. **Goal setting** is a powerful tool for focusing effort, especially when the targeted improvements are measurable. Managers need to be fully involved in the process of setting measurable goals. They set the goals for their department, store, company, or workgroup. They should also help individual employees set goals for themselves. During performance reviews, managers should ask employees about their goals and suggest ways to make individual goals compatible with group objectives.

Goal setting helps establish priorities, as well as determine the sequence and timing of strategy steps. Managers can't fix everything at once, so they should look for the kinds of results that can give the most impact relative to the effort involved—the most bang for the buck. They should first pick the low-hanging fruit. Accomplishing good results with the easier challenges—getting early wins—can motivate the troops to tackle the more difficult problems later. Managers typically need to budget for improvements. Many changes, especially those designed to solve systems or value turnoffs, require the expenditure of money or other resources. You may need to hire more people, provide more training, change the location or layout of the business, purchase additional technology, and so on. All these should be done with an eye to how the change can help employees better meet the organization's service goals. If expenditures don't help employees and customers, they probably should not be implemented.

EMPOWER EMPLOYEES

Managers cannot run the whole organization alone—nor should they. Ultimately, employee empowerment is the key to corporate excellence. **Empowerment** happens when employees are given the authority and latitude to take initiative on behalf of customers. Everyone wins with effective empowerment. First, the customer benefits because the employee can cut through traditional procedures and give them what they need without having to forever get approval of higher management. Second, the employee wins because he or she feels satisfaction in helping customers by asserting creativity and initiative. Third, the company wins because its employees and customers are better satisfied.

Empowerment gives employees the authority to work on behalf of the customer.

Empowering employees can be scary for managers. Many managers are hesitant about letting go of authority. They fear that employees will make mistakes or fail to use good business sense, thus "giving away the store." But employees rarely do and the benefits of empowering far outweigh the potential risk of an occasional mistake.

Empowerment should be accompanied by training. Let people know the impact of their decisions—the potential downside to giving something to a customer that may be out of the ordinary. If, for example, employees give free goods or services to a customer who had a problem, they should understand how that action can impact profits and perhaps their bonus.

TIE THE REWARD SYSTEM TO APPROPRIATE ACTIONS

One of the characteristics of many companies described as great places to work has been the casual, fun-loving, creative workplace with far less attention to decorum or organizational hierarchy. Scenes of high-tech workers on scooters, working in casual dress in a collegial environment has changed the face of businesses worldwide. Companies routinely rated as the best to work for, often have such comfortable cultures. But not all organizations are quite so fun-loving. Many maintain a more formal atmosphere but still provide high employee satisfaction, especially when the reward systems are creative and, well, rewarding. A fairly common problem in some companies is that people are rewarded for the wrong things and may even be punished for doing good things! Traditional compensation that, for example, pays people a flat hourly rate rewards people for *using up time*. The more time you use the more money you make. Likewise, people who try something innovative or unusual (often a desired action in today's rapidly changing workplace) are sometimes punished when the idea fails, thus extinguishing the likelihood that they will ever try to innovate again. Failures of well-intentioned ideas should be *rewarded* if companies are to grow. Managers should be very careful to ensure that their people are rewarded for the right things, and not punished for honest attempts to innovate.

Employees should be rewarded for the right things. Beware of unintended consequences of reward systems.

A small western hospital initiated an A-plus patient loyalty program they called Excel! As part their efforts, they trained every employee in the hospital in A-plus strategy building, got every department involved in idea-generating sessions, and rewarded their people very effectively. Employees earned reward points from a variety of desired actions, including:

- Receiving of a positive comment card from a patient or guest
- Receiving an "atta-boy" or "atta-girl" recognition coupon from a supervisor anywhere in the hospital
- Contributing a helpful suggestion
- Participating in team brainstorming to generate new A-plus ideas
- Reading the monthly newsletter and completing a short quiz
- Attending optional follow-up training sessions after work hours

Employees from each department who received the most points attended a special "Excel-abration" luncheon with games and prizes. At the end of the year, the monthly winners from each department were invited to a lavish "Excel-abration" dinner with substantial prizes such as TVs, mountain bikes, cruise tickets, and cash. Overall, this hospital did it right. The result was long-term, ongoing service excellence and very motivated employees.

The reward process is not mysterious. Managers need to determine exactly what kinds of actions are worthy of reinforcing and then develop a mechanism for rewarding those actions. As with most things, getting employee involvement in the development of the reward program makes sense. People will gladly tell you what they think they should be rewarded for and they will also tell you what rewards will best turn them on. You just have to ask.

A FINAL THOUGHT

In many sales organizations, salespeople who demonstrate world-class performance and build the strongest customer relationships are often "rewarded" by being promoted out of the jobs they do best. All too often, great sales reps become managers or corporate marketers, regardless of whether they have the right talents for those roles. Similarly, outstanding customer service reps become supervisors, then department managers, because that's the only way to earn more money or prestige. A study of one call center showed that it had 11 layers of management—a system that evolved in part as a way to reward outstanding performance. Ironically, reps who were the best at working with customers were literally 10 times removed from ever speaking with a customer again. This may be a good place to repeat a key point made early in the chapter: Not all employees will or should be advanced into management positions. In fact, managing requires special skills not everyone has. Consider creating ways that great employees can still be "promoted" without necessarily becoming managers. Develop incentive opportunities that can afford true engagement by all employees. Ideally a great sales rep or service provider should make more than his or her manager!

That said, good managers play a huge role in any organization's success in developing customer loyalty. Indeed, the first and most important use of a manager's time should be to guide this process. Managers who follow through with the kinds of actions discussed in this chapter will make a positive difference in their organizations—and can be well on the way to creating and sustaining customer loyalty.

Summary of Key Ideas

- Managing is the process of getting work accomplished with and through the efforts of other people.
- A clear vision of the importance of customer loyalty should be at the core of every manager's beliefs. He or she must articulate that vision.
- An effective manager must think about a service strategy looking ahead to what must be done to maintain and improve performance, to solve problems, and to develop employee competence.
- A manager must organize his or her team by assigning responsibilities, giving employees the supporting authority to fulfill their responsibilities, and reducing potential problems caused by systems (staffing, training, work layout, etc.).
- Managers lead by enabling the organization to achieve its objectives. To do this, he or she shows the direction employees must go, generates the energy (motivation) that stimulates subordinates to action, and provides the needed resources.
- Managerial behaviors go a long way toward creating conditions under which employees can feel empowered in the organization. Managers play an important role in shaping an organizational culture. Culture is shaped by a shared sense of vision and values.
- Organizational culture is learned and reinforced by language, stories, material symbols, and rituals.
- Managers should harvest creative, A-plus ideas through the use of brainstorming and NGPs.
- The management function called *controlling* involves comparing actual results to expected or planned-for results so as to identify any deviation from plan.
- Managers should measure specific behaviors (actions) rather than vague outcomes or attitudes whenever possible.
- Managers need to be fully involved in the process of setting measurable goals for their workgroup. They should also help individual employees set goals for themselves.
- Ultimately, employee empowerment is the key to A-plus service. When employees have the latitude to take initiative on behalf of customers, everyone wins.
- Good managers use hoopla and fun to create an environment where people like to work. They also check to be sure they are rewarding the right behaviors.

Key Concepts

brainstorming
emotional
   intelligence
empowerment

goal setting (group and
   individual)
harvesting A-plus ideas
motivation

nominal group process
   (NGP)
organizational culture
reward system

service proposition
tacit knowledge
controlling
vision statement

Reviewing the Facts

1. What are the key distinguishing factors that make management work different from nonmanagement?
2. How can a manager best set a strategy for improving customer loyalty? What steps make sense?
3. How important is organizational culture? What kinds of things create and sustain a culture?
4. Describe brainstorming in your own words. What are the critical elements that must be present for this to work?
5. How can nominal group process (NGP) be useful in processing new ideas?
6. Why is employee empowerment important? What causes some managers to resist empowering employees? Should all employees be equally empowered? Defend your answer.

Applying the Ideas: Getting Employees to Give Great Service

1. Ask three of your classmates, friends, or coworkers to describe the actions of the best and worst manager they have worked for. To what extent do these descriptions relate to the ideas in this chapter? To what extent do these managers fulfill the roles discussed here?
2. Read the most recent copy of *Fortune* magazine's annual feature issue on the "100 Best Companies to Work for In America" (see *www.Fortune.com*). Pick one company you are interested in and compare it against the descriptions of key management challenges described in this chapter. For example, what does the article say about the company culture, the training provided to employees, opportunities for employees to maximize their talents, and so on.
3. Select a company or organization you are familiar with (perhaps somewhere where you now work or have worked) and articulate what you think its vision statement should be. If it

already has a publicized vision/mission statement, how does this compare with what you would express? To what extent does the company seem true to this mission? What contradictions does the company exhibit? Describe your reasoning.
4. Select a company or organization you are familiar with (perhaps somewhere where you now work or have worked) and get a group together to brainstorm some possible A-plus ideas for boosting customer loyalty. Apply the principles of brainstorming described in this chapter and have fun with the process. Write a brief report of your group's ideas with comments about which ideas the company might realistically try. If you are not currently employed or you lack familiarity with the company, use your class as the organization. Brainstorm ways the class could exceed your expectations. Be creative and have some fun with this. Remember that only a few ideas arising from brainstorming can actually be implemented.

Consider this Case

Am I a Manager or Not?

The following request for advice appeared on the company's internal blog. This blog was set up so that employees (internal customers) could freely express concerns and ideas.

> *I'm in a situation where I manage three different groups; however, I am not really the manager but actually in the same job category as the people I "supposedly" manage. The problem is my boss has given me the responsibility of all of these jobs; however, I do not have the authority to delegate to any of the people I manage. They all go crying to my boss. My tendency then is to try to "do it all." I've spoken to my boss about the way I feel, "responsibility but no authority" and*

> *he does not know what I mean. He says just give it to him and he'll find someone to do it. I feel disrespected, overworked, and my self-respect is rapidly diminishing. What approach would be most effective for me to take?*

Probes

1. Suppose you knew who this writer is and that you were the manager of her boss. What would you say to the manager to help resolve this problem?
2. What fundamental violations of good management principles are apparently being revealed by this employee?

Consider this Case

We Can't Go on Meeting Like This

Frieda came out of the meeting shaking her head. She told Terry, "If I have to sit through another one of these meetings, I'm going to put a gun to my head. Such a waste of time!"

"What happened, Frieda?" Terry asked.

"Okay—I'll tell you what happened. Nothing! That's what happens in all these freakin' meetings. Georgette says she wants new and creative ideas for exceeding our customers' expectations. She says 'be creative,' and then when anyone comes up with even a slightly 'out there' idea, she gets into an immediate debate about why that won't work or she says 'we tried that before,' and that kills that. Then we all sit there and look at each other until Georgette pipes up with her latest, lame idea.

"This whole 'let's get creative' emphasis is so bogus. Everybody in that room has good ideas, but she can't seem to let go of control or open her mind enough to try something new. So, our meetings spend hours justifying what she thinks we should do instead of generating new ideas. The woman drives me nuts."

Probes

1. What advice would you give Georgette for better use of meetings?
2. How typical is Freida's response? Describe similar experiences you have had with meetings.
3. What could Freida and the other employees do to improve this situation? How can they be assertive in recommending changes to Georgette?

Notes

1. A fictitious company.
2. David Ulrich, consultant and professor at the University of Michigan, in a lecture delivered upon receiving an award from the Dyer Institute for Leading Organizational Change, Marriott School of Management, Brigham Young University, March 10, 2006. (See also *http://www.daveulrich.com*)

APPENDIX

How to Lead or Participate in an A-Plus Idea-Generating Meeting

Use the Group Process to Boost Customer Satisfaction and Loyalty

In this appendix, we will focus on 12 specific tips that will enable you to conduct or participate in meetings designed to generate A-plus ideas. When focused on improved service, such meetings can tap the ideas of the group to provide a gold mine of profitable customer service ideas. These 12 action tips help run an effective A-plus meeting.

ACTION TIP 1. MAKE THE MEETING'S PURPOSE ABSOLUTELY CLEAR

Meetings are of two general types: informational and problem solving. Don't confuse them. The most legitimate use of the group process is to bring a variety of inputs on a specific problem or decision. A-plus idea generation requires good group skills. Don't waste time at the meeting just giving out information.

Clarify the specific topic up front so that people come to the meeting with the right mind-set. Tell participants that the meeting will seek to generate A-plus ideas from each of the three categories of ways to exceed expectations: value, information, and convenience and timing.

ACTION TIP 2. INVITE THE RIGHT PEOPLE

People invited to a meeting should:

1. Have some expertise. However, don't discriminate against people in lower organizational positions. Typically customer contact people have the most experience with A-plus opportunities, but others may also have ideas.
2. Have a vested interest in the outcome of the discussion—they have shown a desire to participate in efforts to improve customer loyalty.
3. Have some skills in group decision making and they should be able to express themselves reasonably well. Avoid narrow-minded, inflexible people or those who may dominate the group.
4. Share the overall values of the organization. If participants are antagonistic or in disagreement with the company's goals or vision, it makes no sense to have them participate in decisions affecting the company's direction.

In addition, be sure, to invite the right *number* of people. Have enough to represent a variety of opinions but not so many that the process bogs down. A-plus meetings work best with 4 to 12 participants. Five to seven is usually optimal.

ACTION TIP 3. ASSIGN ADVANCE PREPARATION

Participants should know what the meeting is about and what kinds of information and/or ideas they may need to gather and bring with them. If the central focus of the meeting will be on generating A-plus ideas to enhance customer *convenience*, telling people in advance will let them think about competitors' tactics, creative ideas being used by other companies, and perhaps needed data such as sales results others have experienced. If the focus will be on A-plus information, encourage participants to carefully observe ways companies share information with customers. Get people thinking on the right wavelength even before the meeting.

ACTION TIP 4. START ON TIME AND USE A REALISTIC SCHEDULE

A major concern of meeting attendees is the meeting's failure to start and end on time. Don't wait "a few minutes until the rest of the folks get here" or you'll find yourself doing so every time. Get a reputation for prompt starts and people will get there on time. Likewise, don't run over time. If you've scheduled 90 minutes, stop at or before that deadline. If you really want to shock people, end the meeting early! When the work is done, quit.

Schedule breaks. Have refreshments. Encourage people to walk around the room, draw on flip charts, and sit where they like. Do whatever is necessary to make the experience pleasant and satisfying.

ACTION TIP 5. CREATE A POSITIVE CLIMATE

If you are the leader, thank people for coming to the meeting. Let people know that they were selected because they can contribute valuable insights and ideas. Set a good psychological climate by your example. Let people know that the discussion can be casual and that they are encouraged to be creative.

Also set up the meeting room appropriately so that participants:

1. Can see each other face to face (do not sit in rows, auditorium style)
2. Are provided with table(s) and writing materials
3. Use a whiteboard, newsprint flip charts, or transparencies to capture ideas
4. Are encouraged to move around the room freely to relieve tension or fatigue
5. Are provided with refreshments if the meeting will run more than a few hours

ACTION TIP 6. BE AWARE OF A "HIDDEN AGENDA"

Although we may agree on the discussion topic, people in meetings often have unspoken objectives called "hidden agendas." These may include such things as:

- Getting some "exposure" (i.e., to favorably impress others)
- Providing a "status arena" where they can assert power or show off their ability
- Providing a chance to socialize with others (This can be okay so long as the socializing doesn't get too far off topic.)
- Diffusing decision responsibility so that one person won't have to take all the heat if a decision fails
- Getting away from unpleasant work duties

If achieving one's hidden agenda doesn't take away from the effectiveness of the group, don't worry about it. If the ulterior motives of the hidden agenda deter the group from accomplishing its work, talk with participants candidly (in private) and solicit their cooperation in putting the group's needs above their own.

ACTION TIP 7. REWARD GROUP MEMBER INPUT

Never let a group member's input be met with silence. To do so will quickly extinguish further input from that person—and from others. Bear in mind that stating an opinion or idea can be somewhat risky for people. They risk being perceived as wrong, naive, unimaginative, or any of dozens other possibilities. When their comments are met with dead air, it may be seen as punishing—causing them to be embarrassed.

By acknowledging contributions, we create a climate where more will be offered. A simple "good thought" or "you might be on to something there" can go a long way toward drawing out further input. Even if the idea doesn't make much sense to you, you can come up with a neutral response like "okay" or simply "thanks."

ACTION TIP 8. MONITOR PRESSURES TO CENSOR

The problem of pressure to censor information is a bit more complex. Two common forms of such pressure are:

- Individual dominance
- Groupthink

Individual dominance happens when certain individuals dominate a discussion by force of their personality, organizational position, or personal status. These people may be particularly charming (and thus disproportionately influential because everybody likes them!) or highly autocratic or hard-headed. Reduce this dominance by drawing other people into the discussion.

Groupthink describes a condition of like-mindedness which can arise in groups that are particularly cohesive. While cohesiveness is normally a good condition in groups, it can be carried too far. This can happen when the group members' desire for consensus or harmony becomes stronger than their desire for the best possible decision. Here are seven symptoms of groupthink:

1. An overemphasis on team play and getting along harmoniously.
2. A "shared stereotype" view that competitors or those in opposition to us are inept, incompetent, and incapable of doing anything well.
3. Self-censorship of group member; personal doubts are suppressed to avoid rocking the group's boat.
4. Rationalization to comfort one another and reduce any doubts regarding the group's agreed-upon plan.
5. Self-appointed "mindguards" (who are sort of like bodyguards who protect us from "bad" thoughts) that function to prevent anyone from undermining the group's apparent unanimity and "protect" the group from information that differs from their beliefs.
6. Direct pressure on those who express disagreement.
7. An expression of self-righteousness that leads members to believe their actions are moral or ethical, thus letting them disregard objections to their behavior.

Each of these symptoms of groupthink damages creative or original thinking and effective decisions or idea generation.

ACTION TIP 9. DON'T ALLOW CONFLICT TO BECOME DESTRUCTIVE

Traditionally, it has been assumed that conflict should be avoided in meetings. The term "conflict" conjures up images of fistfights or people screaming at each other. In reality, conflict is simply a state of incompatibility. It is neither good nor bad. What creates conflict problems are the participants' reactions to it.

We typically respond to conflict in one of several ways:

1. We can attempt to *avoid* conflict by not expressing opposing views and by withholding any disagreement. Here we keep from rocking the boat and minimize the possibility of being subjected to rejection or reprisals from others. (Groupthinkers respond this way.) The drawback here is that some good ideas—ideas that can best impact the group's effectiveness—may be withheld in the interest of avoiding conflict.
2. We get into a win-lose orientation, leading to a no-holds-barred, open warfare among participants.
3. We *manage conflict* to regulate it but not eliminate confrontation. Recognizing that the abrasive actions of opposing views—like sandpaper on wood—polish the final product, the skillful leaders seek free exchange of information but without the win-lose destructiveness of unregulated conflict. Accomplishing this calls for communication skills that encourage the generation of information without inhibiting or turning off participants.

This third response, managing conflict, is by far the most useful. Incidentally, a sense of humor helps. Laughter can be the most potent, constructive force for diffusing business tension. Humor is what brings back perspective.

ACTION TIP 10. AVOID OVERCENTRALIZED LEADERSHIP

Effective meeting managers work to move the group away from the traditional leader toward group-centered leadership or self-managed teams. The leadership process of guiding and directing the group's activity should move from person to person within the group rather than be centered in one individual. Having each group member take some part of the leadership role can overcome dominance and conflict problems. The result is what is called "group-centered leadership." This is contrasted with traditional leadership in the following list.

Traditional Leadership

1. The leader directs, controls, polices the members, and leads them to the proper decision. Basically it is his or her group, and the leader's authority is acknowledged by members.

2. The leader focuses attention on the task to be accomplished, brings the group back from any diverse wandering, and performs all the functions needed to arrive at the proper decision.

3. The leader sets limits and uses rules of order to keep the discussion within strict limits set by the agenda. He or she controls the time spent on each item lest the group wander fruitlessly.

4. The leader believes that emotions are disruptive to objective, logical thinking, and should be discouraged or suppressed.

5. The leader believes that a member's disruptive behavior should be handled by talking to the offender away from the group; it is the leader's task to do so.

6. Because the need to arrive at a task decision is all-important in the eyes of the leader, needs of individual members are considered less important.

Group-Centered Leadership

1. The group, or meeting, is *owned* by the members, including the leader. All members, with the leader's assistance, contribute to its effectiveness.

2. The group is responsible, with occasional and appropriate help from the leader, for reaching a decision that includes the participation of all and is the product of all. The leader is a servant and helper to the group.

3. Members of the group take responsibility for its task productivity, its methods of working, its assignments of tasks, and its plans for the use of the time available.

4. Feelings, emotions, and conflict are recognized by the members and the leader as legitimate factors in the discussion process.

5. The leader believes that any problem in the group must be faced and solved within the group and by the group.

6. With help and encouragement from the leader, the members come to realize that the needs, feelings, and purposes of all members should be met so that an awareness of being a group forms.

ACTION TIP 11. USE BRAINSTORMING TO GENERATE CREATIVE IDEAS

Remember that the term "brainstorming" is not just some generic way of creative thinking. Brainstorming is a specific technique using explicit rules for idea generation and development. This approach requires a communication climate in which free expression of all kinds of ideas is valued and encouraged—no matter how offbeat or bizarre they may seem. The approach works well for generating A-plus ideas. Brainstorming uses four underlying beliefs:

1. *No idea may be criticized.* No comments; no grunts or groans; no thumbs down gestures. Just let it come out and be recorded.
2. *No idea is too wild.*
3. *Quantity* of ideas generated is important. Push to get as many ideas without regard to whether or not they make any sense at this point.
4. *Hitchhiking is important.* Participants should add to or amplify ideas suggested by others.

The climate set by the meeting's leader can promote or hamper the use of brainstorming. A climate that encourages humor and informality will work best.

ACTION TIP 12. ASSIGN SPECIFIC FOLLOW-UP ACTIONS

Be sure that group members have their "marching orders." A brilliant A-plus idea will be of no value if it isn't implemented. The people who made the decision are the best ones to direct implementation.

Follow-up assignments typically include informing people of the new action, training people in how to implement it, and communicating to key people about the action and its timing. Don't end the meeting without giving people specific assignments.

A FINAL THOUGHT

Meetings hold the potential for generating good ideas if they are handled well. A meeting aimed at generating A-plus ideas will be more successful if you apply the tips presented in this appendix. Now, let's try on the behaviors and see what great ideas we can generate.

Applying the Ideas: Plan and Run a Brainstorming (A-plus) Meeting

Select one of the seven organizations that follow and run an A-plus meeting. Come up with at least two ideas for each of the A-plus categories (i.e., value, information, and convenience and timing).

1. The company you are currently working in (After the meeting, prepare a memo describing your ideas and present it to your boss.)
2. Your university bookstore
3. A restaurant you frequently patronize
4. Your favorite supermarket
5. An electronics or appliance store
6. An upscale clothing shop (boutique)
7. Your class imagined as a "company" interested in developing A-plus ideas for making the students (customers) more satisfied with the course

Try your skills at setting a climate, articulating the topic, running the meeting, capturing ideas, and planning the follow-up necessary to implement the ideas your group produces. Prepare an oral report of your findings—both ideas generated and observations about the group process—to your class.

INDEX